THE DARDANELLES

CAMPAIGNS AND THEIR LESSONS.

Tirah, 1897. By Colonel Sir C. E. CALLWELL, C.B., etc. 5s. net. With maps.

Bohemia, 1866. By Major NEIL MALCOLM. 5s. net. With maps.

The Campaign of Liao-Yang. By Major H. ROWAN ROBINSON. 6s. 6d. net. With maps.

The Marne Campaign. By Lieut.-Col. F. E. WHITTON. With coloured maps. 10s. 6d. net.

OTHER VOLUMES IN PREPARATION.

THE DARDANELLES

BY
MAJOR-GENERAL SIR C. E. CALLWELL, K.C.B.

WITH MAPS

The Naval & Military Press Ltd

Reproduced by kind permission of the Central Library,
Royal Military Academy, Sandhurst

Published by
The Naval & Military Press Ltd
Unit 10, Ridgewood Industrial Park,
Uckfield, East Sussex,
TN22 5QE England
Tel: +44 (0) 1825 749494
Fax: +44 (0) 1825 765701
www.naval-military-press.com

© The Naval & Military Press Ltd 2005

In reprinting in facsimile from the original, any imperfections are inevitably reproduced and the quality may fall short of modern type and cartographic standards.

INTRODUCTION

THE contest for the control of the Dardanelles in 1915 brought about a struggle by sea and land which was in the main conducted quite independently of occurrences in other theatres of the Great War. That being so, it can in a military and naval sense be treated as a distinct incident in the world-wide disturbance. It constituted a campaign by itself. Its course, nevertheless, was appreciably affected by belligerent events elsewhere, by the military situation in Western Europe on various dates—by the progress of the conflict on the western and south-eastern borders of Russia, for instance, by acute strategical developments in Serbia, and even by martial proceedings in the vicinity of the Nile Delta and in Mesopotamia. Such influence as the conditions in distant regions exerted over the fight for the Straits took, however, almost entirely the form of diverting to other fields military and naval resources which, but for this, might have been profitably employed in and about the Gallipoli Peninsula.

It was the Allies who especially suffered in this respect, and they suffered particularly on land. For, lack of troops and munitions was unquestionably one cause of their failure to wrest domination of the Hellespont out of the hands of the Turk. But the inadequacy of the means in respect to men and munitions placed at his disposal, which so shackled Sir I. Hamilton, were primarily —if not indeed wholly—due to the fact that men and munitions were urgently needed in other theatres of war and especially in France and Flanders. To go into the question as to whether the policy adopted in this matter by the Governments concerned was right or was wrong, would manifestly be inappropriate in a volume that only pretends to deal with one particular campaign of the

World War. To become immersed in such comprehensive problems would involve a strategical disquisition concerning the Homeric struggle as a whole. So, when mentioning the relative weakness of the Allies' military forces committed to the Dardanelles enterprise, and the failure of the responsible rulers to despatch the reinforcements and the war material that were called for if the undertaking was to be successful, it will simply be assumed that the reinforcements and the war material could not be provided. The question whether they ought or ought not to have been provided will not be debated.

To review a campaign at a stage when the available information concerning it is derived entirely, or almost entirely, from one only of the two contending sides, must ever be unsatisfying. We unfortunately are at present almost wholly dependent for information as to what occurred upon documents and works emanating from the Entente side. No detailed accounts of the operations are to hand from Teutonic nor yet from Turkish sources. The three published German brochures which do deal with the campaign—their titles are given in Appendix I—are unconvincing and superficial efforts, and they manifestly were written with an eye to their effect upon the general public in Germany, while doing full justice to the valour and grit of the Turks. As Marshal Liman von Sanders observes in a signed Preface, dated the 15th of July, 1916, to one of them, "Only when there shall no longer be need to conceal anything can the truth as to facts and numbers be told. Any narrative of the Dardanelles struggles written to-day for the benefit of friends at home can only serve to throw a passing light over what occurred, for it will not be possible to deal with events exhaustively." Some of the statements in these unpretentious works do, however, bear an almost unmistakable stamp of truth, and these add somewhat to our restricted knowledge of what went on in and behind the Ottoman lines. For all practical purposes, however, this volume is to be regarded as written from the Allies' point of view, and Germans and Turks are throughout called the enemy in its pages.

INTRODUCTION

The following chapters do not pretend to furnish a history of the great adventure. They concern themselves especially with the broad strategical aspect of the operations, and with certain phases of the fighting that illustrate unwonted classes of tactical work and that throw light upon the art of conducting amphibious warfare. Thus, the naval attempt to force the Straits without military aid is treated in some detail. The famous landing on the shores of the Gallipoli Peninsula on the 25th of April is dealt with fairly exhaustively. The successful evacuation some nine months later of the sea-girt patch of Turkish territory which had been the scene of so much heroism and so much bloodshed, is discussed at length in so far as information as to that most memorable operation of war is forthcoming. On the other hand, some of the principal combats, combats that involved furious fighting and that gave rise to serious losses in the ranks of the contending forces, are dismissed briefly because their story suggests no special lessons concerning the art of war. This applies to the protracted contest at the Helles end of the peninsula after the landings had been made good, and to the sanguinary affrays which took place in the month of August for the possession of the Sari Bair mountain mass. The work is in fact designed to be a study of certain phases of the campaign rather than as a formal record of its course, and such comments and deductions as are sprinkled through its pages are meant to be suggestive rather than didactic, seeing that the majority of the problems discussed are in reality matters admitting of considerable diversity of opinion.

The author's special acknowledgments are due to Scout Fred Giles of the 1st City of Westminster Troop for his invaluable and skilled aid in preparing the maps and plans to illustrate the text. A list of the authorities consulted is given in Appendix I. Some valuable unpublished information has also been at his disposal. The campaign has given rise to a number of interesting and instructive works to supplement official reports. The late Mr. Schuler's account of the Anzac operations gives a most graphic description of the services performed by the troops from the Antipodes, alike in battle and in making possible their stay in a singularly unsatisfactory tactical position. Major Cooper's story of the doings of the 10th Division is so informative as to make one regret the short stay of his division in the peninsula. Even a less remarkable and dramatic series of operations than those executed by the Allies in their immortal gamble for possession of the Hellespont would inevitably provide attractive reading in the hands of Mr. Masefield. The virtues that have been claimed for "words of an eye-witness" are to be found in ample measure in the *Gallipoli Diary* kept by Major Gillam, who saw the business through from start to finish with the famous 29th Division, and in the fascinating pages of *A Naval Adventure*. Mr. Nevinson's *The Dardanelles Campaign* provides a complete history of the operations and of the events leading up to the initiation of the attack upon the Straits, by one who was on the spot during some of the most dramatic incidents of the struggle and who remained with the Expeditionary Force to the very end. Mr. Morgenthau, Mr. Granville Fortescue and Mr. Schreiner have placed it beyond doubt that the batteries barring passage through the Straits only suffered limited damage from the heavy bombardments to which they were subjected by the attacking fleet.

CONTENTS

CHAPTER I

THE INITIATION OF THE CAMPAIGN

Pages

The entry of the Ottoman Empire into the European War—The objects to be gained by success in the Dardanelles—The strategical and tactical problem to be solved—The pitting of warships against coast defences—Application of military force generally necessary when coast defences have to be reduced—The minor operations against the Dardanelles in 1914—The Russian appeal for aid—Means at disposal for bringing pressure upon Turkey—Methods by which pressure could have been brought to bear upon Turkey at this time—The decision to attack the Dardanelles—Preparations for the enterprise 1–13

CHAPTER II

THE NAVAL ATTEMPT TO FORCE THE DARDANELLES

The naval forces assembled for the undertaking—The task—The attacks on the outer forts—Comments—Operations to the middle of March—The early attacks upon the defences of the Narrows—Comments—Need for military assistance becoming apparent—The attack of the 18th of March—Comments. 14–26

CHAPTER III

THE ORGANISATION OF THE MILITARY EXPEDITION

The concentration of troops for the defence of Egypt—First steps towards utilising military force in the Dardanelles campaign—Comments—Weather conditions in the Ægean—The development of the military plans—The delay in employing the military forces detailed—The reorganisation of the Military Expeditionary Force at Alexandria—Promises of Russian co-operation . . . 27–37

CHAPTER IV

THE MILITARY PROBLEM PRESENTED BY THE DARDANELLES

Pages

Alternatives to actually attacking the Gallipoli Peninsula—Operations on the European side—Question of operations on the Asiatic side—The disposition of the Turkish forces in the middle of March—The Gallipoli Peninsula the obvious military objective—The disadvantages of selecting the peninsula as objective—Sir I. Hamilton's decision to attack the peninsula—The strategical and tactical problem presented by the peninsula—Sir Ian Hamilton's plan—The tactical problem that arises in the case of a military landing in face of opposition—Ought the land campaign to have been abandoned at the last moment ? 38–57

CHAPTER V

THE LANDING

The opening scene of the enterprise favoured by good weather—The general plan of attack—Turkish preparations and the distribution of the defending forces—Marshal Liman von Sanders' first dispositions—The distribution of the attacking force at Helles—The landing at Beach Y—Comments—The landing at Beach X—The landing at Beach W—Comments on the fight for W Beach—The landing at Beach S—The landing at Beach V—Comments on the landing on V Beach—The camber east of Sedd-el-Bahr—Some observations on the landings at Helles—The landing at Kum Kale—The feint in the Gulf of Saros—The general scheme for the Anzac landing—The approach—The landing—Comments—The question of landing at dawn—Merits of landing at a topographically inconvenient spot—The importance of making good as much ground as possible at once—The value of portable artillery on these occasions—Partially trained troops—Conclusion 58–105

CHAPTER VI

THE CONSOLIDATION AT HELLES AND ANZAC

The situation at Helles on the morning of the 26th—The advance from V Beach—Reinforcements landed at V Beach—Turkish dispositions with respect to Helles—The withdrawal from Kum Kale—The operations at Helles on the 27th—The situation at Helles on the night of the 27th—The position at Anzac on the morning of the 26th—The 26th and 27th at Anzac—The situation at Anzac on the night of the 26th as compared with that at Helles—The fighting qualities of the Turks—Sir I. Hamilton's division of his forces—Boat accommodation and beach space available—Possibilities at Helles—The question of Kum Kale—Possibilities north of Gaba Tepe—Conclusion 106–131

CONTENTS

CHAPTER VII

THE GENERAL STRATEGICAL SITUATION PRODUCED BY THE LANDINGS

Pages

The Expeditionary Force definitely committed to a certain plan—Turkish communications with, and in, the Gallipoli Peninsula—Ottoman powers of concentration—The Allies' power to threaten descents upon other portions of the coast, and its consequences—Possibilities of severing the Turkish communications—The bases of the Allies—The Allies' communications—The Allies' powers of concentration—Question of drafts—The withdrawal of the Russian Expeditionary Force from Odessa 132–146

CHAPTER VIII

THE FIRST THREE MONTHS AT HELLES

The topographical conditions of the Helles area—Sir I. Hamilton's difficulty—The action of the 28th April—From the 29th of April to the 5th of May—The struggle of the 6th–8th of May—From the 13th of May to the 4th of June—From the 5th to the end of June—The month of July—Comments . . . 147–165

CHAPTER IX

THE FIRST THREE MONTHS AT ANZAC

The topographical features of the Anzac area—Events during the first few days after the 27th—The great Turkish attack upon Anzac—From the 25th of May to the end of July—Comments—Ought the fleet to have given more assistance with its artillery than it did after May 166–181

CHAPTER X

POSSIBILITIES OF SUCCESS

The impossibility of achieving the object with the forces available—The reinforcements—Sir I. Hamilton's appreciation—Comments—The Expeditionary Force's weakness in artillery—Aviation—The naval position 182–191

CHAPTER XI

THE GREAT EFFORT OF EARLY AUGUST

Sir I. Hamilton's plan in outline—The Turkish disposition of force at the beginning of August—The combats at Helles—The operations from Anzac. Preparations—The frontal attacks from the Anzac position—The start of the attack upon Sari Bair—The fight for Sari Bair from the 8th to the 10th—Observations on General Birdwood's operations from the 6th to the 10th—Operations at Suvla Bay—Special conditions of the landings—The orders for the IXth Corps — The landings — Operations on the 7th after 8 a.m.—Comments on the first twenty-four hours of the Suvla operations — The events of the 8th — Sir I. Hamilton's direct intervention—Comments—The events of the 9th and 10th—The splitting up of the 10th Division—Conclusion . . . 192–240

CHAPTER XII

THE CLOSE OF THE AUGUST OFFENSIVE

Pages

The situation on the 11th of August—Operations from the 12th to the 16th—Sir I. Hamilton's request for large reinforcements—From the 17th to the 20th of August—The battle of the 21st of August—From the 22nd of August to the end of the month—Review of the August offensive as a whole 241–255

CHAPTER XIII

THE THREE AUTUMN MONTHS

The situation at the beginning of September—An uneventful period in the peninsula from the tactical point of view—The blizzard of the 27th of November—The Balkan situation between April and October—The effect of the overthrow of Serbia on the Dardanelles campaign—Sir I. Hamilton relieved by Sir C. Monro—General Monro's instructions and his conclusions—Government indecision; Lord Kitchener proceeds to the Ægean—Partial withdrawal ordered—The sailors' insistence on the retention of Helles—General Monro's digest of the communications situation at the peninsula 256–275

CHAPTER XIV

THE EVACUATION OF ANZAC AND SUVLA

General Monro's instructions to General Birdwood—General Birdwood's general plan—From the 10th to the 18th of December—The final evacuation of Anzac—Comments on the final evacuation of Anzac—The final evacuation of Suvla—The withdrawal of the left sector of the Suvla force—The withdrawal of the right sector of the Suvla force—Comments on the evacuation of the Suvla area—The German account 276–304

CHAPTER XV

THE EVACUATION OF HELLES

The decision to withdraw from Helles—The problem—The situation on the 28th of December—General Monro's instructions with regard to the carrying out of the evacuation—The preliminary stage of the operation—The unfavourable weather—Change of plan as to the final evacuation—Events of the 7th—The situation on the 8th—The final evacuation—The German version—Comments on the operation 305–331

CHAPTER XVI

SOME OUTSTANDING LESSONS OF THE CAMPAIGN

Pages

The vital necessity of exhaustive examination of the conditions before embarking on a warlike adventure, and of evolving a comprehensive plan of campaign for its conduct—The great size of modern armies tends to impair the effectiveness of amphibious forms of war—An advanced base needed in case of a maritime descent upon an enemy's shores—The influence of the submarine upon undertakings of the Dardanelles type—Comparative ineffectiveness of boardship gunfire against shore targets—Vital importance in the case of a maritime descent upon hostile territory of securing a large area immediately on landing—Reserves to replace wastage must be provided on the spot in the case of distant campaigns—Conclusion . . 332-347

APPENDICES

APPENDIX I. List of authorities consulted 348
APPENDIX II. Order of battle of the Expeditionary Force . . 350
APPENDIX III. The arrangements made with regard to water for the Suvla landing 355
APPENDIX IV. Marshal Liman von Sanders' views and statements . 357

LIST OF MAPS

		Page
I.	The Helles Area (with insets of Lemnos and Imbros)	62
II.	The Landings on " V " and " W " Beaches	70
III.	Kum Kale	88
IV.	Anzac	94
V.	The Anzac and Suvla Areas	168
VI.	Evacuation of the Left Suvla Sector	294
VII.	The Dardanelles	361
VIII.	General Map	361

CAMPAIGNS AND THEIR LESSONS

THE DARDANELLES

CHAPTER I

THE INITIATION OF THE CAMPAIGN

The entry of the Ottoman Empire into the European War.—Although Turkey delayed acts of war against the Allies until the 31st of October, 1914, two months after the commencement of the European conflict, it had been patent to the world for some weeks previously that hostilities were imminent. The unopposed entry of the German battle-cruiser *Goeben* and her consort, the cruiser *Breslau*, into the Dardanelles, had clearly indicated the existence of a definite, if secret, understanding between the Central Powers and the Sublime Porte, and had made it certain that the Ottoman Empire intended to take sides against the Entente sooner or later. That being the case, the question of a possible attack upon the Dardanelles, as a preliminary to securing mastery over the maritime route from the Mediterranean to the Black Sea and to dealing Turkey simultaneously a staggering blow, had not escaped the attention of the British Admiralty and War Office. The objects to be achieved by the successful execution of such an enterprise were so manifest, the consequences of a military triumph in this quarter were bound to be so far-reaching, that no special knowledge of the factors was indeed required to enable the importance of the matter to be realised.[1]

The objects to be gained by success in the Dardanelles.—It is only proposed to deal with the actual Dardanelles campaign in this volume. At the same time it is indispensable, if a correct

[1] Maps VII and VIII at the end of the volume illustrate Chapters I to IV.

appreciation of the circumstances attending the initiation and prosecution of the venture is to be arrived at, that there should be no misunderstanding as to the scope of the undertaking as originally designed. By those responsible for setting the campaign in motion, the conquest of the Hellespont was rightly regarded as merely a preliminary to further combinations of war. The real objective that they had in view was Constantinople and the Bosphorus—especially the latter. For they realised that the acquisition of this remarkable maritime defile by British, French, and Russian naval and military forces would assure to Russia the means both of exporting the agricultural produce which she possessed in abundance and of importing the war material of which she stood sorely in need, would effect a cleavage of the Sultan's dominions into two parts, and would set up an insuperable barrier against that Teutonic pressure towards the east of which signs had been apparent even before the dramatic events of August, 1914, provided Germany with an opportunity for gratifying her Oriental ambitions. The fall of Constantinople would exercise a tremendous moral effect throughout Turkey and the whole Mahomedan world. So daring and decisive a stroke delivered by the forces of the Entente could, moreover, hardly fail to secure an attitude of benevolent neutrality towards the Allies on the part of the Balkan States, and it might well induce all those kingdoms definitely to make common cause with belligerents who had given a demonstration so convincing of their fighting potentialities and of their capacity for conducting war. As it turned out, the project in reality never got beyond its introductory stage. The attempt to win the Dardanelles, first by naval effort and afterwards by the superposition of a military expedition on a great scale upon the original operation, came to naught. Hence it has followed that the enterprise, in spite of what was contemplated to start with, has come to be looked upon merely as a campaign undertaken for the mastery of those Straits.

The inception and the conduct of the adventure have provoked bitter controversy. But by no person of intelligence has it ever been suggested that the game would not have been worth the candle had the means for playing it effectively been available and had it been played with skill. A project, which had everything to commend it in itself, failed for all practical purposes at the outset owing to faulty strategical and tactical conceptions as to how it ought to be executed, and owing to its being embarked on and carried out with insufficient fighting forces. Under the circumstances, it remains open to question whether the objects aimed at would have been gained even if the preliminary stage—the conquest of the Dardanelles—had been successfully passed. But that remains a matter of conjecture, seeing that the campaign for the Bosphorus and Constantinople broke down at the start.

The strategical and tactical problem to be solved.—The Franco-British naval forces possessed complete command of the Ægean at the end of October, 1914, but this circumstance in reality conferred no special liberty of action upon them in respect to operations to be undertaken for the conquest of the Bosphorus. In view of the considerable Turkish military forces gathered around the capital of their country, of the absence of communications alike in Thrace and in Anatolia, and of the lack of ports well adapted to act as bases for a land campaign on an important scale, the only suitable avenue to the objective ran through the Dardanelles. That great waterway joining the Sea of Marmora to the Ægean must be mastered somehow if the straits connecting the Sea of Marmora with the Black Sea were to be won. Command of the Sea of Marmora had to be established if the further operations were to be prosecuted with vigour and were to be brought to a triumphant conclusion. It was necessary for the Allied fleet to reach this middle water-area via the Dardanelles, and consequently the first problem that presented itself was how this was to be accomplished.

But the mere appearance of the Allied flags in the Marmora would not in itself give their navies permanent control of its waters; the communications of the fleet after it had passed the lower straits must give no cause for anxiety if the operations were to be continued. Moreover, in the event of military effort being needed to compass the downfall of Constantinople and to succour the warships in mastering the Bosphorus—and military effort inevitably would be needed—unopposed navigation of the Dardanelles for transports must be regarded as a *sine qua non*. But the Dardanelles were effectively fortified, and they were furthermore eminently adapted by nature for confronting attack on the part of hostile ships of war. Topographical conditions provided elevated sites for batteries to dominate the channel. Its lack of breadth, its length and its winding character all favoured defence. The existence of a well-defined current flowing down from the Sea of Marmora inevitably offered encouragement to the Turk. It was a case where nature, supplemented by art, created in some respects an almost ideal maritime defile. But, on the other hand, the fact that the region forming the European side of the famous straits represented merely a narrow peninsula, tacked on to the mainland of Thrace by the still narrower isthmus of Bulair, was not without encouragement to a commander of amphibious forces engaged on devising schemes for conquering the passage, and this geographical phenomenon seemed to point unmistakably to the means by which success might be achieved should adequate land and sea forces be available.

A British fleet had mastered the Hellespont on a former occasion, flouting the Crescent. That event had occurred in 1807, when Sir John Duckworth forced the pass at the head of a formidable squadron of two and three deckers—in itself a memorable feat of arms and of sailorship. But the intruders did not tarry long in the Sea of Marmora. The impossibility of provisioning his ships while hostile batteries that remained unimpaired in their powers of doing mischief could play upon the narrow channel which constituted his sole line of communications, constrained Duckworth to retire; and in its transit down the Dardanelles his armament was handled somewhat roughly. For the enterprise to have turned out a profitable one in 1807 it had been essential that those straits should not merely have been forced, but that they should also have been subsequently held. In this important respect the broad strategical features of the problem had undergone no transformation when the possibility of pushing an armament from the Ægean into the Sea of Marmora came to be considered in the autumn of 1914.

The problem had, as it happened, been carefully examined by the British Admiralty and War Office some years earlier. A memorandum had been drawn up in 1906 by the General Staff, in which there occurred a passage that clearly indicates the conclusion which expert sailors and soldiers had then come to as to the expediency of attempting to force the Dardanelles by ships alone. "Military opinion," runs this passage, "looking at the question from the point of view of coast defence, will be in entire agreement with the naval view that unaided action by the fleet, bearing in mind the risk involved, is much to be deprecated." The memorandum, moreover, took a discouraging view of the prospects of conjunct naval and military operations for securing possession of the Straits. The position taken up in the document was that a purely naval attack would not be justifiable under any circumstances, while an amphibious undertaking was bound to prove a most difficult and dangerous operation of war.

The pitting of warships against coast defences.—For many years preceding the outbreak of the European War, sailors and soldiers had agreed that for warships to attack coast fortresses was in principle a mistake. This, needless to say, presupposes that the fortresses are reasonably well armed and equipped for the fray. Weak or ill-manned batteries can naturally be vanquished readily enough by an efficient fleet. Of comparatively recent years, for instance, a British squadron has overcome coast defences at Alexandria, a few American vessels have disposed of the fortifications that protected the harbour of Manilla, and Italian battleships and cruisers have destroyed shore batteries at Tripoli as a prelude to the disembarkation in the harbour of an accompanying expeditionary force; but in none of these cases were the works capable of offering a serious resistance. The failure of the naval attack upon Sebastopol, on the other hand, and the damage sustained by the Italian squadron which assailed the defences of Lissa in 1866, serve as examples of warships being virtually beaten off in ill-advised undertakings against land fortifications.

Occasions no doubt will arise from time to time in war where floating forces have no option and are obliged to throw down the gauntlet to shore defences that are strong enough to give a good account of themselves—Blake's daring assault upon the Porto Farina batteries which sheltered the corsair flotilla that he meant to destroy, and Nelson's intrepid action at Copenhagen, can be cited as instances. But most experts declare that such ventures are to be avoided if it is possible. The justifiable disinclination of sailors to risk their ships on such unpromising enterprises has been well illustrated within the last few years by the refusal of Admiral Shafter to attempt to force his way into the harbour of Santiago de Cuba, and by the non-committal attitude so rigidly preserved by the Japanese naval authorities with regard to the coast batteries that protected Port Arthur during the prolonged operations undertaken for the capture of that stronghold from the Russians.

The Dardanelles presented the case of a narrow channel that was more or less fringed with works furnished with heavy ordnance. Up to the time of the introduction of mines and torpedoes, warships often succeeded in running past efficient defences protecting channels and rivers, without incurring much injury—as Duckworth did on the occasion quoted above. Farragut was in his element in such work in the days of the War of Secession. But submarine devices have rendered enterprises of this kind incomparably more difficult for floating forces to carry through successfully than they were a few decades ago. The essence of a running past operation is that the ships engaged on the venture should proceed rapidly through the defile, bringing so intense and violent a fire to bear upon the defending batteries that the gun detachments in these are driven from their emplacements. But the mine and the torpedo have vastly increased the risks inseparable from a resort to such uncompromising tactics. Indeed, if these engines of destruction are skilfully employed by the defenders, and if they are available in sufficient quantities, rushing a channel so protected may be wholly out of the question. To attempt the feat may mean the destruction of the entire flotilla.

Application of military force generally necessary when coast defences have to be reduced.—Seeing that it is in general objectionable to oppose warships against coast defences, but that circumstances in time of war may render imperative the reduction of the works, the duty of dealing with them usually falls upon land forces. Records of past campaigns will produce a dozen examples of the fall of maritime fortresses brought about by the action of soldiers, against one example of the task having been accomplished by sailors. The conquest of Port Arthur in 1895 was achieved by the military, and history repeated itself when the same great place of arms was again assailed in 1905. The coast batteries of Prevesa and of Salonika were dealt with from the land, and not from the sea, side in the Balkan War of 1912. It was the United States army and not the navy that overcame Santiago. Sebastopol fell to military force. When this country felt itself called upon to attack Copenhagen so as to gain possession of the Danish fleet seven years after Nelson's exploit, the method adopted was to land troops in the vicinity of the place. It indeed is hardly too much to say that a purely naval attack upon reasonably efficient coast defences would in practice never take place were it not for the difficulty that so often presents itself in conveying troops to the locality. For, in the nature of things, an enemy's maritime fortress will probably be too remote to permit of the army intended for its reduction marching thither from its own territory.

On broad strategical principles, therefore, attack upon the Dardanelles presented itself in 1914 as an operation that ought not to be undertaken without military assistance, if it was undertaken at all. This had been fully recognised by the British naval and military authorities in 1906. It continued to be recognised during the early months of the European War, and, had the question received that close and detailed examination by sailors and soldiers in consultation that the case demanded when it was suddenly brought into prominence in the early days of 1915, it is difficult to believe that any other verdict would have been given.

The minor operations against the Dardanelles in 1914.—A combined British and French squadron bombarded the batteries at the mouth of the Dardanelles on the 3rd of November, the ships firing at long range for a few minutes. The works replied, and from their feeble performance it was possible to deduce the capabilities of the Turkish guns. Nothing further worthy of note happened after this affair till the 13th of December, when a British submarine proceeded up the Straits and succeeded in sinking an old Turkish battleship—a very fine feat of arms in view of the rows of minefields under which the vessel had to pass. There was, however, no intention of undertaking serious operations in this quarter until the early days of January. Then, however, matters were unexpectedly brought to a head.

The Russian appeal for aid.—On the 2nd of January a telegram was received at the British War Office from Russia containing a request that a demonstration of some kind should be made against Turkey, so as to relieve the very serious pressure that was being put upon the Russian forces in Transcaucasia by a superior Ottoman army at the moment. To this Lord Kitchener, the War

Minister, sent a reply promising compliance, at the same time expressing doubts whether a demonstration would achieve the object in view. But an appeal of this kind from an Ally who had risked and encountered a disaster four months before in a loyal effort to afford assistance indirectly to the Franco-British armies when these were in serious straits in France, could not possibly be disregarded, and the British Government felt itself bound to consider very seriously what form of demonstration, that could be regarded as feasible, would be likely to draw Turkish troops away from the theatre of war in Armenia. It may not, however, be out of place to observe here that, thanks to masterly leadership and to a display of rare martial qualities on the part of the soldiery, the Russian forces at the threatened point had by their own unaided grit and skill relieved the pressure of the enemy upon them before any action was taken to help them from the side of the Mediterranean.

Means at disposal for bringing pressure upon Turkey at this time.—The aggregate of warships of the Allies gathered in the Mediterranean at this juncture represented force sufficient to maintain a virtually undisputed command of those waters, always provided that no new enemy disposing of maritime resources should intervene. The demands made upon it by its duties in connection with keeping careful guard over the respectable and well-handled Austro-Hungarian marine in the Adriatic, and by its responsibilities in connection with ensuring a rigid blockade of the Ottoman coast and watching the Dardanelles, however, practically absorbed its whole fighting capabilities. There was little margin left in hand justifying its embarking on adventures that might weaken it. For it to have committed itself to a serious attack upon the formidable defences of the Hellespont at the moment when Russia called for aid, would have been to impose a greater strain upon the squadrons of which it was composed than these might have been able to endure.

Nor had the Allies at this time adequate military forces available in the Near East, or capable of being promptly despatched thither, to justify their undertaking a land campaign against Turkey designed on an ambitious scale. To have detached troops from the theatre of war in France and Flanders in the midwinter of 1914–15 was out of the question, and not more than a few thousand adequately trained and fully equipped units could have been found elsewhere for the task. It is true that the need of defending Egypt against threatened Osmanli attack from the side of Syria had brought about the assemblage of a numerically considerable army in the Nile Delta. India had sent its quota of regulars, and Territorial units had been despatched from home. These troops had been, and were being, supplemented by considerable forces drawn from Australia and New Zealand for which the country afforded favourable training ground in good climatic conditions. But it was not an army that could have provided at the moment a serviceable fighting force on the scale qualifying it to launch out on extensive operations. For it consisted largely of depots, it was weak in organised artillery formations, and it included many corps, made up of exceptionally fine material but of material that still needed welding into shape. So it came about that at the juncture when the British Government was called upon to take some step calculated to afford succour to the Russian troops in Armenia, those responsible had neither the requisite naval forces nor the requisite military forces at their disposal for dealing the Ottoman Empire a telling blow forthwith.

Methods by which pressure could have been brought to bear upon Turkey at this time.—Leaving the question of insufficiency of land and sea forces for making an effort out of consideration, it may be stated at once that an attack upon the Dardanelles as a prelude to threatening Constantinople and the Bosphorus offered by far the most effective means of bringing pressure to bear upon Turkey, when Russia asked for aid. For, so long as the Sublime Porte entertained any solicitude concerning the safety of the approaches to the Golden Horn, great Ottoman forces were automatically fettered to this part of the empire. The moment, moreover, that the Allies should embark upon any enterprise directed against those approaches, summonses would assuredly go out to commanders in distant provinces to despatch reinforcements to the threatened point, and the Sultan's lieutenants in Armenia would be called upon with the rest to make sacrifices. There is, however, one feature in connection with the strategical situation here involved which must not be overlooked. So long as they were merely more or less directly threatened, the Dardanelles and Constantinople placed a trump card in the hands of the Allies. Without risking a ship or a soldier, the Entente Powers could keep great Turkish forces occupied. Rarely does it occur in war that geographical and strategical conditions offer a belligerent such facilities for exercising "bluff," as the situation in the Near East and the Levant presented in the opening days of 1915. "He that commands the sea," as Bacon observed, "is at great liberty, and may take as much or as little of the war as he will." The naval forces of the Entente dominated the Ægean. Swarms of British and Australasian and Indian soldiers were concentrated in Egypt. Any rumour skilfully propagated in the bazaars of Cairo and of Alexandria as to a contemplated venture against the seat of the Caliph was sure to echo ere long in the streets of Stambul. The islands of Tenedos and Imbros and Lemnos were available, inviting detachments to set foot on land that must excite remark. A bombardment of somewhat more vertebrate character than that inflicted upon the outer defences of the Dardanelles on the 3rd of November, would give just that colour to stories of tremendous impending events that would ensure their causing panic in Constantinople. Nor should it be forgotten that a threat of this kind could be always repeated at later stages of the war if desired, and that it would only cease to be an asset in the hands of the Allies if the operation was undertaken in reality—and failed.

But it must not be supposed that there was no other way of affording some relief to the Russian troops in Transcaucasia, than by demonstrations or operations directed against the Turkish capital. The nearest point on the Ottoman coast to those rugged uplands east of Erzerum where the Tsar's forces were hard pressed happens to be the Gulf of Alexandretta, and the littoral of this gulf was in 1915 of great importance to the communications of Ottoman forces on the warpath in Mesopotamia and Palestine. Turkish garrisons in this region were known to be small. The shore provides satisfactory facilities for effecting landings and for setting on foot a suitable military base. Enough serviceable troops were to be found in Egypt, after providing for its security, to permit of an expeditionary force being detached, adequate for the purpose, should it be decided to undertake such an operation. Transports to convey the armament to the scene of action could have been very rapidly got together, seeing that ships were constantly steaming into Suez with contingents from India and

Australasia. Another merit that could be claimed for an undertaking directed against Alexandretta and its environs, was that such a project could readily be combined with demonstrations directed against the Hellespont. There was in fact undoubtedly much to be said in its favour. Dealing as this volume does merely with the Dardanelles campaign, it would be inappropriate to further discuss in it the possibilities offered by enterprises to be undertaken against other portions of the Ottoman Empire. But it has been necessary to point out that the course actually adopted, that of concentrating effort upon a scheme involving a hazardous operation of war of the first class, was not the only one that was open to her Allies when Russia in early January, 1915, appealed to them for succour.

The decision to attack the Dardanelles.—It was on the 3rd of January that the British Admiralty invited Admiral Carden, who was in command of the British naval forces in the Mediterranean, to report whether he regarded forcing the Dardanelles by ships alone as a practicable operation. He replied two days later that he did not think that the straits could be rushed, but he added that in his opinion they might be forced by extended operations with a large number of ships. A method of proceeding such as the Admiral here suggested had never been seriously considered before in this particular connection, and the proposal consequently attracted much attention. It was exhaustively considered by the naval experts in London and gained a certain measure of approval from them, one great merit claimed for the plan being that the undertaking could always be abandoned without difficulty should the task prove to be too formidable from experiences gained in its opening stages. The General Staff in London, on the other hand, who had examined this problem very thoroughly in 1906 as a more or less academic question, were not called upon to give a considered opinion now that the question had become a practical one. The War Council, which governed the general conduct of the operations, was favourably impressed with Admiral Carden's plan. The idea that the project could be given up after having once started seems to have carried weight with this body, and on the 13th of January a decision was arrived at couched in these quaint terms : " The Admiralty should prepare for a naval expedition in February to bombard and take the Gallipoli Peninsula, with Constantinople as its objective." Thus came to be launched an undertaking which, whatever may be said concerning its expediency and concerning the prospects of success that it involved in theory, brought about one of the most remarkable campaigns recorded in the history of war.

Preparations for the enterprise.—Steps were straightway taken to augment the Allied naval forces in the Mediterranean, and to get together a fleet composed of the class of vessel considered to be particularly well adapted for trying conclusions with the Turkish coast batteries. It was adjudged inadvisable to detach any considerable number of battleships or battle-cruisers of the most modern type from home waters, in view of the heavy responsibilities that the strategical situation imposed upon the Grand Fleet. But the Admiralty had at their disposal several semi-obsolete battleships, as well as one or two others of somewhat superior class but scarcely a match for German Dreadnoughts, which seemed admirably suited for carrying out the work in hand. All of these mounted heavy ordnance superior to the guns that were known to be emplaced in the Turkish batteries, and even if vessels of this type were to meet with mishap in the Hellespont, their loss would not jeopardise the well-established domination of the Allies' navies over those of the enemy outside of the Mediterranean. So a number of these battleships were despatched to Malta and the Ægean from home waters, and the French also managed to allot some analogous units to augment Admiral Carden's fleet. Flotillas of mine-sweepers and other small craft, adjudged to be suitable for the work in hand, were got together. By the middle of February the imposing armada that had been designated to carry the operation through had, with the exception of a very few vessels still on the way, assembled in the vicinity of the Dardanelles, and only favourable weather was now needed to begin.

The decision that had been arrived at by the War Council in London on the 13th of January was confirmed by another decision to the same effect, arrived at on the 28th of the month, which finally committed the Allies to an attack upon the Straits by naval force alone. But although these decisions specifically imposed the duty of winning the avenue to the Sea of Marmora upon the fleet, it appears always to have been realised in a vague sort of way that a certain amount of assistance on the part of bodies of troops might become indispensable even during the process of forcing the Dardanelles. The subsequent programme would in any case demand the presence of an army of some kind. Moreover, just at this juncture, there occurred a military incident which appreciably altered the situation in so far as troops were concerned. For an Ottoman expedition against the Suez Canal, after successfully traversing the inhospitable region that lies between the canal and Palestine, met with signal discomfiture at the hands of the defending troops, and fled eastwards in disorder. All anxiety as to Egypt was thus for the time being at an end, the bulk of the forces assembled in and about the Nile Delta became available for service elsewhere, and the nucleus of an army to share in the impending combinations for the reduction of Constantinople was found to be available at no great distance from the scene of coming action. The despatch of troops from the United Kingdom had also received a certain amount of consideration.

But it will be convenient to defer recording the genesis of the military expedition, and to postpone indicating the organisation and the disposition of the land forces that took part in it, until the arrangements for active intervention by British and French soldiers in the campaign come to be dealt with in Chapter III. In any case it cannot, in the interests of historical accuracy and of placing a correct interpretation on the striking lessons which the opening phases of the Dardanelles affair teach, be too strongly insisted upon that, at the date when the operations started, trust was still officially being placed in ships, unaided by military force, to secure the Straits.

CHAPTER II

THE NAVAL ATTEMPT TO FORCE THE STRAITS

The naval forces assembled for the undertaking.—A powerful fleet had been assembled in the Ægean in view of the operations that were to take place. It included *Queen Elizabeth* with her eight 15-inch guns, the most formidable fighting ship in commission at the moment, and included *Inflexible* with eight 12-inch guns, a vessel classed as a battle-cruiser but which for the work in hand can more conveniently be regarded as a battleship. The remainder of the battleships were for the most part out of date for a fleet action against vessels of the most modern type; but the majority of them mounted four 12-inch guns—*Agamemnon* and *Lord Nelson* being further furnished with ten 9·2-inch guns—and all of them carried a serviceable secondary armament. There were furthermore a number of cruisers, and an adequate flotilla of destroyers, mine-sweepers, and other small craft had also been got together. The majority of the ships were British; but the fleet included a squadron of French battleships, and a Russian cruiser arrived during the operations. The whole armada was under command of Admiral Carden. The islands of Tenedos, Imbros and Lemnos had been occupied, the latter providing the naval forces with a magnificent, if entirely undeveloped, harbour in the great landlocked inlet of Mudros. Large supplies of naval stores of all kinds and of ammunition had been collected, arrangements for aerial observation had been made, and elaborate " squared " maps on a large scale had been prepared to assist the gunnery experts in the allocation of targets and in the control of indirect fire.

Information as to the details and armament of the coast defences protecting the Straits at the disposal of the assailants was upon the whole sufficient, and it proved to be generally accurate when the operations began. There was naturally some uncertainty as to the position of hostile minefields, as to the resources of the

Turks in respect to drifting mines, torpedo tubes and so forth, and also as to the reserves of ammunition accumulated in the forts. Still, the naval authorities had sufficient knowledge of the kind of opposition that they would have to cope with, to enable them to frame their plans with some measure of confidence, and to prepare a detailed programme of the operations contemplated in advance.

The task.—For practical purposes, the operation about to be embarked upon can be divided into three stages. Each stage could be more or less definitely foreseen and could therefore be effectively provided for. To start with, the batteries at the entrance to the Dardanelles had to be rendered innocuous before the fleet could enter the Straits. Then there were extensive minefields, and also some batteries, that must be disposed of before the assailants could act effectively against the defences of the Narrows. When these two preliminary obstacles to progress had been overcome would come the real trial of strength—the destruction of the batteries in the Narrows and the clearing away of the minefields with which this defile was sown.

Assuming that all three stages were got through successfully and without suffering so great loss as to cripple the naval fighting forces, there would still remain the problem of guarding the communications of the fleet when this passed on into the Sea of Marmora. Military forces were, however, assembling in the Ægean and in Egypt, and it was reasonably certain that by the time that the sailors had forced the passage of the Straits there would be soldiers available who might possibly be able to secure their communications. Inasmuch as the naval attack failed when it arrived at the third stage, this question of the communications never arose, and it is therefore unnecessary to speculate concerning a portion of the programme which, if the truth must be told, had received little scrupulous consideration at the moment when the die was cast.

The attacks on the outer forts.—The attempt to force the passage of the Straits by naval power unaided commenced on the 19th of February. On that day the batteries and works guarding the entrance to the waterway were assailed by a fleet of eight battleships (five British and three French), mounting forty-six guns of 9·2-inch calibre and upwards, of which thirty were 12-inch pieces.

The defences were not of a formidable kind. They consisted on the European side in the main of a modern earthen battery at Cape Helles equipped with two 9·2-inch guns, and of the old-fashioned fort of Sedd-el-Bahr with six 10-inch and two 6-inch guns. On the Asiatic side the battleships were confronted by the old works at Kum Kale, which boasted of four 10·2-inch guns, and by a modern earthen battery mounting two 9·2-inch guns near Yeni Shehr. The Sedd-el-Bahr and Kum Kale forts, low-lying and rather conspicuous, offered excellent targets to the ships' guns; the two 9·2-inch batteries had both some little command and with their respectable armament had to be more seriously considered. But the assailants enjoyed the great advantage of having ample sea-room for manœuvring, with deep water fairly close in, and of feeling no solicitude with regard to mines or torpedoes. The ships' guns out-ranged those on shore, and the fact is that this preliminary part of Admiral Carden's task represented as simple a problem as a naval armament can fairly expect to be called upon to solve when it is a case of attacking shore defences worthy of any consideration at all.

A morning bombardment at long range took place which seemed from the decks of the attacking vessels to have done a good deal of damage. Operations were resumed in the afternoon, but it was then found that the destruction wrought in the works had hardly been so great as had been supposed; six battleships, however, steamed in to comparatively short range, and by the evening all the batteries except the 9·2-inch one at Yeni Shehr had become mute. No ship was hit, although in the afternoon the attacking vessels had been well within range of the shore artillery; for the Turkish gunnery was very eccentric throughout. A fresh bombardment was initiated next morning; but bad weather came on, so operations had to be suspended until the 25th. When work began on that day it was speedily discovered that the defences had by no means been definitively placed out of action by the cannonade of the 19th. For it took an hour and a half to silence the 9·2-inch battery on Cape Helles, *Queen Elizabeth* eventually accomplishing this feat when lying a long way out. The works on the Asiatic side also gave appreciable trouble, the gunnery from the land being more effective on this occasion than it had been on the first day, although actually doing little damage.

THE DISCOURAGING START 17

Before dark, however, all firing from the shore had ceased, in spite of some of the ships being close in and offering most tempting targets, and the operation of destroying the defences at the entrance to the Straits by bombardment had been brought to a successful conclusion. Ten battleships took part in this second attack.

Comments.—This prologue to what was recognised on all hands to be a decidedly hazardous operation of war, had admirably illustrated the difficulties under which a fleet of warships labours when it endeavours to overcome the resistance of coast defences. The combat had been almost ludicrously one-sided. It had been a case of target practice for the ships and not a battle. The Turkish gunnery had been virtually innocuous when the attacking vessels closed in to ranges well within the scope of the shore guns, and it had always been possible to bring fire to bear from the sea at ranges which the shore guns could not compass. And yet it had been found by no means easy to silence the coast artillery. The first day's cannonade had served to show that a shore battery must not be assumed to have been silenced simply because it ceases fire. It is indeed very difficult for the sailors to ascertain if they have really put the work out of action or not, unless it has been observed that the guns of the battery have been hit, or unless the air service can report that the battery is abandoned. The attacks on the outer forts afforded upon the whole but scanty encouragement to naval men, who fully realised that these ill-contested affairs could only be regarded as preliminary skirmishes. The results of long-range bombardment had upon the whole proved disappointing. It had been a little disquieting to find the shore defences so lively on the second day, after they had been well battered six days earlier. The truth is—and it is a truth that was well known before the Dardanelles venture was decided upon—that it is one thing for ships' guns to drive coast gunners from their guns for the time being, and that it is quite another thing to render the armament of the coast batteries permanently harmless.

Operations to the middle of March.—The mine-sweepers got to work as soon as darkness fell on the 25th and were little interfered with from the shore. They had soon cleared away the minefields actually barring the entrance to the Straits, and before morning had opened a route for the bigger ships to a point four miles within the channel. Next day three battleships entered the lower

C

reach of the Dardanelles and engaged some batteries on the Asiatic shore, while landing-parties completed the destruction of the forts on the European side. The ammunition was blown up and the guns, the majority of which were found to be intact, were demolished; there was no opposition. Then came two more days of bad weather. But from the 1st to the 4th of March warships each day steamed into the Straits and bombarded batteries near Kephez Point without result. The sweepers, moreover, during the dark hours cleared another four miles to the front, opening a way for battleships to advance to within two miles of Kephez Point. During their efforts to accomplish this, and on subsequent nights, the vessels were subjected to a good deal of annoyance from concealed field guns and howitzers, the enemy searchlights being very effective, and it was made evident that this type of artillery was likely to exert a considerable influence over the further progress of the undertaking to which Admiral Carden was committed. As it had been observed that the Turks were maintaining a grip upon the ruined works about the mouth of the Straits, landing-parties were put ashore on the 4th both at Sedd-el-Bahr and Kum Kale. The task was accomplished with little trouble on the European side; but on the opposite shore the enemy offered a stubborn resistance and the landing troops were hustled back into their boats, suffering appreciable loss. Still, this did not much affect the situation in respect to long-range attack upon the defences of the Narrows, an operation which had been rendered practicable by the success of the small craft in clearing the channel up to within about 10,000 yards of Chanak.

The early attacks upon the defences of the Narrows.—The batteries and works about the Narrows were from every point of view far more formidable to an attacking fleet than those about the entrance to the Straits. As will be noted on Map VII, a sharp kink occurs in the waterway at the point where this contracts into a defile. The consequence is that the defence works for practical purposes divided themselves into two groups—those which bore down the long reach below the angle, and those which guarded the channel above the angle. The lower group comprised several batteries terraced on the southern slopes of the Khilid Bahr plateau or nestling at its foot, and two on the Asiatic

EARLY ATTACKS ON THE NARROWS 19

side about Chanak; their armament included a number of guns of heavy calibre, and, in view of the lack of sea-room and of manœuvring space at the disposal of an attacking squadron, their destruction by ships' guns was bound to be a work of difficulty. The channel was mined, there was every reason to believe that the defenders had torpedo-tubes at their disposal, and the floating forces had to face the perils created by drifting mines dropping down the channel with the current.

Operations began on the 5th. On that day *Queen Elizabeth*, accompanied by two other battleships, repaired to the outer side of the Gallipoli Peninsula, and from thence her 15-inch guns were brought to bear upon three of the Khilid Bahr batteries in succession, using indirect fire under control of aeroplanes, a form of observation still in its infancy. A magazine was blown up in one battery and the others were damaged, but the effect was in reality small; hidden howitzers that opened a harmless fire upon the vessels could not be properly located. Next day *Queen Elizabeth* resumed, making the batteries near Chanak her target, but the result of this bombardment was disappointing; in the meantime five battleships within the Straits were engaging the batteries near Kephez Point and one opposite, and were fired at from one of the batteries on the Khilid Bahr slopes which *Queen Elizabeth* had dealt with the previous day. Much had been expected from the indirect fire from outside the peninsula by the most powerful guns afloat, but the results had not come up to anticipations, and were in reality even smaller than was supposed in the fleet, and the plan was consequently abandoned during subsequent operations.

On the 7th several battleships continued the attack from within the Straits. Two of them, *Agamemnon* and *Lord Nelson*, which had modern guns, bombarded the Khilid Bahr batteries at long range, while the remainder moved further up the channel and engaged the batteries lower down and the concealed mobile guns. The Khilid Bahr batteries returned the fire for a short time, but ceased after discharging a few rounds. Next day *Queen Elizabeth* steamed in and engaged the batteries of the Narrows at very long range, while six other vessels moved further up; but the weather on this occasion was not favourable. It was noticeable that even the big armoured ships during these operations suffered some annoyance from the field guns and howitzers, which almost invariably proved quite irrepressible. On this day, moreover, some of the permanent batteries replied with spirit, if not very effectively, and information since come to hand goes to show that the shore defences had suffered very little from all this expenditure of ammunition. It was becoming apparent indeed that the complete destruction of the main defences by gun fire must form an extremely troublesome operation, the fire of concealed artillery was interfering a good deal with mine-sweeping operations, and a lull of some days took place. The small craft, however, continued their labours night after night intent on methodically clearing away the minefields up to and above Kephez Point, but their progress was much slower than it had been when working in wider portions. The craft were insufficient, the crews inexperienced, and interruptions from shell-fire frequent.

Comments.—The operations up to date had served to illustrate at once the advantages and the disadvantages of the system of deliberate, steady progress which was the basis of Admiral Carden's plan. Its advantages displayed themselves in the broad fact that the fleet had forced its way well within the Straits and had strenuously battered the defences on Khilid Bahr and about Chanak, without suffering any loss to speak of; for not one of the bigger vessels had been put out of action, and, considering the hazardous nature of their task and the resolution displayed by the crews, the mine-sweepers and other small craft had sustained no very appreciable damage. But against this had to be set the fact that batteries which had been silenced one day kept manifesting a disconcerting tendency to come to life again on the morrow.[1] There were, moreover, indications that the Turks were gaining valuable experience in respect to employing their movable armament, and it was becoming apparent that this armament was being reinforced. Clearing away the mines was proving more difficult than had been anticipated. The fleet's ammunition supply was beginning to cause anxiety. It was, moreover, not unreasonable to suppose that the defenders would be developing their defensive system about Chanak and Khilid Bahr, that they were

---

[1] "The experience of the *Triumph* at Tsingtau was valuable. She had learnt to distrust silenced forts." *With the Fleet in the Dardanelles* by the Rev. H. W. Price. (*Triumph* had participated with the Japanese in taking Tsingtau.)

PAUSE IN THE OPERATIONS 21

accumulating means of resistance, and that they were gathering together drift-mines, ready to enlarge these engines of destruction when a really favourable opportunity offered itself. There is reason to believe that within the main defences the artillery officers were purposely withholding their fire for fear of running short of ammunition, and so as to reserve this until the attacking ships should press forward to closer range than they yet had attempted. Whether the comparative ineffectiveness of the Turkish gunnery was due to lack of training, or to lack of the requisite adjuncts for ensuring good practice, or to the damage that the batteries had suffered and were suffering, is doubtful—all three factors probably contributed to bring about the result—but for so far the attacking fleet had encountered little hurt from the shore artillery.

Need for military assistance becoming apparent.—It is not quite clear why a lull of several days should have occurred after the 8th, except on the grounds of shortage of ammunition or because it was hoped that a channel through the minefields would be swept up to within short range of Khilid Bahr and Chanak before resuming. The weather, if not ideal, would not seem to have been such as to prohibit a continuation of the bombardment within the Straits. It was obviously desirable to give the Turks no opportunities for repairing the ravages that their defence works had undergone. It almost looks as if the naval authorities on the spot had come to recognise that military assistance in some form or other was imperatively called for if the venture was to prove successful. To anticipate the record of military events that are to be dealt with in the next chapter, it may be here mentioned that considerable bodies of troops had already arrived at the island of Lemnos, that more were known to be available in Egypt, that the despatch of additional forces from home had been engaging the attention of the Government in London even before the naval operations started on the 19th of February, and that Sir Ian Hamilton had been selected to command the army on the 11th of March. Sir Ian left home on the 13th and arrived at Lemnos on the 17th. It is quite true that there was at this time no intention to employ military forces in or about the Dardanelles except in an auxiliary capacity to the fleet. Still, military co-operation was in the air, the idea of bolstering up the original scheme for forcing the passage of the Dardanelles by adopting the device of bringing troops into play probably exercised its influence on naval counsels, and in any case three weeks' experience of the deliberate method of attack suggested that, if the way was ever to be won by the fleet unaided, the operations would have to assume a more resolute character than had signalised them hitherto.

The attack of the 18th of March.—We know from the Report of the Dardanelles Commission that a telegram was despatched from the Admiralty to Admiral Carden on the 11th in which it was suggested for his consideration, " that a point has now been reached when it is necessary to choose favourable weather-conditions to overwhelm forts of the Narrows at decisive range, by bringing to bear upon them the fire of the largest possible number of guns, great and small." To this the Admiral replied on the 13th, " I consider that the stage when vigorous sustained action is necessary for success has now been reached. I am of opinion that, in order to ensure my communications line immediately fleet enters the Sea of Marmora, military operations on a large scale should be opened at once." Admiral Carden was, however, obliged to resign on account of ill-health on the 16th, and was succeeded by Admiral de Robeck, previously second-in-command. On the 17th the new naval chief met Sir I. Hamilton and intimated that he proposed, if the weather proved propitious, to make a general attack on the Narrows on the morrow, and, as it turned out, the 18th proved to be a day admirably suited for the operations that were contemplated.

At about 11 a.m., favoured by clear atmosphere and an unruffled calm, the four most powerful battleships of the fleet steamed up to within long range of the Narrows and engaged the batteries there, while two other battleships, cruising further ahead, busied themselves with the works about Kephez Point and opposite. Then four French battleships, passing through this group of ships and steaming forward to within a couple of miles of Kephez Point, opened a heavy fire on the defences of the Narrows, which was returned. The batteries, however, ceased firing after an hour, whereupon a fresh squadron, consisting of six British battleships, moved up the Straits to relieve the French quartette. The manœuvre of substituting one set of ships for another in front line, however, obliged the attacking fleet practically to suspend the cannonade for the time being, and this encouraged the batteries in the

Narrows to open fire afresh. Nor had the French squadron come unscathed through the contest, for all four ships were more or less damaged, and then, just when its troubles appeared to be over for the day, it met serious misfortunes. For *Gaulois* was holed by shell-fire; and while steaming down channel in Erenkeui Bay, *Bouvet* struck a drifting mine with the result that she sank within a few minutes, losing the greater part of her crew. *Gaulois* was found to be so seriously injured that she had to be run ashore on Rabbit Island[1] to save her from sinking, *Suffren*, holed by shell, had to be docked, and *Charlemagne* was badly damaged. The Turks, realising that this was a formidable attack and that there were many warships in the fairway, were letting loose drift-mines to float down with the current. *Inflexible*, which was the most powerful unit in the fleet next to *Queen Elizabeth*, struck one, after having already been somewhat knocked about by hostile shell, and ran risk of foundering, but she succeeded in withdrawing out of action and in making Tenedos, and was eventually sent to Malta. Another secured a victim in *Irresistible*; this vessel remained above water long enough to permit of the escape of practically all her complement. A little later in the afternoon *Ocean* also fouled a mine, and in her case also most of the crew were got off under heavy fire before she went to the bottom. All this time the shore batteries were maintaining a creditable fight with the fleet, and the mobile guns of the defence were hard at work. In spite of the contretemps the battleships continued their bombardment as long as the light admitted. Then they steamed back out of the Straits, having failed to establish a decisive superiority over the defences that they had undertaken to crush.

The great attack by sixteen battleships upon the Narrows had in fact met with discomfiture. The defences had suffered but, as we now know, not heavily; and a feature in the combat had been that the shore guns had kept up a more effective fire than they had on any previous day since the operations commenced. For the first time the battle fleet had encountered mines, and it had suffered severely

[1] This island is not shown on Map VII or Map VIII. It lies to the north of Tenedos and about half-way between that island and the mouth of the Dardanelles. In the later stages of the campaign monitors used to lie behind it ready to issue out and engage Turkish land batteries on the Asiatic side of the Straits that were firing on the troops about the extremity of the Gallipoli Peninsula.

at their hands, seeing that three ships had been sunk and another put out of action by their instrumentality. Three other battleships had, moreover, been temporarily disabled by gun-fire, so that only nine of the sixteen capital ships that had steamed into the Dardanelles on the morning of the 18th, would have been in a condition to renew the attempt on the morrow had it been proposed that they should do so. There is reason to believe that the guns of heavy calibre in the batteries at the Narrows had expended nearly all their armour-piercing projectiles; but it was not this ordnance that was impeding the work of the mine-sweepers. Mines, fixed and drifting, were the real obstacle to the fleet's progress, and a Turkish shortage of big shell made no very great difference.

It may be observed furthermore that the remarkable results obtained by the Turkish drift-mines could be accepted as a warning that this form of defence was likely to prove even more effective in case the attacking fleet should on some future date venture further forward than it had advanced on the 18th. Sir I. Hamilton, who witnessed part of the engagement, entertained no illusions on the subject, for, telegraphing to Lord Kitchener, he intimated that he was "reluctantly driven towards the conclusion that the Dardanelles were less likely to be forced by battleships than at one time seemed probable." And he added that if the army was to participate, its operations would not assume the subsidiary form that had been anticipated. Admiral de Robeck came to a similar conclusion after two or three days' consideration, and it was virtually admitted that the plan on which reliance had been placed for making good a passage for Allied naval forces into the Sea of Marmora, had broken down.

The attempt to force a way through by naval power unaided was thereupon abandoned. It was decided that henceforward the fleet was, in so far as the Dardanelles were concerned, to revert to its proper function of an auxiliary to military forces that were, somehow, to deal with the defences of the channel. A naval campaign was—somewhat late in the day—converted into an amphibious one. Little of interest consequently occurred within the Straits during the following month, although units of the fleet entered almost daily to ensure that the control over the lower reaches which had been acquired should not pass away.

THE NAVAL FAILURE

Comments.—The battle of the 18th furnishes us with convincing evidence as to the advantages which shore batteries inevitably enjoy over warships, especially when it is a question of securing a comparatively narrow waterway. The sixteen battleships which attacked could claim an overwhelming superiority over the land defences in respect to gun power. The batteries had, moreover, been shaken by previous bombardments and they would seem to have been somewhat short of ammunition. Yet the assailants sustained considerable injury in the artillery duel, even if it was the mines that really decided the issue for the day; and, as a matter of fact, the havoc in the works was not great, for only five or six guns were definitely put out of action, even if parapets and buildings had been badly knocked about in some cases. Whether the armada would have suffered less from the enemy's shell had it ventured on a dash past the batteries it is hard to say; the danger from mines and torpedoes, however, virtually precluded any idea of trying to rush the passage after this fashion, and it imposed upon the sailors a method of operating which necessarily afforded the hostile gunners scope for taking shelter when hard pressed. It must be added that the ships, owing to the restricted space at their disposal, were compelled to cruise slowly while in action, and that on this account they offered particularly favourable targets to the shore artillerymen. But it was the peril of the mines and not respect for the coast batteries which determined Admiral de Robeck to abandon his fleet operations and to await intervention on the part of the army.

The vessels sacrificed on the 18th were replaced within a very few days, so that the attack might speedily have been renewed with naval forces as strong as those which had failed that day. But the fleet would almost certainly have been to some extent crippled in the affray, and the number of semi-obsolete battleships at the disposal of the British and French and available for sacrifice was not unlimited. Any fresh effort must in any case have been postponed for a few days, and all the experience gained since the 19th of February had served to illustrate the advantages conferred upon the defenders by a pause. It has been asserted that the Turks were completely demoralised and had persuaded themselves that all was lost. It has been alleged that victory was within grasp of the fleet on the 18th of March had it persevered, that the whole defensive system of the Dardanelles was crumbling, that—in a word—the game was in the Allies' hands, but that they threw it away. We may learn for certain that this was so some day, but there was nothing in what had actually occurred to suggest to the naval chiefs that their task was so nearly accomplished. All the portents, on the contrary, indicated that the project of winning a way through the Straits by ship power alone had been a blunder from the very outset, a blunder no less from the technical and tactical than from the strategical point of view.

CHAPTER III

THE ORGANISATION OF THE MILITARY EXPEDITION

The concentration of troops for the defence of Egypt.—The exposure of Egypt to hostile attempts from the side of Syria had caused the British Government some anxiety from the time when the Ottoman Empire entered the lists against the Entente. The garrison of British troops in the Nile Delta in September, 1914, was small. Although the arid isthmus of Suez presented a useful barrier to invasion from the east, reconnaissances that had been carried out during recent years had established the fact that this tract was not so waterless as had been supposed. Danger, moreover, threatened not only from without but also to some extent from within. The need of utilising all regular troops that could be got together for the campaign in France had, moreover, caused some units of the garrison to be withdrawn, their place being taken by Territorial units from home. The consequence was that steps were taken at an early date to introduce considerable forces into the country from India, so as to constitute an efficient corps of defence, and by November there were assembled in Egypt strong contingents composed of Native Indian battalions, together with some mountain batteries and Indian cavalry likewise transported from Karachi and Bombay.

When it became apparent that the Turks were making serious preparations for thrusting a force across the Sinai Desert with the object of attacking the line of the Suez Canal, some further troops were brought from India, while the East Lancashire Territorial Division was also sent out from home to swell the garrison. In the early days of December, moreover, there arrived in the Nile Delta the advanced portions of an army which was destined to win great renown in the Dardanelles Campaign. The executives both in Australia and in New Zealand had, on the outbreak of the European War, called upon those young nations to produce military forces by voluntary enlistment to bear a share in the struggle, and they had not called in vain. Infantry, mounted troops, artillery, and all the other auxiliary services that go to form a mobile army, had been got together with astonishing rapidity, and they had undergone some little preliminary training while awaiting the transports that should carry them west from the Antipodes. The leading échelon was already nearing the Red Sea when it was determined that the Australasian contingents should land in Egypt, a decision arrived at, partly owing to the need of still further strengthening the forces gathered in the Nile Delta, and partly as a consequence of the difficulty of accommodating these additional troops in the United Kingdom where all barracks and hastily devised cantonments were already full to overflowing. It was obvious, moreover, that the climate of Egypt in the winter season would be more suitable for a soldiery recruited in warm latitudes than that of England, while the desert would provide an almost ideal training ground for newly enlisted troops. The consequence was that in the early days of 1915 there were concentrated, in addition to large numbers of Indian troops and of Territorials from the United Kingdom, very nearly the equivalent of two complete divisions drawn from the Antipodes. Lieutenant-General Sir J. Maxwell was in supreme charge on the Nile, while command of the Australasian forces had been confided to Major-General Birdwood.

A considerable portion of the forces, consisting mainly of Indian troops, were disposed along the Suez Canal, while the Australasians and the Territorials were busily engaged in training at convenient localities selected for the purpose. The Indian troops being for the most part regulars were fully qualified to take part in serious military operations, but, being composed largely of Moslems, they were not too well adapted for encountering the soldiery of the Caliph. The Territorials had been mobilised for several months and had reached a fair state of efficiency. The Australasians, although consisting of exceptionally fine material, however still had a good deal to learn. It was, moreover, becoming daily more certain that the enemy intended to make a serious attack upon the line of the Canal. Thus, when the question of an attack upon the Dardanelles was raised within the War Council of the Cabinet in England, the position in Egypt was such that, while Sir J. Maxwell had under his orders a force which on paper stood for many thousand men, he could not have detached a sufficient number of efficient troops for operations against the Straits even if the Nile Delta had not been threatened at the time.

First steps towards utilising military force in the Dardanelles campaign.—We have seen in Chapter I how, on the 13th of January, the British Government decided to prepare a naval expedition which was, in the following month, to set about forcing the Dardanelles by a gradual operation, Constantinople being the objective. Now, it was obvious that, even should the Allied fleet succeed in forcing the Straits single-handed, a considerable military force would be required to assist in executing the later portions of the programme. Therefore it can safely be assumed that those responsible for this venture gave serious consideration to the question whether a military army should be prepared for the purpose. But, as shown above, Egypt could not at the moment produce such an army. Nor could any troops be spared from France nor from the United Kingdom. Moreover, seeing that it had been calculated that it would take the fleet a month to force the Dardanelles, and seeing that the attack was not to begin for several weeks, there was no great urgency for preparing a military expedition which would not be called upon to act for some considerable time unless it was required to help the navy within the Straits. Be that as it may, no definite decision on the point was arrived at until the 16th of February, three days before Admiral Carden commenced his operations, and on a date when the Allied warships were already assembled in the Ægean ready to begin. In the meantime the repulse of the Turkish attack on the Suez Canal and the withdrawal of the hostile forces from the Sinai Desert, coupled with the fact that the Australasian troops had been making great strides towards military efficiency during the past few weeks, had completely transformed the situation in the Nile Delta, and Sir J. Maxwell was now in a position to detach a force of approximately three divisions for operations outside the area of his own command should he be called upon to do so.

On the 16th of February the War Council in London came to the conclusion that a military force should be prepared. Arrangements were to be made for troops to be despatched from Egypt "if required." The 29th Division was to be transported from the

United Kingdom to the island of Lemnos as soon as possible. The Admiralty were to take steps for collecting in the Levant small craft, lighters, boats and so forth, such as would be needed for landing large bodies of troops. The idea was that an army should be massed in the Eastern Mediterranean, that could be used as required. It is, moreover, interesting to note that, in a memorandum which had been prepared in the Admiralty on the previous day, it had been laid down that transports carrying troops ought to be in readiness to enter the Straits as soon as the defences had been disposed of. But the memorandum went even further than this. It declared that " strong military landing-parties with strong covering parties " would be necessary to complete the destruction of the works defending the channel, and it pointed out that full advantage of the undertaking would only be obtained if the Gallipoli Peninsula was occupied by soldiers. " The naval bombardment," it went on to say, " is not a sound military operation unless a strong military force is ready to assist in the operations, or at least to follow up immediately the forts are silenced." It was four days after this memorandum was signed, and three days after the War Council decided to prepare a land force to help the fleet " if required," that the fleet attacked the outer forts of the Dardanelles and thus began the campaign.

Comments.—In its first Report, the Dardanelles Commission remarked that after the meeting of the 28th of January (at which the decision of the 13th of January was finally confirmed) " the objective of the British Government remained the same, but the views entertained as to the means of realising it underwent a gradual change. The necessity for a large military force became daily more apparent. The idea of a purely naval operation was gradually dropped." Unfortunately, however, the change in views on this fundamental aspect of the strategical problem took no practical shape between the 28th of January and the 16th of February. This may have been due to the difficulty that presented itself at this time with regard to finding any troops capable of helping the navy ; but the result was that the military side of the task to which the Allies were committing themselves only began to be taken seriously just when the floating forces were about to start work. The Admiralty Memorandum quoted above for all practical purposes insisted upon the presence of troops to lend a

THE QUESTION OF WEATHER

hand in forcing the Straits, and it seemed to put an end to the idea of the operation being executed by warships unaided; but both the Memorandum and the decision by the War Council of the following day were belated.

It must necessarily take time to organise and to equip military forces that may be detailed for an enterprise involving landing on an enemy's shores and carrying out a subsequent campaign. Lemnos, it is true, is only about two days' steam from Alexandria. But to fit out a respectable body of troops in the Nile Delta and to transport them to the island must have required more than ten days, even if definite orders had been issued on the 16th of February and if there had been sufficient ships available. Nearly three weeks would have been needed to get vessels together and to convey the 29th Division from the United Kingdom to the Ægean. A mistake had been made when it was resolved to attempt the passage of the Dardanelles without the aid of troops. A fresh mistake was made when, the necessity of employing troops having been recognised somewhat late in the day, operations were not suspended until such time as an adequate force equipped for the undertaking should be at hand to bear its part in the effort.

Weather conditions in the Ægean.—It may not be out of place to say a word at this point with regard to a factor in the strategical problem which had not been sufficiently taken into consideration hitherto. Except during about five months in the year, the Mediterranean presents by no means a placid sheet of water on most days. On the contrary, its surface is apt to be ruffled by sudden and violent storms between the months of October and May. The sea, moreover, gets up very quickly at any time of the year if a lively breeze sets in. These climatic characteristics are, moreover, especially noticeable in the Ægean, and neither February nor March were months that could be looked upon as promising ones for embarking on an enterprise in which the landing of a force of all arms on exposed beaches was not unlikely to be a feature. We have seen in Chapter II that the weather interfered even with the work of the battleships after the attack upon the Straits began; still, climatic irregularities could not justifiably have been put forward as an argument against warships trying to force the Dardanelles thus early in the year. It was only when the original design, which contemplated a purely naval operation, began imperceptibly to resolve itself into plans for carrying out elaborate amphibious undertakings, that weather became a factor of prime importance in the problem.

As it turned out, the military campaign only began in the latter part of April, owing to circumstances having no relation to climate. It is impossible to say whether the storms and strong winds to which the Ægean is prone at the time of the year would have enhanced the difficulties attending the military expedition, supposing that the troops had been ready to share in the operations at the date when the fleet commenced the attack, or immediately afterwards. But it is reasonable to assume that, had the project been exhaustively examined in all its bearings by military as well as by naval experts when it first found favour with the British Government, professional opinion would not have rested content with deprecating independent naval action. The experts would assuredly also have expressed themselves as averse to opening the campaign much before May for fear of rough water.

The development of the military plans.—The decision of the British War Council that had been taken on the 16th of February had been of a somewhat tentative nature, except with regard to the 29th Division and to the assembling of boats and small craft. But even with regard to the 29th Division the decision was not acted up to; it was found that the troops could not be spared at the moment on account of the situation in the West, and the arrangements for its embarkation had consequently to be countermanded. On the other hand, the French Government determined to prepare a force to co-operate with the British in any land campaign that might become necessary, and two divisions, made up for the most part of colonial troops stationed in Africa, were rapidly improvised. Some British marines had already been landed in the island of Tenedos, and arrangements were made to despatch a division of the troops that had been especially raised by the Admiralty during the progress of the war, to the Eastern Mediterranean. General Birdwood was also towards the end of the month directed to proceed to the Dardanelles to report upon the situation, and one Australian brigade from Egypt was moved to Lemnos.

General Birdwood's instructions were to report "whether it is considered by the Admiral that it will be necessary for troops to be employed to take the forts, and, if so, what force will be necessary; whether a landing force will be required of the troops to take the forts in reverse and generally in what manner it is proposed to employ the troops." His mission in fact was to find out what assistance the naval forces were likely to require in performing their preliminary task of forcing the Straits, a task which they were to have accomplished without any such assistance according to the original programme. His reports, telegraphed to Lord Kitchener at the War Office on the 6th and 7th of March, were not of an encouraging nature, for he expressed strong doubts as to whether the fleet would accomplish its object unaided. The situation in other theatres of war had become more reassuring in the meantime, and so, on the 10th of March, the British Government definitely committed itself to military action. The 29th Division was ordered to embark, Sir I. Hamilton was selected to command the forces in the Eastern Mediterranean, and the French simultaneously gave the necessary instructions for their contingent to take ship for Lemnos, it having been agreed between the two Governments that Sir Ian was to be in supreme command.

The Commander-in-Chief left the United Kingdom on the 13th, and, as we have seen, arrived at Tenedos on the 17th. His instructions did not suggest that one of the main objects that his army was to fulfil would be operations on a great scale undertaken for the purpose of conquering the passage of the Dardanelles, although they did not wholly preclude that possibility. Their tenor was rather to the effect that the soldiers' task in those Straits would be confined to minor enterprises in support of the warships. It was, however, distinctly laid down that before any serious undertaking was carried out in the Gallipoli Peninsula, all the British military forces detailed for the expedition were to be assembled, so that their full weight could be thrown in. Scarcely had the military commander arrived on the spot, however, when events proved that his instructions had been drawn up on an incorrect appreciation of the conditions of the problem. After witnessing the unsuccessful naval attack of the 18th, Sir Ian cabled home to the effect that the work of the army would not be of the subsidiary form in respect to the Dardanelles that had been anticipated in his instructions. "The army's share will not be a case of landing-parties for the destruction of forts, etc., but rather a case of a deliberate and progressive military operation carried out in force in order to make good the passage of the navy." The scheme to which the British Government had given its assent in January had failed completely. An entirely new condition of things had arisen and one for which no proper provision had been made in time.

The delay in employing the military forces detailed.—Numbers of transports full of troops were already in Mudros Bay on the southern side of the island of Lemnos, and others were on their way thither.[1] A considerable portion of the army that Sir I. Hamilton was to command was actually on the water, and the rest of it was ready to take ship from Egypt at short notice. But he found that he would be obliged to re-distribute the troops on the transports, so as to enable them to disembark ready for immediate action. The military forces that he was to command had been shipped at distant ports, without those responsible knowing exactly what this army was going to try to do and before its chief was aware of what was in store for it. The object had been to assemble a large military force in the Eastern Mediterranean which was to act as circumstances might demand, and it was inevitable that a certain amount of reorganisation and re-arrangement would prove necessary when it reached its destination.

The extensive inlet of Mudros provides one of the finest anchorages in the world for a mighty armada. As will be seen from the inset to Map I, on p. 62, the entrance is narrow. There is shelter against winds from every quarter of the compass. Sufficient depth of water exists, covering an extensive area, to permit of the largest vessels afloat making use of the haven. But in spite of these conspicuous advantages Mudros lacked some of the most indispensable qualifications of a military base. There were no jetties, and none of the appliances usually found at a shipping resort existed on the spot. There was difficulty as to water on shore. For numbers of transports to discharge the troops and stores borne in them and to re-embark these after they had been sorted, would have taken weeks under such adverse conditions. Sir I. Hamilton consequently decided that, with the exception of

---

[1] On the 19th a number of transports full of troops, under escort, made a demonstration of effecting a landing on the outer coast of the Gallipoli Peninsula.

REORGANISATION OF THE FORCE

the one Australian brigade which had already landed, the expeditionary force must proceed from Lemnos to Alexandria, and must be reorganised and be freshly allotted to its transports at that admirably equipped port. The 29th Division, still on its way out from home, was directed to the same base.

This involved serious delay, and delay at this juncture was particularly unfortunate. For a month past the Allied fleet had been trying to batter its way through the Dardanelles, and it had failed. Preparations for a military expedition had been going on openly for some weeks in Egypt and its destination was common talk. The mariners of the Cyclades had been sighting transports in great numbers steaming in the direction of the islands of Lemnos and Tenedos. Any delusions as to the operations of the warships in the Ægean merely representing a demonstration against the famous waterway leading up to the Sea of Marmora, that may at one time have been entertained in Stambul, had long since been dispelled by the obvious resolution with which the Allied naval effort was being pressed. The Turks and their German advisers were now perfectly well aware that a great operation for the conquest of the Dardanelles by naval and military forces was afoot. Yet now, at the moment when time was all-important to both belligerents, the side which possessed the initiative, at least in theory, found itself incapable of acting with promptitude. Sir I. Hamilton and his troops had to steam away from the rendezvous, leaving their opponents leisure to prepare undisturbed for the military attack which they foresaw was impending.

The reorganisation of the Military Expeditionary Force at **Alexandria.**—The redistribution of the British and French troops, and their allocation in detail, as a prelude to the forthcoming landing in force on the enemy's shores, took about three weeks, some of the units from home not arriving at Alexandria till the second week in April. Sir I. Hamilton was, however, able to return to Lemnos by the 7th of that month, to be followed thither by the transports in quick succession, and the army had assembled in Mudros Bay within a month of the date when the need for military effort on a great scale if the Dardanelles were to be won, had been placed beyond a doubt.

Further details with regard to the composition of the army will be found in Appendix II. Suffice it to say here that it consisted of the 29th Division, of the Royal Naval Division, of the 42nd East Lancashire Division, of an Australian division, of a division made up partly of Australians and partly of New Zealanders, of the two French divisions, and of some Indian troops. A military force of all arms, comprising seven divisions with a few additional units, ought to have represented a total of fully 140,000 men. But the divisions did not for the most part consist of the full number of units that a division is supposed to include. They were very weak in artillery. A proportion of the battalions were below war establishment when they started. From the nature of the enterprise on which they were about to embark, it was expedient for them to leave large part of their impedimenta and animals in Egypt. The consequence was that the whole army numbered less than 100,000 officers and men, and it is well to remember that, throughout the campaign that was to follow, the expression "division" was always a somewhat delusive one, partly on this account and partly for reasons that will appear later.

Nor could the troops composing the army be regarded as troops of quite the highest class at the outset. Even the 29th Division, consisting as it did of veteran soldiery drawn for the most part from India and foreign stations and including a comparatively small proportion of reservists in its ranks, had practically never been exercised as a division. The Australasian troops had undergone but a brief period of training since their formation. The Naval Division was a recently created body of troops, without artillery and unprovided with the majority of the departmental units that are ordinarily included in a division. The French contingent was an improvisation counting a proportion of native African troops in its ranks. Still, it was a fine force, if not a perfect one, but it was to be called upon to adventure a feat of arms for which there was no real precedent in modern war.

Promises of Russian co-operation.—The effort against the Dardanelles, as a prelude to further operations against the Bosphorus and Constantinople, had been initiated in January in response to a request for aid from Russia ; and, while one of the objects contemplated was the overthrow of the Ottoman Empire by striking at its heart, the project had for its further object the opening of maritime communications with the Russian Black Sea ports in the interests of the Tsar's dominions. As was only right and proper,

Russian assistance, both naval and military, was promised. An army corps was assembled about Odessa, and it was proposed that this should be transported across the Black Sea to somewhere near the northern mouth of the Bosphorus when, the Dardanelles having been forced, the troops and the fleet from the Ægean moved forward to undertake the second stage of the great offensive enterprise against Turkey. Direct co-operation between the troops in South Russia and the military forces assembling for the conquest of the Dardanelles was manifestly impossible until those famous Straits should be in the hands of the Allies. But it may be pointed out here that the concentration of an army on the northern shores of the Black Sea constituted a distinct threat against the Sultan's capital, and that it acted as a magnet holding Turkish troops fast in the neighbourhood of the Golden Horn which might, from the Ottoman point of view, usefully have been employed in some other region.

CHAPTER IV

THE MILITARY PROBLEM PRESENTED BY THE DARDANELLES

Alternatives to actually attacking the Gallipoli Peninsula.—As it turned out, the military campaign came to be virtually confined to the Gallipoli Peninsula. But, before discussing the opportunities which that singular tongue of land offered to a military force bent on securing command of the Hellespont, it will not be out of place to point out that the Allies were not necessarily obliged to deliver their attack here. There were alternatives which must have suggested themselves to Sir Ian Hamilton, when the failure of the great naval effort of the 18th of March made it plain to him that the forcing of the Dardanelles now depended upon what the troops under his command would be able to accomplish in the immediate future. The question of combining operations in Thrace, or else on the Asiatic side of the Straits, with an attack upon the peninsula itself, was bound to receive consideration, and as a matter of fact such operations were suggested more than once at a later date after the army had gained a footing on the peninsula.

Operations on the European side.—As will be seen from Maps VII and VIII at the end of the volume, the Gallipoli Peninsula is linked to the mainland of Thrace by the slender Isthmus of Bulair, a neck of land barely three miles wide at its narrowest part. It should, however, be noted that a chain of low hills running along the spine of this neck hides the Sea of Marmora from view even from the tops of ships of war in the Gulf of Saros, and forbids their intervening in any land combats for possession of the isthmus that might take place on its Sea of Marmora side. The command of the sea which the Allies possessed outside the Straits did not in fact enable them to dominate the approaches by land to the peninsula. Moreover, the lines of Bulair, which had been created by Anglo-French enterprise at the time of the Crimean War,

QUESTION OF LANDING IN THRACE 39

served to bar the way to any military force endeavouring to enter the peninsula from the side of Thrace. The objective of the Expeditionary Force being positions commanding the Straits, the Isthmus of Bulair manifestly became an all-important feature in any project based on effecting a landing on the European side of the waterway, outside of the actual Gallipoli Peninsula.

The northern coast-line of the Gulf of Saros provided several more or less practicable landing-places, rendered somewhat inviting by the fact that the prevailing wind in this region comes from the north-east and would thus be off shore. But an army setting foot on this littoral would inevitably encounter opposition at the hands of the Turkish contingents known to be gathered in Thrace, and Sir I. Hamilton had not sufficient troops under his control to court combat with such formidable forces. To reach the Isthmus of Bulair the army of invasion would also be obliged to make something of the nature of a flank march. Finally, supposing that the flank march was accomplished and that the hostile forces in Thrace gave less trouble than might reasonably be expected, the lines of Bulair would still have to be stormed, while the attacking army ran the risk of being simultaneously assailed in rear. It should be noted that the victorious Bulgarians, three years before, had signally failed in their efforts to capture these lines at a moment when Thrace was at their mercy, that the Turks were known to have strengthened the entrenchments since that date, and that reconnaissances from on board ship had ascertained that in March and April the defences were held in considerable force. Furthermore, although possession of the Bulair Isthmus would cut the defenders of the Gallipoli Peninsula off from direct communication by land with the European portions of the Ottoman Empire, these would still be able to draw their reinforcements and supplies unhindered from across the Dardanelles. When the arguments for and against a plan of operations contemplating attack upon the peninsula from the side of Thrace came to be placed in the balance, the disadvantages of selecting such a line of advance were found entirely to outweigh its advantages.

Question of operations on the Asiatic side.—There was much more to be said for a campaign on the Anatolian side of the Straits. The strategical position in that region offered roughly two alternatives. It would have been possible to put the attacking army ashore at points some considerable distance from the Dardanelles, where there was good shelter in case of bad weather. Or the landing might be effected only a few miles outside the mouth of the Straits at more exposed localities—a plan that found considerable favour in some quarters both in March, 1915, and at a later date.

As regards the first alternative, the Island of Mitylene affords excellent protection to the sound separating it from the mainland, and within this sound are a number of small ports where troops might have been landed readily enough ; the nearest of them is, however, about 70 miles from the Dardanelles. Further to the south lies the great maritime city of Smyrna, situated at the head of a land-locked gulf, which would in itself have provided an admirable base for an invading army. But the harbour of Smyrna was guarded by fairly powerful batteries, and to have acquired possession of the environs would have involved a special campaign as a preliminary. Moreover, Smyrna is about 150 miles from the Straits, Anatolia is a region that is backward in respect to communications, and the undertaking of a campaign in such territory, having for its objective positions quite a fortnight's march distant, would have called for the assembling of a mass of transport, for the establishment of an elaborate system of communications, and for the services of an army considerably larger than that which Sir I. Hamilton had at its disposal.

The other alternative was more promising. Besika Bay opposite the Island of Tenedos offered marked technical advantages as an actual landing-place, seeing that it possessed a suitable beach with deep water fairly close in, while Yukyeri Bay a few miles to the south also presented similar features. These two bays are situated respectively about a dozen, and about twenty, miles from Kum Kale at the mouth of the Dardanelles. Facing west as they do, both of them are exposed except when the wind comes from south-east, east or north-east ; but, as stated above, the latter is the prevailing quarter. In any case, the Ægean is generally smooth during the summer.

It was known that the Turks were not unprepared to meet a landing in Besika Bay, and that some entrenchments existed ; but it is doubtful whether any serious opposition would have been offered to actual disembarkation in the more southerly

QUESTION OF AN ASIATIC LANDING 41

bight.[1] On the other hand, the distance from these landing-places to the Narrows of the Dardanelles is considerable—fully twenty-five miles from Besika Bay and nearly thirty-five from Yukyeri Bay. Moreover, the valley of the Mendere (the plain of Troy) is marshy, is extensive and is reputed to be unhealthy. To gain possession of the Asiatic shores of the maritime defile, an army landing at these points would need a considerable amount of transport, and, owing to their distance from the objective, such a scheme of operations hardly lent itself to the delivery of a sudden and decisive stroke. Had the forces under Sir I. Hamilton been appreciably larger than they actually were, it would have been for consideration whether part of them ought not to undertake operations on the Asiatic side of the Straits, based on these two bays. At the worst troops so landed could almost certainly have gained possession of all the ground about Kum Kale, and would have afforded welcome support to comrades on the other side of the channel during the prolonged contest at the toe of the Gallipoli Peninsula. As it was, there were no troops available in the opening stages of the great venture for undertaking ambitious enterprises outside the peninsula, if simultaneously an army at all adequate to effect the object in view was to be employed on the conquest of that vital tongue of land. Separation of force is seldom justifiable in war unless there is an ample margin of military strength available, and on this occasion that condition did not hold good.

The disposition of the Turkish forces in the middle of March.—It will be convenient at this point to say a word as to the disposition of the Ottoman troops around the Dardanelles, at the juncture when an enterprise that had started as a naval one for securing possession of the Straits was suddenly transformed into a military one having the same purpose in view. But information on this subject is necessarily still somewhat vague, and it was vaguer still during those critical days when the plan of operations was being worked out by Sir I. Hamilton and his staff. Still, while much uncertainty existed as to the actual distribution of the defending troops whom the Allied soldiery were about to encounter, there were certain assumptions that in this connection could safely be made. The presence of a large army in and around Con-

[1] As will be seen further on, on page 60, there were two Turkish divisions in the Kum Kale-Besika Bay district in April. See also Appendix IV, 2.

stantinople was well known, and it was apparent that portions of this could be transferred to the immediate vicinity of the Hellespont at short notice. It was a well-established fact that there was always a considerable garrison actually in the Gallipoli Peninsula and about Chanak, and that the greater part of the troops in the peninsula were stationed either close to the Narrows or else about the Bulair lines. Imposing bodies of Turkish troops were quartered about Smyrna; but, seeing that this important centre of wealth and population was automatically menaced by the Allies' command of the Ægean, it was reasonable to suppose that the Ottoman military authorities would hesitate before they drew largely upon this particular source of fighting personnel to succour other localities.

One of the inconveniences that you are a prey to in war is that, when you elaborate your appreciation of the military situation as a prelude to framing your plan, the enemy is in all probability elaborating an appreciation likewise. The very same points as may be striking you are probably striking him. As a result of your appreciation you decide that your proper course will be to do some particular thing, and as a result of his appreciation your opponent comes to the conclusion that that particular thing is just what you most likely will do. Your intentions are divined, not because your antagonist is a thought-reader, nor a wizard, nor because his intelligence department gains certain illuminating clues from the preliminary dispositions that you may happen to be making, but simply because you, both of you, read the situation in the same way. This is illustrated by the disposition of the Ottoman forces when Sir I. Hamilton attacked.

It is quite true that the Allies enjoyed in this case the great advantage of possessing the initiative. Not only were the Osmanlis unable to foresee for certain—whatever they may have expected—where the blow would fall, but the liberty of action which sea power confers in a case like this necessarily permitted Sir I. Hamilton to conceal to the last moment the point or points where he meant to strike. But, for reasons to be discussed later, the Gallipoli Peninsula was the obvious preliminary objective of the Allied army, and that it was the obvious preliminary objective was apparent to both sides. The consequence was that the Turks and their German advisers saw to it that the bulk of the forces at their disposal for the immediate defence of the Dardanelles were

YUKYERI BAY 43

gathered on the peninsula, and were content that relatively inferior forces should be left to guard the Asiatic shores of the Straits and the approaches to these.

As has been indicated above, Yukyeri Bay offered in itself an attractive landing-place. It is not suggested that a plan of operations based on disembarking the whole, or the bulk, of the Allied forces there would have been the right one to adopt ; but there is reason to believe that if that plan had been adopted the assailants would in the first instance have met with less opposition than they encountered at Cape Helles and at Anzac. It is not unlikely indeed that the landing troops would, within the first few hours and before the Turks could hurry large forces to the spot, have gained possession of a much more extensive tract of country than in the event they ever did on the Gallipoli Peninsula. Even assuming that the Expeditionary Force was in due course brought to an absolute standstill long before getting within striking distance of the Narrows, just as it actually was brought to a standstill near the water's edge on the peninsula, it might nevertheless have penetrated sufficiently far inland in the meantime to have rendered its landing-place—its advanced base— immune from hostile shell fire. And that was a consummation that was never in actual practice achieved on the European side of the Hellespont. On the other hand, the army might have been successfully dumped down in that region several miles south of Kum Kale, and might have been quite comfortable in so far as its piers and its beaches were concerned, and would still have been a long way from achieving the object that it had come for.

The Gallipoli Peninsula the obvious military objective.—So long as the question of the actual disposition of the defending army is left out of consideration, it in reality hardly admits of argument that the Gallipoli Peninsula was the proper military objective of the Expeditionary Force as a preliminary to securing control over the Dardanelles. As had been obvious before any measures for gaining possession of the Straits were taken, and as was conclusively proved during the abortive naval operations of March, 1915, the Narrows were the key of the Hellespont. The task to be accomplished was to get Allied troops, in adequate strength and accompanied by sufficient artillery, into such a position that the Turks would have to abandon the works of various kinds that rendered the passage of ships through the Narrows impracticable. Now, as it happens, these Narrows are dominated to a very remarkable extent by the Pasha Dagh plateau, the big buttress jutting out on the European side and creating the kink at the point where the channel is most contracted. 400 to 600 feet above sea-level this prominent topographical feature looks down upon the Asiatic side of the Straits and the coast batteries defending the Narrows from that shore, and howitzers planted upon it by an invading force, favoured as they would be by ideal observation facilities, could drop their projectiles on any one of them. Whether the occupation of this coign of vantage by the Allies would necessarily have made an end of the enemy's defences above and below Chanak for all practical purposes, remains a matter of conjecture. The question never came to be put to the test. But it is a justifiable assumption that something of the kind would have resulted from an occupation of the Pasha Dagh by the attacking force, and such occupation would in any case have given Sir I. Hamilton possession of all the most important batteries on the European side of the water.

It must, however, always be borne in mind that the importance of the Pasha Dagh plateau was just as apparent to the defenders as it was to the assailants. The Turks were bound to have taken reasonably effective steps to secure a position of such manifest moment. They had hastily thrown up entrenchments protecting the plateau on its inner side at the time of the Balkan War, when there had been some talk of conjunct military and naval operations on the part of the Bulgars and Greeks directed against the Dardanelles. Just as the Gallipoli Peninsula regarded as a whole could be set down as the obvious general objective for the attacking side, so also could this prominent high ground be set down as its obvious special objective. Even had the operations for gaining command over the Hellespont been conducted on sound lines from the outset, i.e. had they taken the form of a surprise military attack by a sufficient force, without a naval *lever de rideau* that was warranted to give full warning to the opposing side, it is reasonably certain that the Ottoman chiefs would have had sufficient troops assembled on the Pasha Dagh to make its capture a task of no light order.

But the fact that this plateau dominated the Narrows was not the sole reason why operations directed against the Gallipoli Peninsula seemed to offer the brightest prospect of acquiring control over the coveted waterway. Initiating the land campaign in this confined tract offered the further inducement that, supposing the whole of the tract were to be made good by the invaders, its subsequent retention would only demand the presence of a relatively insignificant garrison. A few thousand troops would be ample to man the Bulair lines, and the main body of the army could then undertake the accomplishment of the rest of the programme in respect to Constantinople and the Bosphorus which was the dream of those who had committed the Allies to the gamble, or could even be transferred to some entirely different theatre of war should such a course be deemed expedient. Then again, the fact that extensive stretches of convenient beach were to be found immediately north of Gaba Tepe, provided an opening for a line of attack which, if at all successful, must threaten the communications of any defending troops that might be stationed about the toe of the peninsula. These same beaches were, moreover, little more than six miles from the Pasha Dagh heights, the capture of which promised such very far-reaching results, and, as transport was scarce and would in any case take a long time to land, proximity to the immediate objective was in reality of vital importance. This difficulty in respect to transport indeed, furnished another powerful argument in favour of delivering the attack upon the Gallipoli Peninsula, which promised operations in a restricted area, where it would be possible to execute effective combinations of war within short distance of the advanced base of the army carrying them out.

The disadvantages of selecting the Gallipoli Peninsula as objective. —On the other hand, some incontrovertible arguments could be adduced against making the peninsula the preliminary goal of endeavour. The weightiest objection to adopting such a plan of operations has indeed been mentioned already—the advantages which such a mode of procedure promised to the attacking side were so unmistakable that the Turks could be depended upon to have taken steps to meet an eventuality so inconvenient. The possible landing places furthermore were few, so few that the defending army could probably afford detachments to guard most of them. Consequently a military force that proposed to effect a descent upon this region must reckon upon meeting with a certain amount of opposition during actual disembarkation ; and the perils and difficulties of disembarking troops in face of opposition were fully recognised even before the operation came to be tried—practically for the first time under modern conditions—on the 25th of April, 1915. It must be added that in the situation that presented itself when Sir I. Hamilton was called upon to solve the problem of how to compass the conquest of the Hellespont with a land force, the drawbacks to his delivering his attack upon the Gallipoli Peninsula indicated above were rendered all the graver by the ample warning which his antagonists had received that something of the kind was brewing.

Sir I. Hamilton's decision to attack the peninsula.—As a result of his survey of the coast-line on arrival, and after satisfying himself that the naval operations were brought to a standstill, Sir I. Hamilton decided that the correct plan of operations would be to land his army on the peninsula. There had indeed been an understanding between Lord Kitchener and himself before he left home that this course would be the best one to adopt should his troops be called upon to play a prominent part in securing the Dardanelles, although when he left England influential quarters clung to the hope that the fleet would force the passage practically unaided. In his instructions occurs the passage : " Before any serious undertaking is carried out in the Gallipoli Peninsula, all the British military forces detailed for the expedition should be assembled, so that their full weight can be thrown in." It may, moreover, be recalled that when the War Council initiated the venture on the 13th of January, their decision was that the Admiralty were to prepare an expedition, " to bombard and take the Gallipoli Peninsula, with Constantinople as its objective." Launching a naval expedition to take a strongly fortified strip of territory 45 miles long, 12 miles wide at many points and furnished with a considerable garrison, would hardly be the type of war policy to arouse enthusiasm in the mind of the average intelligent soldier ; but we must acknowledge that even in those early days of emotional strategy the War Council appear to have recognised the importance of the peninsula, and to have realised in a vague sort of way that its occupation was desirable. Sir I. Hamilton was in fact scarcely a free agent when making up his mind. It is

THE PROBLEM OF THE PENINSULA 47

not suggested for a moment that the decision was not absolutely the right one—the writer's view is that it was. But it is for the reader to form his own conclusions as to what would have been the best solution of a by no means easy problem.

As we have seen in Chapter III, it was found necessary to reorganise and to rearrange the Expeditionary Force before any landing on Turkish shores with the whole of the available troops would be practicable. The delays which this involved enabled the Commander-in-Chief to study the problem still further, and with the assistance of fresh reconnaissances carried out during the interval. These reconnaissances served to indicate that the enemy was making determined efforts to develop the defences of the peninsula, intelligence derived from various sources pointed in the direction of considerable reinforcements reaching the garrisons around the Dardanelles, and it was ascertained that there were considerable gatherings of enemy troops about Bulair. Sir I. Hamilton, however, never wavered in the decision at which he had arrived at the beginning.

The strategical and tactical problem presented by the peninsula.— But the question at issue was not merely whether the army was, or was not, to land on the peninsula. After this point had been decided in the affirmative the problem still had to be solved as to how this operation should be effected in such a manner as to secure a footing, and such a manner as to secure that footing at a point, or points, from which the troops on getting ashore would stand the best chance of attaining their real objective, the domination of the Narrows. The most cursory examination of the subject would serve to show that several different possible courses of action presented themselves, and that for more than one of them there was much to be said.

It should be noted that Sir Ian Hamilton had been furnished with information as to the various possible landing points, which turned out upon the whole to be remarkably accurate, although at the outset details as to Suvla Bay were defective. Fairly correct information as to the interior of the peninsula had also been placed at his disposal. But, in the absence of regular surveys, the maps supplied to the Expeditionary Force were necessarily untrustworthy in respect to ground not actually visible from the sea ; **and uncomfortable doubts existed on the very important question** of water supply in a region where it could safely be assumed that the few insignificant rivulets that existed were liable to dry up altogether at certain seasons of the year. Quite apart from the uncertainty that necessarily prevailed as to the disposition and strength of the Turkish forces to be overcome, the undertaking of an attack upon the peninsula in fact partook to some extent of a leap in the dark, seeing that thoroughly reliable details concerning the prospective theatre of operations were not in the hands of the directing staff.

The question of possible points of disembarkation was so vital a one in any consideration of the problem of the Gallipoli Peninsula that it will be convenient to indicate here where these points actually were situated. But there is no need to discuss landing-places actually within the Straits except in the immediate vicinity of Cape Helles. So long as the Asiatic shore of the Dardanelles remained in Ottoman hands, the Allies were bound to effect their disembarkation on the outer side of the peninsula, or at its extremity. We have then to consider its coast-line from the Isthmus of Bulair to the neighbourhood of its southern end.

On the Isthmus of Bulair itself there was a well-sheltered little bay, Bakla Liman, where a landing in some force might have been effected had there been no fear of opposition. But this bay lay outside the Bulair lines, was under fire from them, and its selection would have meant that the disembarking troops must storm this extremely formidable position before they could do anything towards occupying the peninsula. Strategical and tactical considerations practically vetoed its use, although landing operations could have been carried on at this point on many days when they would have been impracticable at almost any other locality outside the Straits.[1] Between this point and Cape Suvla, a distance of some thirty-five miles, there is no place adapted for a military landing except the little bight of Ejelmar, by no means an unfavourable point in itself for putting troops on shore as there is good shelter and a convenient stretch of beach; but Ejelmar Bay is too restricted to admit of any considerable force being disembarked within it. As already indicated, details with regard to landing facilities within Suvla Bay were somewhat wanting when Sir I. Hamilton was forming his plans; it was obvious, however, that

[1] See Appendix IV, 2, as to Marshal Liman von Sanders' views.

AVAILABLE BEACHES

the bay provided better shelter than did the open coast-line further south. Actually, there existed suitable beaches on both sides of the bay which were turned to account at a later date.

South of this, and extending for a distance of some six miles to the promontory of Gaba Tepe, were stretches of beach that were fairly favourable for landings at most points, the littoral here admitting of an army disembarking on a very broad front. Vessels of considerable draft could approach within a few cables' length of the shore, and the number of infantrymen that might have been disembarked, on a fine day within a given time, on this strip of the coast-line reduced itself in reality to the strength of men available for putting on shore and to the capacity in boats that could be placed at their disposal. Following the coast from Gaba Tepe on towards the toe of the peninsula, no very suitable localities offered themselves until within about two miles of Cape Tekke.[1] On either side of this there were favourable beaches, known afterwards as Gully Beach, Beach X and Beach W, the latter a really good landing-place. Between Cape Helles and Sedd-el-Bahr there was another convenient beach, which came to be known later as Beach V. Finally, on the eastern side of Morto Bay near De Tott's Battery and within the Straits, there was a well-sheltered beach, afterwards known as Beach S. The beaches about Capes Tekke and Helles and Morto Bay in reality formed a group, none was sufficiently extensive in itself to admit of a large force being disembarked at one time, and they were separated from each other by appreciable intervals of virtually impracticable coast-line.

We may dismiss Bakla Liman from consideration, owing to its being on the wrong side of the Bulair lines. Ejelmar Bay is isolated, and its distance from the Narrows, fully fifteen miles, rendered it so unfavourable a landing-place from the strategical point of view that it is hardly likely that Sir I. Hamilton will have given it much attention, in spite of its technical advantages. For practical purposes therefore, the problem of the peninsula, in so far as points of disembarkation were concerned, resolved itself into making a selection between three localities—Suvla Bay, the beaches north of Gaba Tepe, and the beaches about Capes Tekke and Helles and Morto Bay. Suvla Bay promised fair shelter; but some doubts existed, as we have seen, as to landing-places,

[1] See Map I, p. 62.

the ground about the Salt Lake was known to be marshy at least in the winter months, and the bay is a good dozen miles from the Narrows in any case. Moreover, a disembarkation there meant starting operations in a basin of considerable extent dominated by hills—tactical conditions that would not favour a force desirous of making good a large tract of country rapidly, in case of the enemy proving to be in strength and ready for all emergencies.

The shore line stretching north from Gaba Tepe, however, stood on a different footing altogether. Its vicinity to the Pasha Dagh heights dominating the Narrows has already been referred to. The extensive beaches that offered themselves here, even if they only represented narrow strips of sand overlooked at practically all points by rising ground, provided some of those very conditions which will especially commend themselves to a military commander who finds himself committed to undertaking a landing in force in hostile territory. But Sir I. Hamilton was evidently unaware when originally forming his plans of the length of practicable landing ground that was available in this locality, for he mentions in his despatch describing the opening events of the land operations, that "further to the north of that promontory" (Gaba Tepe) "the beach was supposed to be dangerous and difficult." This stretch of coast is, moreover, quite exposed, and at no point does it offer any facilities for the construction of a sheltered landing-place where stores could always be discharged in ordinary weather. A disembarkation here would, moreover, almost inevitably necessitate the conquest of the rugged Sari Bair mountain mass, before the army could hope to advance undisturbed by flank attacks towards the Narrows. Still, reckoning up advantages and disadvantages, and fortified by the knowledge that we possess to-day, there was much to recommend the selection of this point for a landing in the strongest possible force.

The merits of the toe of the peninsula—it will be convenient to designate it henceforward by the name that was adopted, Helles—as locality of disembarkation, may be summarised as follows: All the beaches along the stretch of littoral inside of Cape Tekke towards the Straits were well protected against the prevailing north-east wind, a matter of great importance in the interests of establishing a permanent landing-place and base. The seizure of the extreme end of the peninsula was calculated to aid naval

SIR I. HAMILTON'S PLAN

operations within the Dardanelles to some extent. The peninsula is so narrow at its extremity that an army which has made good near its end is automatically secured by the sea on either hand against hostile outflanking efforts. Moreover, the troops as they advanced would be able to count on naval assistance on either flank, although owing to the lie of the ground this was not likely to be very effective. These unquestionably were advantages not to be ignored. But there were, on the other hand, some serious disadvantages to Helles as a starting-point for the conquest of the Gallipoli Peninsula. The available beaches, for instance, were of limited extent, they were well defined, and they were sure to be closely guarded and to be adequately defended. Landing here was to be deprecated in that it involved a direct advance in face of the enemy, whereas troops setting foot on shore north of Gaba Tepe, or in Suvla Bay, or even at Ejelmar Bay or Bakla Liman necessarily threatened the communications of any Turks that might be stationed about the Narrows and at Helles. The distance from the Helles landing-places to the Narrows was quite double the distance from near Gaba Tepe. There was also this further unquestionable drawback: Some of the beaches, and a good deal of the ground all about the toe of the peninsula, were within easy artillery range from across the Straits; and experience within the Dardanelles had already proved that warships find it very difficult to cope with mobile shore guns emplaced behind rising ground, so that the army could not reckon confidently upon the sister service relieving it of what was almost certain to prove a serious nuisance.

Sir Ian Hamilton's plan.—Having anxiously weighed the advantages and disadvantages offered by the various landing-places, the Commander-in-Chief decided upon undertaking two main landings, one at Helles and the other north of Gaba Tepe, the former, however, to be supplemented by a descent near Kum Kale on the opposite side of the Straits. The force to land at Helles was to be made up of the 29th Division, with some additional troops. The Australian and New Zealand army corps under Sir W. Birdwood was to disembark north of Gaba Tepe. A contingent of French were to deliver the attack on Kum Kale. Part of the Royal Naval Division was also to make a demonstration in the north. Sir I. Hamilton attached the utmost importance to getting the largest possible force on shore at once, and it seems to have been largely on this account that he determined to make use of so many landing-places while fully realising the strategical and tactical objections attached to such a procedure.

"The beaches," he wrote in his first despatch, "were either so well defended by works and guns or else so restricted by nature that it did not seem possible, even by two or three simultaneous landings, to pass the troops ashore quickly enough to maintain themselves against the rapid concentration and counter-attack which the enemy was bound in such case to attempt. It became necessary, therefore, not only to land simultaneously at as many points as possible, but to threaten to land at other points as well. The first of these necessities involved another unavoidable if awkward contingency, the separation by considerable intervals of the force." It will be convenient to defer comment upon this question of numerous landings until the story of the 25th of April, and of the subsequent consolidation, has been told in the next two chapters. It may, however, be observed here that, as Helles is about fifteen miles by road from the beaches north of Gaba Tepe, the attacks upon these two localities constituted two entirely distinct operations, alike from the side of the assailant and of the defender. It would have taken many hours for the Turks to have disengaged their troops from the defence of either locality and to have transferred them to the other.

The expeditionary army had been gathering in Mudros harbour since the early days of April, after the troops had been reorganised and reallotted to their transports at Alexandria. All was ready by the 20th, but for a day or two the weather remained unpropitious and afforded a warning of the difficulties which the elements were likely to cause the Allies, even if they succeeded in gaining a footing on the Gallipoli Peninsula. By the 23rd, however, the conditions had improved, and on the evening of that day the covering troops of the 29th Division put to sea from Lemnos and proceeded to the Tenedos anchorage, where on the afternoon of the morrow the troops transhipped into the war vessels and minesweepers which had been detailed to convey them over to Helles. The Australians and New Zealanders steamed out from Mudros harbour late on the 24th, proceeding direct towards their appointed landing-place. The commander of an army undertaking a mari-

PROBLEM OF AN OPPOSED LANDING 53

time descent on hostile territory holds a valuable card in his hand in that he can generally, with naval assistance, deceive his opponent as to the true point of danger by means of false attacks. This principle was not overlooked. A pretence of effecting a landing was carried into effect near Enos on the 23rd, which seems to have misled the Turks, for they announced a notable success at this point, claiming to have beaten off a formidable onset; and the Royal Naval Division made a demonstration in the Gulf of Saros and against Bulair on the 25th. The venture was thus fairly launched, and it may therefore not be out of place at this point to discuss whether under all the circumstances of the sase it ought to have been proceeded with, in view of the elaborate preparations which reconnaissances had indicated to be in existence for repelling an attack.

The tactical problem that arises in the case of a military landing in face of opposition.—It must be remembered that the Allies were embarking upon a tactical enterprise for which there was practically no precedent in modern war. Not since Abercrombie got his army ashore at Aboukir Bay, in the days of muskets and of smooth-bore cannon, had a military force landed on an enemy's beaches in face of determined opposition. It is true that in the autumn of 1911 the Italians had succeeded in disembarking a division at Benghazi in spite of some resistance by a motley force of Turks and tribesmen ; but, although the operation had been skilfully carried out by the attacking side and reflected great credit on all concerned, the defenders had consisted of a somewhat tumultuary array, destitute of artillery or machine-guns, which, moreover, had not made the most of its opportunities. But although, owing to the absence of practical illustrations in actual war, military experts depended almost entirely upon theory when examining the tactical problem of an opposed landing, certain factors influencing that problem were fairly patent to those soldiers who had considered the subject.

The progress that has taken place in respect to armament during some decades past was generally acknowledged to favour the defending rather than the attacking side in an affair of this kind. Troops must land in boats, and boats must always offer admirable targets to artillery and to riflemen. At Aboukir Bay our infantry only came under musketry when within a very few score yards of the beach, they were exposed to no machine-guns riddling them with a pitiless hail of lead, and the guns in those days only discharged cannon balls or else shell of the most elementary type. Under the conditions that prevail to-day, a military force proposing to disembark in defiance of serious opposition has to be prepared for a tempest of shrapnel and high explosive projectiles when still quite a long way out to sea. Machine-guns will worry it when a mile or more from shore. Rifle fire is likely to prove murderous when the boats have still hundreds of yards before them ere they can hope to touch bottom. There is considerable risk indeed, supposing the arrangements of the defenders to be skilfully devised and their appliances to be formidable in character, that the troops will for all practical purposes have ceased to exist before the few stricken remnants reach the land and are able to set foot on shore.

It may be urged, no doubt, that progress in science has aided assailants as well as defenders in an affray of this nature, and that is perfectly true. Steam and internal-combustion engines admit nowadays of strings of boats being towed to near the shore by launches of various kinds, and the leading troops can thus traverse the bullet-swept water area that has to be passed, more rapidly than was feasible in an era when it was a case of rowing the crowded craft the whole way from the transports to the selected landing-place. Ordnance and machine-guns aboard of fighting ships are, moreover, incomparably more effective in these times than they were when Abercrombie performed his renowned feat of arms, and they can consequently afford far more valuable support to the disembarking force than was formerly the case. Those are factors favouring the attacking side. But boats towed in batches afford a much better target to the defenders than do boats that are proceeding independently, and this to some extent neutralises the advantages conferred by self-propelled launches. Granted that warships of the present day are furnished with a terribly destructive armament, the fact remains that the conditions render it difficult for ship's gunners to maintain that unerring, that well-sustained and that intensive fire that is indispensable if good defending troops are to be seriously disconcerted, and are to be kept disconcerted up to the moment when the assaulting infantry are wading ashore to make their rush. A landing in face of the enemy has always been held to be a perilous operation of war, and even before

RISK IF BAD WEATHER SETS IN

the immortal exploits of the 25th of April, 1915, it was generally recognised that under the conditions of to-day an enterprise of this kind stood for almost the most desperate undertaking that a soldiery can reasonably be called upon to attempt.

There is another point which must not be overlooked in this connection. The fact of the landing actually being opposed almost necessarily aggravates the anxieties, which are inseparable from a maritime descent at a point where there is no harbour, for this reason. There is always for practical purposes the danger that the weather may change for the worse after the expeditionary force is committed, that the sea may get up, and that communication between the shore and the transports may consequently be interrupted or may even be wholly cut off. This actually occurred to a British force that was landed at Ostend in 1798, with the sequel that the troops who had disembarked were compelled to surrender. It is not merely a question of getting the combatant troops to land, but also of disembarking supplies and impedimenta of various kinds, and this inevitably takes time. It was owing to the failure to land food and artillery before the weather broke, that Charles V's army came to such woeful grief in his attempt against Algiers in 1541. Now, if the landing be opposed, this in itself almost inevitably means delay. It means that the landing troops are harassed by the presence of wounded, and that there is less likelihood of their consolidating their position within a comparatively short space of time ; so that, if atmospheric disturbance supervenes after a start has been made, those portions of the army which have gained a footing in the enemy's country may not be in a position to hold their own until the weather moderates. Sir I. Hamilton's attack upon the Gallipoli Peninsula was deferred till so late in the year that he could fairly count upon favourable climatic conditions ; but, had the venture been launched in the latter part of March, immediately after failure of the fleet imposed definite action upon the army that was gradually assembling, the risk of a sudden change of weather would have appreciably augmented the perils of an enterprise which was hazardous enough in any case.

It ought to be noted in conclusion that one impediment, which troops disembarking in face of the enemy on most littorals have to overcome, does not confront an army which is undertaking this particular class of operation in the Mediterranean. There is practically no tide in that great land-locked sea, a circumstance which no doubt favoured Abercrombie in Aboukir Bay and also the Italians at Benghazi. Rise and fall of tide is apt to add appreciably to the difficulties of an opposed landing, which will almost necessarily be taking place on some beach. In the first place, it is usual for the sea to shoal some distance out from a beach, so that boats will often be unable to get close to land in tidal waters except about the time of flood; this limits the number of hours available for carrying out what is in any case certain to be a critical operation. In the second place, ebb and flow may give rise to an untoward situation should the troops fail to make good their footing after reaching land. Talmash's signal discomfiture at Brest in 1694 would have proved less disastrous than it was, had the tide not fallen while his men were battling desperately on shore and left the boats high and dry when the stricken force was hustled back to the water's edge.

Ought the land campaign to have been abandoned at the last moment?—The risks attending a disembarkation in face of the enemy were well known. It had been ascertained by reconnaissance that the Turks were prepared. The army detailed for the purpose of conquering the Gallipoli Peninsula was manifestly none too large for so critical an undertaking. Reserves ready to fill up the gaps that were bound to occur in the ranks during the combats in prospect, were not available close at hand—it will be seen later what an unfortunate influence this circumstance exerted over the operations. The course of the campaign in France and Flanders had already made manifest the difficulties in the way of compelling a foe to abandon well-entrenched positions under the tactical conditions of to-day. It has been hinted in some quarters that, after reviewing the situation as a whole on the spot and after seeing for himself the localities where his troops would have to fight their way ashore, Sir I. Hamilton ought to have informed the British Government that the enterprise was too hazardous and too unpromising a one to be proceeded with.

But the instructions which had been sent to him by Lord Kitchener in reply to a telegram of his of the 19th March, in which he had announced that his army would have to undertake deliberate and progressive operations in order to open the Dardanelles for the fleet, were explicit. "You know my views that the passage of the Dardanelles must be forced, and that if large military operations on the Gallipoli Peninsula are necessary to clear the way, those operations must be undertaken after careful consideration of the local defences, and must be carried through." It would have been difficult to raise objections at the last moment in face of instructions of this uncompromising character, even had the Commander-in-Chief come to the conclusion that the venture ought properly to be abandoned. It is easy for critics to say now—after the event—that this would have been the proper course to adopt. A soldier must be very sure indeed of his ground before he can be justified in taking up an attitude that will completely upset the plans that his Government have commissioned him to carry out in time of war.

CHAPTER V

THE LANDING

The opening scene of the enterprise favoured by good weather.—The Allies enjoyed good fortune in respect to weather on the night of the 24th–25th, and also on the morrow. The sea was smooth, the temperature was equable and the atmosphere was fairly clear. There was also moonlight lasting nearly till dawn. Such conditions were a matter of considerable importance to Sir I. Hamilton's army, seeing that the troops had to be transhipped by night from warships and transports and mine-sweepers into the boats that were to convey them to the shore. Calm water also necessarily facilitated operations when the boats came to discharge their living freight on the beaches that had been chosen for the purpose. It has already been pointed out that there is little tide in the Mediterranean. On the other hand, there were awkward currents about Helles caused by the outflow of water from the Dardanelles, close by; these as it turned out gave rise to a good deal of inconvenience, and, had the sea been rough, they might have added very greatly to the terrible difficulties that the troops had to overcome even as it was.

The general plan of attack.—As has been already indicated in the last chapter, the Commander-in-Chief had determined on disembarking part of his force north of Gaba Tepe, another portion about Helles, and some French troops on the Asiatic shore at the mouth of the Straits, besides making a feint on an important scale in the Gulf of Saros. Although all three landings were to take place nearly simultaneously, the operations were kept distinct from the maritime point of view. Rear-Admiral Thursby was in charge of the Australasian force, Rear-Admiral Wemyss officiated at Helles, and the French squadron was responsible for putting the French troops ashore. The underlying idea was to get as great

THE TURKISH DISPOSITIONS

a number of soldiers as possible disembarked, partly on the western shore of the peninsula and partly at its extremity, to accomplish this with the utmost possible celerity, and by means of a temporary descent at Kum Kale to prevent the enemy from unduly hampering the operations at Helles by gun-fire across the Straits. The design was concealed from the enemy as far as possible by delivery of the feint against the northern coast of the Gulf of Saros and Bulair, and by warships demonstrating in the direction of Besika Bay on the Asiatic side of the Dardanelles. The threat in the direction of Bulair and about the Gulf of Saros undoubtedly served to cause the commander of the Turkish forces a good deal of anxiety.

The landing at Helles will be dealt with first. But before recounting the details of that memorable exploit of war it will be convenient to give some information as to the distribution of the enemy forces at this time, in so far as this is known, and to record some of the arrangements that had been made on the side of the defenders to meet the impending invasion of the Sultan's territory.

Turkish preparations and the distribution of the defending forces. —On the 25th of March, a week after the repulse of the great naval attack upon the Narrows of the 18th, Marshal Liman von Sanders, a German officer, was nominated by the Turkish Government to command the military forces charged with the defence of the Dardanelles. The marshal lost no time in proceeding to the Gallipoli Peninsula to take charge, and began at once with the assistance of his staff to grapple with the problem of preparing against the expected military attack. Especial attention was paid to the all-important task of developing the somewhat backward road-communications within the peninsula, as also on the Asiatic side. Entrenchments were thrown up at likely landing-places, wire entanglements were elaborated, gun-emplacements were excavated, electric communications were developed in so far as this was practicable with available resources, bridges were constructed, ammunition and supply depots were established at convenient localities, and an adequate hospital establishment was organised. To facilitate communication from shore to shore across the Narrows a pier was run out at Nagara Point. Thanks to the generous military working parties that were at disposal of the high command—the Turkish soldier makes a capital labourer—quite remarkable progress appears to have been made with these works during the closing days of March and during the first three weeks of April. As a consequence, the inevitable difficulties attending a maritime descent followed by an advance of the landing troops, was vastly increased just during that very period when Sir I. Hamilton was engaged in transforming an expeditionary force, that had been detailed and despatched at haphazard with no definite operation in view, into an army organised to undertake a determinate operation of war of inordinate complexity.

The marshal's troops consisted of the 5th Turkish Army, with some additional units, and the distribution of these forces on the day before the landing, appear to have been approximately as follows : About Helles was the 9th Division, while another division was watching the west coast of the peninsula by Gaba Tepe and to the north. The 19th Division was in reserve about Boghali and Maidos (see Map V on p. 168). The 7th Division lay near Gallipoli, and the 5th Division was guarding the Isthmus of Bulair, thus making a total of five divisions defending the peninsula and isthmus. Near the mouth of the Straits on the Asiatic side was the 3rd Division in the direction of Kum Kale and Yeni Shehr, while the 11th Division in reserve watched Besika Bay, these two being under command of a German officer, General Weber. Liman von Sanders' principal subordinate, however, was Essad Pasha, a distinguished Ottoman commander who had held the fortress of Yanina against the Greeks during the Balkan campaign of 1912–13.

Marshal Liman von Sanders' first dispositions.—In addition to the special feints on the European side to which reference has been made on page 53, the enemy was perplexed by having been constantly annoyed around the Gulf of Saros during the preceding weeks owing to the action of British and French warships. The results of this were made apparent by the anxiety which Marshal Liman von Sanders displayed with regard to the possibility of a landing near Bulair. Immediately on receiving news in his headquarters in Gallipoli early in the morning on the 25th that an armada had appeared in the Gulf of Saros, the Commander-in-Chief of the Ottoman forces hurried to the hill Ghazi Tepe, a little in rear of the Bulair lines, and he remained there for the next two days, using the telephone system of a neighbouring fort belonging to

DISPOSITIONS FOR THE HELLES LANDINGS

the lines for transmitting messages. It is claimed that he obtained a wide outlook over the gulf and the entire peninsula from this eminence, but, although it does overlook the gulf as well as the isthmus, much higher hills shut out a view over the peninsula—as will be seen from Map VII.

The marshal heard speedily of the landing near Gaba Tepe, a little later came news of landings about Helles, and he thereupon decided to give the command of the southern half of the peninsula to Essad Pasha, who at once proceeded by launch to Maidos. In the meantime the 7th Division had been assembled close to Gallipoli ready to be sent in any direction. It was kept there all day,—this, although the 5th Division was guarding the isthmus, and although the lines of Bulair could be trusted to delay any attack that could have been made, supposing that a disembarkation had been effected at the landing-place of Bakla Liman. It is a good illustration of the difficulties that beset the commander of a force which is charged with the duty of beating off hostile descents that may fall at various points along a considerable stretch of coast-line. Having given these details with regard to the dispositions of the enemy the narrative of the landings can be proceeded with.

The distribution of the attacking force at Helles.—The plan of operations for securing a footing at the extremity of the peninsula was a somewhat elaborate one. Three main landings were to take place, and these were to be supplemented by a minor landing on either flank. The principal disembarkations were to be undertaken respectively at Beaches V, W, and X (*vide* Map I on page 62), all three of which were in themselves favourable places, apart from the opposition that might be offered. Comparatively gentle slopes rose from the actual beaches in the case of V and W, and promised facilities for moving impedimenta forward as soon as a footing had been made good. In the case of X, on the other hand, the ground abutting on the beach rose somewhat abruptly, giving it the character almost of a bluff; but this circumstance, coupled with the fact that the beach faced west, concealed the environs of the landing-place from Kum Kale and gave reason to hope that the disembarkation at this point would not be interfered with by hostile artillery on the Asiatic side.

The minor landings were to take place at Beaches S and Y. S Beach was narrow and was obviously much exposed to fire from

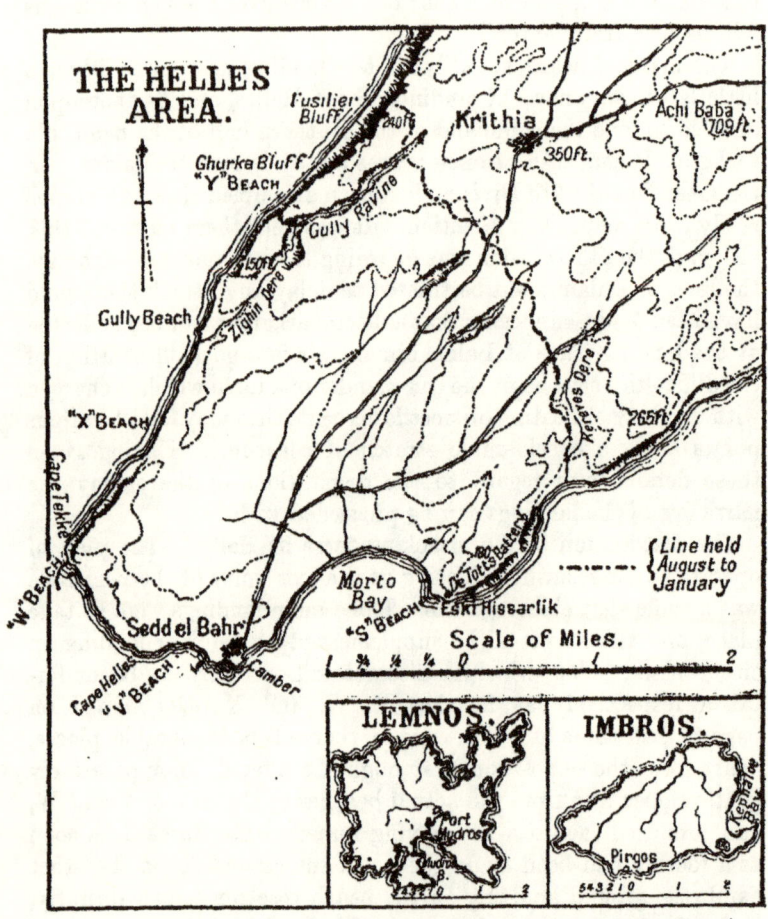

MAP I.—THE HELLES AREA (WITH INSETS OF LEMNOS AND IMBROS)

DISPOSITIONS FOR THE HELLES LANDINGS

across the Dardanelles. Y Beach was situated at the foot of cliffs, was not for that reason adapted for the landing of troops other than infantry and mountain artillery, and was not the kind of spot that would naturally be selected to put troops ashore at. Sir I. Hamilton hoped by means of these two secondary operations to protect the flanks, to disseminate the forces of the enemy and to interrupt the arrival of hostile reinforcements.

The Order of Battle of the 29th Division, commanded by General Hunter Weston, is given in Appendix II. The brigade organisation was, however, temporarily broken up in view of the number of different landing-places that the division was being committed to. The plan was that the Hampshires, the Royal Munster Fusiliers and the Royal Dublin Fusiliers should make Beach V their objective. The Lancashire Fusiliers were to make for the shore at Beach W. The Royal Fusiliers were allotted to Beach X. The South Wales' Borderers, a battalion which had fought alongside the Japanese at the taking of Tsingtau and which was the only one in the division that had already gained fighting experience during the course of the Great War, was told off to disembark at Beach S. The effort at Beach Y was entrusted to the King's Own Scottish Borderers and to the Plymouth Battalion of Marines belonging to the Royal Naval Division. The remaining five battalions of the 29th Division were to land at W, V, or X as circumstances might direct after the attack was once fairly launched. The "Anson" battalion of the Royal Naval Division was distributed in detachments amongst the troops detailed for landing at V, W, and X Beaches. The naval side of the operations was under control of Rear-Admiral Wemyss.

Owing to the fact that the disembarkation at Beach V (for which, as will be seen later, especially elaborate preparations had been made and which was looked upon as the most important landing of all) practically failed in the first instance, it will be convenient to leave it to the last. The different attacks will be taken from left to right, beginning at Beach Y.

The landing at Beach Y.—The King's Own Scottish Borderers had a comparatively easy task in gaining a footing on shore at Beach Y, for the enemy never anticipated that a landing would be attempted at this point. Lofty cliffs rose abruptly from the foreshore, the declivity being so steep that some doubt existed up to the last moment as to whether the troops would be able to scramble up or not, and it is not surprising that the Turks had taken no steps to defend such a spot. The troops were conveyed from the Tenedos anchorage to the vicinity of the beach in the cruisers *Amethyst* and *Sapphire* and in a couple of transports, supported by the battleship *Goliath*. There was only sufficient boat accommodation to provide for half a battalion at a time, so part of the Borderers led the way. They were unopposed, they landed without difficulty, and they had speedily breasted the almost precipitous slopes and established themselves at the top. The rest of the regiment followed on the next trip, and the Marines were brought ashore in a third one. The orders for the force were that after the whole was landed it should move along the top of the cliffs towards Cape Tekke, so as to join hands with the contingent that was disembarking on Beach X two miles off.

But this project proved to be impracticable. The enemy, while wholly unprepared for a landing at Y Beach, had assembled a body of troops at the mouth of the Zighin Dere where a good point for disembarkation presented itself, afterwards known as " Gully Beach." The reserve regiment of the 9th Turkish Division also appears to have been drawn up near Krithia awaiting developments. These hostile troops combined against the Borderers and Marines, and the consequence was that, before the little column had got fairly on the move, the enemy was gathering in great strength to overwhelm and destroy it, fire from *Goliath* and the cruisers proved of no avail, and although the two battalions promptly entrenched they were hard put to it to maintain themselves. The ground fell inland from the crest of the cliffs towards the Zighin Dere ; so that the watchers on the warships could not see the Turks and were thus debarred from lending effective assistance to their military comrades in distress. All day long this isolated British force was exposed to damaging artillery fire, and was called upon to withstand a succession of onsets delivered with unmistakable resolution and pertinacity by antagonists very superior in numbers. The hostile attacks continued far into the night. By dawn on the 26th the position was getting desperate in view of the heavy losses that had been sustained and of the exhaustion of the soldiery. It had become plain that this unsupported detachment was in danger of total destruction if left where it was, so orders were sent for it to be withdrawn. The retirement proved to be less difficult than might have been supposed, for when the troops descended to the water's edge, covered by a small rearguard, the gun-fire from the ships kept the Turks from crowning the crest of the cliffs and firing down on the beach. The retreating force was therefore able to embark almost unmolested, taking with it all its stores and its wounded, but much diminished in effectives. The work of the naval personnel both during the landing and also during the re-embarkation had been remarkably efficient, and all concerned had acquitted themselves with no little credit.

Comments.—In so far as the question of landings in face of probable opposition is concerned, the most useful lesson taught by this isolated effort at Beach Y seems to be this: When, included within the general theatre of operations, there are many localities which from the topographical point of view favour disembarkation and which the enemy will in consequence presumably feel obliged to guard, it may always be worth while to reject them all and to try instead at some point which is not in itself by any means attractive as a landing-place. With the object of avoiding a fight at that critical moment when the boats are discharging the leading troops, it, in a word, may prove profitable to sacrifice what can be described as the technical facilities that a soldier looks for. It is true that the attempt to gain a definite footing on the Gallipoli Peninsula at Beach Y miscarried, but the fact remains that the Scottish Borderers and the Marines did make their way ashore easily enough. It seems likely, moreover, that if a considerably larger force of infantry had been allocated to this particular enterprise the whole force would have disembarked quite comfortably, and that in that case its doings might have played a very prominent part in the operations of the 25th of April as a whole. When the attacks upon Beaches W and V come to be considered, it will be seen what a desperate venture a landing in defiance of determined resistance is under the tactical conditions of to-day. That class of undertaking is one to be avoided at almost any cost.

What, after all, is the problem ? Can it not be summed up in the phrase that you have got to establish yourself ashore, somehow ? May not your best plan be to choose a spot where infantry alone can gain a footing—and that only with difficulty owing to cliffs and so forth—for the sake of disembarking unopposed? Once safely on dry land, the foot soldiers may be able to work along the coast and be able to lay their hands on some spot where troops of all arms can disembark, thus securing a landing-place of the more conventional type.

We are dealing at the moment with landings. But it should be noted that the withdrawal of the defeated force was in some respects the most instructive and striking incident in this affair of Y Beach. The warships then proved of very real service to the troops, thanks to the somewhat peculiar contour of the ground. The Turks could not harry the retiring infantry on the beach owing to the ships' guns; and, as it turned out, this spot in spite of its apparent drawbacks proved itself a particularly satisfactory place to get away from. The subject of withdrawals will, however, be treated more at length when the story comes to be told at the end of this volume of how the Allied Expeditionary Force evacuated the Gallipoli Peninsula many months afterwards.

The landing at Beach X.—X Beach resembled Y Beach in many ways, but its features were less pronounced. It consisted of a strip of sand, about 200 yards long, nestling at the foot of an escarpment; but in this case the escarpment was in no sense precipitous, it rose only about 40 feet or so above the beach, and it therefore offered no obstacle whatever to infantry. The Royal Fusiliers had been brought over in the battleship *Implacable* and a couple of mine-sweepers, and the landing was heralded by the roar of guns from the battleship *Swiftsure;* these began a furious bombardment of the vicinity of the landing-places as soon as there was light enough to see. The troops were taken ashore in two trips, the landing parties on the first trip shepherded by *Implacable*, which crept close in, with the boats on either side of her and an anchor swung out over her bows, lowered sufficiently to drag before the great vessel ran risk of taking the ground. Her fire at close range as she approached the beach kept the Turks from showing themselves in their trenches; these were well constructed, but they were somewhat conspicuous, and, their site being as it were tilted up for the naval gunners to lay on, offered the ship's guns excellent targets. The consequence was that the Fusiliers made good their footing on the beach and mounted the slopes above it without suffering any appreciable loss, and they had thus overcome the

THE LANDING AT X BEACH 67

difficulty of getting ashore at all more easily than had been anticipated. As a matter of fact it was found afterwards that the bombardment had not very seriously injured the hostile defences, but it had none the less done exactly what was needed.

As soon as they were ashore and had breasted the escarpment, the Fusiliers pushed sturdily forward, their task in the first place being to try and join hands with the troops who were to land at Beach W, on the further side of Cape Tekke about a mile away. The high ground intervening between the two landing-places, however, turned out to be held in strength by the enemy, and, no sooner had the Fusiliers gained the crest of the escarpment, than they became heavily engaged with a determined and well-posted enemy. They, moreover, found themselves exposed to a malignant, enfilading shell-fire from a field battery emplaced somewhere near Krithia. They found it hard to gain ground under such conditions. They were, moreover, vigorously counter-attacked by hostile infantry, and were even compelled to give ground slightly under very severe pressure at the hands of superior forces. The situation was, however, completely restored after a time by the arrival of a supporting battalion, the Inniskilling Fusiliers, who were followed by the Border Regiment. These battalions as they came ashore on Beach X pushed partly south to aid the first comers, and partly worked outwards to extend the line. Thanks to their welcome assistance, it eventually became possible to deliver a resolute attack upon the bluffs near Cape Tekke. They were carried by a rush, and connection was thus established with the Lancashire Fusiliers, who by a wonderful feat of arms had won a landing for themselves on Beach W. But, even so, the position was not wholly reassuring. The Turks began coming on in imposing numbers and pressed forward with grim determination, so that, although *Implacable* had silenced the troublesome hostile battery near Krithia, the British were at one time forced back nearly to the cliffs by X Beach. Our troops, however, gradually dug themselves in, they beat off all attacks, and by nightfall they had established a line of entrenchments for about half a mile round Beach X, and extending south-west to link up with the battle front of the troops that had disembarked at the adjoining beach, W.

Judged as a landing in face of opposition, the success of the Royal Fusiliers at Beach X must be set down as a particularly memorable exploit, for the enemy was upon the whole well prepared and was on the look out. The defences which the Turks had contrived were, it is true, decidedly less formidable than those devised for the protection of Beaches W and V. Little use had been made of barbed wire. Nor, owing to the contour of the ground, was it a particularly easy point to defend—the defenders also may not perhaps have had time enough to make the most of such advantages as it possessed. Moreover, the fire of the warships was undoubtedly effective in this instance and it contributed markedly towards easing the way for the troops when they first set about gaining their footing ashore. Still, the actual landing was signally successful, and that particular phase of the general operation was accomplished with scarcely any loss. It is noticeable that the defenders reserved their fire at X Beach, allowing the leading boats to approach the shore undisturbed ; but, as will be seen later, this same procedure was adopted by the Turks at other points—even at Beaches W and V, where a far more determined resistance was offered to the actual disembarkation in the first instance than had been the case at Beach X. The reason why the enemy had devoted comparatively little labour and ingenuity to the fortifications at this locality, probably was that it obviously was not a suitable spot for landing artillery and impedimenta until communications from the beach on to the higher ground had been prepared ; in this respect it was from the attacker's point of view decidedly inferior to the Beaches W and V.

The landing at Beach W.—Had there been no question of opposition, Beach W would have provided an excellent landing-place. At Y and X bluffs rose abruptly from the strand, rendering it difficult (especially in the case of Y) for troops other than infantry to penetrate further. At W, on the contrary, there was, as is shown in the sketch map of W and V Beaches on page 70, a complete break in the cliffs, and as the shore formed a bay, facing south-west, the beach was better sheltered against the prevailing north-easterly winds than were Beaches Y and X. The Turks had not failed to take note of these conditions and they had prepared accordingly for eventualities. Sir I. Hamilton describes the landing-place as follows in his Despatch of 20th May :—

" W Beach consists of a strip of deep, powdery sand some 350 yards long and from 15 to 40 yards wide, situated immediately south of

Tekke Burnu, where a small gully running down to the sea opens a break in the cliffs. On either flank of the beach the ground rises precipitately; but, in the centre, a number of sand dunes afford a more gradual access to the ridge overlooking the sea. Much time and ingenuity had been employed by the Turks in turning this landing-place into a death-trap. Close to the water's edge a broad wire entanglement extended the whole length of the shore, and a supplementary barbed network lay concealed under the surface of the sea in the shallows. Land mines and sea mines had been laid. The high ground overlooking the beach was strongly fortified with trenches to which the gully afforded a natural covered approach. A number of machine-guns were also cunningly tucked away into holes in the cliff so as to be immune from naval bombardment whilst they were converging their fire upon the wire entanglements."

The Lancashire Fusiliers were told off to effect the landing at this point. They were conveyed to its vicinity in the cruiser *Euryalus*, and by 4 a.m. had transhipped into the ship's cutters which were to carry them ashore. It had been foreseen that their task would be an exceedingly difficult one, and it had therefore been decided that the whole battalion should be conveyed to land in one single trip. The arrangement was that eight picket boats, each of them towing four ship's cutters, should start for the shore simultaneously in line abreast.[1]

At 5 a.m. the covering warships got to work and directed a hot fire against the beach and also upon the ground which commanded it; this preliminary bombardment, however, did not—as was ascertained afterwards—exercise the damaging effect on the wire entanglements and the Turkish trenches that had been hoped for. During this opening phase of the contest the defences showed no signs of life; it almost looked indeed as if the disembarkation was to be unopposed, in spite of the preparations made to meet it, of which reconnaissances had established the existence. Then at 6 a.m., the flotilla of small craft got under way for the shore. The steam launches cast off as soon as they reached shallow water. The

[1] A 30′ cutter takes 32 men in marching order and a 34′ cutter will convey 42 men in marching order; besides these it is usual to allot 6 sailors to assist in working the boat. Thus eight of the 30′ type will carry a full company of infantry, while 6 of the 35′ type will suffice for the same load. In this case there were altogether 32 cutters, eight to each company; two picket boats, towing four cutters each, provided for a company. Picket boats draw nearly 5′ astern and, as they are ahead, the cutters have to be cast off while still some distance from the shore; these are then rowed the rest of the way to land.

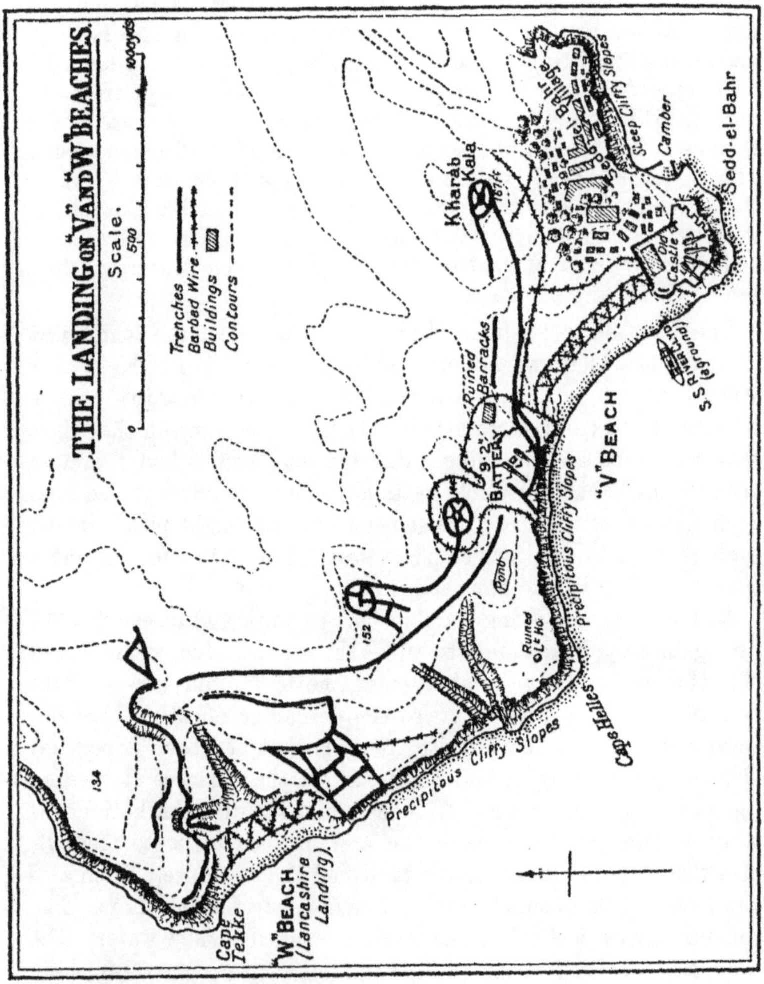

MAP II.—THE LANDINGS ON "V" AND "W" BEACHES

THE LANDING AT W BEACH

majority of the cutters went straight ahead, making direct for the beach; but the company on the left veered away towards Cape Tekke and pulled for the rocks below that promontory. A few boats also diverged to the right, heading for the cliffs at the extremity of the beach nearest Cape Helles.

All this time the Turks were obstinately holding their fire. Only at the moment when the leading boats touched the beach did a murderous, converging fusillade from rifles, machine-guns, and pompoms suddenly greet the assailants as these made their way to land. The losses were extremely heavy as the men struggled out of the boats. Many were shot down in the water, others were hit before they tried to disembark, some were drowned. Nevertheless, undismayed by the hail of bullets and regardless of gaps in the ranks, the Lancashire Fusiliers strove desperately to force their way through the masses of barbed wire which confronted them close to the water's edge, and to press on beyond. But, had it not been for their comrades who had diverged to the left before reaching land, all the efforts of the companies that had held their course straight for the beach might have been in vain.[1]

The platoons which had made for Cape Tekke were skilfully landed on the rocks at the foot of the headland, suffered little loss during the process, and then straightway set about mounting the rugged cliffs that rose above them. They were thus enabled after a short but desperate struggle to dispose with deadly effect of the hidden machine-guns which were sweeping the beach from this side, for the gunners were all bayoneted at their guns. They also from this position in a measure enfiladed the enemy's trenches

[1] It is interesting to note that Wolfe's memorable landing at Freshwater Cove near Louisburg on the 8th of May, 1758, furnishes an incident very similar to the successful landing on the rocks below Cape Tekke. The cove was not unlike W Beach, the actual strand being about of the same length, with rocky bluffs at either end. The French did not hold their fire. On the contrary, their musketry, coupled with the fire of eight guns, was so effective while the flotilla was approaching that Wolfe had actually signalled to call his troops off, when three subalterns on the left flank veered off to that side with their boats and in spite of the broken waters—the sea was somewhat rough—succeeded in landing on the rocks below the bluff at that end of the beach. Wolfe instantly signalled to the other boats to follow. The landing parties poured ashore, overthrew the defenders of the beach by taking them in flank, and gained a firm footing for the British on this inhospitable shore, with the result that the great French stronghold on Cape Breton came to be besieged and taken. Those three subalterns played a big part in moulding the history of the New World.

directly facing the beach, and they thereby afforded some relief to the main body of the regiment in its predicament. This, realising that there was dead ground below Cape Tekke, hurried in that direction and got into shelter below the declivity which the platoons on the left had already scaled, and here the shattered companies were reformed by such of the officers as had not been struck down. They then scrambled up, pushed resolutely on although most of their rifles were choked with sand owing to the men throwing themselves down on the beach, and drove off the Turks, thus establishing themselves firmly on the southern side of the high ground near the cape which the troops that had landed at X were already preparing to attack from the north. In the meantime the party which had landed at the Cape Helles end of the beach had worked its way up the cliffs on that side ; but it was brought to a standstill at the top by a wire entanglement which had been constructed near the edge, under fire from the two infantry redoubts northeast of the promontory. A portion of these detachments contrived to work their way under shelter of the cliff to the lighthouse, getting cover in the small ravines north-west of that point that are shown on the map.

It was now 9 a.m. and much needed reinforcements were beginning to arrive in the shape of the Worcesters who, profiting by the experience undergone by their predecessors, made straight for the rocks below Cape Tekke, got ashore there and, after breasting the bluff, hastened to the aid of the Lancashire men. These, on receiving such welcome support, pushed forward afresh and carried some trenches in their immediate front, which enabled their left to unite with the right of the Royal Fusiliers coming from Beach X. The Worcesters, moreover, about the same time made themselves masters of the gully leading up from the beach. As a consequence of these operations the position on the northern flank and immediately in front of Beach W had, shortly before noon, been rendered fairly secure. But the assailants were not making such satisfactory progress on the other flank, for the Lancashire detachments which had gone in that direction at the outset had found it impossible to advance from the crest of the cliff, or from the small ravines, or eastwards from the lighthouse towards V Beach. So the Worcesters were called upon to move across from left to right and to storm the high ground overlooking Cape Helles.

THE LANDING AT W BEACH 73

This high ground had been appropriately prepared for defence, and it was very strongly held by the enemy. In addition to the two infantry redoubts which have already been spoken of, a substantial wire entanglement ran transversely down from those works to the cliff edge, barring lateral movement from west to east. Further east, again, lay the 9·2-inch battery of Cape Helles which, as we have seen in Chapter II, had been seriously damaged by the fire of *Queen Elizabeth* and other ships during the attack upon the outer defences of the Straits at the end of February. This battery had been transformed into an excellent lair for infantry, and its recesses now swarmed with riflemen. In view of the heavy task confronting the Worcesters, the covering warships opened a warm fire on the position about 1 p.m. Then, when this bombardment had lasted some little time, the battalion advanced to the attack, and after a desperate affray wrested the two redoubts from the Turks. But, owing to the entanglements and to a withering musketry from the 9·2-inch battery, they failed to penetrate further to the right when an effort was made to move in that direction, with the idea of lending succour to the troops who had been endeavouring since early morning to gain a firm footing on Beach V and beyond it.

Some additional reinforcements were now arriving, diverted from the force destined for Beach V. But the Turks were pressing on in formidable numbers, bent on recovering the ground extending from Cape Helles to beyond Beach X that had been wrested from them, so that even with the accessions to their strength, the depleted ranks of the Lancashire Fusiliers and the Worcesters were hard set to hold their ground. Still, a fairly satisfactory position had been established by the close of the day, which was fortunate seeing that the thrusts on the part of the enemy were very determined and were continued long after dark. So critical was the situation for a time, indeed, that every available man had to be summoned into the firing line; but the position was stubbornly maintained at all points. The result of a day of furious combat was that a grip on Beach W had been fixed—although at the cost of heavy sacrifice in life—and that British infantry had proved to the world how, even under the unfavourable conditions that obtain to-day, it is not impossible for troops of the very best class to effect a landing in broad daylight in face of relentless and skilfully conducted opposition. In recognition of the heroism and fortitude that had been displayed in winning a way ashore under the most adverse conditions, the beach which had been the scene of this brilliant exploit was named " Lancashire Landing."

Comments on the fight for W Beach.—The struggle of the Lancashire Fusiliers, backed by the Worcesters, to secure a landing-place at this point ranks as one of the most remarkable and instructive episodes of the Dardanelles campaign. Here was a case of an operation of war similar to Abercrombie's daring feat, carried out successfully under modern conditions against an enemy who had enjoyed far longer warning of what was in store than General Friant had been favoured with when he tried to stay the British landing in Aboukir Bay. The disembarkation took place in daylight. The defenders were fully prepared and had made skilful use of technical devices of all kinds to defeat the attempt. It is true that imposing warships supported the assailants; but the naval assistance was not in reality on a more lavish scale than might fairly be looked for in an enterprise of this class. It was an admirable example in fact of this particular nature of tactical undertaking, the landing was successful, and its story suggests a number of edifying professional lessons.

In the first place, the effect of the projectiles from the ships' guns was disappointing to those who had placed reliance on their support, although soldiers and sailors who had seriously considered the subject ought not to have been surprised. Experiences of somewhat later date in France, in Flanders, and on the Isonzo have proved how heavy an expediture of ammunition and what accurate gunnery are demanded to sweep away wire entanglements. Well designed entrenchments require artillery treatment of a special kind before they can be safely assaulted by infantry, and this treatment a fleet is hardly in the position to apply. The essence of artillery preparation in such a case (supposing that flat-trajectory guns are being employed) is that fire should be maintained up till the very last moment, so that the defenders dare not show their heads; but ships' gunners are not trained for that kind of work, which is an art in itself. Only by dint of high-angle fire can artillery hope to destroy earthworks and to so cow the troops who are manning them that no serious resistance will be offered when the assailants drive home their attack; but warships are not fitted out with the necessary type of ordnance for executing the task, nor could this be used effectively, if they had it, from a moving platform.

A very striking feature in this memorable combat was the stubborn fashion in which the Turks held their fire till the last moment. This was also their attitude, it may be observed, at Beaches X and S; and, as will be seen later, the same procedure had evidently been contemplated at Beach V. It was pointed out in the last chapter, when discussing the problem in the abstract of opposed landings under modern conditions, that one of the advantages which the progress in arms of precision confers upon the defenders nowadays, as compared with their position in the era of muskets and smooth-bore guns, is that a damaging fire can be opened on the advancing boats while these are still a long way from the shore. The Turks deliberately threw away this advantage and permitted the foremost of the assailants of Beach W to reach land untouched. Why was this?

The phenomenon may be accounted for in various ways. The defenders possibly hoped to trap their antagonists, and feared that, if fire were opened as soon as this was likely to be effective, the result would be to scare the quarry away. Or they may have been afraid of disclosing the exact position of their trenches and machine-gun emplacements, and of thereby exposing themselves to a devastating fire from the warships before such fire came to be virtually masked by the advancing boats—it is as a matter of fact open to question whether there were grounds for such an apprehension. It is conceivable, no doubt, that the Turks had failed to realise how damaging their fire ought to be on crowded boats even when these were some hundreds of yards away; but this hardly seems likely. Whatever the reason was, the defenders seem to have made a mistake. Even such ideal troops as the 1st Lancashire Fusiliers consisted of on the 25th of April, 1915, are unable to stand unlimited punishment. Had, say, twenty per cent of that illustrious battalion been placed *hors de combat* before a single boat reached the beach, this additional loss might have just turned the scale and, for the signal triumph which the Lancashire men placed to their credit, might have substituted a sanguinary and mortifying repulse.[1]

---

[1] The range of firearms was of course very different in 1758 from what it represented in 1915; but it is interesting in connection with the landing of

Another point of interest is the somewhat significant contrast between the experiences undergone by those portions of the Lancashire Fusiliers that landed below Cape Tekke, and the experiences which befell the bulk of the regiment landing fair and square on the beach. Had it not been for the company which made its way ashore with no great loss on the rocks below the headland, and which then rushed the bluffs overhanging them, it is not inconceivable that the whole undertaking might have come to naught at this point. The rocks did not offer an attractive landing-place in themselves. Had there been no opposition, troops told off to disembark on Beach W would not have dreamt of selecting so inconvenient a spot, when there was an inviting strand close by offering easy access into the interior. The striking results obtained by the company which made for the flank seem to support the theory, already propounded when discussing the events at Beach Y, that when determined resistance is anticipated to the landing of troops it may pay to choose for disembarkation a point where the facilities for getting ashore are, in the topographical sense, restricted.

Only this remains to be said. Except for the extreme flanks, the general lie of the ground at Beach W rendered defence particularly easy, while its advantages as a landing-place were so obvious that the defenders were bound to take special precautions to guard so dangerous a locality. It was therefore a bad place to select as a point of disembarkation in the first instance. But whether the course that was pursued was unavoidable will be considered when the landings at Helles come to be discussed as a whole further on.

The landing at Beach S.—Although the Turks had made careful

Wolfe's brigade at the cove west of Louisburg, to which reference was made in the footnote to p. 71, to note the following extract from the diary of an officer who took part in the operations: "Had the enemy permitted the troops of the left attack (Wolfe's) "to have landed in the cove, they must certainly have put it out of our power to have troubled them afterwards, as by reserving their fire till then in all probability they would have put us in confusion, and we afterwards must have been at their mercy, the advantage mentioned giving them so much superiority." The advantage mentioned was "their intrenchments being 15 feet above high mark, the approach to which was rendered impracticable by large trees being lay'd very thick together upon the beach all round the cove, their branches laying towards the sea the distance of 20 yards in some places and 30 in others between their lines and the water's edge. Then the surge was extremely violent. . . ."

THE LANDING AT S BEACH

preparations to deal with a landing at Beach S, these were not on the same imposing scale as at Beach W. The place was hardly suitable for putting a large force ashore ; for the beach was narrow and the water to the left shallow, so that there was risk of the boats grounding prematurely if they deviated at all from the proper course. Slopes rose at a sharp incline from the beach, and well-designed trenches had been constructed from which an effective fire could be directed on the troops when they were landing and while they were still on the water. It has already been pointed out that this locality was particularly exposed to artillery fire directed from across the Straits ; it turned out, however, that the annoyance to the assailants from this source was not excessive on the opening day.

The contingent designated for this particular venture comprised three companies of the 2nd South Wales' Borderers, some engineers, and a landing party especially detailed from *Cornwallis*. The troops were brought over from Tenedos in trawlers, convoyed by that battleship, and in Morto Bay they were transferred into ships' boats towed by trawlers, six boats to the tow. Their arrival had been somewhat delayed by the strong current flowing out of the Straits, which hampered the trawlers in making the rendezvous ; the disembarkation therefore only began about 7.30 a.m. It was effected expeditiously and at no great cost, the Turks only opening fire at the last moment when the boats were already close to land. Supported by an effective cannonade from the warships, the Borderers worked their way forward in masterly fashion after setting foot on shore, and by 10 a.m., assisted by the naval landing party, they had captured the main defences that bore upon the beach, and were in possession of De Tott's Battery. They then dug themselves in and, aided by the shell from *Cornwallis* and *Lord Nelson*, were able to repulse a furious counter-attack in the afternoon with no great difficulty. The enemy directed some artillery fire on the beach from the Asiatic side, but this was badly conducted and it did little harm—which may possibly be accounted for by the influence of the French descent upon Kum Kale.

Unquestionably a meritorious performance, the sailors and soldiers of the attacking side sharing the credit for what was a skilfully contrived and admirably executed amphibious operation, the landing at Beach S proves that an undertaking of this character is perfectly feasible if the opposition be not more than moderately formidable. But it has to be remembered that the delay of the defence in opening fire while the assailants were still on the water probably facilitated their task—troops undertaking an enterprise of this class cannot safely count upon such good fortune. In this affair the ships' guns, it should be noted, played an important rôle, their supporting fire proving of great assistance to the landing troops ; owing to the lie of the ground the enemy's trenches were readily seen from the sea, and the battleships here took full advantage of conditions that were wanting at Beaches W and V.

The landing at Beach V.—The difficulties in the way of effecting a landing at Beach V proved very nearly to be insuperable, and they brought about an embittered contest in which the attacking side suffered almost overwhelming loss. A description of the landing-place, and of the elaborate arrangements that had been made by the Turks for securing it against attack, can best be given in Sir I. Hamilton's own words :—

" V Beach is situated immediately to the west of Sedd-el-Bahr. Between the bluff on which stands the Sedd-el-Bahr village and that which is crowned by No. 1 Fort[1] the ground forms a very regular amphitheatre of three or four hundred yards' radius. The slopes down to the beach are slightly concave, so that the whole area contained within the limits of this natural amphitheatre, whose grassy terraces rise gently to a height of a hundred feet from the shore, can be swept by the fire of the defender. The beach itself is a sandy strip some 10 yards wide and 350 yards long, backed along almost the whole of its extent by a low sandy escarpment about 4 feet high, where the ground falls almost sheer down to the beach. The slight shelter afforded by this escarpment played no small part in the operations of the succeeding thirty-two hours.

" At the south-eastern extremity of the beach, between the shore and the village, stands the old fort of Sedd-el-Bahr, a battered ruin with wide breaches in its walls and mounds of fallen masonry within and around it. On the ridge to the north, overlooking the amphitheatre, stands a ruined barrack. Both of these buildings, as well as No. 1 Fort, had been long bombarded by the fleet, and the guns of the fort had been put out of action ; but their crumbled walls and the ruined outskirts of the village afforded cover for riflemen, while from the terraced slopes already described the defenders were able to com-

[1] The 9·2" battery referred to in the account of the landing at Beach W.

mand the open beach, as a stage is overlooked by the balconies of a theatre. On the very margin of the beach a strong barbed-wire entanglement, made of heavier metal and longer barbs than I have ever seen elsewhere, ran right across from Sedd-el-Bahr to the foot of the north-western headland. Two-thirds of the way up the ridge a second and even stronger entanglement crossed the amphitheatre, passing in front of the old barrack and ending in the outskirts of the village. A third transverse entanglement, joining these two, ran up a hill near the eastern end of the beach, and almost at right angles to it. Above the upper entanglement the ground was scored with the enemy's trenches, in one of which four pompoms were placed; in others were dummy pompoms to draw fire, while the debris of the shattered buildings on either flank afforded cover and concealment for a number of machine-guns, which brought a cross-fire to bear on the ground already swept by rifle fire from the ridge.

"Needless to say, the difficulties in the way of previous reconnaissance had rendered it impossible to obtain detailed information with regard either to the locality or to the enemy's preparations."

Although the defensive arrangements described above were necessarily only very imperfectly known to the staff of the attacking side, it was fully realised at the time when the plans were being drawn up that the landing at Beach V was destined to be an exceptionally hazardous operation of war, and especial devices were brought into play with a view to overcoming some of the difficulties that were foreseen. A collier, the *River Clyde*, was especially prepared for beaching, and was to contain the bulk of the assaulting force. Great doors were cut in her sides, giving access to gang-planks, slung by ropes and dipping towards the bows. Although it might prove possible for the troops to wade ashore from the end of the gang-planks, it was expected that lighters would have to be got into position beyond the bows so as to form a pier to the shore; these were prepared for the purpose and were towed astern of the *River Clyde* by a hopper. Maxims protected by sand-bags were mounted on the bows of the ship and on its lower bridge. The Royal Munster Fusiliers, two companies of the Hampshire Regiment, a company of the Royal Dublin Fusiliers and a field company of engineers embarked in this vessel, the total force on board exceeding 2000 of all ranks. The remaining three companies of the Dublins were brought over in a transport and were transferred before dawn to ships' cutters, ready to be towed to land by picket boats. The plan was that half a company was to be put ashore at the camber to the east of Sedd-el-Bahr as an isolated operation—this will be dealt with later—while the other two and a half companies were to land direct on V Beach. The *River Clyde* was to be run ashore as soon as these had disembarked.

A hot bombardment of the beach and environs was started by *Albion* soon after dawn, but this does not appear to have caused commensurate havoc amongst the hostile trenches and entanglements; the Turks, as at Beach W, remained quiescent during this preliminary cannonade. *Queen Elizabeth* and other warships battered the old castle and the village of Sedd-el-Bahr. Then, about 6 a.m., the line of picket boats (five of them, each towing four cutters) made for the land, and only when the leading boats, after casting off, reached the beach did the defences show sign of life. Then the assailants were greeted with a terrific fire, which proved disastrous to the troops as they scrambled out of the boats. Only a very few of the Fusiliers succeeded in attaining the cover of the four-foot escarpment, described above, where they found shelter. The majority were either shot down in the water or else as they reached the beach, or they were placed *hors de combat* while still in the boats. Many of these were seriously damaged, and most of them were rendered unmanageable owing to the sailors in charge being struck down or else by the rowers being killed or wounded. Within a few minutes, this portion of the attack had been to all intents and purposes defeated, the troops detailed for the operation were almost wiped out of existence, and the few survivors were cowering at the water's edge under the inadequate protection of the lip scooped by the waves.

The *River Clyde* took the ground rather nearer to Sedd-el-Bahr than had been intended, and practically simultaneously with the beaching of the boats. It was then seen that the lighters must be brought into play to establish a pier, for the water at the bows was much too deep for men to land. So under a hail of bullets those responsible began to get the lighters into position. It proved no easy task. A strong lateral current running along the shore towards Cape Helles created almost insuperable difficulties, for the lighters swung across under its influence and became unmanageable. How naval officers and sailors stuck to their work in this

THE LANDING AT V BEACH

emergency has been often told. No sooner had the pier been prepared and did troops start for the shore, than a gap occurred between the unwieldy vessels. The leading company of the Munsters was stopped by the gap; but the men thereupon scrambled down into the sea, those wounded being in many cases drowned, and the survivors managed to gain the shelter of the low bank. When the next company tried, the lighters had drifted into a worse position. By a glorious display of valour and tenacity on the part of the naval personnel the pier was re-established after a fashion, and the remnants of the company got ashore. When a third company was rushing forward it found itself exposed to severe shrapnel fire and it suffered so heavily that a pause had to be called. Then some Hampshires started for the land. But the line broke, and the lighters thereupon drifted into deep water with the troops who were lying down on board offering excellent targets for every class of fire from the Turkish entrenchments, General Napier commanding the 88th Brigade was killed, and it was reluctantly decided to abandon a continuation of the heroic attempt till dark. The *River Clyde* was in the meantime being bombarded by hostile artillery, and the vessel was struck several times by big howitzer shell discharged from across the Straits; but the projectiles upon the whole did less harm than might have been expected. In the meantime her machine-guns were doing excellent service, and their fire may perhaps have been the controlling factor in preventing the enemy from delivering a counter-attack upon the troops who were crouching at the water's edge, shielded by the low escarpment, and who would have found it hard to beat off a determined onset.

Towards evening the position was as follows. There were perhaps 400 unwounded officers and men spread out along the beach escarpment, practically unable to move, and about 1000 officers and men remained in comparative security on board the collier. Some units which in the original plan had been destined for Beach V had been diverted to Beach W, because for all practical purposes the attempt to effect a landing immediately west of Sedd-el-Bahr had miscarried in spite of the elaborate preparations that had been made. The losses had been almost overwhelming, and the prospect of successful advance by the parties which had actually gained the shore looked the reverse of promising, although some individuals did manage towards evening to creep forward as far as the lee of the old castle at the south-eastern end of the bay. But, about 8 p.m., the whole of the troops remaining on board the *River Clyde* emerged from their lair and made their way to land along the floating pier without losing a man—a strange sequel to the terrible events of the day and to the untoward experiences which had been undergone by the Dublins, by the Munsters, and by portions of the Hampshire Regiment when trying to reach the beach by daylight. An attempt was then made in the dark to gain a footing in the castle and in the village. But the Turks proved to be fully on the alert, they opened a destructive fire, and further efforts were postponed till the morning.

Comments on the landing on V Beach.—Of the five separate attempts to secure a footing on shore in the Helles region, the fight for Beach V undoubtedly presents the most interesting tactical features. The difficulties were greatest. The preparations by both sides were the most complete. At each of the other four beaches the attack had proved successful early in the day, and the troops detailed for the different operations had effected their purpose of securing a footing on land at the first attempt, whereas at V the hold of the assailants upon the shore when evening approached was in reality so precarious that it might almost have been called non-existent. The expedient of running a steamer, especially fitted out for the purpose, ashore full of troops may be said to have established a new precedent in the art of war. The virtual impossibility of effecting a landing from boats in broad daylight in face of resolute opposition when there is no dead ground to favour the assailants, seems to have been pretty well decided by the fate of the Dublin Fusiliers.

What lessons can be deduced from the striking episode of the *River Clyde?* Is such a device justifiable and expedient when it is a question of effecting a disembarkation on a beach in defiance of the resistance offered by a determined enemy fully prepared for the struggle? Now, the passage of a defile in presence of the enemy is ever likely to prove a hazardous operation, costly in casualties, and it is hardly the class of enterprise that will be attractive to most soldiers. Circumstances will no doubt at times oblige a commander to force such a pass—the Bridge of Lodi and the Dargai Ridge provide examples—but it assuredly is not an

THE LANDING AT V BEACH 83

undertaking to be sought after. When, however, you convey troops imprisoned in the hold of a ship to a fire-swept beach, and when you then discharge them from the bows of the vessel for the shore along gang-planks and a floating pier, you are creating a defile for yourself. You thrust your men along a narrow causeway under converging hostile fire, and in doing so you deliberately set at defiance what is in reality one of the most elementary of tactical principles. Still the fact remains that the expedient of employing the collier must be acknowledged to have proved on the whole less unsuccessful during the daylight hours of the 25th of April at Beach V, than did the normal plan of throwing the assaulting troops ashore in boats. A fair number of infantrymen did manage to get to land unwounded from the *River Clyde* in spite of the extraordinary difficulties that arose in connection with the lighters.

It must also be remembered that Sir I. Hamilton and his staff could not possibly foresee that the Turks would hold their fire until troops actually began to land. Had the defenders opened on the tows that were conveying the Dublin Fusiliers to shore when they were still some hundreds of yards out, it is likely enough that not a man would have gained the beach. On the other hand, seeing that the detachments inside the collier actually suffered very little loss from hostile bullets or shell, there is no reason to suppose that it would have made any appreciable difference to them had the Osmanli soldiery in the trenches started firing on the ship when she was still approaching land ; the 2000 men in her hold would have been no less fit for their task of getting to the beach after she had grounded than they actually were. This is a point that should not be overlooked when an attempt is made to deduce tactical lessons for guidance from the memorable fight for Beach V. For it is, after all, reasonable to anticipate that in future affairs of this particular character, the defenders will make free use of their artillery, of their machine-guns, and of their rifles, from the moment that their antagonists come within range.

As the beaching of the *River Clyde* was carried out early in the day the incident does not throw much light on the question whether this device is likely to prove a success supposing it to be put in force during the night watches. Still the fact that such troops as remained shut up in the vessel when darkness set in, found themselves able to reach land without suffering any loss at all, is instructive. It does seem to indicate that the plan of running a ship full of soldiers ashore may prove to be an excellent way of effecting a landing if the entire operation be carried out at night. There are, however, obvious nautical objections to adopting such a procedure. Even as it was, the *River Clyde* grounded at a point some little way from the spot intended. Had the attempt been made in the dark she might have missed the beach altogether; or she might have brought up where the water shoaled some considerable way out from the shore, necessitating a long floating pier; or she might even have struck a reef too far out to admit of a floating pier being established.

It should be remembered that the absence of tide in the Mediterranean militates against the effective employment of a ship for this particular purpose. In more open seas a vessel can run her nose on to a beach at high water; then, as the tide ebbs, her bows will be left high and dry, enabling the troops to disembark quite comfortably by gang-planks or even possibly to dispense with these adjuncts. Most of the loss that befell the Munsters and Hampshires when they were landing from the *River Clyde* occurred on the lighters and in the water, before they had actually reached land.

The camber east of Sedd-el-Bahr.—Reference was made further back to a half-company of the Dublin Fusiliers who were to land on the camber east of the village of Sedd-el-Bahr. This camber, as will be seen from Map II, was about three hundred yards from the south-eastern end of Beach V, and as it turned out this minor affair was quite distinct from the operations at that point. The half-company disembarked on the camber with less loss than might have been expected, and they then tried to work across to Beach V, below the castle. This, however, they found to be quite impossible. They then strove hard to gain a footing in the village, but they found this also to be beyond them. The warships could give them little help, and in their isolated and very exposed position they naturally suffered heavy losses. Eventually the survivors were got away.

Such an extraneous enterprise undertaken by a handful of troops was hardly likely to lead to any satisfactory result. That the little force was not wiped out altogether was probably due to the enemy not anticipating trouble at so unlikely a spot; the Turks would naturally realise that any attack at such a point was certain to be delivered on a very small scale in view of the narrow front. It has been suggested in earlier paragraphs, when discussing the landings at Beaches Y and X, that an inconvenient locality for effecting a disembarkation may sometimes be a good one to select, because there may be little or no opposition at such a spot. But the camber was so near to Beach V that the defenders were in a position to collect troops very rapidly to bar the way to the half-company of Dublins, even had there been no troops actually on guard in the first instance.

Some observations on the landings at Helles.—It is proposed to reserve a general review of the plan adopted for securing a lodgement on the Gallipoli Peninsula for the next chapter. In this one we deal only with the details of the preliminary disembarkations. But, before turning to the initial operations undertaken by the French at Kum Kale and by the Australasians north of Gaba Tepe, it may be worth while to draw attention to certain significant points in connection with the violent struggles about Helles on the 25th of April that formed such a dramatic opening scene to the land campaign for the possession of the Dardanelles.

Sir I. Hamilton has been criticised for deciding to use so many different points of disembarkation at the extremity of the peninsula. But it is worth noting in this connection that the three beaches chosen for the main attack—X, W, and V—taken together only provided a length of 900 yards. That represents a somewhat narrow frontage when it is a question of getting the largest possible number of troops ashore in the least possible period of time. It is always likely to be the case—as it was to a large extent in April off the Gallipoli Peninsula—that the strength of the force that can be landed on a beach, or on beaches, hinges upon the number of boats that are available to convey the troops ashore. When the matter comes to be examined into, however, it turns out in the case of Helles that it was perhaps hardly so much a question of boats as a question of elbow-room.

The actual disposition of boats was, as we have seen, that enough for half a battalion were allocated to Beach Y, for half a battalion to Beach X, for a whole battalion to Beach W, for three companies to Beach V and the camber, and apparently for about half a battalion to Beach S. To the three main beaches was allowed boat accommodation for nine companies, and, as each company takes approximately two tows of four boats each, this means that 18 tows were told off to a frontage of 900 yards. That allows only about 50 yards between tows, and it promises that there will be a swarm of 72 cutters, with only about 12 yards space to the cutter, approaching the shore simultaneously after casting off. It furthermore means a mass of some 2000 men discharged more or less simultaneously on a front of 900 yards, without cover of any sort, necessarily in considerable confusion and under close fire from a well-posted enemy. Would more tows and more boats and more men have improved the prospects ? It seems extremely doubtful. On the other hand, it must be remembered that a proportion of the boats are bound to be damaged in an affair of this kind—at Beach V a considerable proportion of the cutters were rendered unserviceable—and on this account there is something to be said for keeping some craft in reserve, so that there may be some resources in hand to fill up the gaps in view of landing later troops. Sufficient boats for about a battalion were allocated to Beaches Y and S ; had operations been confined to the three landing-places near Capes Tekke and Helles, these boats would certainly have been of use in hurrying reinforcements to Beaches X and W after the Royal Fusiliers and Lancashire Fusiliers had won their footing.

It is always easy to be wise after the event. Knowing what we do now, no very profound mastery of the art of war is called for to perceive that the best course to pursue might have been to make the main effort at Beach X, to delay the landing at Beach W till a strong force was ashore at X, to keep Beaches Y and V busy with feints, and possibly to have deferred the effort at Beach S till the following day, using a fresh battalion from Mudros. The *River Clyde* could presumably have been beached on Beach X just as easily as on Beach V ; and, if she had been, the troops on board would have poured out of her intact, within a few minutes, because there was less current at that point than there was near Sedd-el-Bahr and because her passengers would have met with no opposition at all until they began to advance from the beach. The unfortunate part of the operations as they actually took place was that three of the battalions—the Lancashires, the Dublins, and the Munsters—should have suffered such tremendous losses while

THE LANDING AT KUM KALE 87

actually trying to get on land, and at a juncture when they were causing no corresponding casualties to the enemy. There was hard fighting all along the line on the 25th of April after footings had been gained; but both sides naturally were losing men during that fighting, and not merely the attacking side, which makes all the difference in the world.

The landing at Kum Kale.—The descent upon the Asiatic shore at the mouth of the Straits was undertaken mainly for the purpose of preventing effective hostile artillery fire being brought to bear upon Helles across the channel. But it served also to some extent as a feint, the efficacy of which was probably enhanced by the action of one of the French battleships which made a demonstration towards Besika Bay. The operation was entrusted to French troops, who were accompanied by General d'Amade, the Commander of the French Expeditionary Force, and the contingent detailed for the task was composed of the 6th Colonial Regiment (one European and two Senegalese battalions), a field battery, and a half-company of engineers, under immediate command of Colonel Ruel. It was conveyed in five transports, one of which carried 4-inch guns, and was under the protection of the three old French battleships, *Jauréguiberry*, *Henri IV*, and *Jeanne D'Arc* and of the Russian cruiser *Askold*. There would appear to have been sufficient boat accommodation to carry about 1400 infantry at a time.

The flotilla sailed from Lemnos about nightfall on the 24th, after having practised disembarkation outside Mudros harbour in the afternoon. Proceeding under slow steam, the armada had arrived within three miles of Kum Kale by dawn, and the four warships soon afterwards opened a brisk fire upon the fort and village of Kum Kale and upon the village of Yeni Shehr. The transports anchored about 7.30 a.m., some of the troops intended for the first trip having already been transferred to boats. It then at once became apparent that, in view of the strong current running out of the Dardanelles and of the low horse-power of the picket boats and tugs that were to undertake the towing, progress towards shore on the part of the tows would be a slow business; some assistance was to be rendered to the tows by destroyers and torpedo-boats.

The map on the next page illustrates this operation. It had originally been intended to carry out the disembarkation north-

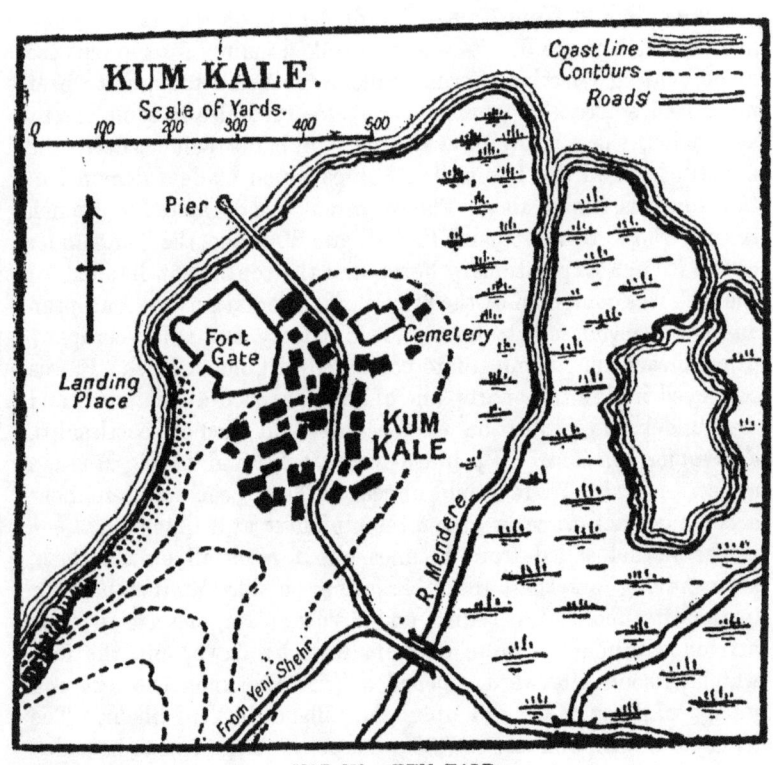

MAP III.—KUM KALE

THE LANDING AT KUM KALE

east of the fort of Kum Kale, near the pier shown, but at the last moment it was fortunately decided to change the venue and to carry out the operation on the other side of the fort, and close to it. The pier and the shore near the pier were exposed to heavy machine-gun and rifle fire from the village and the cemetery, and also to artillery fire from rising ground to the east of the Mendere flats, whereas the beach close to the fort on the other side was dead ground owing to the shelter given by the wall of the stronghold, and it was entirely invisible from the other side of the Mendere. The whole of the first echelon, composed of five infantry companies and the half-company of engineers, had pushed off from the transports by 9 a.m., and it moved slowly against the strong current towards the appointed landing-place. Owing to some misunderstanding, however, the tow under charge of *Askold* made for the pier, came under heavy fire when still some distance off, lost heavily and was compelled to withdraw. Owing to difficulties experienced in towing, the remainder of the first echelon arrived in somewhat straggling order at the beach. But this mode of approach offered certain advantages, seeing that only the end of the beach nearest the fort was really effectively defiladed; as only a small number of boats arrived simultaneously they could all be discharged at the sheltered spot. The Turks did not in this case hold their fire as they did at most points on the Helles side; but they were disinclined to expose themselves owing to the gun-fire from the ships and the actual landing was effected with little loss, the troops being able to form up under cover of the fort wall near the gate. The fort had soon been secured, and the troops then attacked the village and carried it at the point of the bayonet, although they failed to wrest the strongly held cemetery from its garrison.

The second echelon began proceeding towards shore about 11.30, the rafts with guns and horses started about 1.30, and the entire force was on land by 3 p.m. As reinforcements arrived the troops pushed out from the village of Kum Kale and advanced in the direction of Yeni Shehr. They were opposed by considerable part of the 3rd Turkish Division moving up from the south into a position taken up about 800 yards from the village; but they nevertheless managed to move forward some distance, for they were aided by the gun-fire of the warships which took the enemy in enfilade. The defenders were, however, in strong force in Yeni

Shehr, and when night set in the French troops were still held up a few hundred yards south of Kum Kale and also by the staunch garrison of the cemetery.

This operation does not call for very much comment. The Turks were hardly so well prepared to contest the landing as they were in the case of V and W Beaches on the other side of the water, although they disposed of considerable forces. It is noteworthy that owing to the good cover existing at the point where the disembarkation took place this met with little difficulty, whereas the boats which approached the pier, where there was no cover, suffered severely. The difficulties caused by the current and the low power of the steam vessels towing the boats apparently did no great harm beyond delaying things. The experience of *Askold's* tow certainly suggests that in a case like this the defending side should open fire promptly; the boats never reached land, whereas at W Beach, where the defenders held the formidable concentrated fire that they were in a position to bring to bear, the troops got ashore. The fire of the warships would not seem to have been very effective, although the conditions were not unfavourable. But the small French force did what was required of it, the capture of the village of Kum Kale was a dashing piece of work, the Turks suffered appreciable losses in killed and prisoners, and the troops had the satisfaction of knowing that they had indirectly afforded some assistance to their British comrades who were forcing their way ashore on the European side of the Straits.

The feint in the Gulf of Saros.—Before giving an account of the memorable landing of the Australasian forces north of Gaba Tepe, the important feint that was made by an amphibious force in the Gulf of Saros on the 25th and the night following should be mentioned. Part of the Royal Naval Division, escorted by the battleship *Canopus* and some destroyers, proceeded to the Gulf of Saros on the evening of the 24th, the Royal Naval Division carried in their own transports. The destroyers opened fire against various points on the northern shores of the gulf next morning, and later *Canopus* bombarded the Bulair Lines, while preparations as though for a landing were made on board the transports. At night an officer (Lieutenant-Commander Freyberg) swam ashore carrying flares which he lighted on the beaches near the lines, and the destroyers then opened fire, to which the Turks replied.

This feint probably exerted some influence in keeping Marshal Liman von Sanders in a condition of nervousness as to the possibilities of a serious landing in that quarter, and in delaying the despatch of the two divisions, which he had assembled about Bulair and Gallipoli, southwards during the 25th.[1] The operation did not for practical purposes reduce the numbers at disposal for carrying out landings at Helles on the 25th, because there would not seem to have been boats available on that day for the purpose.

The general scheme for the Anzac landing.—The plan of action decided upon for establishing a lodgment on the outer side of the Gallipoli Peninsula, north of Gaba Tepe, differed materially in principle and in its details from the method that was put in force in winning a footing near Helles. Sir I. Hamilton's design for the Australasian Army Corps under General Birdwood was that the troops should begin landing at dawn and all at one spot. It was practicable to beach boats almost anywhere between Gaba Tepe and Suvla Bay, although neither the foreshore itself, nor yet the avenues inland from the foreshore, were equally convenient at all points ; so that a failure to hit off the exact locality selected for the disembarkation did not necessarily involve disastrous consequences. It was therefore justifiable to accept the risks incurred by approaching in the dark. The idea was to effect a surprise. The disembarkation was not to be ushered in here by a roar of ships' artillery. It was hoped that the leading troops would get ashore almost without loss, and the scheme warranted confidence that the advanced echelons as they rowed ashore would not at the worst come under fire till the last moment. We have seen that the Turks deliberately held their fire till the boats reached the beach at Helles ; but that could not be foreseen, and we are not entitled to assume that the same procedure would have been

---

[1] The account given by the anonymous staff officer on Liman von Sanders' staff who wrote *Gallipoli, Der Krieg um den Orient,* when describing how news of the landings reached headquarters, says : "The first information that came to hand" (during the night of the 24th-25th) "intimated that seven hostile transports, surrounded by battleships, cruisers and torpedo-boats, had entered the Gulf of Saros. The division that was assembled at Gallipoli was immediately warned by the commander-in-chief who happened to be there at the moment." He goes on, speaking of the following day : "The fleet of transports that has entered the Gulf of Saros is not taken seriously. When it is observed that the enemy late in the afternoon makes no preparation for landing, the commander-in-chief becomes satisfied that this is only a feint."

adopted elsewhere. The project of commencing landing operations at daybreak therefore had a good deal to recommend it.

The nautical difficulties attending a military disembarkation on an open beach are, however, manifestly augmented if it be effected in the dark or in the half-light of dawn. Navigation, the management of tows, controlling individual boats, actual beaching, and so forth, are obviously easier to carry out by daylight. But as mentioned at the beginning of this chapter the weather on the night of the 24th–25th April was particularly favourable for executing this class of enterprise.

Five battleships had been allotted to General Birdwood's army corps, *Queen, London, Prince of Wales, Triumph,* and *Majestic,* of which the first three carried between them 1500 men of the 3rd Australian Infantry Brigade.[1] These 1500 constituted the first echelon of the covering force. *Triumph, Majestic,* and the cruiser *Bacchante* were to support the landing with their fire. The flotilla also included a number of smaller war craft, besides transports and trawlers conveying troops. The rest of the 3rd Brigade, which constituted the covering force, was to be transferred to destroyers to bring it close inshore, while the bulk of the 2nd (Victoria) Brigade which was to follow the 3rd made the voyage in trawlers; these likewise were to push in near to the landing-place so as to facilitate discharging their troops by boat.

The approach.—The armada, as we have seen in the last chapter, quitted Mudros harbour on the evening of the 24th. It steamed slowly with all lights extinguished until it reached the appointed rendezvous, about five miles from Gaba Tepe, about 1 a.m. Ships' boats were then promptly lowered, the troops from the three battleships took their places in these, and the picket boats moved to their stations to take the cutters in tow (12 picket boats towing 4 cutters each—48 cutters in all). The entire operation proceeded without a hitch, the 3rd Brigade having been practised in this kind of work while at Lemnos. At the same time the rest of the 3rd Brigade transhipped from transports into destroyers. The moon which had been shining brightly set at 2.30 a.m., and the flotilla then proceeded slowly ahead, with the covering warships leading. At 3.30 a.m. it had arrived within 2500 yards of the

[1] One battalion Queensland, one South Australia, one West Australia, one made up from South Australia, West Australia and Tasmania.

shore, the outline of the hills beginning to show up, and the tows were thereupon ordered to make for land, followed half an hour later by the destroyers.

It had been intended to carry out the disembarkation on a stretch of beach a few hundred yards north of Gaba Tepe, which reconnaissance had indicated to be favourable. A broad depression here led into the interior of the peninsula, there was some fairly level ground near the shore, and, apart from the question of opposition, the locality offered a favourable landing point for a force of all arms. As it turned out, however, the set of the current running northwards along this coast had carried the flotilla out of its course, and the point actually hit off by the tows was just south of Ari Burnu which is some two miles from Gaba Tepe. Rugged hills here rise abruptly from the foreshore, and, although there is an indentation in the coast-line, immortalised under the name of Anzac Cove, the enemy had manifestly not expected a serious attack at that particular point on account of the inconvenient topographical features. On the other hand, there is every reason to believe that the Turks were fully prepared to deal with attack at the point which had actually been selected, and that they had there prepared defences almost, if not quite, as elaborate and formidable as those which confronted the 29th Division on W and V Beaches near Helles.

The landing.—The beach on which the landing was actually effected is a very narrow concave strip of sand, about 1000 yards in length, fringing the indentation shown as "Anzac Cove" on Map IV. "At its southern extremity," writes Sir I. Hamilton, "a deep ravine,[1] with exceedingly steep scrub-clad sides runs in a north-easterly direction. Near the northern end of the beach a small but steep gully runs up into the hills at right angles to the shore. Between the ravine and the gully the whole of the beach is backed by the seaward face of the spur which forms the north-western side of the ravine." This was not in fact a spot that could be looked upon as a favourable locality for disembarking an army. The beach was so narrow that there was no elbow-room, the rugged hills that encroached upon it offered no conveniences for moving forward ordinary transport and military stores, and there was no shelter whatever in case of the sea getting up. Nevertheless it

[1] This was christened "Shrapnel Gully."

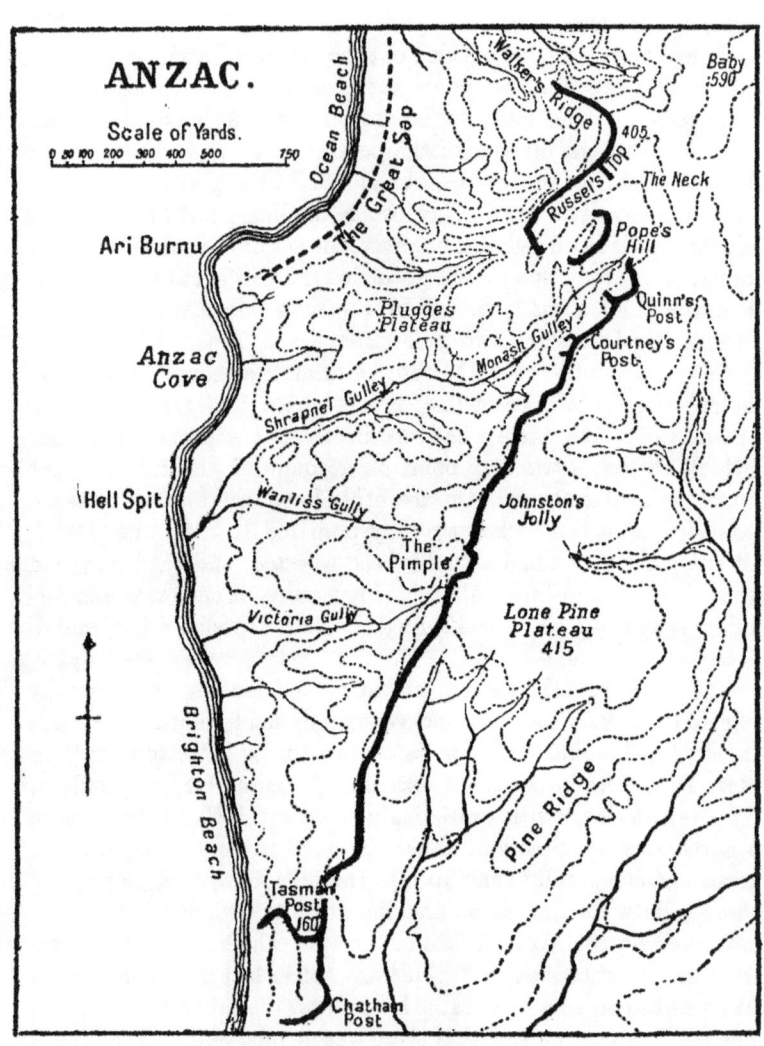

MAP IV.—ANZAC

had its advantages, for the Turks do not appear to have detected the approach of the flotilla until the tows were very near the shore, and they had made no elaborate arrangements for defence. But about a battalion of them were perceived in the dim light to be running up from the south to intercept the landing parties at the last moment, and fire was opened and caused some casualties before the boats actually reached the beach. Vice-Admiral de Robeck in his despatch gives 4.20 a.m. as the hour at which they grounded.

The troops instantly scrambled out and went for the enemy with the bayonet, their antagonists fleeing before them up the rugged hill-side. The small gully mentioned by Sir I. Hamilton, and the spur between this and Shrapnel Gully (afterwards called Maclagan's Ridge after the commander of the 3rd Brigade), were secured almost at the first attempt, the active Australian infantry breasting the declivities like mountaineers and then rushing after the fugitives down into Shrapnel Gully. Meanwhile, the rest of the 3rd Brigade were landing from the destroyers. But no satisfactory line was taken up such as a "covering force" is supposed to secure, so as to enable the following troops to assemble in good order. So sudden and uncompromising had been the rush of the first comers, however, that the enemy offered no very determined resistance at any point for the first hour or two. The Turks had no sooner become aware that a landing was taking place near Ari Burnu, than their guns at Gaba Tepe brought a heavy and, considering that it was still almost dark, extremely accurate and destructive fire to bear from about Gaba Tepe on the troops as they were proceeding ashore, and on the narrow beach itself. Their shrapnel caused considerable losses and some boats were sunk by high explosive shell; owing to its being enfilading the fire was particularly effective and trying. At one or two points there was barbed wire below the surface, which added to the difficulties of getting ashore. While the troops first landed were striving hard to establish themselves on the heights, their first reinforcements were losing heavily in getting ashore and immediately after they set foot on land, the half-light seriously aggravating the inevitable confusion on the beach.

The 3rd Brigade were, after some delay, followed by the 2nd Brigade, which was accompanied by an Indian mountain battery.

As these troops landed they hurried forward in support of the first arrivals, and seeing that different battalions and companies were landing simultaneously and that there was no space for forming up on the beach, there was necessarily some confusion of units even before they were thrust into the fight; the 2nd Brigade in general worked south-eastwards across Shrapnel Gully, on the right of the 3rd Brigade, extending the front. The operation of putting troops following the 3rd Brigade ashore was somewhat delayed by the transports having to lie a considerable distance out in order to avoid the howitzer and field gun-fire brought to bear on them, and also projectiles from the Ottoman warships stationed in the Narrows.

It is difficult to give a connected account of the disjointed encounters that took place during this day of fluctuating battle. The further the assailants pushed inland from the beach the more difficult the terrain became, and the more formidable grew the resistance of antagonists, who displayed marked skill in utilising the plentiful cover afforded by the scrub and by the very broken character of the ground. There had been intermingling of companies and battalions even at the moment of the first rush from the beach, and this naturally became aggravated during a succession of haphazard, but sanguinary, affrays in gullies and on the hillsides. In the eagerness of pursuit, parties of Australians pushed far ahead, became isolated, and were swallowed up in the ravines by much stronger bodies of Osmanlis. Substantial success was obtained at many points, and a three-gun battery was taken in brilliant style. But as they recovered from their preliminary surprise on finding themselves assailed at a point where they had not anticipated a landing in force, the Turks rapidly assembled strong bodies of infantry to confront the invaders. The 19th Turkish Division was hurried into the fight in support of the troops especially detailed to guard this portion of the coast, and, owing to the inevitable delays that took place in getting the 1st and 4th Australian Brigades and the New Zealanders ashore, the defenders were able to concentrate on the battlefield more rapidly than did the attacking side.

The 1st (New South Wales) Brigade was, however, on shore and fully engaged before noon, taking up a general direction to the left of the 3rd Brigade, and apparently making good some of the ground about what afterwards came to be known as Courtney's Post. It was followed by the New Zealand Brigade which worked off to the left, occupying Plugge's Plateau and pressing on in the direction of Russel's Top, besides pushing out a small force along the low ground to the north of Ari Burnu and seizing a spur which came to be known as No. 1 Post.[1] Fire from that direction had been particularly severe when some of the boats tried to disembark troops north of Ari Burnu. All this time the beaches and the various craft and boats standing close in were being subjected to a heavy artillery fire from the direction of Demajalik Bair and Ismail Oglu Tepe (see Map V, p. 168), and coming from the guns skilfully concealed about Gaba Tepe. *Majestic*, *Triumph* and the cruiser *Bacchante* did something towards keeping the fire from this promontory down, but it kept bursting out afresh, and the comparative failure of the warships to crush the Turkish guns and aid the troops in the boats was one of the most instructive incidents of the day. It is indeed noteworthy that the very heavy losses sustained actually in the boats, and on the beach after the landing had been made good by the 3rd Brigade, were in fact mainly due to hostile gun-fire, whereas during the landings at Helles, and immediately after the troops had gained their footing on those southern beaches, they suffered rather from rifles and machine-guns than from artillery.

The direction taken by the first four brigades to land necessarily tended to create a great gap between the Australian 1st Brigade and the New Zealanders. Early in the afternoon, however, the 4th Australian Brigade, under General Monash, pushed up to fill in this gap and succeeded in doing so after a fashion, but by no means completely. The one Indian mountain battery which had landed with the 2nd Brigade proved invaluable by the encouragement which its presence gave, and the troops gradually formed a more or less continuous line, except about the head of Monash Gully. But as the afternoon wore on the enemy kept coming on in ever-increasing numbers, and a good deal of loss was also suffered on the heights from converging shrapnel fire. The truth was that, although the heights immediately dominating Anzac Cove had been captured in the grey of the morning, there would seem to

[1] This is not shown on Map IV ; it was about half a mile north of the point.

have been more spontaneity and valour than of method in the early hours. The necessity which had arisen almost from the outset of pushing on troops in driblets as they reached the shore, the intricacy of the ground, the lack of training from which the troops suffered, and the very determined opposition offered by the enemy, all combined to create confusion and dissemination of units and rendered the duties of command on the part of superior officers extremely difficult. The front actually taken up was a fortuitous one. It was impossible to dig in rapidly on such ground. The process of replenishing ammunition was rendered especially arduous by the declivities up which it had to be carried. The confused character of the fighting furthermore greatly handicapped the naval gunners in respect to selecting targets when endeavouring to afford direct support to the infantry who were heavily engaged on the heights. It is not quite clear what positions exactly the five brigades that had disembarked were holding at nightfall, but these would seem to have followed roughly the lines shown on Map IV—but not extending so far south in the direction of Gaba Tepe and including the more or less detached No. 1 Post, spoken of above. The line would not seem to have run quite so far forward about Quinn's Post, Pope's Post, and Russel's Top, and there were gaps there and at other points. The front appears to have been especially thin along the section extending roughly between Courtney's Post and The Pimple, largely owing to the very severe attacks delivered by the enemy during the afternoon here—probably because this locality was the one most conveniently approached from the direction of Koja Dere and Maidos where the Turkish reserves had been assembled.

As darkness fell the situation was disquieting. General Birdwood, besides General Bridges and Godley, the commanders of the two divisions, had come ashore and they found much confusion prevailing on the beaches and between these and the straggling front. The Turks were most aggressive and were now in considerably superior force, as far as could be judged. Over 2000 wounded had to be attended to and got away from the shrapnel-swept beach. Ammunition was scarce and there was difficulty as to water. The question of evacuation was seriously discussed and Sir I. Hamilton appears to have been communicated with. But the Commander-in-Chief's instructions received during the night were un-

PLAN OF LANDING AT DAWN

compromising. The troops must hold on, although additional naval help would be provided early next morning.

Comments.—The landing of the Anzacs on the outer coast of the Gallipoli Peninsula on the 25th of April was a very memorable feat of arms, and one for which all the preliminaries had been admirably arranged by the Royal Navy. Its story suggests a number of interesting points for consideration, and as already observed this particular enterprise differed in its procedure very materially from the operations that were going on simultaneously at Helles. The experiences undergone by General Birdwood's force throw a valuable light upon one way of solving the problem presented by an obligation to effect a landing in force in defiance of the efforts of the enemy to repel it.

The question of landing at dawn.—Although the leading echelon of the attacking force did not reach the beach actually in the dark, the light was still bad at that critical moment. The armada of warships, transports, and small craft had, moreover, approached the appointed locality near the shore under cover of darkness. The consequence was that the leading troops enjoyed all the advantage of surprise, but that they arrived at the wrong place, thus illustrating at once the advantage and the disadvantage of undertaking an enterprise of this kind at dawn of day. Making the land at the wrong spot may, as it turned out, possibly have proved a blessing in disguise in this instance; but such a contretemps would in the majority of like cases produce inconvenient and possibly disastrous results. Owing to the great length of foreshore north of Gaba Tepe along which boats could be beached, there was ample justification for approaching in the dark—a justification that could not have been pleaded at Helles supposing that the landings had been attempted there before daylight. At Helles it was a case of striking certain short lengths of beach, separated from each other by stretches of coast-line where disembarkation, even on so calm a morning as that of the 25th of April turned out to be, would have been almost if not wholly impracticable.

That the leading echelon of the Australasian contingent did, as a matter of fact, have its task appreciably lightened by the hour selected for initiating operations, hardly admits of question; for although the 1500 men of the 3rd Brigade who formed the vanguard suffered some loss before disembarkation, and as they dashed out of the boats, on to the beach, the casualties in the ranks at this juncture were not really serious, and the troops had made good their landing and had scaled and secured the heights immediately dominating Anzac Cove before the enemy fully realised what was afoot. In the race between the two contending sides to achieve numerical superiority at the point where General Birdwood's army corps was making its descent upon the Gallipoli Peninsula, the attacking side got off with a flying start, thanks to the dim light. They in fact won the first trick in the game, as a consequence of the hour chosen.

Merits of landing at a topographically inconvenient spot.—Anzac Cove was very far from being an ideal place for a force of all arms to land at, which was undertaking the invasion of hostile territory. Had no hostile resistance been anticipated, nobody would have dreamt of pitching upon such a locality for the purpose. It was in a technical sense about the worst point to be found within three miles of Gaba Tepe. The rugged hill-sides encroached more closely upon the foreshore here than anywhere else, and they were, moreover, particularly steep and rugged. There is every reason to believe that the beach much nearer to the promontory, which the flotilla was supposed to be making for, was from the technical-topographical point of view incomparably more suitable as a landing-place than the spot where the Australian leading echelon found itself. But it is almost certain that if the armada had not unwittingly diverged to the north and if the disembarkation had been attempted at the appointed place, the losses suffered in gaining a footing would have been very heavy. It is not impossible indeed that the effort to land might have failed altogether. The point has already been raised when discussing certain of the landings near Helles, that where it is a question of getting ashore in defiance of expected opposition there is a good deal to be said for choosing a technically unattractive spot, simply because such a spot is not unlikely to be weakly defended and may even be wholly undefended. The great thing is to get ashore somehow.

Still, the fact remains that a locality like Anzac Cove makes a very bad starting-point for further operations. The cove came to be a base—and a most indifferent base—for an army of many thousand men during several months. There can be little doubt that, if a successful landing had been carried out at the spot intended by Sir I. Hamilton, the subsequent operations on the western shores of the Gallipoli Peninsula would have proved far easier to conduct than did the operations based on that slender fringe of beach south of Ari Burnu. The accident by which the invaders brought up at the wrong place may have been a blessing in disguise, but we cannot be sure of this.

The importance of making good as much ground as possible at once.—When undertaking a landing in face of opposition there is one fundamental principle to be observed. That is to frame plans with a view to getting a maximum number of troops ashore at the start in a minimum period of time. For you want to secure as extensive a bridgehead, so to speak, as is practicable before the enemy can mass forces to oppose you. Upon the possession of the bridgehead, and upon its extent, will largely depend the question whether the main body of the landing army and its artillery, and later the rest of its impedimenta, can be rapidly disembarked without their suffering damage while still on the water and while they are actually setting foot on shore. But, for the attacking side to fully act up to this principle, it is indispensable that the means exist for landing the vanguard and the leading echelons very quickly. Therefore, assuming that the troops exist and that the transports are available for conveying them to the coast where the landing is contemplated, it comes to be primarily a question of boats, and of the picket boats or other self-propelling craft required to tow the boats to shore.

Now the Australasians only had at their disposal sufficient boat accommodation to land 1500 men at a time. The rate of disembarkation was, it is true, accelerated by a liberal use of destroyers and of trawlers that were able to steam in close to the beach. Still, even allowing for this, it is obvious that if more boats had been available the operation could have been carried out more speedily than it was, always taking it for granted that there was sufficient length of beach to admit of additional tows approaching land without causing undue crowding. During the furious affrays that took place on the hill-sides and ridges and amongst the gullies and ravines after 7 a.m. on the 25th of April, victory or defeat almost hinged upon the result of the competition that took place between the contending sides as to which of the two would gather the quicker on the battlefield in strong force. The Turks were not prepared for a hostile landing at Anzac Cove, and at first could only rush reinforcements from positions to the south and the north where the possibility of attack had been foreseen. The numbers that could be drawn from these sources were not large, so additional troops were hurried across the peninsula from Maidos. All this took time, and, in the event, neither side seems to have had the advantage in respect to establishing a very decided superiority of force during the forenoon, although the defenders were perhaps always rather the stronger after about 8 a.m.

Even with the limited number of boats available, three infantry brigades were put on shore by noon, i.e. some 12,000 men were landed in under eight hours. Had double the number of boats been at the disposal of the troops, those three brigades would have been on land by 9 a.m. and they would have enjoyed a decided advantage in numbers over the enemy at that time; all five brigades would have been in battle-line by noon or one o'clock in the afternoon; a satisfactory line, instead of a haphazard one, would have been taken up; and it is reasonable to assume that the losses suffered by the attacking side would have been less severe than they were. Double the number of boats would in fact have ensured the triumph of the Australasians in the race for securing decisive superiority of force during the critical early hours on which so much depended. The question arises whether there would have been sufficient beach-space for so large a number of tows, and the subject of space taken up by the transports and larger craft also manifestly enters into this problem. But there was in reality plenty of room at Anzac Cove and on either side of that indentation in the coast. Indeed, given sufficient boats, there appears to have been sufficient frontage to land quite two brigades at a time, representing about 8000 men; they would have needed about 250 cutters, arranged in about 60 tows, and if we allow 50 yards between tows would have taken up roughly 3000 yards of beach; quite that length of foreshore was practicable for beaching boats about Anzac in a flat calm such as prevailed on the morning of the 25th of April.

No criticism of the arrangements is intended, in so far as the operation as planned is concerned. The Royal Navy had only a certain number of cutters and picket boats at their disposal, and this governed the dispositions as a whole. But if ever in the future a considerable force of troops formed from the British Empire is called upon to undertake a task analogous to that which General Birdwood's army corps was required to perform on the 25th of April—the task of landing in face of opposition on a shore where the topographical conditions admit of disembarking on a broad front and on a calm day—it is to be hoped that there will be a sufficiently large flotilla of boats at hand to permit of full advantage being taken of tactical and technical conditions which from their nature greatly benefit the attacking side.

The value of portable artillery on these occasions.—The inestimable service performed by the single Indian mountain battery, that was put ashore early and was promptly brought into action on the heights, deserves a word of notice. Portable guns are particularly useful when carrying out a landing because, the equipment being light, it can easily be handled in boats and can be rapidly disembarked from them, and because this form of artillery can traverse practically any ground that infantry are able to advance over. Two mountain batteries accompanied the infantry when the Italians landed at Benghazi in 1913. Anzac Cove, overhung by declivities rising abruptly from the foreshore, presented conditions where no other kind of artillery could have been brought into action within an hour or two of the leading troops reaching land. Published accounts of the day's fighting indicate that the arrival of these Indian mountain guns close to the firing line, at a moment when the leading Australian troops were hard put to it to hold their own, was of signal import. Their presence afforded invaluable moral support to the infantry, and it created a feeling of confidence in the ranks just at the very juncture when this was most needed.

Partially trained troops.—There is a point suggested by the events of the 25th of April at Anzac to which attention must be drawn. It is evident from the official despatch, as also from certain published narratives by Australians justly proud of Australian deeds on this great day, that the assailants suffered to some extent from a lack of cohesion and as a result of excessive individuality in the ranks. In many cases small, isolated parties pushed intrepidly on into this wilderness of hills and scrub, wholly unsupported and with fatal consequences to themselves. In the enthusiasm of victorious advance a portion of the infantry clearly got somewhat out of hand at the start, and this serves to illustrate a weakness that is inherent in raw troops—the expression is not used in an invidious sense, but in its true meaning of soldiery who are not broken to habits of instinctive military submission. It was not in the Gallipoli Peninsula alone that the contrast between fully trained and partially trained troops manifested itself in the field during the early months of the World War. Our "New Army" divisions, even when composed of the best material and after shaping extremely well before actually meeting the enemy, did not at the outset of their career in the war zones compare favourably with divisions of older standing. They fell short in respect to automatic interdependence between units and portions of units. Their officers and non-commissioned officers had not acquired confidence in themselves nor controlling influence over those under their authority. All ranks lacked experience, even though they knew their duties and could handle their arms. Only a very few weeks at the front were needed to transform them into absolutely the right stuff; but their start was not always wholly satisfactory.

At the date of the opening of the attack upon the Gallipoli Peninsula, hostilities had only been in progress for eight and a half months, and the contingents from the Antipodes which played so glorious a part in the Dardanelles campaign from the outset had only come into being within that period. One month of the time furthermore had been spent on board ship. They had hardly undergone more than four months of profitable training as fully equipped and efficiently organised troops when they were called upon to join in an exceptionally difficult and trying operation of war. That is not time enough; for it must be remembered that we are not here discussing a question of drafts about to be incorporated in regiments of long standing, but of entirely new units. The landing at Anzac would have offered a crucial test to the best of troops, and it is surely no indication of incapacity on the part of subordinate leaders nor of indiscipline amongst rank and file if, under such circumstances, the forces but recently raised in Australasia failed to combine with their valour and their grit and their enterprise that steadiness in advance which comes almost like second nature to the personnel of veteran battalions.

Conclusion.—This has been a long chapter, but for this its subject

A DAY WITHOUT PRECEDENT

is the best excuse. It deals with the most interesting and illuminating day's fighting that took place during the greatest of all wars. Up till the 25th of April, 1915, it had for years been purely a matter of conjecture as to what would happen were a resolute effort on an important scale to be made to effect a landing in face of opposition under the tactical conditions of to-day. There was no precedent to point to and no example to quote. The subject had been studied tentatively and as a matter of theory, and certain conclusions may have been arrived at, but few works treating of the art of war concerned themselves with the matter at all, and the problem involved had hardly received the consideration to which it was entitled either from the point of view of the attacking or of the defending side. Still, all soldiers who had devoted attention to the subject were in agreement on one point. They realised that an opposed landing represented one of the most hazardous and most difficult enterprises that a military force could be called on to undertake, and the events at Helles, and to a somewhat less extent at Anzac and at Kum Kale, proved that they had interpreted the prospective situation aright.

A criticism of the general plan that was adopted for securing a footing ashore on the confines of the Dardanelles will be reserved till the end of next chapter, wherein will be recorded and discussed the consolidation of Sir I. Hamilton's hold upon the fringes of the Gallipoli Peninsula. This chapter, for practical purposes, has been concerned only with the actual landings, and with suggestions as to certain tactical deductions that may be drawn from the events that took place. But one point should always be borne in mind when formulating theories as to the conduct of enterprises of this class, based upon the dramatic episodes of the 25th of April, 1915—the achievements of the assailants were in some cases so brilliant and so extraordinary on that occasion that the incidents of that day of conflict can hardly be accepted as necessarily establishing tactical principles, nor as giving a true picture of what a disembarkation in defiance of determined resistance is likely to involve in warfare of the future.

CHAPTER VI

THE CONSOLIDATION AT HELLES AND ANZAC

The situation at Helles on the morning of the 26th.—Determined fighting took place at several points along the scattered, partially consolidated, thinly held Helles front during the night of the 25th-26th, as has been recorded in the last chapter, fighting in which the Turks displayed marked enterprise and in which they gave evidence of considerable daring. Especially bitter were the affrays near Y Beach, as also along certain portions of the defensive sector that had been established between X and W Beaches. Sufficient troops had, however, already been got ashore to permit of a stalwart opposition being offered to the Ottoman offensive efforts, and the consequence was that the line which had been taken up by the late hours of the previous afternoon was held at practically all points in spite of the severe hostile pressure exercised against it. But the position of the Scottish Borderers and Marines on the bluffs above Y Beach was, as we have already seen, rendered virtually untenable during the night. Therefore the situation about Helles as it presented itself in the early morning hours of the 26th of April may be summed up as follows :—

It had been decided to withdraw from Y Beach and to transfer the troops landed there to X Beach. The disembarkation of personnel and stores at X and W Beaches had been proceeding all night, and the British force based on those two landing-places was occupying a position that coincided with high ground which stretched, parallel with the shore, from a little north of X Beach round to near the dismantled 9·2-inch battery that lay between Cape Helles and V Beach. This high ground constitutes the watershed of the basin draining into Morto Bay, a basin of which the rim is adjacent to the outer shore of the peninsula right round to the back of Sedd-el-Bahr village. Thus the topographical features are

ADVANCE FROM V BEACH

such that troops put on shore anywhere between X Beach and the Sedd-el-Bahr camber had only to push inland a very short distance to gain ground from which they overlooked the basin. But the companies that had managed to land on Beach V and that had suffered so terribly in the effort, had been unable to penetrate beyond the outermost fringe of the beach except close to the old castle ; there they had gained some little ground and they enjoyed a certain amount of cover. As for the detached force formed by the South Wales Borderers which was planted down near Beach S, this had dug itself in in a favourable position above the landing-place, and it could reckon upon holding on unless assailed by great numbers. A footing had in short been won at four points, viz. at Y Beach, at X and W Beaches, at V Beach, and at S Beach ; but of those four points Y Beach was about to be abandoned, and such grip as had been fixed upon V Beach remained in the highest degree precarious.

The advance from V Beach.—It was imperative that the somewhat critical situation at V Beach should be improved without delay. The general position of affairs demanded that the front which had already been made more or less good by the invading troops should be extended so as to include Sedd-el-Bahr and the high ground immediately above the village. The acquisition of additional landing accommodation had, moreover, become urgent, and it should be borne in mind that, but for its being particularly exposed to shell-fire from across the Straits, V Beach was about the best landing-place in the entire Helles area. The extrication of the detachments of the Dublins, Munsters, and Hampshires from the position where they found themselves, still at the water's edge after nearly twenty-four hours of combat, was a matter of immediate concern. So, realising all this, General Hunter Weston arranged with Admiral Wemyss that a strenuous bombardment should be directed upon the enemy's entrenchments about the beach by the warships as soon as there was sufficient light, and in pursuance of this compact *Albion* and other vessels poured a hurricane of projectiles from an early hour upon the village of Sedd-el-Bahr, upon the castle, and upon the Turkish entrenchments that furrowed the amphitheatre dominating the beach itself.

The naval gunners having done their work, the remnants of the three battalions, their spirit wholly unsubdued by what they had gone through, rushed the castle, and by 9 a.m. they were already beginning to force their way into the village. It was only by slow degrees, and after gaining the mastery in an infuriated house-to-house contest, that the assailants had by about noon succeeded in gaining possession of the place. The triumph had, moreover, been somewhat dearly purchased in respect to killed and wounded.

There followed a prolonged pause, which was seized upon by *Albion* for the delivery of a fierce cannonade, taking the redoubt of Kharab Kala for target. This work, which crowned the eminence behind the village and was held in strength by the enemy, now engaged the attention of the victorious troops. Spent as they were with fatigue but still undaunted, they emerged from the village as soon as the battleship had done her work and began pressing resolutely up the bullet-swept incline that led to the redoubt. Although greeted by a veritable tempest of musketry, nothing could stop this unconquerable band of Irish and English soldiers. The Turks offered a staunch resistance and they caused the assailants many casualties; but in spite of their fatalistic fortitude they were compelled to give ground, and the fortress was eventually carried by storm—a glorious feat of arms under the circumstances. In memory of the brave staff officer who had done much during the night to reorganise the weary troops cowering on V Beach, who had led them all the forenoon, and who fell at the last almost in the moment of victory, the redoubt was thenceforward known as Fort Doughty Wyllie.

Other parties of the force landed the previous day, which had been detached from the main body when in the village, had in the meantime worked their way off to the left, had ejected the enemy from the elaborate trench system which bore upon the landing-place, had occupied the ruined barracks overlooking the western end of the beach, and had joined hands with the extreme right of the troops that were based upon Beach W. For detachments from that side had at last succeeded in expelling the riflemen from the 9·2-inch battery whence they had given the Worcesters so much trouble on the previous afternoon. As a result of these combats the landing-place was definitely in the hands of the attacking side by about 3 p.m., and the little body of infantry which had accomplished such great things was at last able to take rest for a while.

Reinforcements landed at V Beach.—No sooner had the enemy been turned out of his trenches that overlooked Beach V than additional troops were pushed ashore in hot haste. French infantry, to the amount of four battalions (other than the troops which had landed at Kum Kale), was got ashore rapidly and proceeded along the coast towards Morto Bay. The Turks had shown remarkable grit and valour on the 25th, and again during the contest for Sedd-el-Bahr village and for the Kharab Kala redoubt; but the loss of this latter very important tactical point would seem to have caused a profound discouragement in the enemy's ranks in this part of the battlefield. For it was found possible to work right round Morto Bay by the evening and to gain contact with the South Wales Borderers at De Tott's battery beyond S Beach—an important acquisition of ground and gained quite easily. In the meantime, guns and stores were being landed freely at W and V Beaches, both being immune from direct rifle fire owing to the lie of the country now that the Allies held all the high ground which has been described above as the rim of the basin draining into Morto Bay.

Turkish dispositions with respect to Helles.—According to German accounts, Marshal Liman von Sanders, ensconced on Ghazi Tepe at the Bulair end of the peninsula, was not made fully aware of the condition of things at Helles until 9.30 p.m. on the 25th. He then received a message running as follows :—

"The enemy has occupied the coast just east of Sedd-el-Bahr. The landings at the Zighin Dere and by Cape Helles are proceeding afresh. An enemy battalion has dug itself in above Eski-Hissarlik. The division[1] is going to attack in full force after night has set in."

This information was by no means correct in respect to detail, but it intimated to the chief of the defending side that his opponent had made good a footing at the extremity of the peninsula. The marshal promptly ordered both the 5th and 7th Divisions to proceed by ship to Maidos—there were craft assembled for the purpose should such a move become necessary—and to march thence towards Helles. The leading battalion of the 7th Division is reported to have reached the heights above Eski-Hissarlik on the morning of the 26th, and a second to have appeared near Helles shortly after-

[1] Evidently the 9th Division.

wards; but these units cannot still have been at Gallipoli at 9.30 p.m. the previous night, taking into consideration the time required to embark them, to move them to Maidos, to disembark them there, and then to march them in the dark a distance of from ten to a dozen miles. They were probably somewhere near Maidos on the 25th and marched straight from there. On the other hand, we may assume that the infantry of the 7th Division was arriving on the Helles battlefield during the latter part of the day on the 26th, and should all have got to its destination by morning on the 27th. Unless the Turks were very well off for shipping of a suitable kind it would hardly seem likely that the whole of the 5th Division can have reached the Helles area till late on the 27th.

The withdrawal from Kum Kale.—During the night of the 25th–26th the Turks made resolute efforts to recover Kum Kale village, and they delivered their onsets in such strong force that, after desperate hand-to-hand fighting amongst the alleys and houses, large part of the place passed back into their hands. About dawn, however, the French succeeded in regaining the upper hand. They not only expelled the enemy from the village, but they also stormed the cemetery, which the Osmanlis had stuck to stubbornly on the previous day, after it had been effectively bombarded by *Latour Tréville*, which had only arrived on the previous evening. As the morning drew on it, however, became apparent that the enemy was in strong force to the south—the entire 3rd Turkish Division appears to have been on the ground—and it was realised that to advance towards Yeni Shehr with a body of troops only 3000 strong was under the circumstances out of the question. General D'Amade, who had landed, moreover received instructions from Sir I. Hamilton that the French force now at Kum Kale was to be transferred to Helles. The French warships continued to bombard Yeni Shehr and the positions held by the Turks nearer to Kum Kale all day, and it was made possible by this means for the troops, who had been very highly tried during the night, to keep the enemy busy without their delivering an actual attack. As the gun-fire from the vessels took the Turks in enfilade considerable losses were inflicted upon them, and they manifested a marked readiness to surrender—more than their comrades evinced either at Helles or at Anzac.

General D'Amade decided to defer the retirement until dark,

and it was then effected successfully in spite of the hostile efforts at interference. 400 prisoners were carried off, and more had been taken and could have been removed had there been the requisite boat accommodation available. The French losses in the two days' fighting had amounted to 788 killed, wounded, and missing, or just about a quarter of the force. That the grip fixed upon the nearest point on the Asiatic shore to Helles and maintained upon it for the two critical days, the 25th and 26th, proved of value to the British troops in their contests for the possession of Sedd-el-Bahr, and also to the French when after landing on V Beach on the 26th they pushed round the edge of Morto Bay to gain touch with the British battalion at De Tott's, there can be no question. For there was in reality little interference by artillery fire from across the Straits during the Helles operations, compared to what might have been expected had this diversion at Kum Kale not taken place. But it does not necessarily follow on that account that the troops which were landed on the Asiatic shore on the 25th, together with the boat accommodation which they absorbed, would not have been more profitably employed in the Gallipoli Peninsula instead.

The operations at Helles on the 27th.—The Allies could fairly claim that the position of the landing army in the Helles area was decidedly more satisfactory on the night of the 26th–27th than it had been the previous night. The Allies now held all the ground near the coast from about X Beach right round to De Tott's Battery, the whole of the infantry of the 29th Division and several French battalions were already ashore, some guns had been landed, and considerable accumulations of stores were already collecting on the principal beaches, W and V. But there was urgent need of securing more elbow-room, quite apart from the question of giving the enemy battle. It was also most desirable to gain possession of additional wells. Sir I. Hamilton in consequence felt himself obliged on the 27th to call upon his troops for a fresh effort. The object was partly to push the fighting units further forward from the immediate vicinity of the landing-places where it had become imperative to start establishing regular store depots, partly to occupy the lower portions of the basin near Morto Bay so as to acquire possession of additional watering places, and partly to take up a better tactical line from which to launch fresh offensive operations. The Allies on the morning of the 27th were drawn up, as against the enemy, on a concave arc of a circle; the Commander-in-Chief wished the troops to make their front the chord of that arc.

A general advance accordingly took place, except on the extreme right, and the objective was gained with comparative ease. The Turks, although the 7th as well as the 9th Division must have been present with possibly some units of the 5th Division, only offered a very half-hearted opposition. The 29th Division pressed forward on the left and in the centre, while on the right four French battalions, pivoting on the South Wales Borderers, swung their left forward and so completed the new line. By the evening a satisfactory front had been secured that extended from near De Tott's Battery across to the mouth of the Zighin Dere about two miles north of Cape Tekke. The consolidation of the landing at Helles could thus be regarded as accomplished.

The situation at Helles on the night of the 27th.—The Allies now occupied the toe of the Gallipoli Peninsula for a depth of about two miles, and the two main landing-places, W Beach and V Beach, were at least safe from musketry and machine-gun fire. Additional French troops had landed, some more guns had been got ashore, much useful work had been performed in improving the landing-places, and the Turks had had to acknowledge defeat at all points except at Y Beach. But the 29th Division had suffered very heavily during the severe fighting which it had undergone, the losses being by no means confined to those battalions which had been hit especially hard in the actual landings; about a third of the infantry of the division was indeed already *hors de combat*, and there were no reserves at hand to fill up the yawning gaps in the ranks. The French had up to the present fared better in this respect; but the absence of any machinery for making good wastage amongst the troops on shore and amongst those shortly expected was already casting a shadow over the undertaking. Moreover, sufficient ground had not been gained at the end of three days' fighting to protect the landing-places, upon which the force depended for its existence, against fire from the feeblest of guns that the Turks might be able to bring into action, while the enemy had apparently assembled at least three divisions on the spot and probably enjoyed the advantage in respect to numbers.

The position at Anzac on the morning of the 26th.—It is now necessary to turn to the efforts of the Australasian force to con-

SITUATION AT ANZAC

solidate its hold upon the very inconvenient landing-place, and upon the position covering this, which General Birdwood's army corps had occupied more or less by accident on the previous day. The situation at Anzac on the morning of the 26th was by no means wholly reassuring. The enemy was manifestly in formidable strength. It may, indeed, be observed here that the Turks and their German advisers had from the outset realised the vital importance to them of the extensive beaches that stretched north of Gaba Tepe, in view of the propinquity of these to Maidos and to the Narrows of the Dardanelles, and that they had assembled substantial reserves in the vicinity in anticipation of a landing. The Australasians had found little leisure for improving their hastily constructed defences during the night, owing to the persistent hostile attacks. Some field guns had, however, been landed and had been hauled up on to the high ground by dint of great exertions. A beginning had been made with the disembarkation of stores, and a certain amount of order had been established on the congested beach. But companies, battalions, and even brigades, had become intermingled to some extent on the previous day, as was almost bound to happen with newly organised, partially trained troops when flung into battle under particularly trying conditions ; and the situation ever since had been too anxious and critical to admit of their being re-sorted.

Although it protected the landing-place against frontal fire or direct counter-attack, the position which had been taken up on the high ground, to some extent at random, remained very far from being an ideal one. It suffered from the grave drawback of forming a sharp salient, and it therefore almost invited enfilade, and even reverse, fire from such enemy's artillery as might be brought into action on the flanks. Any effort to extend and improve the line carried with it the obligation of expelling hostile detachments from a rugged, tangled, scrub-clad terrain, which offered these rare opportunities for putting up an obstinate defence. The fighting front could only be gained from the beach by an arduous climb up steep declivities, and the problem of conveying food and ammunition to the firing line was a particularly awkward one. The situation in respect to water also gave grounds for much solicitude, for there was very little of it to be found within the occupied area. The beach, again, was so lacking in depth that its unsuitability for constituting the base of a force of all arms was obvious; moreover, in addition to its inconvenience it was exposed to shell fire, alike from the side of Gaba Tepe to the south and from the hilly ground jutting westwards towards Suvla Bay to the north. Nevertheless, there were features in the position of affairs that were not without encouragement. Such as it was, the footing that had been gained almost at the first rush on the previous morning had developed into a grip, and, if the Turks were fighting stubbornly, the invaders from the Antipodes had already proved themselves masters of the Osmanlis, man for man. *Queen Elizabeth* had, morever, steamed round from Helles and opened fire with her huge shrapnel shell upon the Turkish positions soon after daylight on the 26th.

The 26th and 27th at Anzac.—Scarcely had day broken when the Turks were descried gathering in force and evidently contemplating attack. Fresh units were seen to be joining up from various points, and as far as could be judged the enemy was in greater strength than on the previous day. It is not easy to arrive at a clear idea either as to the sequence of events or as to the tactical aspects of the fighting in the case of the many encounters that took place around the Anzac position during the opening days of the land campaign. Vivid descriptions have appeared from the pen of participators in those grim combats amid the wilderness of ridges and gullies and spurs which constituted the battle area; but they deal with the subject piecemeal, and it is difficult to knit them into a well-balanced record. It would seem, however, that the struggle of the 26th began in earnest about 9 a.m. when, after a heavy preliminary bombardment of shrapnel, a most determined onset was launched by the enemy, the shock being especially violent along the front that had been taken up beyond Shrapnel Gully, facing south-eastwards. Severe fighting lasted for some time, without the assailants gaining any appreciable advantage. The warships joined in the fray and gave the defenders no little encouragement. Towards noon, however, there came a pause; but soon afterwards the Turks delivered a fresh assault, which was beaten off decisively. Thereupon the Anzacs rushed out from their flimsy breastworks, thrust the enemy back in dire confusion, and by this well-timed and vigorous counter-stroke eased the situation for the rest of the day. The entrenchments were improved and consolidated during the afternoon and during the following night, and the line was

SITUATION AT ANZAC

somewhat pushed forward at a number of points, for the struggles that had taken place had indicated the spots that stood in need of special care. The 1st Division had suffered the most heavily in the furious encounters, the losses during the 25th and 26th mounting up in the 3rd Brigade to 1900, in the 2nd Brigade to 1700, and in the 1st Brigade to 900—a total of 4500, or about two-fifths of the infantry of the division.

More guns were brought into action by the Turks on the 27th, and they rained shrapnel upon the position, causing many casualties ; they also bombarded the beach and even fired on the warships. No serious infantry attacks were, however, attempted, so that the Anzacs were enabled to yet further strengthen their works. By the evening the trenches and breastworks were indeed so solidly constructed and so skilfully arranged and designed that they might almost be considered capable of defying any infantry attack that had not been preceded by a destructive bombardment with heavy shell. Much work had also already been done in respect to improving communications. The steepness of the slopes towards the sea, even if they had the disadvantage of making connection between the beach and the greater part of the front most cumbersome, had on the other hand the merit of providing many welcome patches of dead ground that were immune from the enemy's projectiles. Masses of stores were already accumulating about the landing-place, and subsidiary depots were being organised in convenient, sheltered localities, higher up. General Birdwood's corps had in fact consolidated its hold on a morsel of the peninsula, and it could confidently reckon upon retaining the ground that it had seized against almost any attack that the Turks might be expected to deliver on it.

The situation at Anzac on the night of the 26th as compared with that at Helles.—It is interesting to note what a marked difference existed between the positions that the Allies had secured and consolidated respectively at Helles and at Anzac on the night of the 26th. At Helles the invading army held the whole of the extremity of the Gallipoli Peninsula, having as it were bitten off its end ; at Anzac the Australian troops had on the contrary merely bitten slightly into its flank. At Helles, the left flank abutting on the sea was safe, and the right flank abutting on the Straits was secure except against shell fire from across the water ;

at Anzac, on the contrary, neither flank was completely sheltered by the coast-line, although the left flank was somewhat assisted by the indentation in the shore north of Ari Burnu. At Helles the front was already fully two miles in advance of the two main landing-places, the Beaches W and V; at Anzac the outermost point of the line of defence was not 1000 yards as the crow flies from the one landing-place. At Helles the Allies had two satisfactory beaches at their disposal, both furnished with fairly good avenues leading inland; at Anzac the only avenues leading inland from the narrow, cramped beach climbed up steep inclines and only offered particularly inconvenient means of communication. In so far as the question of the landing-places being under shell-fire was concerned, there was not much to choose between the two positions; but, taking all the various considerations together, there can be no question that the position of affairs at Helles was for the moment decidedly the less unpromising of the two.

The ground wrested from the Turks at Anzac has already been described as constituting a haphazard position as regards the actual defensive line taken up. But it was also an eminently haphazard one as regards its fitness to serve as a starting-point for further offensive operations. As will be seen from Map V on p. 168, the ridges and bluffs which formed such conspicuous features within the area that the Australasian forces had appropriated, merely represent outlying lower spurs of a rugged mountain mass called Sari Bair, which culminates in a hill-top known as Koja Chemen Tepe, 1000 feet above sea-level and situated about three miles to the north-east of the landing-place. It will be convenient to defer a more detailed description of the peculiar topographical features around Anzac, until an outline of the operations in this theatre of war during the next three months comes to be given in Chapter IX; suffice it to say here, that, although General Birdwood was firmly established on the outer coast-line of the Gallipoli Peninsula, he was planted down at a locality from which it was particularly difficult to advance, and where the maintenance of a steady flow of supplies to his troops in front line, a few hundreds of yards from their base, presented a most awkward problem. The failure of the flotilla, as it had groped its way forward in the grey of the morning on the 25th, to hit off the point that it was aiming for, may peradventure have saved the Australasian corps

THE TURKS 117

from a sanguinary repulse at Gaba Tepe. But it had led to the troops from the Antipodes being put ashore at a spot on the coast that was singularly unpromising for an advance on the Narrows.

The fighting qualities of the Turks.—Critical discussion of the general plan for effecting landings on the Gallipoli Peninsula has been deferred till this chapter; Chapter V only touched upon the tactical aspects of the actual disembarkations. But, before examining further into this subject, it may not be out of place to refer to a factor which exerted no small influence over this campaign from start to finish, and to which the stirring experiences of the first three days of land operations had already drawn attention.

The military forces of the Ottoman Empire had by no means covered themselves with glory in their bout of 1912 with the legions of the Balkan kingdoms. The story of that contest had been little better than a tale of successive discomfitures encountered by the Turks at the hands of enemies whom they had affected to despise. Their organisation had proved to be lamentably defective, their armies had been outmanœuvred and outfought in almost every engagement, and their troops had given little evidence of retaining those martial virtues for which the campaigners of the Caliph in times past had been justly renowned. Even when defending prepared positions—a form of combat for which the Osmanli had manifested an exceptional bent during his many struggles with the Russian in the past—the Sultan's infantry had shown themselves incapable of repelling the onsets of Bulgarian, of Serb and of Greek foot-soldiers. So it came about that when the Allies embarked upon the Dardanelles venture they reckoned to some extent upon the enemy offering but a feeble resistance. The first few hours of struggle at Helles and at Anzac, however, made it plain that there was plenty of fight still left in the defenders of the Ottoman Empire when this came to be threatened at its heart.

For, not only did the Turks offer an obstinate resistance to the landings, and not only had they made admirable arrangements (at least at Helles) for bringing the efforts of their antagonists to naught; they had also delivered counter-attacks with a verve and with a resolution that was eminently worthy of a warrior race of renown dating back to the days of Soliman the Magnificent. Even troops so seasoned as, and fortified with an *esprit de corps* so bracing as that which bestirred, the 29th Division, found the guardians of the Dardanelles to be foemen by no means unworthy of their steel. There had been an untoward miscalculation. The idea which had been cherished in influential quarters that Ottoman resistance would crumble up, so long as the Allies displayed sufficient vigour and resolution, had within a few hours of the first British soldier setting foot on Turkish soil proved to be a delusion and a snare. Those signal episodes of war, the historic landings of the 25th of April, had already proved beyond the possibility of a doubt that, in deciding to undertake the conquest of the Hellespont, the Western Governments had committed themselves to an eminently precarious adventure, that—if the expression be admissible—those executive bodies had bitten off at least as much as they could comfortably chew.

Sir I. Hamilton's division of his forces.—Separation of forces is always to be deprecated on the part of the side possessing the initiative in time of war, supposing that the enemy is thereby placed in a position to act on interior lines. You may hold the strings; but if you get your people all over the place the enemy may catch some of them and give them a dressing down. Sir I. Hamilton did disseminate his troops. Was he right?

The Commander-in-Chief separated the divisions that he had at his disposal for gaining a footing on, and conquering, the Gallipoli Peninsula into two roughly equal groups, and he launched those two groups against two objectives separated many miles from each other. In doing so he in reality gave his adversaries no opening for acting on interior lines during those very critical hours when the 29th Division at Helles and the Australasian divisions at Anzac were forcing their way ashore, and were consolidating their hardly won positions after they had got ashore. The Turks were not so disposed on the 25th of April as to be able to turn the principle of interior lines to account. They could not have transferred troops from north of Gaba Tepe to the extremity of the peninsula, or vice versa, and have brought such troops into action on the new ground, between sunrise and sundown on that day. The distance was too great. Allowing for inevitable delays in issuing orders and in extricating the units to be transferred from one point to the other during the course of actual fighting, there was not time enough. As a matter of fact, the Commander-in-Chief carried separation of force still further, seeing that he detailed a French contingent and the available French shipping and boats for Kum Kale, but that additional dissemination likewise afforded the Turks no opportunity to act on interior lines. For the Ottoman troops to have moved from the vicinity of Kum Kale to Anzac would have taken quite two days. For them to have moved from Kum Kale to Helles via Chanak could hardly have taken them less than three. Sir Ian's deliberate splitting up of his forces did not in fact furnish the Turks with an opportunity of acting effectively against him on the most precarious day of the campaign—that of the first landing.

But this question has also to be looked at from the other point of view. The Allies possessed the initiative and, thanks to command of the sea and to their power—speaking in general terms—of starting an attack at any point where there happened to be a favourable beach, they enjoyed uncommon liberty of action. Although the disposition of the enemy forces was not well known, it could safely be conjectured that these would be distributed, some at Helles, some about Gaba Tepe, some at Bulair, and some at Kum Kale and on the coast to the south, with main reserves at Maidos and Chanak. Without going into questions of detail for the moment, it may be asked whether it would not have been in accordance with principles of sound strategy to strike with all available forces at one point.

Certainly it would if practicable; and that point ought to have been either Helles or Anzac, for Kum Kale and Bulair need hardly be seriously considered here. Supposing it to have been feasible to throw ashore the whole of the troops available on the 25th at one place or the other, the enemy could not have concentrated his entire strength to meet the attack on a single day, and the balance of advantage in respect to numbers would therefore clearly have rested with the Allies. Thus the question arises :—

Would it have been feasible to land the whole of the available troops on the 25th either at Helles or at Anzac ?

And the answer to this question obviously hinges upon the amount of boat accommodation upon which the troops could reckon, and upon the extent of beach in the two rival areas where landing was practicable. It will therefore be necessary in the first place to examine into these aspects of the question.

Boat accommodation and beach space available.—The Allies would seem to have had sufficient cutters and other boats at their command on the 25th of April to land quite 5500 infantrymen in one single trip. They could, moreover, utilise the *River Clyde* once. They were thus in a position to disembark 7500 men as a first effort, and could follow this up with successive contingents of 5500 each, always provided that boats did not come to grief during the landing process. Now, given ample beach space, the number of men who can be put on shore within any given times does not depend only upon the number of boats that are being used. It depends also upon the distance that the tows have to travel each time, or, in other words, upon the distance at which the larger vessels in which the troops will have been conveyed to the vicinity of the landing-place are obliged to lie out from the shore. It is a point worth noting in this connection that at Kum Kale, where the troops laboured under the disadvantages of relying on old-fashioned picket boats for towing purposes, and of being seriously inconvenienced by the contrary current when the tows were proceeding inshore, loaded, 3000 men and four field guns reached land within six hours. Even in spite of the difficulties of transportation and navigation involved, quite 6000 men could therefore have landed at this spot between daybreak and sundown on an April day. At Anzac, again, with apparently only sufficient boat accommodation for 1500 men available at a time, five infantry brigades, and some guns—say 16,000 men—were got ashore on the one day.

At Helles, on the other hand, with the necessary means of conveying at least 2500 men to land in one trip without counting the *River Clyde*, it was not until after eight o'clock in the evening that all twelve battalions of the 29th Division were on shore ; and this in spite of the fact that the disembarkation had begun soon after dawn. As a question of statistics, the results achieved at Helles were disappointing when compared with what was effected at Kum Kale and at Anzac, and, seeing the devoted exertions of all concerned and the admirable nature of the naval arrangements, this can only be accounted for by the lack of beach space at the toe of the peninsula, and by the stubborn resistance that was encountered in this sector. All the available beach space was turned to account except at one point, the mouth of the stream flowing down the Zighin Dere, mentioned on page 64 as having later gone by the name of Gully Beach. As a matter of fact, this Gully

Beach was, next to W and V Beaches, the best landing-place in the Helles area; but previous reconnaissances had established that the locality was elaborately prepared for defence, and any attempt to gain a footing there would almost certainly have met with stern resistance. Indeed, it was largely due to the action of the Turkish forces which had been told off to defend Gully Beach that the K.O.S.B.'s and the Marines were unable after disembarking at Y Beach to make their way along the coast to X Beach according to programme.

Assuming, however, that this additional landing-place had been made use of on the 25th, and that troops such as had been told off to deliver the attack there had managed to fight their way ashore, it is reasonable to suppose that two or three battalions, in addition to those of the 29th Division, could have been disembarked in the Helles area on that day. But a total of about sixteen battalions would seem to have been almost the limit of what could have been got on shore at the extremity of the peninsula at the first start. In other words, not half of the infantry force that was on the water on the night of the 24th–25th could during the all-important opening day of the land campaign have been landed in this area. And this circumstance was not due to lack of boats, but to the absence of extensive beaches and to the sturdy opposition offered by an enemy who was well prepared for what was coming.

When, on the other hand, we turn to the rival scene of operations, to the coast-line stretching away to the north of the Gaba Tepe promontory, we find totally different conditions. There, beach accommodation was, comparatively speaking, plentiful. First of all there was the stretch near the promontory that had been selected for the landing of General Birdwood's force, but which the flotilla missed; further north there was an extensive beach south of Anzac Cove afterwards known as Brighton Beach; then there was Anzac Cove itself; beyond that again the foreshore was practicable for a long way. The only really satisfactory spot may have been the one chosen in advance; but infantry could have been put on shore on that still April morning at almost any point between Gaba Tepe and Suvla Bay. Bearing in mind that in actual practice nearly 16,000 Australasian infantrymen were disembarked at Anzac Cove by the afternoon of the 25th, it is difficult to avoid the conclusion that the entire infantry force that was immediately at the disposal of Sir I. Hamilton, viz. the 29th Division, some battalions of the Naval Division, the Anzacs, and the 1st French Division, could have been planted down on the western coast of the Gallipoli Peninsula within a very few hours by making use of all the boat accommodation that he had at disposal, reinforced by the *River Clyde*. To the question whether it would have been feasible to land the whole of the available troops on the 25th either at Helles or at Anzac, the answer in fact is that it would not have been feasible at Helles, but that it would have been feasible at Anzac.

Possibilities at Helles.—Sir I. Hamilton's plan of utilising five distinct beaches for landing at in the Helles sector has been criticised in some quarters on the grounds that it necessarily led to tactical dispersion of force. But, so far from this multiplication of landing-places being contrary to sound principles of conducting war under the conditions that existed, it would almost seem to be a matter of consideration whether the Commander-in-Chief would not have been well advised to have taken advantage of a sixth beach, viz. Gully Beach, even admitting that troops directed to that point would almost certainly have had to fight hard to gain a footing. It has, however, to be remembered that it was only proposed to land the infantry of the 29th Division at Helles on the 25th. Supposing that the French force, which made its way ashore at Kum Kale, had been directed on the Helles sector instead, there certainly would have been good reason for turning Gully Beach to account; for it was manifestly of vital importance to disembark as large a force as was practicable in a minimum of time.

In debating these matters it must never be forgotten that we know much now that the Commander-in-Chief and his staff did not know when they were framing the plan and issuing orders for its execution. We know now that V Beach was so effectively defended that, to all intents and purposes, landing there on the 25th only became practicable after dark, and that no real footing was made good till the following morning. We know now that a single battalion met with no serious difficulty in fixing its grip upon Turkish soil near S Beach, in spite of the isolation of that point. We know now that the disembarkation of troops at Y Beach and at X Beach proved quite a simple operation, and that dangers

POSSIBILITIES AT HELLES

only thickened in these quarters after the detachments were safely on shore. We know now that the Turks were in strong force at Krithia, and we are entitled to assume that reinforcements kept reaching the enemy by the road through that village during the afternoon of the 25th and during the night of the 25th–26th. We are in a totally different position from that occupied by the headquarters of the Expeditionary Force on the 24th of April, 1915, and the following observations are not therefore intended as criticisms of the plan of operations.

It will be convenient first to consider the situation on the extreme left of the British attacks. Now, the two battalions which disembarked at Y Beach, but which had perforce to be withdrawn on the following morning, might have been of great assistance to a force landing at Gully Beach. Their failure to get far when they moved south along the coast was largely due to the presence of the Turkish detachments guarding Gully Beach, where no attack was actually delivered. If troops had landed, or even tried to land, at that point, the situation would obviously have been considerably modified. The attacking side would have been so much stronger on this left flank that it might have held its ground against any attacks that the enemy could make upon it on the 25th and during the following night. A force securely planted down at Gully Beach would, moreover, have constituted a serious threat to the communications of the defenders fighting in the vicinity of X and W Beaches. Still, even with the aid of a friendly force approaching from the side of Y Beach, troops landing at Gully Beach might have been beaten off, or they might have fared no better than the Dublins, Munsters, and Hampshires did at V Beach.

Supposing that the general plan had been for the whole of the available force to disembark in the Helles sector, Gully Beach would no doubt have been made use of. But as it was, troops to land there must have been obtained at the expense of some other point. The defences there do not seem to have been so elaborate as were those which proved too formidable for the three battalions told off to V Beach. Knowing what we know now, it is interesting to speculate what the result might have been if those three battalions and the *River Clyde* had been allocated to Gully Beach instead of to the landing-place where they suffered so terribly. Given the Dublins, the Munsters, the Hampshires, the K.O.S.B.'s, and the

Marine battalion firmly established about Gully Beach, with another force ashore based on X and W Beaches, and with the South Wales Borderers at De Tott's, it is likely enough that the enemy would have withdrawn on the night of the 25th–26th to the line which the Turks did not actually take up till the 27th. The French could in that case have begun landing unopposed at V Beach on the morning of the 26th, instead of the afternoon.

Turning now to the other flank, to the vicinity of S Beach and De Tott's Battery, the fact that the South Wales Borderers, retarded as their disembarkation was by the current, got ashore at this landing-place and held on where they were with no great difficulty till supported by the French on the afternoon of the 26th, is one of the most singular incidents in the fight for a footing at Helles. Had more infantry and more boats been available on the 25th, and had some of them been detailed to reinforce the one battalion that had established itself at this point, the result would have been to assemble a somewhat formidable body of troops on the extreme left flank of the Turks, and this must have caused the Ottoman staff anxiety. It would have made the position of the defenders of V Beach a very uncomfortable one. Nor is there any reason to suppose that reinforcements would have found much difficulty in disembarking on S Beach, apart from navigation troubles. With the knowledge that we now possess, it does seem a pity that more advantage was not taken of the somewhat unexpected facility with which the enterprise entrusted to the South Wales Borderers achieved its object. Still, troops could only have been obtained on the 25th for this objective at the expense of some other point. Moreover, supposing that some spare battalions had been available, these might well have been employed to still greater advantage on the other flank—at Gully Beach, say, as suggested in the previous paragraph.

Had the untoward outcome of the effort to land upon V Beach on the 25th been anticipated, Sir I. Hamilton would naturally have refrained from directing troops thither, except possibly as a feint, and would have used the three battalions that actually operated against it in some other manner. All three could no doubt have been landed at X Beach before noon; or they could have proceeded to Gully Beach; or they might have been employed wholly or in part at S Beach, although owing to the shallows the conditions there would not seem to have suited the *River Clyde*. The results, had any one of these alternatives been adopted, would probably have been more satisfactory than those actually accomplished by the very gallant assault upon V Beach. The three battalions might even have disembarked at Y Beach ; but that was so bad a landing-place in the technical sense that to have piled up five battalions there would have practically meant gambling on the chance of the Turks withdrawing from the extreme end of the peninsula under threat of this force planted down on their right flank. It may be remarked here that the venture at Y Beach, although it turned out to be a mistake, did undoubtedly have the effect of occupying the attention of considerable bodies of Turkish troops which otherwise would have been available for confronting the forces landed at other points.

Knowing what we do now, it almost looks as if the best disposition of the 29th Division for the great landing would have been a main operation directed upon X Beach, using the *River Clyde* and six or seven battalions, coupled with the disembarkation of three battalions, instead of one, at S Beach. Some of the troops put ashore at X Beach could have taken W Beach in rear before any attempt to land at that point was launched, which should have made this latter operation a comparatively speaking easy one for the two or three remaining units. Even now, when we have cognisance of the conditions that obtained, the problem of what could be done and of what ought to have been done admits of wide diversity of opinion. In the conditions of uncertainty that prevailed before the event the problem was one of singular complexity.

The question of Kum Kale.—Exception has been taken by some critics to the diversion of the three thousand French troops to Kum Kale. The purpose of this departure from the rule that in war effort should be concentrated, was to relieve the troops that were to land at Helles from some of the artillery fire from across the Straits that they were otherwise likely to experience. It is not clearly established that the capture of Kum Kale in reality made very much difference in this respect. Although the promontory at the mouth of the Hellespont on the Asiatic side represents the nearest point to the Helles area, that tongue of land squeezed between the Mendere flats and the Ægean did not provide the Turks with gun positions that the warships of the Allies could not effectively deal with. It was rather from the undulations about In Tepe than from Kum Kale that the extremity of the Gallipoli Peninsula was exposed to artillery annoyance. Moreover, even supposing that the deflection of an important fraction of the available force to the far side of the Dardanelles did serve to check Turkish gun-fire across the Straits, it remains a matter of opinion whether the three French battalions would not have been more advantageously employed in the Helles area on the 25th.

The paramount object to work for on that day in this theatre of attack was to get as large a force as possible ashore at the extremity of the peninsula, and with that force to wrest as much ground as possible from the Turks before nightfall. The French regiment put ashore at Kum Kale, provided as it was with boat accommodation for landing purposes, would have been invaluable as a reinforcement to the 29th Division on that strenuous day. Various possibilities of allotment of the division have been discussed. But however its battalions were told off it is manifest that an addition to their number of 25 per cent must have proved of great advantage. The French might for instance have been allocated to S Beach, allowing the South Wales Borderers to take their place at some other point. In so far as the question of keeping down Turkish artillery fire across the channel is concerned, it may be observed that the three French battleships and *Askold* were mainly engaged on the 25th in shelling the vicinity of Kum Kale and afterwards that of Yeni Shehr; had there been no landing on the Asiatic side their guns would have been available for dealing with enemy artillery that was directing its fire on the Helles area.

While on the subject of artillery bombardment from across the Straits, it should be pointed out that, while such fire did constitute an unpleasant threat to S Beach and V Beach and to a less extent to W Beach, the three landing-places on the outer coast of the peninsula—X Beach, Gully Beach, and Y Beach—were much less menaced. Even transports and warships lying off those outer beaches were practically invisible from the Asiatic shore owing to the intervening high ground, while the beaches themselves were wholly concealed. During the months that followed, W and V Beaches were constantly scenes of bustle and activity, and the Turkish long-range gun-fire was a great nuisance. Still, those later experiences hardly suggest that the landings even at S Beach and V Beach would have been very seriously interfered with had no attack been made simultaneously upon Kum Kale.

Possibilities north of Gaba Tepe.—What might have been accomplished in the other arena, the littoral north of Gaba Tepe, is unfortunately a matter of conjecture depending on very indeterminate premises. The possibility of achieving a substantial success in this quarter and one leading to far-reaching results, hinged on a factor full of uncertainty. For the truth is that we cannot possibly tell now whether a landing on that beach just north of the promontory, which was the real goal of the Australasian corps on the morning of the 25th of April, would have succeeded or not. We do know that the enemy was well prepared to meet attack in this locality, that elaborate devices for beating off any attempt from the sea were in existence, and that considerable reserves of Turkish troops were within hail. We are entitled to assume, therefore, that a disembarkation would only have been effected at the cost of heavy casualties, if it proved feasible at all.

The environs of this particular stretch of foreshore were obviously such as to aid defending troops in protecting it against attack. The headland of Gaba Tepe, seventy-five feet above sea-level, dominated it in flank. A low spur of the Sari Bair mountain fronted it at less than a mile distance. It was overlooked from the north by other, higher spurs of this mountain rising from the position which the Australasians secured on the 25th. There appear to have been wire entanglements as at W and V Beaches, and Gaba Tepe was a mass of trenches. It is difficult to believe that if the first half of the 3rd Australian Brigade, which led the way from the beach of Anzac Cove and rushed the bluffs above it within a few minutes of quitting the boats, had fetched up at this more southerly point instead, those dashing soldiers from the Antipodes would not have found the task of securing a footing incomparably more difficult than it proved to be at the point where they actually made their way ashore. They might well have fared no better than the Royal Dublin Fusiliers did when their cutters grounded on V Beach to meet with the tempest of fire which almost wiped them out.

On the other hand, assuming that the landing under the shadow of Gaba Tepe had proved successful, that the leading troops had been promptly followed by others as occurred at Anzac, and that under the impulse of ever-gathering forces the defenders had won their way inland far enough to secure some sort of battle-front, the situation ought to have been decidedly more promising than it came to be in practice a couple of miles further north during the early hours of the 25th. General Birdwood's troops would have been in the position of having secured one end of a line of operations which led somewhere, instead of their merely clinging to a wilderness of rugged scrub-clad spurs which led nowhere. As will be seen from Map V on page 168, the beach by Gaba Tepe is only five miles distant from Kilia Liman, the bight on the European side of the Dardanelles a short way north of Maidos and at the upper end of the Narrows. The intervening ground, although undulating, partakes of the nature of a trough separating the mass of Sari Bair and of the hills to the east of it, from the Pasha Dagh hill system extending from Kilid Bahr almost across to the outer coast-line of the peninsula. This trough represents the shortest route from the outer coast-line to the vicinity of the Narrows. Strategically it may almost be called the natural gateway for a military force to the Dardanelles. The drawback to it has already been mentioned in Chapter IV—its importance was just as obvious to the Turks as it was to the attacking side. A landing force was consequently sure to meet with most determined opposition in any attempt to win its way through a depression of such manifest strategical significance.

Had the attack on the 25th actually been delivered according to programme upon the beach just north of Gaba Tepe, it would very likely have met with discomfiture. But the result might well have been different supposing that the entire invading army had made this portion of the Gallipoli Peninsula its goal. For in that case the stretch of foreshore by Gaba Tepe would merely have represented one extremity—an important extremity no doubt—of the battle-front. The flotilla of cutters approaching the shore would have done so on a frontage extending from the promontory at least as far north as Ari Burnu. Any detachments attempting to gain the land about dawn would no doubt only have represented advanced parties, the bulk of the first echelon of troops waiting until daylight to make sure of arriving at their appointed spots on the coast. Starting with a misadventure on the southern flank need not then necessarily have implied that the coveted beach at that end of the line could not have been secured later, seeing that its defences would almost automatically have been taken in flank by troops thrown ashore to the north of it. The 29th Division, the Australasians and the 1st French Division, together, would almost certainly have enjoyed for several hours a very decided superiority in numbers over the Turks—they would indeed probably have remained the stronger side for the whole of the 25th. Neither the 5th nor the 7th Turkish Division, from the Bulair end, could have reached the scene of action for many hours ; and even if Liman von Sanders had been prepared to withdraw troops from Helles they could not have arrived before evening.

Had all gone reasonably well the Allies might, before their antagonists could meet them on level terms or nearly level terms in respect to numbers, have established their hold upon a very useful area near the shore. They might indeed well have won their way two or three miles forward before sundown on the 25th in the direction of Kilia Liman and have thus on the first day created a situation decidedly more promising than that which actually was brought about at Helles, at Anzac and at Kum Kale within the same period of time.

Still, it has to be acknowledged that it would have been a daring venture to have poured out some 40,000 infantry upon these two or three miles of foreshore, which were believed at the time to be none too favourable for effecting military landings. Opposition was inevitable. Formidable entrenchments had been observed. The littoral was overlooked by hills that must be in hostile possession. A plan of operations framed on the suggested lines would have been a case of putting all one's eggs in one basket, and, even supposing the enterprise to start as auspiciously as could fairly be hoped for, it meant disembarking four divisions, with more to follow, at a locality where the landing-place, or places, were much exposed in the event of bad weather, and where troops ashore would run some risk of finding themselves cut off from their transports and from their base. There was a good deal to be said against the scheme, in fact, as well as for it.

Conclusion.—Nevertheless, if we take into consideration the disappointing course that the campaign was to follow—as will be recorded in later chapters—it is difficult to escape from the impression that, what would no doubt have appeared to those on the spot to be the boldest if not indeed to be an actually foolhardy, plan might have been the right one to adopt. But we enjoy a great advantage over those who were burdened with the responsibility of deciding what was to be done. We know numbers of facts germane to the issue, of which the Commander-in-Chief and the naval authorities were either wholly unaware, or of which they were only partially cognisant. We know how very formidable the defences were at the Helles end of the peninsula. We know that the foreshore for long stretches north of Gaba Tepe was perfectly practicable for boat-landings on a calm day. We know that at the actual moment of disembarkation the Turks were not particularly well prepared to meet attack north of Gaba Tepe except at the particularly favourable spot close to the promontory. We know that the enemy would take a tremendous lot of beating no matter what the scheme of attack was, and that merely gaining a footing on shore—which many thought meant half the battle— was in reality but a short step towards the attainment of the goal.

The truth of the matter is that, under the circumstances which ruled the situation in the latter part of April, 1915, the throwing of one half of the available forces on shore at Helles and Kum Kale, and the throwing of the other half of those forces ashore north of Gaba Tepe, could only by extraordinarily good fortune have achieved the object that was sought after. That object presumably was the occupation by the first comers of a sufficient area of the Gallipoli Peninsula, in the right place, to permit of a triumphant offensive being launched from thence as soon as the remainder of the troops had disembarked. But the fairly large area acquired almost at once at Helles was not in the right place. The forces detailed for the other operation, the landing north of Gaba Tepe which was the right place, were numerically insufficient to acquire immediate possession of an adequate area there.

That the plan chosen failed for all practical purposes, was not so much the consequence of topographical conditions nor of the disposition of the enemy forces nor of bad luck, as it was the upshot of a factor that had not been sufficiently taken into account. This factor was the rare fighting qualities that the Osmanli soldier was to display in the campaign. The troops who had come so badly out of the struggle with the Bulgars and Serbs

THE REAL MISTAKE 131

and Greeks two years before, turned out to be an extremely tough proposition. But if Sir I. Hamilton and his staff at the outset possibly underrated Ottoman valour and grit, if they assumed too readily that the opposition that would be offered by this soldiery would not be of the most whole-hearted type, they were only following the lead of Governments which, in a happy-go-lucky mood and confident that the enemy would crumble up before a show of bluff, had despatched the expedition on a mission of which they had failed to realise the danger, and for which suitable preparations had not been made by them in advance.[1]

[1] In thus advocating the plan of projecting the whole force upon the littoral north of Gaba Tepe, the writer may be pronouncing himself too confidently concerning a subject which is, when all is said and done, essentially a matter of opinion. But he was called upon in 1906 to consider, more or less as an academical proposition, the problem of an attack upon the Dardanelles. He had to consider it afresh a few weeks after the World War broke out, because the possibility of employing Greek military forces for the purpose in concert with Allied warships, was officially raised. As those responsible in this country early in 1915 were gradually drifting into the Gallipoli adventure, he had to examine the problem yet again. From the outset of those successive investigations, no other plan of operations ever appeared to him as comparing with that of making the main effort at the one point where it was feasible to land large bodies of troops rapidly on a broad front within striking distance of the Narrows. Nor have the dramatic events which followed, and the additional information acquired from their story, caused him to change that view.

CHAPTER VII

THE GENERAL STRATEGICAL SITUATION PRODUCED BY THE LANDINGS

The Expeditionary Force definitely committed to a certain plan.—Before continuing the narrative of military events at Helles and at Anzac, it will be convenient to indicate some of the more important strategical considerations that were involved in the land campaign now definitely initiated, and to this the present chapter will be devoted. Two distinct landings having taken place, both of them on an imposing scale, one at the extremity of the Gallipoli Peninsula and the other on its western coast, the army of the Allies was definitely committed to two distinct operations although both of them aimed at the same objective, the occupation of the ground dominating the Narrows on the European side of the Straits. By the night of the 27th–28th the position of both forces had been consolidated. To withdraw either of them from the area which it had managed to secure would even at this early stage have proved a difficult operation. It was bound to become an even more difficult operation from hour to hour, as artillery, impedimenta of all kinds, and stores of food and ammunition were discharged on the beaches. Sir I. Hamilton's plan had been almost automatically disclosed to the Turks, who undoubtedly had been well informed of the concentrations of British and French troops at Alexandria and on the islands of Lemnos and Tenedos. Uncertainty as to where the blow would fall was at an end in the enemy's camp.[1]

Confronted with a *fait accompli*, the bilateral invasion of the Gallipoli Peninsula in its southern portion, the Ottoman military authorities and their German advisers had two main questions

[1] Owing to the many islands in the Ægean and to the character of their population and of that of Alexandria, it was almost impossible to keep movements secret.

THE TURKISH COMMUNICATIONS   133

to take into consideration. The first was how to reinforce the troops already collected in the peninsula for its defence. The other was how to supply their army in the peninsula now and in the future with the munitions and food which it would stand in need of if it was to keep the field. Both depended upon the problem of communications, and it is necessary therefore to give some information with regard to these.

Turkish communications with, and in, the Gallipoli Peninsula.—The Sea of Marmora, and the Dardanelles above Kilid Bahr and Chanak, were in the hands of the Turks and there was in consequence safe water communication with the peninsula. The towns of Gallipoli and Maidos offered certain landing facilities, and owing to their position in restricted waters these ports, such as they were, were not much dependent on the state of the weather. It was also possible to land personnel and stores at Kilid Bahr, and there were two or three localities like Kilia Liman, at the angle north of Maidos, where jetties could easily be erected so as to enable lighters and boats to discharge. As the campaign progressed arrangements for disembarking goods, as well as roads, were a good deal improved about Maidos and Kilia Liman.

Land communications within the Ottoman Empire are notoriously most defective, and those leading to the Dardanelles were no exception to the rule. The nearest point to the peninsula on any Turkish railway was to be found on the line between Constantinople and Adrianople at about seventy-five miles from Bulair, while the nearest point on the Asiatic side, within a few miles of Smyrna, was quite 130 miles from Chanak. The road communications leading to the latter place were, however, fairly serviceable, and there was incessant military traffic across the Straits between Nagara Point or Chanak and Maidos during the campaign. There was also the very important road leading from Thrace to Bulair and Gallipoli, a well laid out *chaussée* ; but where this route traversed the Isthmus of Bulair it ran along the Gulf of Saros side of the defile and it was consequently under fire of Allies' warships if any happened to be on the spot. A road was, however, laid out along the Sea of Marmora side of the isthmus during the campaign, which proved very useful to the Turkish army that was defending the peninsula in the later stages of the operations.

There were thus three principal lines of communication at the disposal of the Ottoman military authorities for pouring troops and stores into the theatre of active operations. There was the water route via the Sea of Marmora. There was the water route across the Straits from Chanak, which latter place was in road communication with the towns in Anatolia. There was the land route from the interior of Thrace to Bulair. All three lines were made use of freely at different stages of the campaign.

Communications within the peninsula itself were few and indifferent. As shown on Map VII two roads ran from near Gallipoli to near Maidos, but neither of them would seem to have been well laid out routes in good repair. There was a moderately good road leading from Maidos to Krithia and from thence on to Sedd-el-Bahr. This strip of Ottoman territory which was to be the scene of one of the most memorable of campaigns is a hilly region, the hills generally being rugged and broken. Most of the streams that run into the Straits or into the Ægean follow a course at right angles to the coast-line ; and as such country tracks as are available after a fashion for wheels mostly followed the valleys, the communications, regarded as a whole, were necessarily winding and inconvenient from the military point of view. It may be remarked here that, since the invading forces never penetrated far into the peninsula, the unsatisfactory character of the communications within its area was a handicap to the defending rather than to the attacking side.

Ottoman powers of concentration.—Situated at no great distance from Constantinople and from Smyrna, and with water communication available to act as a link with the Golden Horn, the environs of the Dardanelles formed a section of the Sultan's dominions where substantial military forces could be assembled without those delays taking place, which have as a rule so hampered Turkish operations in most portions of their Empire. Constantinople and its neighbourhood constituted at all times by far the most important centre of military activity in the State. In 1915 there, moreover, already existed railway communication connecting the Bosphorus with Aleppo, Palestine, and the Hejaz, interrupted only for short distances at two points owing to the tunnels through a couple of mountain ranges not yet being completed ; distant regions could therefore be tapped from the capital for troops, and the troops thus obtained could be sent on by water

ALLIES' LIBERTY OF ACTION 135

to Gallipoli or Maidos, or by land to Bulair or Chanak. All three routes from about Constantinople seem to have been used both when mustering the army for defence of the Dardanelles and when despatching reinforcements to that army during the campaign subsequent to April, 1915.

It seems doubtful whether large forces were transferred to the vicinity of the Straits, from the original garrison of Smyrna and its environs. Exposed as it was to maritime attack at the hands of the Allies, the Ottoman authorities were hardly in a position to denude so important a city of its troops. But Smyrna is the terminus of a railway system which connects up with the line above mentioned that leads from the Bosphorus to Syria, and it is not unlikely that soldiers from far-off portions of the Empire were brought to the Dardanelles via the city, following the land route thence to Chanak.

The Allies' power to threaten descents upon other portions of the coast, and its consequences.—While on the question of Ottoman facilities for concentration, it may be pointed out that the liberty of action which command of the sea conferred upon the Allies enabled them to tie Turkish forces down to districts other than the actual area of operations about Helles and Anzac. The possibility of effecting a military landing in force outside of the Bulair lines was seriously considered by Sir I. Hamilton in conjunction with Admiral de Robeck, even after operations in the Gallipoli Peninsula were in full swing. The possibility of such an operation on the part of their antagonists must have caused the Turkish and German authorities some anxiety, and, as we know from German admissions, tended to keep Ottoman detachments stationed about the town of Gallipoli and in the lines. Both sides, moreover, must have realised in about equal degree that there were promising openings for the British and French on the Asiatic shore near the mouth of the Straits and further to the south, at Besika Bay and beyond. But, whereas the Commander-in-Chief of the Expeditionary Force was aware whether he was going to commit himself to ventures in this direction or not, the Turks could not tell what their opponent's intentions might be. They were consequently forced to keep troops watching Kum Kale and the possible landing-places between that place and Yukyeri Bay, prepared to meet attacks that in the end were never delivered. In this matter the invaders undoubtedly enjoyed an important advantage. They compelled their adversaries to disseminate forces while remaining in a position to keep their own concentrated.

Even on the night of the 27th–28th, when the British and French forces had established themselves at two points on the Gallipoli Peninsula and when the defenders were hard put to it to hold these invaders in check, it was probably almost as well known to the Turkish staff as it was to the staff of the Expeditionary Force that additional forces of the Allies were to be expected almost at once. But the Turkish staff could not know where these fresh troops would be thrown ashore, whether at Helles, or at Anzac, or near Bulair, or on the Asiatic side, and so they had to be prepared at all points. Did we possess the distribution "states" of the Ottoman forces operating around the Dardanelles during the eight months' campaign, we should probably ascertain from them that on the average about one-third of the whole of the Fifth Turkish Army was disposed at points where it exercised no influence whatever on the course of the struggle.

Possibilities of severing the Turkish communications.—So long as the naval forces of the Allies remained below the Narrows of the Dardanelles, the enemy's communications by water could only be severed or interrupted either by means of such submarines as succeeded in passing the minefields and reached the upper portion of the Straits and the Sea of Marmora, or else by gun-fire from warships directed across the peninsula from somewhere off Gaba Tepe—always assuming that the Expeditionary Force did not reach some spot from which it would dominate the channel above the Narrows. Some very daring and skilfully conducted raids by individual submarines were carried out, and they interfered more and more with the transfer of Turkish troops and stores to the scene of military action by water as the operations proceeded. The fire from warships also caused inconvenience to the enemy about the Narrows and compelled ships to discharge at Ak Bashi, a cove east of Kilia Liman (not shown on Map V), where there were at first no facilities whatever. But such interruption as was caused to the Ottoman communications by water was in the nature of things of a somewhat fitful character, and was effective against transit down the Sea of Marmora and the Straits, rather than traffic across the Narrows.

ARRIVAL OF ENEMY SUBMARINES

It has been mentioned above that the question of a military descent on the Bulair Isthmus received serious consideration at the hands of the chiefs of the Allies. Such an operation, assuming it to have been successful, would have effectually severed the important land line of communication leading from Thrace to the peninsula. Moreover, had such a descent been undertaken, and had it led to the forcing of the Bulair lines and to the occupation of ground about the town of Gallipoli, it would have meant a very serious interference with the Turkish water route from the Sea of Marmora to Maidos, for even field guns would have dominated the upper reaches of the Dardanelles by day from the European side. Marshal Liman von Sanders evidently realised this and therefore kept portions of his force near the isthmus. Traffic along the road which traverses the Bulair Isthmus was a good deal interfered with by the fire from British and French warships, but these could not prohibit the passage of transport by night. There can be no doubt that a military operation directed against this important line of Turkish communication might have achieved most important results, but the Turks were prepared for such an eventuality and such a project would consequently have involved a landing in face of serious opposition. But there was also another strong objection to undertaking an offensive in this quarter, and it may be as well to mention this here, because the point will serve to introduce the question of the Allies' water communications.

Almost simultaneously with the successful landings at Helles and Anzac the danger of enemy submarines, a danger which had been fully foreseen for some weeks previously, began to cause Admiral de Robeck serious concern. It had been ascertained that one or two under-water vessels had passed the Straits of Gibraltar, and there could be little doubt that sooner or later these craft, which were known to possess a wide radius of action, would appear in the Ægean. Within a very few weeks subsequent to the 25th of April, the system of bringing troops to the landing-places on the Gallipoli Peninsula in ocean-going transports and great warships had, as we shall see, to be abandoned in favour of utilising trawlers and tugs for the purpose, such craft being much less likely to be struck by torpedoes than vessels of large size and drawing many feet of water. This factor of enemy submarines would not have affected the question of a landing about the Bulair Isthmus had such an operation been undertaken at the end of April or in the early days of May ; but, later on, the naval authorities entertained very strong objections against despatching a flotilla of small craft from the bases in the islands of Lemnos and Imbros on so long a voyage as one to the upper end of the Gulf of Saros. The Bulair project, in fact, came, at an early date after the Expeditionary Force had gained its footing at Helles and Anzac, to be precluded by maritime consideration almost more than by military ones.

The bases of the Allies.—In discussing the strategical aspects of the Allies' communications, it will be best to touch in the first place upon the various bases from which the British and French drew their reinforcements of personnel and their supplies of all kinds, and at certain of which final details of organisation were in some cases adjusted before the despatch of troops actually to the Gallipoli Peninsula was carried out. The principal base throughout was the Nile Delta, with Alexandria as its natural outlet. Malta was made use of to some extent. Then there were the three islands of Lemnos, Imbros, and Tenedos lying near the mouth of the Dardanelles, each of which played its more or less notable rôle in the campaign for the Straits. Finally, there was the island of Mitylene which was also utilised to some extent in later stages of the operations.

Alexandria, emporium of commerce and first-class port as it is, furnished with abundant wharfage and fitted out with most of the modern appliances that exist for discharging and loading up ships, needs no description. In Egypt were gathered together the training units and reserve depots of the Australasian contingents, as also the depots of such Indian troops as participated in the contest for the Gallipoli Peninsula. We have already seen in Chapter III how, when it was decided to undertake land operations on a great scale in substitution for the original plan under which the military were merely to act as auxiliaries to the fleet, the leading portions of the Expeditionary Force, British and French alike, were reorganised and repacked into their transports at Alexandria during the latter days of March and the opening ones of April. It is to be noted, moreover, that the divisions which were sent out from the United Kingdom to the Ægean, as also the Australasian divisions when these were completed after arrival in Egypt, had with them most of the artillery and of the transport which forms part

MUDROS AND KEPHALOS 139

of the normal authorised war establishment of such units. Many of the batteries and most of the transport were left in Egypt for a time; and latterly guns and impedimenta arriving from the United Kingdom were usually sent straight to the Nile Delta, while the infantry with certain selected detachments proceeded straight to Lemnos or Imbros. This depositing of artillery in Egypt was mainly due to the lack of facilities for disembarking heavy weights and for landing animals on the open beaches which had to serve for advanced bases in the peninsula. The guns were subsequently from time to time transferred to the fighting zone as the campaign developed; but large part of the transport was never required at all and it stopped where it was.

Although Malta was of service chiefly as a port of call, it was made use of by the Expeditionary Force in the later stages of the struggle for hospital purposes. Valetta, moreover, constituted the main base of the fleet, all heavy repairs being carried out at the naval dockyard in the Grand Harbour.

The remarkable physical features of the inlet known as Mudros Bay and Port Mudros in the island of Lemnos have already been mentioned in Chapter III, and its merits and its disadvantages set out. It is situated approximately fifty-five miles from Helles and somewhat further from Anzac, so that transit from this base to the Gallipoli Peninsula was necessarily a matter of several hours. Another objection to Lemnos was that the island was Greek territory and therefore at least nominally neutral soil, with the result that it was by no means easy to prevent intelligence of military movements being conveyed from thence to the enemy. But in spite of these defects, Port Mudros and its surroundings gradually, as the weeks passed, developed into a great military centre and became the headquarters of the line of communications of the Expeditionary Force. Piers were constructed, the water supply was seen to, new roads were prepared and old ones repaired, stretches of light railway were introduced, and store-buildings, hospitals, and rest camps were set up. The harbour, moreover, served as an advanced base and anchorage for the Allies' naval forces, its narrow entrance being easily made secure against enemy submarines.

The Bay of Kephalos, situated on the eastern side of the Island of Imbros (*see* the inset to Map I), also became an important military base, and its shore was chosen by Sir I. Hamilton as the site of his General Headquarters, as the distance therefrom to the nearest point of the Gallipoli Peninsula was only about fourteen miles—a twenty-five minutes' run by destroyer. Owing to its geographical position, the bay was completely sheltered from west and south, but it was, on the other hand, quite open to the northeast, and this was the direction from which came the prevailing wind. Kephalos served in a sense as a complement to the landing-places at Helles and Anzac, seeing that the peninsula beaches were exposed to the west and south; small craft engaged on naval and military work off the peninsula would run across to Imbros for shelter if it came on to blow from those quarters. The bay did not possess natural advantages in the shape of a narrow entrance such as Port Mudros enjoyed, and consequently provided by no means an ideal anchorage; the safeguarding of so open a stretch of water against the enemy's under-water craft also taxed the ingenuity and resource of the sailors, and such floating piers and jetties as were established were always liable to sudden destruction if the wind got up from the bad quarter. Nevertheless, the proximity of Imbros to the actual theatre of conflict invested the island with a special significance and made its improvised port a scene of much activity. The island which was somewhat barren had few inhabitants, and these were easily controlled as the place was Turkish territory.

Tenedos, which likewise formed part of the Ottoman Empire, was used principally by the fleet, offering as it did a well-sheltered anchorage under its lea. This island was at first utilised freely by the Royal Naval Air Service in view of its convenient position with reference to the peninsula. After the port of Kephalos had been developed Tenedos was used mainly by the French, and it remained their aviation base to the end.

Then there was also the large, fertile, and populous island of Mitylene which belonged to the Greeks. Mitylene possesses two fine natural havens, each of them a land-locked sheet of deep water with narrow entrance, and one of them covering a considerable area. But owing to the distance of the island from the Dardanelles —the harbour nearest to the Straits is nearly eighty miles away— Mitylene hardly provided a very suitable base for troops operating in the Gallipoli Peninsula, especially after the submarine danger had become acute. However, as will be seen, this jumping-off place was used under special circumstances at a critical juncture of the campaign.

The Allies' communications.—From the nature of the contest, the communications of the Allies were necessarily maritime, and in view of the distance of the Ægean from Great Britain and France—to say nothing of the Antipodes—they were also necessarily of great length. It must be remembered that while Egypt, as well as Lemnos and certain other islands, served as bases of varying military importance for the Expeditionary Force, the communications of that force were not confined to the stretches of sea between those bases and the peninsula. They extended from the bases back to English ports in the case of troops from the United Kingdom, to Australia and New Zealand in the case of General Birdwood's corps, and to France or to Tunis according to circumstances in the case of the French contingent. A voyage from Southampton or Avonmouth to the Ægean or Egypt might be reckoned as a rule to take more than a fortnight, one from Marseilles to Lemnos would take fully a week, and the transit from Australasia to Egypt was a matter of several weeks. In certain cases of exceptional urgency troops and munitions from the United Kingdom were transferred by rail to Marseilles and sailed from thence; but unless special arrangements had been made for a move of this kind little time was saved by adopting the overland route. Nor was the number of days required for the passage from home territory to the zone of active operations dependent solely upon the period occupied in the long sea voyage. Transhipment was almost always necessary before reaching the final destination, and in some cases (especially where personnel or goods went in the first place to Egypt, as everything from the Antipodes did) there was double transhipment, once in Egypt, and a second time in Mudros harbour or at Imbros. We may take it that rarely did a detachment of troops or a consignment of stores take less than three weeks to find their way from the United Kingdom to the shores of the peninsula. This was a vital consideration when it came to be a question of getting out drafts to fill the gaps caused by casualties in action or by sickness.

We have seen in Chapter V that when Sir I. Hamilton delivered his attacks on the 25th of April, the troops were for the most part conveyed either in large warships or else in ocean-going transports to the vicinity of the beaches where they were to disembark, although some detachments made the trip in trawlers. Transports continued to be used for taking troops to near the landing-places for the next few weeks; but on the 22nd of May the presence of submarines was detected, and on the 26th the battleship *Triumph*, suddenly attacked off Gaba Tepe in broad daylight, was torpedoed and sunk. On the very next day the battleship *Majestic* met with a similar fate off W Beach. The consequence of these two maritime mishaps was that from that date forward large ships were seldom used for conveying either personnel or material from the islands to the peninsula; their place was taken by trawlers and tugs, of which types of craft a great flotilla was gradually got together. This arrangement suffered from the drawback that the voyage took longer; but, on the other hand, the smaller vessels could get in nearer to the shore, and when piers came to be constructed at W and V Beaches and at Anzac it became possible to carry out some of the discharging direct without having recourse to cutters or lighters.

It should be noted that the submarine menace did not affect the question of the direct shipments to the peninsula alone. The danger to troop-transports and freight ships on their way to Mudros, to Imbros, and at a later stage to Mitylene, caused the naval authorities of the Allies much anxiety, and the protection of such vessels necessitated a certain diversion of floating force from the immediate neighbourhood of the Straits to the sea routes leading thither from far afield. As a matter of fact the safeguard so afforded and the skill displayed in the naval dispositions proved most effective; for losses were few. Nevertheless, a large transport carrying 1600 troops on board was torpedoed on the 14th of August, with the loss of about 1000 of the passengers and crew, and untoward mishaps befell certain other vessels at various times.

The Allies' powers of concentration.—In respect to reinforcements, as apart from drafts, the Expeditionary Force was obliged to look almost entirely to the United Kingdom. It is true that British troops might have been transferred from France and Flanders to the Ægean had the situation on the Western Front permitted of it, and that the move might perhaps have been carried out more expeditiously than one from the home country; but the conditions on the Western Front never did permit of such depletions. A few

QUESTION OF DRAFTS

additional units were obtained from Australasia ; but during the early months of the Dardanelles operations the military authorities in the Antipodes were obliged to devote their attention rather to the problem of providing drafts for the existing army corps in the Gallipoli Peninsula than to that of creating new formations. The not inconsiderable forces of Indian troops stationed in Egypt had the defence of the Nile Delta to occupy them, and they could not therefore be drawn upon for the Dardanelles, while the military resources of India itself were, as it was, so severely strained by commitments in Mesopotamia and East Africa that nothing could be expected from that quarter. The French Government contented itself with trying to maintain at their proper establishment the two divisions that it had allotted to Sir I. Hamilton's army. So it came about that if reinforcements were to come from anywhere they had to come from the United Kingdom.

Question of drafts.—But from the very outset, the question of drafts to fill up the gaps in the ranks was an acute one and one more pressing even than that of reinforcements. Casualties were heavy at the start, as we have seen. Later on there was much sickness amongst the troops in the peninsula, and the wastage due to this cause, added to the drain in men arising from losses in action, seriously depleted units and created very heavy demands for drafts ; and as the casualties during the almost incessant combats naturally fell chiefly upon the infantry, it was that branch of the service that gave especial grounds for anxiety. Moreover, to make matters worse, infantry battalions from the United Kingdom (especially those belonging to Territorial divisions and to the Royal Naval Division) too often took the field short of establishment. It has been explained above that the transfer of detachments from English ports to the scene of action was bound to take quite three weeks. No provision had been made—or ever was adequately made—for maintaining reserves of infantry officers and soldiers more or less on the spot, ready to fill gaps within a day or two after these occurred. The consequence was that the infantry from the United Kingdom was always below strength, for what happened was this. By the time that the drafts intended to make good the wastage that had taken place during any particular period had arrived from English ports in the war zone, large numbers of additional casualties had already occurred. So replenishment was always in arrear. The infantry battalions recruited in the British Isles were throughout the campaign from 25 per cent to 40 per cent below establishment.

The truth is that reserves in infantrymen amounting to from 20 per cent to 33 per cent of the total numbers in the field that had to be fed from English ports, ought to have been constantly at hand. Those reserves—or a proportion of them—ought to have been kept as near to the peninsula as possible, at Imbros say, or at Lemnos, or else in Mitylene. None of them should have been further away than Malta or Egypt. But, that some arrangement of this kind was not made, must not necessarily be attributed to bad management on the part of the military authorities. They could not produce what they had not got. A serious shortage of armed and trained personnel existed almost continuously in the British Islands until compulsory service was introduced in 1916; for new divisions were constantly being formed and the demands for drafts from the Western Front were uniformly heavy. Sir I. Hamilton may have got his fair share, or more than his fair share, of what there was going; but what was going was not enough. As has already been pointed out in the Introduction, a discussion concerning the relative importance of the supply of men and munitions to the Dardanelles Expeditionary Force, as compared to needs arising in other quarters, would be outside the scope of this volume. We simply have to take note that the requirements in respect to infantry drafts from the United Kingdom were not met. It must, however, be observed here that, although the percentage of wastage arising from casualties in action proved to be considerably higher during the European War than military authorities in general had anticipated beforehand, the Dardanelles land campaign was not initiated until March, 1915, seven months after the outbreak of hostilities. The wastage to be expected could therefore to some extent be foreseen when the land campaign was being initiated. The fact that the production of reserves to fill gaps in the ranks could not be depended upon, ought indeed, if the matter was thought of at all, to have provided a powerful argument against embarking on the undertaking.[1]

---

[1] Sir I. Hamilton made representations on this subject before leaving England, foreseeing that it would not be practicable to make omelets without breaking eggs.

The Australasian troops were, upon the whole, better supplied with drafts than those from the United Kingdom. As for the French, their arrangements were as appropriate as could reasonably be expected; they maintained a goodly contingent of reserves in the Island of Lemnos except just at first, and their infantry was consequently fairly well up to establishment at most stages of the drama. But, as has already been indicated, it was the troops from the United Kingdom that constituted the bulk of the Expeditionary Force, except during the first few weeks. No critical account of this memorable undertaking of war would be other than misleading that did not give a due prominence to the persistent failure to keep reasonably full the majority of the infantry battalions that took part in the operations. It is no exaggeration to say that many divisions were, in respect to the principal arm of the service, at times only divisions in name. This was not the least of the causes which contributed to bring to naught the hopes of winning command of the Dardanelles entertained by the Allies in the early months of 1915.

The withdrawal of the Russian Expeditionary Force from Odessa.
—Another circumstance that impaired the Entente's prospect of success in the Gallipoli Peninsula must be mentioned here. We have seen in Chapter III how the Russians at an early stage of the preparations for the venture undertook to co-operate in due course in the contemplated operations for mastering the Bosphorus and occupying Constantinople, and how, with this end in view, they had massed troops about Odessa who were intended to participate in the campaign when the time came. But during the months of April and May the course of the war in other theatres—in Galicia and in Poland—obliged the Russian commander-in-chief to recall this force from the Black Sea coast; and from that time forward there never was any question of a host from the north co-operating with the British and French soldiery who were endeavouring to penetrate to the Golden Horn from the side of the Ægean.

It had never been suggested that Russia could assist directly in a struggle for the Dardanelles, and there is no occasion to speculate here as to what effect absence of help from across the Euxine might have created had operations against the Bosphorus and Stambul actually taken shape. But the disappearance of a considerable Allied force from the vicinity of Odessa exerted an appreciable

L

influence over the struggle for the Hellespont. So long as the German and Turkish military authorities were hampered by anxiety lest hostile armaments from the far side of the Black Sea should imperil the capital, they were compelled to maintain an ample garrison at the heart of the Empire. The removal of the Russian threat liberated numbers of battalions and batteries for service elsewhere, and a proportion of these repaired to the Gallipoli Peninsula during May, appreciably augmenting the strength of the Ottoman army which Sir I. Hamilton was called upon to overcome.

CHAPTER VIII

THE FIRST THREE MONTHS AT HELLES

The topographical conditions of the Helles area.—It is not proposed to deal at any length with the operations that took place at Helles and Anzac during the first three months of the land campaign. Although events in both regions took the form of a stern and a most continuous struggle, often at very close quarters, the incidents were not especially illuminating or instructive from the tactical point of view, even if they provided plentiful opportunities for a display of grit and valour which was not confined only to the side of the Allies.' The contest indeed partook to a large extent of the monotonous characteristics inseparable from trench warfare. Moreover, as will be seen from the narrative, the general military situation in the Gallipoli Peninsula was not very materially altered from that which had been arrived at on the night of the 27th–28th, by anything that occurred between that date and the end of July.

It will be convenient in dealing with Helles to give consideration in the first place to the topographical features of the tract in which the invaders were about to operate, and to the difficulties which these features necessarily placed in the way of carrying out the formidable task that the troops planted down at the extremity of the peninsula were called upon to perform.

As will be seen from Maps I and VII the ground rises towards the interior of the peninsula from the basin west of Morto Bay, and a belt of high ground stretches practically from shore to shore. The highest point of this belt is the well-defined hill-top of Achi Baba, about 700 feet above sea-level, and nearer to the Straits than it is to the Ægean. The slopes leading up to this upland from the basin are gradual and form long easy spurs, the ground in general being not markedly broken. Two deep gullies, however, run up into it—Zighin Dere, already mentioned in Chapter VI, and Kerevez Dere on the opposite side of the peninsula. Moreover, a couple of long depressions run up in the middle representing the valleys of two streams that find their outlet in Morto Bay. The village of Krithia is near the highest part of the belt of uplands on the Ægean side and lies about 350 feet above sea-level ; the cart route from Sedd-el-Bahr to Maidos passed through the place in 1915.

The ground beyond the elevated belt is necessarily hidden from the low ground about Helles ; and it was not as a matter of fact ever seen by the troops operating in this area except on occasions when they proceeded along the Ægean coast by sea, to and from Anzac. But it may be as well to briefly indicate its main features. To the south and south-west of the great depression or trough mentioned in Chapter VI as running across from about Gaba Tepe to the bight of Kilia Liman near Maidos, the ground at most points rises abruptly from the Dardanelles and the high ground is mainly to be found on that side of the peninsula. Rugged plateaux extend from Achi Baba to the Pasha Dagh or Kilid Bahr tableland broken into only by two deep ravines opening on the Straits, that nearest Achi Baba known as the Soghanli Dere. The slopes towards the Ægean are more gradual, and on that side (except where the belt mentioned above makes, as it were, a buttress right across the peninsula) there are open valleys which are fairly well cultivated. The Pasha Dagh, and a good deal of the high ground between it and Achi Baba, are from 550 to 700 feet above sealevel, so that the Narrows as well as the country in their vicinity are invisible from Achi Baba ; on the other hand, Gaba Tepe and some of the spurs about Anzac can be seen. In some respects the portions of the Achi Baba belt of high ground that are nearest to the Ægean were of more tactical importance to the troops operating from Helles than the peak itself, seeing that they overlooked the valleys and depressions on that side of the peninsula, stretching away towards Gaba Tepe.

The possession of the culminating point of Achi Baba was nevertheless calculated to be of great benefit to the Allies supposing that they were to secure it. It necessarily provided an admirable observation point in the event of operations taking place between it and the Pasha Dagh. It dominated the undulations on the

QUESTION OF IMMEDIATE ADVANCE 149

Asiatic side of the Dardanelles about Eren Keui Bay, where folds of the ground provided excellent sites for hostile batteries intended to fire across the Straits. Its occupation would almost automatically bring about the capture of the whole of the high ground on either hand, and would thus give the Allies control of the entire belt of plateau land extending athwart the peninsula. Most important of all, perhaps, the loss of Achi Baba and of this plateau land would rob the Turks of their artillery positions for bombarding the Helles landing-places, and it would deprive them of all observation of the effect of fire from any long-range guns or howitzers of theirs which they might manage to emplace further back. The fact that the enemy throughout the Dardanelles campaign always had good artillery observation posts at his command, while the Allies had not, was undoubtedly a contributory cause of the ill-success that the Allies' efforts met with as a whole.

Sir I. Hamilton's difficulty.—Fully realising the urgency of pressing forward if possible and of thereby winning Achi Baba and the high ground at and beyond Krithia, the Commander-in-Chief was on the night of the 27th–28th placed in a dilemma. All the advantages that the power to surprise confers upon a combatant force had now passed out of his hands. The enemy had had ample time to transfer reserves to the scene of action from about Maidos, and might at the end of three days even be assembling troops, drawn from Chanak and the Asiatic side of the Hellespont,[1] to give him battle. The fact that the Allies had contrived to make progress on the 27th, virtually unopposed, offered no guarantee that twenty-four hours later the Turks would not be in a position to present a resolute front were any fresh advance to be attempted, seeing how strong was the likelihood of their forces on the spot having been substantially augmented in the meantime. The British and French troops, especially the former, were, moreover, somewhat exhausted; the 29th Division had suffered exceedingly heavy losses, several of its battalions having shrunk to very modest proportions and being lamentably short of officers.

On the other hand, a certain amount of artillery had now been landed and was ready for action. There were grounds for hoping that the enemy was somewhat discouraged by his discomfitures at

[1] According to *Gallipoli, Der Kampf um den Orient*, one whole division and part of another had crossed the Straits by the 28th.

the landing-places and by the heavy losses that had been sustained. Although considerable reinforcements were on their way from Egypt, or were preparing to sail from thence, these would only arrive gradually during the next ten days. There was not much object in waiting for them, seeing that the enemy within the same period would probably bring up troops from Bulair and from the Asiatic side of the Straits. So Sir I. Hamilton decided to carry out a fresh advance on the 28th, and he gave orders to that effect.

The action of the 28th April.—The plan was that the whole force should move forward at 8 a.m., pivoting to some extent upon the extreme right near De Tott's Battery. The 29th Division was on the left, the 1st French Division on the right, with the South Wales Borderers on the extreme right; of the 29th Division the 87th Brigade was on the left, with the 88th on its right and the 86th in reserve. The troops advanced without meeting with very stiff opposition at first. But the further they pressed on the more determined they found the resistance that was offered by the Turks. Moreover, by the afternoon ammunition began to run short, owing to there being insufficient transport as yet available on shore to ensure a consistent supply. About 3 p.m. the enemy counter-attacked with the bayonet against the centre and right of the line, obliged the assailants to give ground to some extent, and caused some confusion.

Practically the whole of the troops had been absorbed into the firing line by this time, and the Allies found themselves hard pressed; but they succeeded in holding their ground at most points and at the end of the day were in possession of a position considerably in advance of that which they had occupied during the preceding night. It extended from the Ægean shore a few hundred yards short of Y Beach, to a point about a third of a mile south-west of the outlet to the watercourse descending the Kerevez Dere; the 29th Division had, incidentally, made good the mouth of the Zighin Dere ravine, with Gully Beach—both important acquisitions. But the French had suffered very severely in the affray, and there had also been heavy casualties in some of the battalions of the 29th Division, depleting their ranks still further.[1] The line held on the night of the 28th–29th was, moreover, somewhat longer

[1] The 86th Brigade on the 29th had only 36 officers and 1,850 other ranks effective.

FIGHT OF 28TH APRIL

than that which had been taken up twenty-four hours before, and its defenders were necessarily somewhat scattered. Still, the day had on the whole been crowned with a very fair measure of success, and the results that had been obtained justified the decision to attack without awaiting the arrival of further troops.

The Turks, it should be noted, had borne themselves most gallantly in this engagement. They had by no means confined themselves to a defensive attitude, and their onsets had been delivered with an almost reckless disregard of losses. Nor was there any reason to suppose that their strength would not go on being augmented from day to day. The formidable character of the opposition that was being offered, coupled with the increasing numerical weakness of the 29th Division and of the French contingent, and with the fact that there were no reserves anywhere near the theatre of war to fill the yawning gaps in the ranks of the 29th Division, was by this time bringing home to the responsible leaders on the spot the exceedingly difficult nature of the problem with which the force landed at Helles was confronted.

From the 29th of April to the 5th of May.—The 29th and 30th of April and the 1st of May were, comparatively speaking, quiet days. They were chiefly marked, in so far as the invaders were concerned, by the arrival of two more battalions of the Royal Naval Division, and of the 29th Indian Brigade. These additions to the force considerably increased its numerical strength for the moment and they added appreciably to its security. Some more batteries, British and French, were also landed. The brief lull, however, was brought to an end on the night of the 1st by the Turks delivering a furious and well-directed attack, the full force of which fell upon the Allies' centre about the junction of the British with the French contingents. A captured order showed the assailants to have numbered 16,000, with 2000 in reserve. The position was decidedly critical for a time ; but the prompt arrival of reinforcements sent up from in rear sufficed to restore the situation. Towards morning the British troops delivered an effective counter-offensive and drove the Osmanlis back some distance, but before noon the whole line was back in its former position. The Turks had lost very heavily in this affair, especially from artillery fire when retreating, and they had upon the whole the worst of a well-contested engagement.

Undeterred by their repulse on this occasion, the enemy, however, attacked again on the night of the 2nd-3rd and yet again on the next night; but they were repulsed on each occasion. The French, however, had many casualties—so much so that a portion of their line was taken over by the 2nd Naval Brigade on the 4th, during which day an important reorganisation and redistribution of available forces was carried into effect on the side of the Allies. On the 5th, the Lancashire Fusilier Brigade, the first brigade of the 42nd East Lancashire Division to arrive, disembarked, and during the following night the 2nd Australian Brigade and the New Zealand Brigade (infantry) quietly took ship at Anzac and were brought down to Helles, where they landed during the 6th. Sir I. Hamilton's first despatch carried the story up to the evening of the 5th, and it may be recorded here that he therein gave the figure of his losses to date as just short of 14,000, exclusive of the French—a serious wastage. These heavy casualties had occurred mainly in the ranks of the infantry of the 29th Division and of the two Australasian divisions, reducing their strength by about two-fifths.

The struggle of the 6th-8th of May.—Anxious to secure possession of Achi Baba and of the high ground stretching across the peninsula on either side of that hill-top, if possible, the Commander-in-Chief had resolved to make a fresh effort to press forward, and it was in view of the contemplated operation that the two Anzac brigades had been transferred from the west coast to Helles, as recorded above. The British contingent of the Allied forces at the extremity of the peninsula was especially reorganised for the operation. The Lancashire Fusilier Brigade and the 29th Indian Brigade were added to the 29th Division, a composite division was formed out of the two Anzac brigades and the 1st Naval Brigade, while the 2nd Naval Brigade remained attached to the French contingent; the composite division was to be employed as a general reserve during the coming combat. On paper, the troops destined to carry out the undertaking represented a formidable total, in so far as infantry was concerned, for three divisions and a spare brigade at war establishment would represent about 40,000 infantrymen; but battalions had started short of establishment, as has already been indicated, and losses in action had been so heavy that the total did not approach such a figure.

There was every reason to believe that the Turks had been

substantially reinforced. They had held practically their present position ever since the fight of the 28th. They had dug themselves in, had emplaced numbers of machine-guns, and had introduced wire entanglements to strengthen awkward points. They more or less overlooked the ground occupied by the Allies and they enjoyed a great advantage in respect to artillery observation, thanks to their holding Achi Baba and the uplands on either side of it. On the other hand, the Allies were decidedly better off in respect to the number of guns landed than they had been on the 28th of April, and they could furthermore reckon upon the warships lending them some effective aid.

The attack of the 6th brought about a battle which lasted for three days almost without intermission. A little ground was gained on the first day by the 29th Division, as also by the French on the right; but such progress as they could lay claim to had only been purchased at the cost of many casualties. On the 7th a little more ground was made good; on this day the New Zealand Brigade, detached from the Composite Division in reserve, was partially thrown into the fight. The 8th found the Allies attacking again. They were unable to make much progress during the early part of the day, but in the afternoon, following on a very heavy bombardment by artillery ashore and afloat, a general advance was ordered and this secured a certain measure of success; the Anzacs were prominent in this final effort, and that night the whole force of the Allies dug itself in on a line that was from 400 to 600 yards further forward than the position that they had held on the night of the 6th–7th. Several Turkish trenches and works had been captured during these three days of obstinate combat, in spite of the sturdy resistance of the enemy and of the murderous fire of the hostile machine-guns. The high ground, however, had not been conquered, the invaders' left still found itself some distance short of Krithia, and the casualties incurred within their ranks had again been serious. The 2nd French Division under General Bailloud landed at V Beach between the 6th and 8th and began reinforcing the 1st Division.

The 9th proved a more or less quiet day; but the Turks delivered a fierce assault at nightfall, and their attacks continued until morning. This nocturnal struggle was prosecuted with especial violence on the Allies' right, but the Osmanlis were eventually beaten off at all points, and the discomfiture met with on this occasion appears to have disheartened them, for they refrained from embarking on a serious offensive for some time to come after their bitter experiences of that night. It was found possible to withdraw the 29th Division from the front line on the 11th, relieving it by the 42nd Division under General Douglas, the two remaining brigades of which had completed disembarkation on the 8th. The troops at Helles then perforce settled down to the monotony of trench warfare, which, however, was enlivened on the 12th by a particularly successful tactical enterprise, and one that appreciably ameliorated the position on the extreme left, adjacent to the Ægean.

Steep slopes interspersed with almost perpendicular cliffs rise abruptly from the foreshore for a considerable distance north-east of Gully Beach, although there are occasional narrow strips of strand at their foot, such as Y Beach. As shown on Map I, the ground rises as one proceeds north-east and the declivity consequently becomes higher and higher. Since the 25th of April the Turks had been crowning a prominent bluff just beyond Y Beach and had prepared a strong entrenchment on it. A party of the 1/6th Ghurkas had crawled along the lower part of the escarpment on the night of the 10th-11th in hopes of surprising this work, but the project had failed. It was, thereupon, decided to undertake a more formal attack, and, early on the 12th, the two cruisers *Dublin* and *Talbot* steamed suddenly round from Cape Tekke and opened a brisk bombardment of the fortress, while a demonstration was carried out directly towards it by infantry and artillery on either side of the Zighin Dere ravine. In the meantime a company of the Ghurkas were creeping along the declivity overhanging the shore and, the attention of the defenders of the work being otherwise occupied, this little force succeeded in rushing the bluff unexpectedly, more Ghurkas pressed forward, and speedily the captured ground had been united by entrenchments with the line held further back and to the right flank. The result was that the extreme left of the Allies had been pushed forward more than a quarter of a mile, and that their hold upon the lower end of the important ravine had been considerably strengthened.

From the 13th of May to the 4th of June.—For nearly a month after this the operations were confined to minor raids and to methodical sapping work, in which the Allies contrived from time to time to gain a little ground. The 2nd Australian and New Zealand Brigades had returned to Anzac after the struggle of the 6th–8th ; but on the other hand, the artillery of the 2nd Division of the French corps had disembarked by the 14th, on which day General D'Amade handed over command to General Gouraud. The battleship *Goliath* had been sunk by an enemy destroyer while anchored in the Straits covering the flank of the French on the night of the 12th–13th. The 29th Division, 42nd Division, and Royal Naval Division were formed into the VIIIth Army Corps under General Hunter Weston, the British contingent continuing to hold the left of the Allies' line while the French held the right.

The troops at Helles in general, as also the landing-places, were from the outset subjected to a good deal of desultory and spasmodic, but none the less somewhat damaging, artillery fire. This at times caused appreciable losses. It emanated mainly from behind the enemy's positions facing the front of the Allies ; but a certain amount was also directed from across the Straits, and this took the invaders in flank and even to some extent in reverse. Transports and other vessels lying off the extremity of the peninsula were occasionally taken by the Turks as their target and were sometimes hit. Partly owing to the length of the range, and partly also owing to howitzers being used as well as flat trajectory guns, this fire was of a very searching, plunging character, and, seeing that it was also in a measure converging, perfect shelter against it could not readily be found or be devised at any point. The two principal landing-places, V and W Beaches, suffered somewhat severely from hostile shell at times, and the fact that there was scarcely one single spot within the area which the invaders had succeeded in occupying, that was not liable to be hit by a Turkish projectile at any moment, threw a constant strain upon the troops, besides often causing material injury. As a consequence of their being on the right, the French naturally suffered particularly from the hostile pieces that were emplaced on the Asiatic side of the Dardanelles.

The landing-places were being constantly improved by skilled workers. At W Beach a serviceable breakwater was gradually constructed running out from Cape Tekke, alongside which small craft and lighters could discharge even when the sea was moderately rough; a pier was also added, sheltered by this breakwater, and one or two small boat jetties were thrown out from the beach. The *River Clyde* served for a useful bulwark at V Beach and was joined to the shore, one or two modest jetties being added, and the French, who had charge of this landing-place, converted it gradually into a satisfactory and well-arranged advanced base. A small pier was in due course constructed at S Beach. These various harbour works naturally took time to develop, and they were continually being elaborated and rectified for the first three or four months of the occupation, light railways being laid down at W and V Beaches. Roads and communications of all kinds were also taken in hand, and the water arrangements were placed on a satisfactory footing. As a matter of fact, it had turned out that there was a fairly good natural water output within the area, so that this particular matter did not cause much anxiety at Helles, although a portion of the supply needed had to be imported.

The weather was rapidly getting hotter, and by the end of May the ground was already in that parched condition that is customary in summer time in warm latitudes. Vegetation dried up, the dust began to cause serious inconvenience and discomfort, and a plague of flies set its hold upon bivouacs and hospitals. Such conditions naturally bred sickness after the early weeks, and this created a serious drain on the fighting strength of the force. Such inconveniences were not, however, confined to the side of the Allies; for the Turks also suffered, and in view of their very defective sanitary arrangements their wastage from disease was probably fully as high as that of their opponents.

From the 25th of May to the 3rd of June there was much intermittent fighting on a minor scale, in which both British and French gradually improved their position and gained some little ground. The Turks, who in former times had often displayed a quite peculiar aptitude for contriving earthworks, had laboured hard to fortify the slopes of Achi Baba and the ground about Krithia, and they had converted the whole of the high ground confronting the Allies from shore to shore into a veritable fortress. The trenches were deep and were skilfully constructed. There were ample covered communications along which reinforcements could be pushed unseen. Skilful use had been made of any accidents of ground that could be turned to account for defensive purposes. They had,

THE 4TH OF JUNE

moreover, received reinforcements and were holding their line in strength; but, on the other hand, Sir I. Hamilton had received some drafts for his British troops and the gaps in the ranks of the French caused by the severe fighting of the 6th–8th of May had to a great extent been filled up. The Commander-in-Chief, therefore, decided upon delivering another general attack, to take place on the 4th of June, and in this combat the 29th Division, the 42nd Division, the 2nd Naval Brigade (these three mustering between them 20,000 bayonets) with the 2nd French Division and 1st French Division, in the order named from left to right, were engaged. It will be remembered that the appearance of enemy submarines in the latter days of May, coupled with the sinking of *Triumph* and *Majestic*, had made it somewhat awkward for warships to assist in the land operations of the Allies; but by the beginning of June both British and French were fairly well supplied with field artillery, and on this occasion the affair opened with a prolonged bombardment from the Allies' guns on shore, the British having six batteries of French 75's placed especially at their disposal. Then, at noon, the whole line advanced.

All went encouragingly at first, except on the left of the French where the troops were unable to gain ground, and on the British left where also great difficulty was experienced in making any advance. Any success achieved at the outset was, however, only temporary, for after having made a most successful start the French on the right were very heavily counter-attacked and were forced back. This set-back exposed the right flank of the 2nd Naval Brigade, already somewhat *en l'air* owing to the left of the French having been unable to advance at the beginning, and as a consequence the right of the Naval Brigade had to fall back with heavy loss. The 42nd Division, and especially its Manchester Brigade, had made a substantial advance; but as a result of what had occurred on the right and in the right centre, these troops were taken in enfilade from that flank, and although they held on grimly all the afternoon they had to be withdrawn from what had come to be a critical position in the evening, suffering severely during the retirement. The net result of the day's operations was a gain of from 200 to 400 yards along the whole of the centre, involving the capture of the Turkish front lines of trenches in this part of the field which had been won in the first few minutes of the action ; but the Turks could upon the whole claim to have had the best of the encounter as they had repulsed the assailants on the right. The casualties had been heavy on both sides.

This combat affords an interesting illustration of the tactical value of an immediate counter-attack by the defending side after losing ground in consequence of a hostile assault. The French had made a brilliant advance at the outset, taking one particularly strong redoubt and securing a number of enemy trenches ; but the Turks counter-attacked in formidable force before the victors could consolidate, and by doing so practically regained all the ground that they had lost. The story of the fight also illustrates another point, the importance of which was impressed upon combatants on the Western Front on numberless occasions during the World War—in trench warfare it is seldom of much avail for portion of an attacking force to gain ground. The whole force engaged must make progress more or less simultaneously and the same distance, otherwise a salient is created or else a flank is exposed in the battle line. Because the extreme left of the French was held up, the right of the Royal Naval Division was compromised ; because the Royal Naval Division had to fall back, the Manchester Brigade found itself thrust out considerably in advance of the troops on its right, and, as we have seen, its position eventually became untenable. The experiences of this day, indeed, almost seem to suggest that an attack on a broad front is a mistake in warfare of this type unless, owing to previous overwhelming bombardment with heavy artillery, or owing to known weakness of the defending side, or in virtue of complete surprise being rendered practicable by the circumstances of the case, success at all points is reasonably certain. Before the end of June two very satisfactory actions were to be fought by the Allies in the Helles area ; but, as will be noted, neither of them covered a broad front.

From the 5th to the end of June.—Early in June the British force at Helles was strengthened by the arrival of the 52nd (Lowland) Division, raising the number of divisions in this area to six ; but like all Territorial divisions it was short of establishment when it arrived. In view of the losses incurred in the struggle of the 4th of June and of those that were constantly occurring, and of the incessant wastage caused by sickness, the army of invasion at the extremity of the peninsula did not really represent six divisions, or anything like it. For the first few days after that combat the Turks made several attempts to regain some of the few hundreds of yards that the Allies had deprived them of as a result of it; but these efforts all proved unavailing, being invariably repulsed and often with considerable loss to the assailants.

Then, on the 21st, the French Corps under General Gouraud brought off a most gratifying minor success. Attacking at dawn, the 2nd Division on the left and 1st Division on the right, the 2nd Division carried a number of entrenchments on the forward slopes of the big spur west of the Kerevez Dere. The 1st Division was, however, less successful; for although it gained ground satisfactorily to start with, prompt counter-attacks on the part of the Turks recovered from them much of what they had won. Then, late in the afternoon, the 1st Division attacked afresh and this time its infantry established themselves firmly in the enemy's nearer trenches, thereby safeguarding the 2nd Division in the positions that it had taken up as a result of its brilliant assault of the morning. The Ottoman troops lost very heavily in this day's fighting, which in the end had gone entirely in favour of the French, and the Allies had good reason for congratulating themselves on the results, seeing that valuable ground had been secured on the extreme right on the heights that flank the Kerevez Dere from the west.

A week later the Allies scored an even more important success on the opposite flank. For this operation General Hunter Weston made use of the 29th Division and the 52nd Division, and its object was to push the extreme left flank of the line forward from Ghurka Bluff, and thereby to gain possession of a long stretch of the Zighin Dere—or Gully Ravine as it had come to be called—pivoting the attack upon a point about a mile from the sea. The cruiser *Talbot*, closely guarded against possible enemy submarines by a curtain of destroyers and small craft, took part in this action, and her fire, and that of the destroyers *Wolverine* and *Scorpion* which stood close in, proved useful in enfilading the Turkish trenches nearest the coast. The attack was completely successful, planning and execution alike being beyond reproach. As regards the front as a whole it was a sectional operation, all guns along the line that would bear taking part, and it was carried out in waves, a fresh force on two occasions passing through troops that had gained

the objectives which they had been detailed to make good, and
the artillery co-operating before each successive advance. The
timing was admirable and the entire programme was carried out
practically without hitch. The result of the combat was that,
when fire died down, the extreme left flank resting on the edge of
the declivity that overhung the shore had been pushed forward
from Ghurka Bluff to "Fusilier Bluff," and that several hundred
yards of the important Gully Ravine, with the ground on either
side of it, had fallen into the hands of the 29th Division.[1] The
losses on the side of the assailants were, moreover, relatively
small considering the value of the gains, and the enemy would
seem at this time to have been somewhat short of ammunition.

Nevertheless, the Turks counter-attacked vigorously on the two
following nights. Their efforts to eject the victors from the trenches
that had changed hands, however, proved of no avail, they cost
the Osmanlis a number of casualties, and that such counter-strokes
should have been delivered indicated unmistakably that the
Ottoman staff realised the importance of the ground that had been
lost. The affair of the 28th, following as it did so closely on General
Gouraud's stroke on the opposite flank, seemed to suggest that if
there had been plentiful reserves to throw into the scale at this
juncture on the Helles front, this might have proved the psycho-
logical moment for initiating a determined effort to secure Krithia,
the high ground beyond that coveted village, and even possibly
Achi Baba itself; no such reserves were, however, available. The
month of June ended with a grave misfortune for the Allies.
General Gouraud was very seriously wounded on the 30th, the
command of the French corps devolving upon General Bailloud
who had previously been at the head of the 2nd Division. It is
interesting to note, as indicating how thoroughly the troops on
both sides were settling down to trench warfare, that hand grenades
began to be largely used at Helles in the latter part of June.

The month of July.—The bulk of the Expeditionary Force

[1] Mr. Nevinson in his *The Dardanelles Campaign* writes in regard to
the advance on the immediate right of the Gully: "These rapid successes
were mainly due to two trench-mortars lent by General Gouraud and dropping
bombs containing some 30 lb., some 70 lb., of melinite, vertically into the
trenches at short range. The British force at this time possessed a few
Japanese trench-mortars—very effective, but numbering only six, and these
very short of ammunition. We had no others of any kind. Yet in the
scarcity of howitzers, trench-mortars were more needed than any gun."

originally detailed for the undertaking that was to ensure the passage of the Dardanelles by the Allies' fleet, had now been planted down at the extremity of the Gallipoli Peninsula for about two months, and yet its front followed a line that was barely four miles in advance of W and V Beaches at any point, and that was barely a quarter of the way from those landing-places to the Kilid Bahr plateau which was the immediate objective. At this rate of advance the Helles army would not reach the plateau before Christmas—trench warfare is a slow process even when progress is continuous and when a terrific artillery preparation can be indulged in at frequent intervals. The affairs of the 21st and 28th of June had been satisfactory enough in themselves and had given much encouragement to the invading troops; there was reason to believe that the Turks had suffered even heavier losses during the continuous fighting since April than had the Allies, and yet it could not be said that from the tactical—still less from the strategical—point of view the situation in this section of the theatre of war was reassuring. Early in July the Turks in the peninsula were considerably reinforced—by as much as five divisions it would seem. But it will be convenient to defer a further consideration of the general situation, as this will be discussed in Chapter X.

The events in the Helles area during July hardly call for detailed description. The Turkish defence works were constantly being strengthened. A new trench system guarding Achi Baba on the Krithia side had also been devised which necessarily added to the difficulties that confronted the Allies, because owing to its existence the capture of that village and of ground immediately beyond it by no means rendered Achi Baba untenable by the enemy. The successes on either flank in the closing days of June had, no doubt, improved the outlook of the Allies, but hardly sufficiently for such progress as had been made to ensure further tactical triumphs. This indeed was proved on the 12th–13th of July, when a general attack was delivered all along the Ottoman front extending from the Krithia–Sedd el Bahr road to the Straits, but which upon the whole only secured a moderate measure of success.

The two French divisions and the 52nd Division delivered this attack. Advancing after a heavy bombardment had been directed upon the Osmanli's lines, the assailants began in promising style. The first two lines of enemy's trenches were secured at once, and the 4th K.O.S.B.'s, belonging to the 52nd Division, even captured the third line in front of them—only, however, to be thrust back with heavy loss. But the Allies had to rest content on that day with the capture of the two front lines of trenches, whereas the third line had been their objective. As usual the Turks counter-attacked that night with great determination; but they failed to shake the French, and they only obliged the 52nd Division to give way somewhat on its left. On the 13th three battalions of the 1st Naval Brigade were pushed up in support of the 52nd Division on its left so as to secure that flank, and the French thrust their right down to the mouth of the Kerevez Dere. The result of the two days' fighting, however, merely produced an advance of from 200 to 400 yards, and it did not very appreciably alter the situation. But 500 Turkish prisoners had been secured, and although the fight had been well contested the Allies had not lost unduly; the French, however, had to deplore the death of General Masnou, commander of the 1st Division, who was mortally wounded during the combat.

In this affair Sir I. Hamilton had been somewhat embarrassed by want of artillery ammunition, only having sufficient in hand to justify his committing himself to one single serious operation during the month. The shortage consequent upon the heavy expenditure incurred on the 12th and 13th precluded any idea of a further offensive during July, and no important combats took place in the Helles area during the remainder of the month. It should, however, be noted that, although the actual advance made on the two days, the 12th and 13th, amounted to less than a quarter of a mile on the average along about half of the front, the ground that had been gained on this occasion had in the words of the Commander-in-Chief provided "far the best sited line for defence with much the best field for machine-gun and rifle fire" that had hitherto been secured on the peninsula. A few days later General Hunter Weston left the scene of action, ill, and was succeeded temporarily by Lieutenant-General Sir F. Stopford, who had arrived in advance of the IXth Army Corps. This corps was on its way out from the United Kingdom, as part of large reinforcements which were being despatched somewhat belatedly to swell the Expeditionary Force. One of its divisions, the 13th, under General Shaw, arrived at Helles towards the end of the month, and for the time being relieved the 29th Division on the left of the line.

Comments.—The story of the first three months at Helles is instructive as illustrating, in the case of a campaign that originates in landing on an enemy's coast, the vital importance of gaining ground at the outset with the utmost rapidity. The Allies' front on the third day after disembarkation had commenced ran roughly from Gully Beach to De Tott's. That was not nearly far enough forward to create a situation that could be regarded as encouraging. Three months later the front ran roughly from Fusilier Bluff to the mouth of the Kerevez Valley, two miles having been gained on the left and little more than one mile on the right. The disappointing results of the operations between the 28th of April and the end of July are directly traceable to what occurred between the 25th and 27th of April.

The dispositions made for the original landing have been discussed in Chapter VII, and that point need not be referred to further here. But after a careful study of the course of events during those early months of conflict at the extremity of the Gallipoli Peninsula, it is difficult to escape from the conclusion that, had it been possible to get the infantry of a couple of divisions ashore on the first day (the 25th of April), and had the troops so landed been able to win their way forward on that same day to somewhere about the line that was not actually secured till two days later, Krithia and even possibly Achi Baba would have fallen within less than a week. For the forward thrust could have been started before the Turks had recovered from the effects of their initial defeat at the landing-places, and before they had brought up large reinforcements from the vicinity of the Narrows. We know from German accounts that two Ottoman divisions from about Bulair arrived on the 26th and 27th. It is not suggested that this would have meant a strategical success in the sense of clearing a path to Kilid Bahr. That consummation would by no means have followed as a matter of course. But the capture of the buttress of high ground stretching from shore to shore across the peninsula which faced the 29th Division and the French on the 26th and 27th of April, and which continued to face the invaders of the Helles region till they withdrew from it many months later, would have made the situation of the Allies in this area incomparably more comfortable than, in the event, it ever came to be at any time during their prolonged sojourn in that patch of Ottoman territory.

The campaign in this part of the Gallipoli Peninsula took the form of trench warfare from an early date in May, of trench warfare in which neither side was well supplied with the guns, the howitzers, the trench mortars, and the ample stores of hand grenades that have come to be regarded as indispensable for effectively prosecuting operations of this class. Invaders and invaded developed their artillery resources as time went on, but these never dominated the situation as they did on the Western and the Italian Fronts during the World War, while the Allies, and also at times their antagonists, were harassed by an insufficiency of ammunition. Reference has been made in preceding paragraphs to bombardments preparing the assaults delivered by the Allies; but these bombardments were carried out almost entirely with field guns. The British gradually brought a few field howitzers into play as the operations proceeded, and got a few 60-pounders ashore; but the French had no field howitzers, and it took a long time to get any heavier pieces of this type landed. The British gunners, moreover, were always restricted in respect to rounds, although the French were adequately supplied.

Even for the latest attack mentioned in this chapter, that of the 12th–13th July, the artillery preparation meant nothing in the slightest degree approaching to the volume of that, for instance, which had introduced the advance of the infantry at Neuve Chapelle in the preceding February, still less could it be compared to the intense bombardment which was to usher in the struggle around Loos in the following autumn. Nor did gun-fire from the warships afford much assistance, the trajectory of naval ordnance being so ill-adapted to fulfil the object of overwhelming deeply excavated trenches in anticipation of an infantry assault. Moreover, naval gun-fire almost came to an end for several weeks after the later days of May, pending the arrival of craft especially contrived with an eye to immunity from submarine attack. On the other hand, the ships' artillery did undoubtedly prove of much assistance on one or two occasions, when by its direction it enfiladed enemy trenches—as, for instance, in the case of the combat for Ghurka Bluff.

As appears from the narrative, the Turks by no means confined their activities to a passive defensive during these Helles operations. On the contrary, they almost invariably, sooner or later, hit back hard on any occasion when ground or trenches worth the keeping were wrested out of their hands. Their counter-attacks generally proved especially effective when they were delivered at once, or almost at once, and therefore before the assailants had had time to settle down in the conquered position. This was the case on the afternoon of the 28th of April, it was the case at one or two points during the combat of the 6th–8th May, and it was the case on the 4th of June, when territory that had been wrested out of the hands of the Osmanlis in masterly fashion by the French in the morning, was recovered by the enemy that same afternoon and with untoward consequences to the Allies all along the line of battle. The Helles campaign indeed teaches us an important tactical lesson in this particular connection. Some of its most conspicuous and dramatic incidents illustrate the virtue of the immediate counter-stroke in striking fashion.

Bearing in mind how successful counter-attacks delivered by the Turks on a number of occasions were owing to their having been delivered with promptitude, it is singular that the enemy's bent should have so long remained one for tarrying till nightfall before attempting to restore a situation. Those nocturnal offensives of theirs were often repeated for several nights in succession. They almost invariably failed, these belated ripostes, and there are good grounds for assuming that the Osmanlis got decidedly the worse of the deal in the majority of cases in so far as casualties were concerned. Leadership would indeed seem to have been somewhat at fault in this matter on the Turkish side. But Chapter X will show that a very different procedure was to be the order of the day during the furious encounters that were to take place in the Anzac region in the month of August. That alteration in method may have been the result of lessons somewhat slowly learnt in the theatre of operations at the extremity of the peninsula.

CHAPTER IX

THE FIRST THREE MONTHS AT ANZAC

The topographical features of the Anzac area.—Some references have already been made in Chapters V and VI to the topography of the region about Anzac and Gaba Tepe, and to that trough which extends right across the Gallipoli Peninsula from near Gaba Tepe to the vicinity of Maidos and the Straits above the Narrows. A more detailed description of some of the principal physical features of the rugged tract in which the Australasian army corps had succeeded in planting itself down as a result of the successful landing of the 25th of April, will not be out of place before proceeding to give an outline of the events in this quarter during the first three months of the land campaign. As an introduction, it will be convenient to point out how the peculiarities in the conformation of the tumbled hill mass of Sari Bair affected the military position. As will be seen from Map V (p. 168) the troops from the Antipodes had forced their way ashore at the spot where commanding spurs of this hill mass approach most nearly to the shore, and the result of this was that unless further advance was to diverge at a tangent northwards or southwards, practically along the coast, any further thrust must inevitably be directed right into these jagged, furrowed, jungle-clad uplands.

Now, as will be seen from Map V, Sari Bair takes the general form of a central ridge or spine running from south-west to north-east, starting, so to speak, from the big, pear-shaped spur to the south-east of Anzac Cove that came to be known as Lone Pine and Pine Ridge, and finishing up near the Biyuk Anafarta village. Its culminating point at Koja Chemen Tepe is situated nearly three miles to the north-east of Lone Pine. But it should also be noted that the slopes on the north-western side of the ridge are abrupt and that the spurs on that flank are generally short, while

THE ANZAC AREA

the slopes on the south-eastern side of the ridge are gentler and the spurs are elongated. These extensive spurs on the south-eastern side of the ridge and the valleys between them, moreover, run roughly north and south at an acute angle to the direction of the ridge, whereas the spurs and valleys on the other side are roughly at right angles to the ridge. A consequence of the direction and of the length of the spurs and valleys on the south-eastern side of the ridge was that, if the force at Anzac wished to advance straight across the peninsula or if it were to take a direction slightly to its right front direct for Kilia Liman, it was necessarily called upon to traverse a succession of ridges and depressions. A consequence of the general direction of the main Sari Bair ridge was that, should the force at Anzac propose to secure possession of its higher portions, Chunuk Bair and Koja Chemen Tepe (from which the Narrows and the reach of the Dardanelles immediately above them could be seen), it was almost bound to advance obliquely nearly at right angles to the direct line to Kilia Liman.

One ravine, however, and one which played a very important part in the Anzac operations, has a general direction eccentric to the rest. This is Shrapnel Gully, already mentioned in Chapter V, the upper portion of which came to be known as Monash Gully. (In this wilderness of crags and declivities and depressions it was necessary to give names to minor physical features; these came to be called after officers who had distinguished themselves in combats around them.) As will be seen on Map IV, Monash and Shrapnel Gullies run from north-east to south-west, almost in prolongation of the higher portions of the main ridge, although they are situated to the north-west of the great Lone Pine spur. This pear-shaped spur separates Monash and Shrapnel Gullies from an extensive valley situated to the east and south-east, the stalk end of the pear-shaped spur forming a neck between Monash Gully and the valley. From this neck—it came to be known as " The Neck "—the ridge keeps rising to the north-east, more or less overlooking the two gullies. The conformation of the ground about The Neck and the head of the two depressions played a very prominent part in shaping events at Anzac, owing to the troops not having secured at the outset what experience was to prove to be a point of vital tactical importance. It dominated the Shrapnel-Monash artery of traffic after a fashion, and it furnished the stage

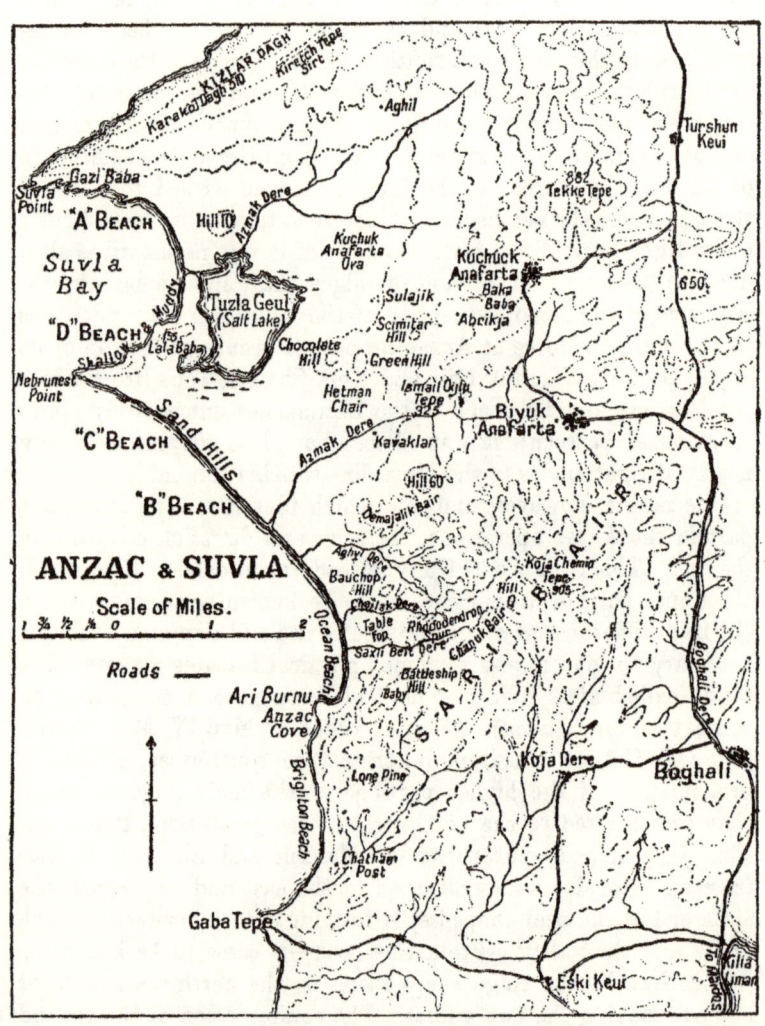

MAP V.—THE ANZAC AND SUVLA AREAS

THE ANZAC POSITION 169

for many infuriated affrays between invaders and invaded during the early weeks of the struggle.

Australian troops had made themselves masters of the slopes and under-features of Lone Pine spur almost at once, and they maintained an effective line of defence along these from the first day. The Lone Pine spur partakes, however, to some extent of the nature of a plateau, and most of it remained in the hands of the Turks. On the other side of Monash and Shrapnel Gullies there is a sharply defined ridge that runs in a direction rather south of west from The Neck towards Ari Burnu. At first it forms a narrow table-top with almost precipitous sides, which was christened Russel Top ; it then drops considerably, to rise again and form Plugge's Plateau, and from thence it falls abruptly down to the shore. To the north of this, also starting from near The Neck, a minor spur known as Walker's Ridge runs north-westwards, falling rapidly to near Ocean Beach. At the start, the left of General Birdwood's force only occupied Plugge's Plateau and part of the ridge leading thence to Russel Top ; but Walker's Ridge was taken up as the line of defence on the left flank after a day or two. It may be observed that the distance from the mouth of Shrapnel Gully up to the head of Monash Gully is fully a mile, while the upper end of the depression is barely 1000 yards as the crow flies from the nearest point of the shore. The lie of the ground in fact is such that the position taken up by the Anzac corps almost inevitably assumed the trace of a right-angle triangle, with one long side extending from near The Neck along the Shrapnel Gully side of the Lone Pine spur to Brighton Beach, and with a short side descending more abruptly from near The Neck to Ocean Beach.

The main ridge of Sari Bair mounts gradually above The Neck, with prominent bluffs at intervals marking steps, as it were, in the ascent. The nearest of these steps came to be known as Battleship Hill, further along was Chunuk Bair, then about a mile beyond Chunuk Bair the ridge after a sharp drop rises again and reaches its highest point at Koja Chemen Tepe. At the back (i.e. to the east) of the Sari Bair hill system lies a well-defined depression, the valley of a stream which passes the village of Boghali and flows into the Dardanelles a little above Kilia Liman ; along this depression runs the route from Maidos to the two Anafarta villages. To the south of Sari Bair is the trough already spoken of as marking a natural approach from Gaba Tepe to the Straits. To the northwest of the mountain stretches a plain extending to Suvla Bay, which was destined to play an important part in the campaign from August onwards; but it did not affect the course of the operations at Anzac during the first three months of the operations and need not therefore be considered here.

Events during the first few days after the 27th.—A brief lull ensued after the furious combats of the first three days. This pause was very welcome to the Anzacs, exhausted as they were with their long-drawn-out efforts; for it gave them the leisure to get thoroughly re-sorted, to draw up supplies from rear to front, and to commence the construction of systematic road communications within the conquered area. Four battalions of the Royal Naval Division and the 1st Australian Light Horse Brigade arrived as reinforcements on the 28th and 29th. This pause must, however, also have been welcome to the Turks, who cannot have been less exhausted than their antagonists at the end of the three days of continuous fighting. It afforded them an opportunity for developing their hastily improvised defences at points like The Neck and on the Lone Pine plateau and joining these up, and it in fact enabled the Ottoman forces to start a close blockade on the land side of the position held by the Australasian corps. By establishing themselves firmly on the front that they had taken up to some extent by hazard, they were enabled to confine the invaders rigidly to the cramped, tangled patch of heights which these had made themselves masters of on the opening day.

General Birdwood had contemplated a general advance on the 30th, convinced of the vital importance of extending his conquest before the enemy should have fenced him in with elaborate lines of circumvallation. The contemplated offensive had, however, to be abandoned after orders for its execution had been issued; but this change of plan appears to have been unavoidable. The truth was that he had not reserves at his disposal to restore his units to the establishment at which they had entered upon the furious contest. The 1st Australian Division had suffered very heavily, many of its battalions having shrunk almost to skeletons. No fresh troops had come to hand other than Light Horse and the four naval battalions, and these latter as it happened were very short of establishment. Serious difficulties presented themselves to anything in the nature of a general advance owing to the conformation of the ground in front of the Anzac position, because a thrust outwards meant advancing on both sides of the Sari Bair ridge and therefore created a divergent movement. To undertake such an operation with depleted forces in face of an enemy who enjoyed all the advantages of position would have been to run a serious risk, and General Birdwood was no doubt well advised when he cancelled his orders.

Apart from an almost incessant bombardment maintained by the Turkish artillery, the situation remained quiescent until the 2nd of May; but an important local offensive was undertaken on the evening of that day. Its object was to clear the head of the Monash valley of the enemy, and to secure possession of those portions of The Neck from which hostile riflemen and machine-guns —now firmly dug in—were able to fire down the ravine. The Osmanlis fought with no little spirit on this occasion. The combat lasted all night and such ground as the Anzacs succeeded in making good was only won after hard fighting. Practically every point that had been secured during the night had, moreover, to be given up again in the morning, as found to be untenable by daylight. One patch of ground that had been acquired had to be abandoned owing to destroyers mistaking their target and firing into an Australian battalion which was hard pressed at the moment—an unfortunate occurrence, illustrative of the danger of introducing gun-fire from on board ship into a hotly contested scuffle at close quarters of this kind. On the 4th a party was landed near Gaba Tepe as an experiment; it found both the beach north of the promontory (where the disembarkation had been intended to take place on the 25th), and the promontory itself, very elaborately prepared for defence.

The 2nd Australian and New Zealand Brigades were moved from Anzac to Helles on the night of the 5th, as already mentioned on page 152. This weakening of the force at Anzac rendered any offensive operation in this quarter out of the question for the time being, and there was consequently a lull for a fortnight. Both sides employed themselves busily in developing their fortifications and in adding to their artillery. But in this latter respect the Turks enjoyed a decided advantage; they managed indeed to bring a number of heavy guns and howitzers into action, with which they shelled exposed portions of the Anzac position and maintained a troublesome fire on the beach. The Australians were all this time suffering a good many casualties from snipers and from shrapnel, and on the 15th they sustained a severe loss in General Bridges, commanding the 1st Australian Division, who was mortally wounded while going his rounds. He was succeeded by General Walker. The two brigades returned from Helles on this day. In the meantime the communications were much improved and were to some extent converted into covered approaches; but the labour of conveying ammunition, food supplies, and water (especially the latter) from the shore to the high ground where the bulk of the troops were located was tremendous. The water problem may indeed be said to have remained almost acute throughout; very little was found in the area occupied, the springs dried up as the season advanced, and distribution was always a most troublesome business.[1]

The great Turkish attack upon Anzac.—On the 18th it was ascertained by aeroplane reconnaissance that a fresh division of Turks was being landed near Maidos, and that afternoon an intensive bombardment was directed upon the Anzac position, a number of heavy guns and howitzers that had not previously been located taking part in the cannonade. At midnight that night a violent musketry fire was opened by the enemy all along the line, accompanied by heavy bombing at points where the opposing trenches were in close proximity. This, however, died down for a short time, the intention of the Turks apparently being to lull the Australasian troops into a false sense of security, for at 4 a.m. a determined assault was delivered on the right centre of the Anzac position. This was beaten off, but it was taken up at other sections along the line; at one or two points Turks indeed actually reached the defenders' trenches, but they were all killed or taken. These attacks were delivered throughout in dense formation, and the assailants in consequence suffered very severe losses from musketry and machine-gun fire. The combat continued after daylight and it lasted till near noon, resulting in a complete victory for the defenders, whose losses amounted all told only to about 100 killed and

[1] It may be observed here that the Australian soldier will get on with much less drinking water than the British soldier finds necessary.

500 wounded. The enemy's casualties, on the other hand, were very high, over 3000 dead lying in the open in view of the trenches. 30,000 Turkish troops appear to have taken part in an undertaking which not merely failed completely, but which in reality greatly strengthened the position of the invaders. From that day forward no serious anxiety was ever felt as to the security of the Anzac position, except in respect to water and to communications.

During the following four days the Turks carried on negotiations for a suspension of arms with the object of burying their slain, and this was eventually assented to for the 24th. The agreement was loyally observed and great numbers of Ottoman dead, some of whom had been killed earlier than the big attack of the morning of the 19th, were interred. It may be observed here that, although a few instances of outrages did occur both at Helles and at Anzac, the Turks generally acted scrupulously in accordance with the rules of civilised warfare during the Gallipoli operations and thereby gained the respect of their antagonists.

From the 25th of May to the end of July.—The two months subsequent to this suspension of arms were signalised by only two actions of importance, which took place on the 28th of June and on the night of the 29th–30th of June respectively. Minor affairs, raids on a small scale and surprises, were constantly taking place at various points along the front; either side from time to time took the initiative, although this usually rested with the Australasian troops. The two fortified points, Pope's Hill and Quinn's Post, guarding either side of a little ravine at the head of Monash Gully were the scene of many such broils, the antagonists being at very close quarters at this point and the Turks enjoying some advantage in respect to position. Quinn's Post served as a centre of much activity ; sorties were delivered from thence on the 4th and 5th of June to distract Ottoman attention from Helles, where the attack recorded on page 157 was about to be delivered. These two localities gradually developed into very formidable little strongholds.

Other strong points along the front were the commanding Russel's Top, a salient in the line known as The Pimple which confronted a particularly elaborate hostile entrenchment system on Lone Pine plateau, and Tasman and Chatham Posts near where the extreme right of the Anzac position dropped down on to

Brighton Beach. The trenches were virtually continuous, although at one or two spots where it was impracticable to excavate there were short gaps kept closely under fire from positions near at hand in flank and in rear. The enemy, it may here be noted, enjoyed a decided superiority in artillery at this time and indeed throughout, although German accounts indicate that ammunition was scarce. It was especially in respect to suitable howitzers that General Birdwood found himself at a disadvantage; pieces of that type were wanted to search the ravines and depressions all round the Anzac position—a work for which field and mountain guns were not adapted. Moreover, in addition to the lack of artillery material under which the Australasian corps suffered, it was by no means easy to find suitable gun position within the cramped space that was available.

As the days passed, the work strenuously carried out in respect to developing communications began to bear fruit. A network of routes spread itself through the position, defiladed for the most part either by epaulments or else by being excavated so as to secure cover. The "Great Sap" shown on Map IV was run out from Anzac Cove along the foot of the spurs that rise abruptly from Ocean Beach, and by this means a sheltered highway came into being extending northwards, which proved very useful at a later date. Nor were the labours of the working parties confined to road construction. Condensing plant was set up, pumping arrangements were devised and reservoirs were prepared; but water always remained a source of anxiety.[1] Dugouts for personnel were constructed at many spots, and sheltered magazines for ammunition and supplies created. Seeing that the area in occupation of the invaders at Anzac was much more limited than was the case at Helles, and that the position was, moreover, hemmed in on a half-circle by the enemy, General Birdwood's troops suffered more from the desultory fire of the Turkish artillery than their comrades at the extremity of the peninsula. The Anzac beach was indeed particularly exposed to hostile shell-fire. Con-

[1] Water was conveyed to the peninsula from Egypt and from Malta. Some, drunk by the troops, had even been brought out as ballast from home. The demand on Malta became so heavy that the supplies nearly gave out, and in the later stages of the campaign the army depended largely on a slow-steaming tank ship which brought Nile water to the peninsula at considerable risk of being torpedoed.

sidering how frequently it was swept by the enemy projectiles it is almost surprising that more harm was not done. The weather during these early summer months, it may be added, was generally fine and favoured the landing of stores ; but the sea occasionally got up and caused interruption.

While the men from the Antipodes toiled at their positions and communications, the Turks were not idle. Always on the watch and gathered in strong force, the enemy lost no opportunities of developing his counter-works. As at Helles, the Osmanlis manifested no little skill and resource in improvising defences, in elaborating them into formidable works and in linking these up with the rear by means of covered approaches. Their trench system was especially laid out with the object of barring any advance from the Anzac position in the direction of Boghali and Kilia Liman. Lines stretched down from the higher ridges of Sari Bair along the extensive spurs that thence jut southwards and which provided natural defensive positions. The Lone Pine spur and plateau were particularly strongly fortified. The positions of the Ottoman lines of trenches were reported to the Anzac staff by aeroplane reconnaissance, and photographs were obtained ; but the British aviators found it particularly difficult to locate the enemy's gun emplacements as the scrub that covered the hill-sides and the valleys greatly favoured concealment.

Reinforcements in the shape of several mounted units without horses and of certain other corps arrived from the Nile Delta during June and served to swell the numbers of the Anzac army. The troops furnished by Australia and New Zealand were in no better plight than those recruited in the United Kingdom at first as regards being maintained at their war establishment. The grievous losses sustained during the first few days, and those undergone by the two brigades that were transferred temporarily to Helles, were not made good for some little time. But, thanks to the exertions of the Governments concerned and to the existence of substantial depots in Egypt, the failure to replace wastage did not upon the whole hamper the forces at Anzac so seriously as it did the British troops at the extremity of the peninsula during the early months of the campaign.

The combats of the 28th of June and of the night of the 29th–30th, mentioned above, although they occurred within a period of three days were not closely connected with each other. The first affair resulted from a wish expressed by Sir I. Hamilton that some activity should be displayed with the object of preventing the transfer of Turkish force to Helles on the occasion of the attack intended to take place in that area on the 28th. It took the form of a very realistic and effective demonstration. On the afternoon of the appointed day a force advanced from its trenches near Tasman Post on the extreme right of the line and occupied portions of the lower spurs of Pine Ridge. The Turks speedily brought up reinforcements from the direction of Eski Keui, moving these by roundabout routes up the valleys from the south in the hopes of the columns remaining unobserved. They were detected, however, and were subjected to a most damaging artillery fire both from the position and also from destroyers which were co-operating and were making demonstrations against Gaba Tepe. In the evening the force was quietly withdrawn to its trenches.

The combat of the night of the 29th–30th was better contested, although the result was never seriously in doubt. Soon after midnight the Turks delivered strong attacks upon the line about Quinn's Post, Pope's Hill, and Russel Top, some of the assaulting parties succeeding in forcing their way into the trenches at one or two points, only to be quickly disposed of. The assailants were in strong force and they fought with desperation, the struggle lasting till daylight; but they were ultimately beaten off at all points decisively and they suffered heavy losses. The lesson taught the enemy by the reverse suffered on this occasion, following as it did upon the bloody repulse that the onslaught of the 19th of May had met with, created a marked disinclination in the hostile ranks to commit themselves to any further efforts to expel the invaders from the position that they had won and which they had so strongly fortified. As no special object was to be gained at this time by offensive action on the part of General Birdwood's troops, the consequence was that the month of July passed quietly.

Comments.—It has been suggested in some quarters that the troops from the Antipodes planted down at Anzac served no useful purpose during the first three months of the Gallipoli campaign, beyond causing the Ottoman forces heavy losses in the Homeric encounters that took place between them. But there is no warrant for such a contention. The German and Turkish military authorities

ADVANTAGE OF HOLDING ANZAC

from the outset manifested uncommon solicitude with regard to the possibility that their opponents might contrive to force a way through to the Straits from the extensive stretches of beach that marked the coast-line north of Gaba Tepe. At the moment when the Australasians effected their landing on the 25th of April, there was a hostile army near at hand which, as we have seen, speedily confronted them in superior strength. From that time forward till the end of July the Anzacs were always containing at close quarters hostile forces at least equal in numbers to themselves, besides obliging the enemy to maintain strong reserves about Kilia Liman and Maidos. The anxiety that the Turks felt with regard to this body of invaders thrust ashore close to the narrowest portion of the peninsula, is well illustrated by the way that reinforcements were hurried up from Eski Keui on the occasion of the demonstration from about Tasman Post on the 28th of June. Once General Birdwood's corps was thoroughly dug in in its position, and after the Turks had definitely tried conclusions with it and failed, as they did on the 19th of May, some of his troops might perhaps have been transferred to Helles by night to take part in the offensive operations carried on in that quarter. But sufficient forces to alter the situation in the other arena very appreciably could not safely have been withdrawn from Anzac. Moreover, as will be seen in the next chapter, an entirely new framework of operations was to be erected on that restricted area of hilly wilderness upon which the Australians and New Zealanders had fixed their grip.

It has to be admitted that their failure to gain possession of a more extensive territory at the start exercised—as at Helles—an almost paralysing influence over the subsequent career of the troops from the Antipodes. It is not suggested that the failure was due to blameworthy errors in design and execution on the part of the force which had been emptied out, so to speak, upon a patch of abnormally awkward ground, ground that was unreconnoitred and unknown and that furthermore happened not to be the locality that the force was aiming for. Only a supernatural eye for country, for instance, would have realised the tactical significance of The Neck and of the Lone Pine plateau during the swaying conflict that took place in this bewildering terrain during the first few hours on shore. Nor, even had the tactical significance of those localities been realised, does it follow that they could have been secured and held. Nevertheless, their possession would have been of incalculable advantage to the Anzacs during the first three months of the struggle. The Neck was almost vital from the defensive point of view. Occupation of the Lone Pine plateau would have been a priceless asset from the offensive point of view. It was only after the Turks had dug themselves in and after the situation had settled itself that the value of such points became apparent.

Those parties of gallant Australians of the 3rd and 2nd Brigades referred to on page 96, who pressed on unsupported into the heart of the hills after the first rush and were never heard of again, no doubt blundered. But, none the less, quite apart from their eagerness to close with the foe, they were animated by a sound instinct —the craving for elbow-room. In the case of effecting a landing in presence of the enemy you have got to grab as much ground as you can before you are brought up short by gathering hostile strength. You are without artillery and you are likely to remain so for some hours. The enemy is almost bound to be taken by surprise to some extent, as until the boats head for the shore he does not know where you mean to land. If you do not occupy an adequate area at the start you may never have another chance. There is perhaps no strategical and tactical situation arising in war that demands more imperatively that hay shall be made while the sun shines. Commander, staff, subordinate leaders, rank and file, everybody, ought to be thoroughly imbued with that idea when they are committed to an enterprise of this character. The principle is fundamental. Its recognition on all hands is likely to prove the keystone of success.

The speed with which, within a very few weeks of their arrival on the shores of the Gallipoli Peninsula, the Australians and New Zealanders transformed themselves out of a body of relatively raw troops into a soldiery of the very highest class, is a signal illustration of the value of experience in presence of the enemy to newly created contingents of fighting men—especially if those fighting men be endowed by nature with martial qualities of a high order. From the many vivid accounts of the performances of these recently constituted battalions and batteries and engineer companies that have appeared, it is evident that their efficiency increased by leaps and bounds during their early days at Anzac,

HILL TERRAIN AND ARTILLERY TARGETS 179

owing to their close contact with gallant and skilfully handled foemen—this, moreover, in spite of the fact that many of the most brilliant of the officers and men had gone down in the bitter combats of the first few days. The troops from the Antipodes who watched the Turkish burying parties carrying out their gruesome task on the 24th of May, were no longer troops to fall into such confusion as occurred on the 25th of April and who consequently very nearly had that night to abandon what had been so bravely won. They would have retained their cohesion instinctively in spite of difficulties caused by awkward ground, by strange surroundings and by the grim resistance that was being encountered. Within one single month they had learnt their job.

One other point deserves a brief reference. A hilly terrain is wont to provide particularly inviting targets for the artillery arm under certain conditions. This is because the ground, so to speak, stands up facing the batteries and thereby at once favours observation of fire and assists the gun-layers. This, however, only holds good when slopes and crests present comparatively smooth surfaces, and when the topographical features are moulded on grand lines. When the ground is, on the contrary, rocky and clothed in scrub, when the hill-features—as was the case at Anzac—are framed on a small scale and are tangled and intricate, the conditions are unfavourable for artillerists. The guns of the warships were most helpful to the Australasian troops on shore on several occasions ; but the task of those directing their fire was a very anxious one as a rule. Owing to the nature and the configuration of the ground that the troops were engaged on, it was very difficult to distinguish from aboard ship what exactly was going on—the more so seeing that the affrays were generally fought out at close quarters. The Turks also were able to hide their reserves in the elongated valleys that run north and south at the back of the main Sari Bair ridge. These valleys could not be seen into or searched by gunners in vessels lying west of Anzac, and they could only be seen into very partially and enfiladed to a limited extent from ships stationed off Gaba Tepe and to the south of that promontory.

But in discussing the work of artillery whether ashore or afloat there is always this to be said : The value of guns to a side is not wholly material. Their effect is not alone to be judged by the actual havoc that their shell cause in the hostile ranks. Their influence is also moral, and on many occasions at Anzac the mere fact that naval projectiles were flying overhead gave welcome encouragement to General Birdwood's men, even though the damage that they were doing to the Turks at the moment may have been inconsiderable.

Ought the fleet to have given more assistance with its artillery than it did after May? The above remarks suggest consideration of a question that has been raised as to the attitude of the naval authorities on the spot after the German U-boats appeared on the scene. It has been suggested in some quarters—notably by Mr. E. Dane in his informative work *British Campaigns in the Near East*—that in spite of the disasters to *Triumph* and *Majestic* the battleships and cruisers ought to have continued hanging about off the shores of Helles and Anzac aiding the army with the fire of their guns, that they ought to have risked being sent to the bottom by hostile torpedoes instead of thenceforward remaining as a rule behind nets in Mudros Bay. It may be remarked that ships must anchor or else must cruise very slowly if they are to do the slightest good with their gun-fire at targets ashore, and that under such circumstances they are particularly liable to come to grief if hostile submarines are about. Still there might be something to be said for accepting the risk if their support were of any great value to the troops on shore, especially as the Dardanelles fleet consisted so largely of almost obsolete vessels. But even if the vessels were of no great value the crews were of the highest class and were almost irreplaceable, and the truth of the matter is that naval artillery fire, even from monster guns, is not particularly effective when directed against an enemy on shore. The ordnance is not of the right sort, the business is not properly understood by those directing the gunnery, and establishment of that close cooperation between the artillery and the infantry, dependent on forward or overhead observation, which is the very basis of latter-day tactics on land, is virtually impracticable—certainly as regards forward observation.

Even with well-defined targets to practise at, their positions accurately marked on large-scale maps, the naval bombardments of the batteries defending the entrance to the Straits and guarding the Narrows had caused very little damage at the cost of a heavy expenditure of ammunition. The task of the naval gunners at a

EMPLOYMENT OF WARSHIPS

later stage became a far more difficult one, except on a few special occasions where there happened to be some conspicuous object to fire at, and when the exact position of the friendly troops near that object was known. Such situations did not, and could not, often arise, the more so as Marshal Liman von Sanders, who realised the difficulties under which warships labour in this sort of work, gave special instructions that the Turks should always try to establish their trenches as close to those of the invaders as possible. Nothing hampers the artillerist more than the fear of shelling his own side. The theory that constant support from the warships would have greatly aided the army in its operations is based on a misconception.

Nor should it be forgotten in this connection that the sinking of one of the Allies' warships would be bound to give great encouragement to the enemy. *Triumph* and *Majestic* were sent to the bottom in broad daylight in full view of the Turkish trenches. German and American accounts make it quite clear that those events caused great enthusiasm, not only in the Ottoman lines near the Dardanelles but also in Constantinople, following as they did on the successful night attack upon *Goliath* within the Straits.

CHAPTER X

POSSIBILITIES OF SUCCESS

The impossibility of achieving the object with the forces available.—Already early in May it had become manifest that the campaign undertaken by the Allies in the Gallipoli Peninsula was bound to prove a failure, unless the strength of the force which had been originally detailed for the enterprise and which had initiated the venture was to be substantially increased. Foiled as it had been in its attempt to acquire domination over the Narrows of the Dardanelles by a sudden descent upon the enemy's shores, brought to a standstill by a hostile array superior in numbers to itself and better equipped with guns and howitzers, the expeditionary army could not hope to accomplish its purpose without considerable reinforcements. If any uncertainty had been entertained on the point after the troops at Helles, although reinforced from Anzac, had been unable to gain more than a few hundred yards by their determined offensive of the 6th–8th May, doubt must have been dispelled by the combat of the 4th of June and by the stalemate at Anzac following on the great Turkish effort of the 19th of May. A good deal of perplexity always existed as to the numerical strength of the Ottoman army, even if the number of divisions and their approximate distribution in the immediate theatre of operations was usually known. Still it could be foreseen that this army would grow as time went on and as Ottoman resources about the heart of the Empire were developed under German guidance.

The Commander-in-Chief was under no illusions as to his prospects. He realised that, as matters stood during May and June, the odds against him were too great to justify his indulging in any hopes of a strategical triumph with the army then at his disposal. So early as the 10th of May he had cabled home asking for two more divisions; and a week later, apprised in the meantime that no assistance was to be expected from the Russians even in the indeterminate shape of threats to Constantinople from across the Black Sea, he followed this message up with another requesting that two additional army corps should be sent him. But although arrangements were at once made by the War Office in London to ship the 52nd Division to the Ægean—as we have seen on page 158, it arrived early in June—it was not until June that the Home Government decided to send out the further troops that Sir I. Hamilton had asked for. The course of events on the peninsula during the three weeks following his second message had indeed shown almost conclusively that it had become a question between withdrawing the Expeditionary Force, with all the dangers military and political which such a course involved, and complying with the demands of the man on the spot. The delay of the British Government in arriving at a decision appears to have been to some extent due to a political crisis, the "Coalition Government" replacing the Liberal Government previously in power.

The reinforcements.—Sir I. Hamilton was informed that his army was to be augmented by three complete divisions and by the infantry of two more Territorial divisions, all of them coming from the United Kingdom. They were timed to arrive between the 10th of July and the 10th of August—a striking illustration of the number of days needed to embark and to move a force of all arms, mustering considerably less than 100,000 men, oversea on a fortnight's voyage. The new divisions actually selected were the 10th, 11th, and 13th (which latter it will be remembered was utilised at Helles at the end of July) belonging to the "New Army," together with the 53rd (Welsh) and 54th (East Anglian) belonging to the Territorial Forces; the accession of these additional troops would raise the strength of the expeditionary army to thirteen divisions,[1] besides the Indian brigade and four Anzac mounted brigades.[2] The infantry composing thirteen divisions and five independent brigades would on paper represent about 160,000 bayonets. But, as has already been indicated, the infantry (and especially the Territorial infantry) was almost always short of establishment when it joined. Drafts were invariably seriously in arrear. Some of the divisions had

---

[1] The 10th, 11th, 13th, 29th, 42nd, 52nd, 53rd, 54th Royal Naval, 1st Australian, Australian and New Zealand, 1st French and 2nd French.
[2] For order of battle, see Appendix II.

not their proper complement of twelve or thirteen battalions even on paper. In actual practice Sir I. Hamilton apparently never had more than about 110,000 bayonets under his orders, and he only had that number for a very few days.

His chances of success were, moreover, prejudiced by the fact that the whole of the reinforcements were not to be available until so late a date as the 10th of August, three and a half months after the successful landing of the 25th of April. Although the Allies were assailing the Ottoman Empire very near its heart, the enemy's facilities for despatching troops, munitions, and food supplies to the point of danger were limited; the extent to which this was the case has been already explained on pages 133 to 135. Time therefore meant much. Could the additional contingents from the United Kingdom have arrived several weeks earlier, there would have been a strong probability of their forestalling the Turks in respect to assembling a preponderance of force in the peninsula. The question of the despatch of British forces from the United Kingdom to the Ægean in the early summer of 1915, however, depended upon a variety of strategical considerations, amongst which Sir I. Hamilton's requirements only represented one item. It is not proposed to discuss the merits of the attitude taken up by the Home Government in this matter; but, not to mention the fact that the delay in sending out the additional troops to the Dardanelles was detrimental to the prospects of securing possession of them, would not be justifiable in a record of the campaign for the Straits.

Sir I. Hamilton's appreciation.—Once he had been made aware of the forces that he could reckon upon, Sir I. Hamilton was in a position to frame his plans, and in the despatch written on laying down his command in the following October he summarises the situation as it presented itself to him at this time.

" Eliminating the impracticable," he writes, " I had already narrowed down the methods of employing these fresh forces to one of the following four :

    (a) Every man to be thrown on the southern sector of the peninsula to force a way forward to the Narrows.

    (b) Disembarkation on the Asiatic side of the Straits, followed by a march on Chanak.

SIR I. HAMILTON'S PLAN

(c) A landing at Enos or Ebrije for the purpose of seizing the neck of the Isthmus of Bulair.

(d) Reinforcement of the Australian and New Zealand Army Corps, combined with a landing in Suvla Bay. Then with a strong push to capture Hill 305,[1] and, working from that dominating point, to grip the waist of the peninsula."

He goes on to explain that he rejected the first alternative because there was not room enough for a large force, because of the special defences erected for the security of Achi Baba, and because any landing on the coast south of Gaba Tepe at the narrowest point of the peninsula would have to be carried out under artillery fire from Achi Baba and the Kilid Bahr plateau.

The objection to the second alternative was that there would not be troops enough for a serious undertaking on the Asiatic side unless the force actually on the peninsula was to be reduced to a strength that would render it incapable of effective operations. The Commander-in-Chief admits that the project of an advance on the Asiatic side was from some points of view attractive. He does not discuss the possibility of making such an advance the main operation; but in this he was probably influenced to some extent by the consideration that, as pointed out on page 41, such a plan would have involved the employment of a large amount of transport.

The arguments that could be adduced against the scheme of a landing north of the Gulf of Saros were that the landing-places were unsatisfactory; that Admiral de Robeck objected strongly to disembarking troops at so great a distance from the concentration points, Mudros and Imbros, and under conditions exposing the transports and covering ships so much to submarine attack; and that, even supposing a force landed successfully and after overcoming such opposition as might be met with securing possession of the Bulair Isthmus, it did not follow that the enemy would abandon opposition to naval passage of the Dardanelles. To cut the Turkish communications in the peninsula, artillery fire must be brought to bear upon those communications whether they were by land or were by water.

Sir Ian therefore decided in favour of the fourth alternative, that of capturing Sari Bair and effecting a landing in Suvla Bay

[1] Koja Chemen Tepe, the culminating point of Sari Bair.

simultaneously, and in his appreciation he goes into his reasons for coming to this conclusion fully. He hoped by means of a vigorous offensive from Anzac, combined with a surprise landing to the north of it, to win through to Maidos, leaving behind him a well-protected line of communications starting from Suvla Bay. This inlet would provide a submarine-proof base, only a mile further from the islands than Anzac, and affording satisfactory shelter against bad weather except from the west and south-west. He realised the difficulties that broken country and lack of water might create, but " it can only be said that a bad country is better than an entrenched country, and that supply and water problems may be countered by careful preparation." As his plan involved landing large numbers at Anzac without the enemy becoming aware of it, as well as surprise disembarkation at Suvla Bay in the dark, it was necessary to deliver the stroke during the short period when the moon was hidden ; and, as the bulk of the reinforcements would be available by that time, the dark nights early in August were selected for the undertaking.

Comments.—It will be more convenient to comment on the actual plan that was adopted when the operations come to be narrated. But there are one or two points in connection with the discarded alternatives that invite a few observations. Sir I. Hamilton seems to have considered the possibility of effecting landings south of Gaba Tepe, although he rejected such a plan of operations for fear of artillery fire ; the idea has generally prevailed that there were no suitable landing-places anywhere between Gaba Tepe and Gully Beach, but reconnaissance may have proved this to be an error. If practicable beaches really existed, that fact would strengthen the arguments in favour of the whole of the Expeditionary Force having been put ashore on the western coast of the peninsula at its " waist " at the start. The plan of landing at Ebrije or Enos was undoubtedly, as the Commander-in-Chief expressed it, " a better scheme on paper than on the spot." It was just the kind of project to commend itself to a body like the " Dardanelles Committee " sitting at 10 Downing Street. There can be no doubt that the seizure of the Isthmus of Bulair would have caused the Turks great inconvenience, even if no attempt had been made to force the lines and press southwards ; the enemy constructed a road during the campaign along the shore of the isthmus on the inner side, where traffic could not be molested by the Allies' warships owing to the intervening high ground. But a plan on such lines would have meant further dispersion of force, the matter has already been discussed on pages 38 and 39, and in any case the naval objections were conclusive. Sir I. Hamilton no doubt gave serious consideration to the possibilities of making the Asiatic side of the Straits his main theatre of operations, although he did not discuss the merits of such a disposition of forces in his despatch. A plan of campaign on these lines always found some supporters, especially among the French; but the objections to it were very strong. It would have been difficult to withdraw any considerable force from the peninsula to swell the numbers of the five divisions that were coming as reinforcements. The Anzacs, clinging to their singular position, were doing invaluable work in containing great numbers of Turks; for the enemy could not afford to run risks at this point, with antagonists not six miles from Kilia Liman; a brigade or two of General Birdwood's force might have been withdrawn for service elsewhere, but not more than that. Troops could no doubt have been spared from Helles, where there were nominally six divisions; but it would have been dangerous to remove more than two out of the six. By adopting an almost purely defensive attitude on the peninsula, the Commander-in-Chief might in fact possibly have transferred three divisions to the Asiatic coast, creating an army of eight divisions for an effort on that side.

Operations based on Besika and Yukyeri Bays have already been discussed in Chapter IV, and the drawbacks to such a plan of campaign from the point of view of a sudden stroke have been indicated. There could be no question of a sudden stroke now, and, even assuming that there would have been awkward defences to overcome at the landing-places, a more or less formal military advance on this side of the Dardanelles would no doubt have been feasible. But the distance to be covered to the Narrows was far greater than that from Helles or Anzac or Suvla, there was no position on the Asiatic side that commanded the defile as the Kilid Bahr plateau did, and a more or less direct move from Besika and Yukyeri Bays towards Chanak did not threaten Turkish communications as an advance from Anzac or Suvla Bay on Maidos did. Had ten divisions been joining the Allied army instead of five, four or five of them might well have been landed on the Asiatic side as a secondary operation. That would have greatly worried the Turks, have drawn off some of their numbers from the peninsula, and have decidedly improved the position of the troops at Helles. As it was, there was very little to be said for starting such an undertaking.

The Expeditionary Force's weakness in artillery.—It may not be out of place to refer here to what undoubtedly was one of the contributory causes to bringing about the failure of the Dardanelles venture. Sir I. Hamilton's army was very badly off for artillery—not so much perhaps in regard to actual number of guns placed in the field, taking the peculiar conditions of the campaign into consideration, as in regard to the nature of the ordnance employed and in regard to the volume of ammunition placed at the disposal of the batteries. There were obvious administrative objections to the getting together of a great assemblage of guns in arenas of operations such as Helles and Anzac. The demands involved on ship-tonnage, the problem of horses and of their forage and their water on shore, the lack of sites for batteries within the Anzac position, the landing difficulties in respect to disembarking heavy ordnance, all these considerations dictated a reduction of pieces to a minimum. But, on the other hand, that being the case, it became all the more imperative, if there was a limit on the number of guns and howitzers, to ensure that the right types were allotted and that those employed should have ample stores of ammunition at their disposal.

The insufficiency of field howitzers was undoubtedly a serious impediment to success. Tactical operations in the Sari Bair hill mass demanded the comprehensive searching of gullies and the sweeping of steep, reverse slopes with shell, and neither field guns nor the armament of warships was adapted for work of that kind. The Turks, moreover, had evolved deeply sunken trench systems alike at Helles and at Anzac, and to make defences of that character untenable howitzers of some sort were almost indispensable. Owing to the nature of the terrain and to transport difficulties, field howitzers were the class of ordnance especially desirable ; but a very few medium howitzers would also have been a great boon to the invading army. A few, old pattern, 6-inch guns provided by the French and mounted on the right flank of the Helles area

WEAKNESS IN ARTILLERY

proved very useful for counter-battering work across the Straits, and the few 60-pounders landed did good service of the same kind; but searching fire was lacking.[1]

In so far as field guns were concerned, the army was reasonably well fitted out with this form of artillery from June onwards, even in spite of the Territorial divisions in some cases having none; but the ammunition allowance was inadequate throughout. It had been almost inevitable that the Allies should be short of guns in the early days, even had large numbers been detailed to form part of the Expeditionary Force, and in the fights of April and of May a want of guns was much felt. But that would always be likely to occur in the case of a maritime descent upon an enemy's shores. It is at the start that landing difficulties are most troublesome, and in April and May several batteries were kept in Egypt waiting for ship-transport and for the development of jetties, and so forth, at the beaches. But such obstacles had been pretty well overcome before the August operations were initiated, and there would then have been no difficulty in disembarking and in distributing an abundance of ammunition. At the end of July there were 124 guns at Helles and about 70 guns at Anzac, these latter in many cases emplaced in very inconvenient position owing to lack of space and of suitable localities.

As regards trench mortars it should be remembered that weapons of this kind were still in their infancy in the first half of 1915. The improved types of this form of armament that made their appearance in later stages of the European War would have been invaluable in the Gallipoli Peninsula. The opposing trenches were very adjacent to each other, and, in view of topographical conditions, mobility and lightness were almost a *sine qua non* in the case of any war material that was to be employed in such a theatre of war.

Aviation.—A word will not be out of place here as to air-work during the early months of the campaign, and as to the general position in respect to aviation at the end of July when Sir I. Hamilton was giving the finishing touches to his plan for a great offensive in the coming month. Although the Royal Navy had

---

[1] A brigade of field howitzers was sent out from the United Kingdom at the last moment under special arrangements late in July, proceeding to Marseilles by rail and being shipped on from thence; but it arrived too late for the critical opening days of the August offensive.

employed aeroplanes with a fair measure of success for " spotting " operations during the attacks of the warships on the Dardanelles defences in March, and although airmen had carried out some extremely informative reconnaissances before the April landings, aviation hardly played a very important part in the conduct of the struggle on the peninsula during the first three months. But, as the weeks passed, a moderate number of machines, British and French, gradually came upon the scene and made Tenedos their home. That island, however, gradually came to be looked upon more and more as a French preserve, as Imbros became more and more suitable for an advanced base on its harbour being made secure; and so, towards the end of June, an aerodrome was established at Imbros for the British air service. By the end of July there were about sixty British planes there, and the French had about twenty at Tenedos. Half would generally be available at any one time.

The British airmen from the outset performed excellent service in the way of reconnaissance and bomb-dropping; but it took the naval flyers time to master the art of effective co-operation with the artillery on shore, a service that was new to them. Another weak point about this service was the lack of fighting machines. Owing to this it was not easy to prevent the enemy from carrying out raids with their large planes for the purpose of observation and of bomb-dropping. Hostile machines would appear very suddenly, and they occasionally dropped bombs on Imbros and even so far away from home as Mudros. Some small airships used for naval service also had their hangar at Imbros; they were employed chiefly to look out for enemy submarines in the waters traversed by shipping connected with the operations. The atmospheric conditions, it may be observed, were almost ideal for aeronautics during the summer about the Ægean. Skies were generally unclouded, the weather was calm, and visibility left little to be desired. The nature of the terrain on the Gallipoli Peninsula rendered concealment very easy owing to the rocks and the scrub. Allied aviators found it very difficult to locate enemy guns, and the hostile flyers no doubt experienced similar difficulty in detecting the artillery positions at Anzac and Helles.

The naval position.—Reference has been made in earlier chapters to the subject of the submarine menace and to its effect upon the activities of the Allies' fleets. No sooner had it become obvious that German and Austro-Hungarian under-water craft were likely to hamper the work of battleships and cruisers very seriously, than steps were taken by the British Admiralty to despatch some shallow-draught monitors, carrying very heavy ordnance, to the Ægean. The sides of these vessels bulged out a distance of about ten feet below the waterline, making a protective waist-belt in the event of a hit by a torpedo ; this, if it gave security, necessarily reduced their speed considerably. Three old cruisers, *Endymion*, *Talbot* and *Theseus*, were treated in like fashion as to equipment with the protective waist-belt. Most of these freak craft had become available before Sir I. Hamilton launched his August offensive, and they performed useful service during those operations and subsequently. But it stands to reason that a limited number of such vessels, aided by destroyers, did not represent the aggregate of gun-power that the imposing armada of great warships which had co-operated with the land operations at the time of the first landings had boasted of, and that, in so far as naval artillery support can be made effective in such cases, the army was less well supported than it had been in April and May. Such German accounts as have appeared of the Dardanelles campaign always lay the utmost stress upon the aid that naval forces afforded to the British and French troops, and they suggest that these troops always had the support of a great fleet of the most powerful ships of war. But owing to the submarines that was not the case subsequently to the month of May.

British submarines, handled with rare daring and skill, were managing occasionally to pass up the Dardanelles in spite of minefields and other obstacles, and to reach the Sea of Marmora ; but it was always a most difficult and hazardous operation. These raids were of the utmost service to the army ashore in that they harassed the enemy's water communications. On the 8th of August the old Turkish ironclad *Barbaroussa* together with a torpedo-boat were sunk above the Narrows. But a much more sustained and continuous effort would have been necessary to bring about serious interruption of the traffic across the Straits from about Chanak, or absolutely to have put an end to the despatch of supplies and warlike stores from the Golden Horn in small vessels to Marshal Liman von Sanders' army in the peninsula.

CHAPTER XI

THE GREAT EFFORT OF EARLY AUGUST

Sir I. Hamilton's plan in outline.—The general scheme of operations which the Commander-in-Chief had decided to carry into effect as soon as his reinforcements were all on the spot comprised three distinct, but interdependent, undertakings. They may be indicated in outline as follows :—

The most important of the three sets of operations consisted of an attack to be carried out from Anzac upon the Sari Bair mountain, with the object of securing its topmost ridges, from which the Dardanelles were visible and the possession of which would provide observation posts enabling artillery to be directed upon the communications of the Turkish forces guarding the Narrows on the European side. The capture of these dominating ridges would, moreover, be a first step towards accomplishing a thrust eastwards and south-eastwards, which would carry the troops from Anzac to Kilia Liman, to Maidos, and to the Kilid Bahr plateau. Against a direct advance being undertaken by General Birdwood from the position that he held as against those three points, his adversaries were well prepared, alike in respect to disposition of available troops and to alignment of entrenchments. His plan of action, which was accepted by Sir I. Hamilton, was therefore to strike at the Turks from a direction that they would not anticipate attack from, to move out from his Anzac position northwards near the shore and then to wheel to the right and assail Sari Bair on the side where its slopes were abruptest, viz. the north-west; the operation was to be a surprise and must therefore be carried out by night. But although the bulk of the forces under his orders were to be detailed for this enterprise, attacks were also to be delivered from Anzac against the hostile positions extending from The Neck to the Lone Pine plateau, partly with the object of

SIR I. HAMILTON'S PLAN

occupying the attention of the enemy, but partly also for the purpose of gaining ground on that side, as a preliminary to further advance should the assault of the higher ridges of Sari Bair prove successful. To carry out this set of operations General Birdwood's force was strengthened by the addition of the 13th Division from Helles and of the 29th Brigade of the 10th Division which had newly arrived in the war zone, bringing it up to a total of approximately 37,000 rifles, with 72 guns. He was to be supported by two cruisers, four monitors, and two destroyers.

Of almost equal importance with the task to be undertaken by the troops at Anzac was the project for landing a fresh force in and near Suvla Bay, with the twofold object of securing a new base and of throwing forward a force on General Birdwood's left to co-operate in his offensive. There was every reason to believe that the enemy forces near the bay, and occupying the hills looking down on the flats that stretch eastwards from the bay, were not formidable. The landing was to be a surprise and was therefore to be carried out by the bulk of the infantry by night, the design being kept secret from all except the principal officers concerned until the last moment. The date was dependent to some extent on the moon; this, in its last quarter, rose so late as 2 a.m. in the morning on the 7th August, and the night of the 6th/7th was therefore selected as the earliest; this indeed fixed the date of the offensive as a whole. Sir F. Stopford was to be in command, and his troops were to consist of the 10th Division, less the 29th Brigade, and the 11th Division. The 11th Division was assembled at Imbros; but the 10th Division was awaiting the move to the peninsula partly at Mitylene (six battalions) and partly at Mudros (three battalions), and the Royal Navy thus had to arrange to bring considerable bodies of troops from three different points, respectively 15 miles, 60 miles, and 120 miles from the point of disembarkation, and to get them all ashore within a few hours of each other.

The third of the three undertakings comprised in the Commander-in-Chief's general scheme of operations was an attack to be delivered by the force at Helles. Its primary purpose was to hinder the enemy from sending any troops from that area to aid those defending Sari Bair; but the Higher Command also hoped that ground would be gained by the attack and that the front would be improved locally in consequence,

It was recognised that the Turks were bound to learn that large British reinforcements were arriving in the islands, and special steps were therefore taken to hoodwink the enemy and to deceive Liman von Sanders and his staff as to the plan that was actually in contemplation. A surprise landing of a small force was carried out on the northern shore of the Gulf of Saros. The arrival of part of the 10th Division at Mitylene served as a diversion in itself, and the effect of this was increased by demonstrations on the part of French warships against the Anatolian coast opposite the island ; Sir I. Hamilton and Admiral de Robeck, moreover, made a parade of an inspection of its environs. Soundings and the registration of guns were also carried out by monitors along the littoral south of Gaba Tepe—operations which served their purpose, for we know from the German account that the enemy diverted a couple of regiments to the neighbourhood before it was discovered that the affair was merely a feint. Reports were spread by the Intelligence Department calculated to deceive the opposing side, and there is reason to believe that the sum of these various devices proved effective in misleading the defenders of the peninsula as to the Allies' plan up to the last moment. In giving a brief account of the very remarkable series of operations carried out in prosecution of Sir I. Hamilton's design, it will be convenient to dispose first of the fighting that took place at Helles, seeing that this presents no points of any special interest as illustrating the art of war. But before doing so it is necessary to indicate the distribution and dispositions of the Ottoman forces at this important juncture of the campaign, in so far as these are known at the present time.

The Turkish disposition of force at the beginning of August.—Although the General Headquarters Staff of the Allies was probably fairly well acquainted with the " Order of Battle " of the Ottoman army and with the disposition of its various divisions, few details on this subject have as yet appeared in published narratives of the campaign. There is reason to believe that at the beginning of August there were more than a dozen Turkish divisions on the spot, but only the following have been definitely indicated as being located within the area : the 3rd, 4th, 5th, 7th, 8th, 9th, 11th, 12th, 15th and 19th, together with one or two others referred to by the name of their German commander. Only some of these are mentioned in the accounts of actual combats and it is therefore

DISTRIBUTION OF TURKISH FORCES

difficult to identify the position of most of them. We, however, know that Marshal Liman von Sanders always had two groups, a "Northern Group" facing Anzac, and a "Southern Group" facing Helles, and that in addition to these there was a special group up in the north about Bulair. No general reserve about Maidos is mentioned; but it is remarkable that we find the 4th Division to have been transferred from the Southern to the Northern Group late, if not after dark, on the 6th and yet to have arrived on Sari Bair early on the following day, and this seems to suggest that part of the Southern Group was stationed about Maidos and not immediately fronting Helles.

At the time when the important August operations began, we know that the 9th Division was facing Anzac and that, as mentioned above, the 4th Division was in a position to be moved to Sari Bair at short notice. The only other divisions of which the position is indicated were the 7th and 12th which were near Bulair. A German major had been especially looking to the defence works about Suvla Bay; but according to enemy accounts there were only three battalions and some artillery in that part of the zone of operations, two of the battalions being gendarmerie.

The combats at Helles.—The great offensive on the Gallipoli Peninsula was to commence on the 6th of August and during the following night. On the afternoon of that day an attack was delivered on a section of about 1200 yards of the Turkish trenches near the centre of the enemy's Helles front, coupled with minor thrusts more to the left. Some little ground was gained on the left at the outset; but the defenders were found to be in unexpected force all along the front, the trenches as well as the communications leading to them from in rear were crammed with troops, and the resistance was marked by the utmost determination. The consequence was that the main British attack was repulsed; and certain short lengths of hostile trench that had been secured on the left at the start had perforce to be abandoned during the night in face of the heavy counter-attacks of the Osmanlis. It turned out that the Turks had themselves been just about to launch an offensive, when they were forestalled, and that two new divisions had very recently arrived to relieve two others that had been roughly handled in previous encounters.

Next morning the Turks in their turn embarked on an offensive;

but their assaulting troops were beaten off with no great difficulty, and portions of the 42nd and 52nd Divisions thereupon advanced afresh to the attack. This led to very severe fighting. Ground was as usual gained at the first rush, but what was won at the outset had speedily to be relinquished owing to the prompt and fierce Turkish counter-strokes, all except a certain vineyard west of the Krithia road which was held unyieldingly in spite of all efforts of the enemy to reconquer it. On the day following Lieutenant-General Sir F. J. Davies arrived, and he took over command at Helles while the conflict for the vineyard was still in progress. On the 9th activity by both sides was somewhat relaxed, but on the night of the 12th–13th the enemy succeeded by a sudden onset in wresting the vineyard from the troops that were holding it. This Ottoman success was, however, short lived, because next day the bone of contention was retaken by the British and thenceforward it remained in their hands.

Such advantages as had been gained by the Allies in this Helles fighting represented so little in themselves that the combats of the 6th–8th of August could only have been regarded as a reverse, but for the influence that the outbreak of activity at the extremity of the peninsula probably exerted upon the course of events further north. Sir I. Hamilton claims that Turkish reinforcements were actually drawn south to aid in holding the Krithia-Achi Baba position. This does not quite fit in with the German story that the 4th Turkish Division was transferred from the Southern to the Northern Group as a consequence of the operations from the side of Anzac, and that the transfer was carried out in spite of the remonstrances of General Weber commanding the Southern Group. But it is reasonable to suppose that the Helles attacks at all events prevented any more Ottoman troops being withdrawn, and it is likely enough that the transfer of the 4th Turkish Division was merely a nominal arrangement, that division being located in reality near Anzac, while reserves were being drawn down from about Maidos to reinforce the enemy's forces actually engaged about Krithia.

Seeing that they must have had a shrewd idea that their task was only a subsidiary one, the Lancashire and Lowland Territorials had acquitted themselves admirably in these affairs. That the actual successes in respect to gaining ground were not more marked

PREPARATIONS AT ANZAC 197

can probably be attributed largely to the want of really effective artillery preparation. The entrenchments to be assailed had been developed from day to day for weeks past—indeed almost for months past. The Osmanli bent for elaborating earthworks, furnished with head-cover and laboriously scooped out to a considerable depth underground, had been a feature in the Turkish mode of making war since dates long before the German General Staff came upon the scene within the Sultan's dominions. Searching howitzer fire—and plenty of it—was needed to pave the way for an infantry triumph over obstacles so formidable. In view of the observations regarding counter-attacks on page 165, the success of the Turkish counter-strokes on the night of the 6th-7th and on the 7th should be noted.

The operations from Anzac. Preparations.—The problem which General Birdwood had to solve was not merely one of tactics. He and his staff had also to devise such arrangements that the fact that his force was being substantially augmented should remain unknown to the enemy. They had furthermore to provide for the new arrivals, and had to accumulate food, ammunition, and water in conformity with the tactical plan about to be carried into execution.

" All the work," writes Sir I. Hamilton in his final despatch, " was done by Australian and New Zealand soldiers almost entirely by night, and the uncomplaining efforts of these much-tried troops in preparations are in a sense as much to their credit as their heroism in the battles that followed. Above all, the water problem caused anxiety to the Admiral, to Lieutenant-General Birdwood and to myself. The troops to advance from Suvla Bay across the Anafarta valley might reckon on finding some wells—it was certain, at least, that no water was waiting for us on the ridges of Sari Bair. Therefore, first, several days' supply had to be stocked into tanks along the beach and thence pumped up into other tanks half-way up the mountains ; secondly, a system of mule transport had to be worked out, so that, in so far as was humanly possible, thirst should not be allowed to overcome the troops after they had overcome the difficulties of the country and the resistance of the enemy.

" On the nights of the 4th, 5th and 6th of August the reinforcing troops were shipped into Anzac very silently at the darkest hours. Then, still silently, they were tucked away from enemy's aeroplanes or observatories in their prepared hiding-places. The whole sea route lay open to the view of the Turks upon Achi Baba's summit and Battleship Hill. Aeroplanes could count every tent and every ship at Mudros or at Imbros. Within rifle fire of Anzac's open beach hostile riflemen were looking out across the Ægean no more than twenty feet from our opposing lines. Every modern appliance of telescope, telegraph, wireless, was at the disposal of the enemy. Yet the instructions worked out at General Headquarters in the minutest detail (the result of conferences with the Royal Navy, which were attended by Brigadier-General Skene of General Birdwood's staff) were such that the scheme was carried out without a hitch. The preparation of the ambush was treated as a simple matter by the services therein engaged, and yet I much doubt whether any more pregnant enterprise than this of landing so large a force under the very eyes of the enemy, and of keeping them concealed there three days, is recorded in the annals of war."

The troops thus gathered together in the restricted Anzac position were to assume the offensive on the 6th and on the following night; the Helles operations commenced, it will be remembered, on the afternoon of the 6th. German accounts of the operations suggest that the enemy remained wholly unaware of the great accessions to the strength of the Anzac army until their presence was made apparent in the fighting that ensued.

The frontal attacks from the Anzac position.—As has already been indicated when describing Sir I. Hamilton's plan of operations in outline at the beginning of this chapter, General Birdwood's troops were to undertake two more or less distinct tasks. Besides the main effort against the higher ridges of Sari Bair from the north-west, there was to be a frontal attack from the Anzac position against the Turkish trenches extending from above The Neck to the Lone Pine plateau, and it will be convenient to tell the story of the secondary operations first—the more so seeing that they actually commenced some hours before the main operation was set in motion. Map IV on p. 94 illustrates these frontal attacks best.

During the 4th, 5th, and 6th the works on the enemy's left and centre were subjected to a slow bombardment. Then, on the afternoon of the 6th, an assault was delivered upon a series of formidable works on the Lone Pine plateau, the nearest point to which in the Anzac line was the salient known as "The Pimple." The line from

Russel's Top to the sea near Tasman Post was being held by the 1st Australian Division under General Walker and the 1st and 3rd Australian Light Horse Brigades, and the attack upon the Lone Pine trenches was carried out by the 1st Australian Brigade. The barbed-wire entanglements and the loop-holed, roofed galleries (which had not been seriously damaged by the preparatory bombardments) proved to be even more elaborate than had been anticipated. They were nevertheless taken after a furious combat, and the victors at once set to work to consolidate themselves. At 7 p.m., and again during the night, the Turks delivered counterattacks in great force, which were only beaten off with considerable difficulty, hostile detachments penetrating into the works at certain points. Another formidable counter-attack was delivered at 1.30 p.m. on the 7th, and a last one on a great scale was tried about dawn on the 9th. But the 1st Australian Brigade, reinforced later by two battalions from other brigades, held on grimly to the end to what it had won, in spite of the heavy losses incurred in a struggle which had throughout been maintained against very superior forces.

The operations on Lone Pine were supplemented by others further to the left. At midnight on the 6th–7th an attack was delivered upon an enemy work situated north of Johnston's Jolly, about midway between The Pimple and Quinn's Post; but this effort proved unsuccessful. Then, at 4.30 a.m., an advance on a more ambitious scale was made from about Russel's Top by the 2nd Australian Brigade and a regiment of Light Horse against the Turkish trenches on The Neck and Baby. But although some of the hostile breastworks were carried at the first rush, it was found impossible to remain in occupation of them in face of the concentrated machine-gun fire of which they were made the target, and eventually the troops had to fall back to their original line.

Even taking into account the stirring achievement of the 1st Australian Brigade on the Lone Pine plateau, it has to be admitted that these frontal attacks from Anzac hardly brought about any really important improvement in the tactical situation along the sections of front where they were delivered. They were in themselves, in fact, crowned with but a limited measure of success. They, nevertheless, no doubt accomplished their main object—that of hindering the transfer of Turkish forces on this front from left to right to meet the turning movement which General Birkwood was developing against the higher portion of Sari Bair. As a consequence of the menace that they offered to such vital localities as The Neck and the eastern edge of the Lone Pine plateau, large bodies of enemy troops remained on guard on the 7th in the entrenched line stretching from Baby down to the extremity of the Turkish defences opposite Chatham Post. The repeated efforts, efforts that were continued for several days, of the Osmanlis to re-take their works on Lone Pine plateau, necessarily meant so many fewer battalions available on the enemy's side to participate in the struggle on the more dominating spurs and ridges and summits of the Sari Bair hill-mass, the story of which has now to be told. The capture of those particular works, moreover, did strengthen the right centre of the Anzac position from the defensive point of view, and it constituted a pronounced step towards acquiring the whole of the plateau and of the spurs dropping down from it towards Gaba Tepe. It may be remarked that the limited success attending these frontal attacks by the 1st Australian Division and the Mounted Brigades was probably largely attributable to the absence of really effective artillery preparation by howitzers or trench mortars. With opposing lines so closely in contact, trench mortars, of short range but throwing heavy bombs, must have been extraordinarily effective had they been available.

The start of the attack upon Sari Bair.—We come now to the consideration of what constituted the most important item in Sir I. Hamilton's comprehensive scheme for a general offensive in the Gallipoli Peninsula—the attack upon the higher ridges of Sari Bair from the west and the north-west that was to be executed by bodies of troops issuing from the northern portion of the Anzac position. This undertaking was to bring about fighting of the most determined character, but as its various incidents and phases can only be followed on a large scale map it is only proposed to give an outline sketch of what was a very memorable struggle. The opening stages of this operation were fixed to take place after dark on the 6th. General Birdwood proposed to use for it the Australian and New Zealand Division, the 13th Division, the 29th Brigade of the 10th Division, the 29th Indian Brigade, and the New Zealand Mounted Brigade.

It will be seen on Map V (p. 168) that three valleys debouching on

SCHEME OF ATTACK ON SARI BAIR

to Ocean Beach bite into the hill-mass on this side. The two nearest to Anzac, the Sazli Beit Dere and the Chailak Dere, lead up to that portion of the main ridge that is known as Chunuk Bair. The other, further to the north, the Aghyl Dere, runs up towards Hill Q and Koja Chemen Tepe, which latter is the culminating point. All three of these pronounced depressions partake of the character of gullies and ravines rather than of valleys ; they are deep, winding, rocky, rise rapidly, and are choked with scrub, while the spurs between them, as also the minor promontories separating the small gullies that fork out from the main depressions, are steep-sided, serrated, and in some cases crowned with craggy hillocks most difficult of access. Sari Bair is not an eminence of commanding altitude, for its topmost crest does not reach a height of 1000 feet above sea-level—in Switzerland it would not be reckoned a mountain, and even in Carnarvonshire it would be held of mean account. But the side of it where the above-mentioned valleys cut deep into the heart of the mass, partakes almost of the nature of an escarpment, and for assaulting columns to breast such declivities and to work their way along ravines so intricate in the dark, was an undertaking warranted to try the very best of troops and calling for skilful leadership and highly efficient staff work.

General Birdwood's plan was for a right assaulting column to move up the Sazli Beit Dere and Chailak Dere, with Chunuk Bair as its objective, and for a left assaulting column to move up the Aghyl Dere, aiming for Hill Q and the prolongation of the main Sari Bair ridge between Chunuk Bair and Koja Chemen Tepe. The assaulting columns were to be preceded by two covering forces. Of these the right covering force was charged with the duty of securing the foot-hills about the mouths of the Sazli Beit Dere and the Chailak Dere and to capture Bauchop Hill, and it was furthermore to gain possession of the jagged ridge between the two valleys together with the rugged eminence known as Table Top. The left covering force was to push right on to the mouth of the Aghyl Dere and was then to seize the Demajalik Bair hill, and was thereby at once to guard the outer flank of the left assaulting column and to establish a connecting link of the Anzac troops with the force to be landed about Suvla Bay. In addition to these four bodies of troops there was a reserve. The different forces varied in strength from two battalions to a couple of brigades; the whole was under charge of General Godley, commander of the composite Australian and New Zealand Division, and it was made up of that division, of portions of the 13th Division, and of the 29th Indian Brigade. The four days' fighting for the possession of the Sari Bair mountain which followed took place in exceptionally intricate ground, and it was signalised by numberless stirring incidents in which Australian, New Zealand, English, Irish, and Indian troops alike bore themselves with rare fortitude and valour. Their Moslem adversaries, moreover, vied with them in their display of martial qualities. The struggles were of such a nature, however, that, as already stated, they can only be followed satisfactorily on a large scale plan of the ground, and it is therefore only proposed to indicate their general course.[1]

An encouraging start was made. The left covering column had carried Demajalik Bair by 12.30 a.m. in brilliant style. The right covering force gained possession of Bauchop Hill and of the jagged spurs between the Sazli Beit and Chailak gorges; then by a brilliant feat of arms it stormed the precipitous-sided, strongly fortified Table Top. The left assaulting column, its flanks secured by these conquests, began working its way up the Aghyl Dere at as early an hour as could reasonably be expected. Part of the right assaulting column was delayed for some time at the mouth of the Chailak Dere by a very formidable wire entanglement; but this difficulty was in due course overcome and, in two bodies, the column pressed on up the twin gorges, but not without suffering considerable loss. Then progress became extremely slow and laborious. For the few hours left before dawn, both assaulting columns were struggling with topographical difficulties of no common order in the night watches, their progress seriously impeded by rifle and machine-gun fire from nooks and crannies commanding the routes that they were endeavouring to follow. For troops starting by day from Ocean Beach to reach the topmost ridges of Sari Bair, would probably not have taken two hours if unopposed. But, as it was, the leading detachments were still some distance short of their objectives when day broke, and the Turks, apprised before midnight that hostile forces were in movement at a number

---

[1] Sir I. Hamilton in his final despatch gives a detailed account of this epic contest, as do also Mr. Schuler in his *Australia in Arms* and Mr. Nevinson in his *The Dardanelles Campaign*.

of points between Ari Burnu and Demajalik Bair, were mustering on the heights in swarms to bid defiance to the advancing foe.

As has been mentioned on page 195, the 4th Osmanli Division, although properly speaking included in the Turkish Southern Group, was early diverted to the Anzac area, and its leading units appear to have reached Chunuk Bair during the night, or soon after dawn, to reinforce the detachments already entrenched on the main ridge. The troops of General Godley's assaulting columns were too exhausted after their all-night contest with nature and with the slowly retiring Turks to be in a position, after securing possession of Rhododendron Spur, until 9.30 a.m. to launch a formal attack upon Chunuk Bair; and, although some battalions were hurried up to help from the reserve, it was apparent before noon that the project of winning the heights by surprise had failed. A fine advance had been made, much ground had been won, but the attacking troops were worn out and the enemy still firmly held the dominating ridge. It was therefore decided to stand fast and to organise a fresh attack from the new positions that had been taken up for the following morning. In the meantime, however, the enemy was hurrying reinforcements to the threatened point, and much more formidable opposition was to be expected than if, as had been hoped, the assaulting columns had been in a position to assail Chunuk Bair and Hill Q at dawn on the 7th.

The plan had been a daring one. To move a number of columns into such a terrain in the dark in presence of a brave and vigilant enemy was to throw a very heavy strain upon officers and men. Only efficient battalions composed of genuine fighting material could indeed have undertaken such an enterprise at all with any reasonable hope of success. The difficulties had, however, proved to be greater than had been expected, progress at all events had been slower than the staff had been prepared for, and consequently the troops when the time came for the final effort were too spent to push an onset victoriously home.[1] The plan was perhaps somewhat ambitious. It suggests itself that, had the units—or some of them—composing the left covering force and the left column been detailed instead to closely follow the right assaulting column,

[1] In his orders to General Stopford with regard to the Suvla operations Sir I. Hamilton stated that General Godley's advance would be "timed so as to reach the summit of the main ridge near Chunuk Bair about 2.30 a.m."

their instructions being to push through this if necessary so as to deliver the attack upon Chunuk Bair with reasonably fresh troops, the ridge might possibly have been secured soon after dawn. Confident battalions, unexhausted by fighting all night in extraordinarily difficult terrain, might perhaps have struck a decisive blow from Rhododendron Spur before 8 a.m., at an hour when the enemy was still comparatively weak on the heights. But it is easy to criticise after the event and when in possession of knowledge that was not at the disposal of General Birdwood and his Staff.

The fight for Sari Bair from the 8th to the 10th.—It was arranged that the renewed effort should be made in three columns on the following morning, starting at 4.15 a.m. The plan for this operation of the 8th inst. was that the right and centre columns should assail Chunuk Bair, while the left column, starting from the position near the head of the Aghyl Dere which had been secured early on the previous day, was to advance against Hill Q. This hump of the main Sari Bair ridge, it should be noted, is separated from Koja Chemen Tepe by a well-marked depression ; its elevation is about fifty feet above the highest part of Chunuk Bair, to which it is joined by a neck. It will be noted that the experience of the night of the 6th–7th and of the following forenoon had already decided Generals Birdwood and Godley to restrict their objectives, as compared to what these had been in the original plan. It had been intended on the 6th that the left attacking column should head for Koja Chemen Tepe as well as for Hill Q. In the project for the 8th the front of attack was shortened, Koja Chemen Tepe ceased to be a point aimed at, and the extreme left of the assaulting troops was not to extend beyond the approaches from the upper part of the Aghyl Dere to Hill Q.

The right column did well. For after a severe struggle it succeeded soon after dawn in forcing its way on to the south-western end of Chunuk Bair. The centre column did not fare so favourably, for it met with a stout resistance, and was unable to attain its objective. Nor did the left column accomplish much ; after it had made some ground to its front, it found itself stubbornly opposed and then counter-attacked, and it was obliged, after maintaining what had been won for a time, to fall back to the line that it had started from. Still, if the centre and left column could claim practically no success,

FIGHTING ON THE 9TH OF AUGUST 205

and although the attacking side suffered heavy loss this day, a substantial gain had been registered in that a footing had been gained on one point of the main ridge. This was the more satisfactory seeing that help which had been hoped for from the force that had landed about Suvla Bay during the night of the 6th–7th had not been forthcoming. On the other hand, the Turks were gathering strength rapidly, still less than on the previous day was there now any question of surprise, and the enemy enjoyed all the advantage of position as at the start.

Yet another attack was devised for the morning of the 9th—to take place in the form of three separate groups. The right group was merely called upon to hold the stretch of Chunuk Bair that had been made good on the previous morning and to consolidate this captured ground. To the centre group was assigned the task of delivering an assault upon the neck joining Chunuk Bair to Hill Q. The left group was to play the most important part in the operations ; it was to attack Hill Q itself, and was numerically the strongest force of the three. The advance was to take place after a heavy bombardment by every gun ashore and afloat that could be brought to bear.

The centre group achieved a signal triumph at the outset, succeeding in its task of gaining the main ridge and in capturing a commanding height on the neck between Chunuk Bair and Hill Q, from which it was able to look down upon the Dardanelles. But the left group was unable to perform the all-important task assigned to it in the general scheme of operations, and this proved to be most unfortunate seeing how much depended upon its effort. Seriously delayed by difficulties of ground in the dark and by losing its way, this force was late, and the result was that the centre group found themselves deprived of the support of troops on their outer flank when in a critical position. For the Turks, fully realising the vital importance of the portion of crest near Hill Q which they had lost, made desperate endeavours to recapture this. A salvo of big high-explosive shells landed at the critical moment amongst the 6th Ghurkas and 6th South Lancashires, the troops that had made themselves masters of the height ; the enemy counter-attacked in force ; and so it came about that, after a brief spell on the ridge that had been won, the assailants were flung back down the hillsides on the top of the left group which had now reached their rendezvous.[1] Such formidable attacks were at the same time delivered by the Osmanlis upon the right group that was holding the portion of Chunuk Bair taken on the morning of the 8th, that this was hard put to it to maintain itself. The 7th Turkish Division, which had marched from about Bulair, appears to have to some extent intervened on this day from about Biyuk Anafarta, although partly occupied with the British attack from Suvla.

At the end of the day on the 9th the position was much the same as it had been twenty-four hours earlier, in so far as the actual ground held by the contending sides was concerned. But the Turks were now in strong force and they enjoyed all the advantage of ground, while General Birdwood's troops were not merely harassed by the enemy, but were also in difficulties as to water— the enemy did not suffer to the same extent as regards this because water is to be found in the valleys running southwards from Chunuk Bair and Koja Chemen Tepe. No help, moreover, was coming to the Anzac force from the side of Suvla Bay. The situation was in fact far from reassuring.

The troops on Chunuk Bair were relieved during the night. The new-comers were heavily attacked at daybreak before they had settled down and after having been exposed to a concentric bombardment, with the result that they were swept off the heights with very severe loss and with the enemy at their heels. The Turks had been reinforced by a fresh division, the 8th, and they now advanced with much confidence and on a comparatively broad frontage; but once over the crest they came under the full blast of the invaders' guns, naval and military, and were mowed down in swarms. In spite of the casualties suffered, the Osmanlis, however, pressed forward and obliged their opponents to yield a good deal of the ground that they had won early on the 7th and had held ever since; and, although checked after a time, the enemy undoubtedly had the best of the morning's struggle, for no attempt was made then, or later, by General Birdwood's troops to initiate a fresh effort against the heights.

[1] Doubt appears to exist as to the source of the disastrous salvo of high explosive shell, which had so much to do with driving the troops that had established themselves on the crest off that dominating position; but the nature of the detonation made it clear that they were British and not Turkish projectiles; it has been assumed too readily that they were naval 6-inch shell. The fact that there was only a single salvo is additional evidence that this cannot have come from the Turkish side.

END OF THE FIGHT FOR SARI BAIR

At the end of four days the enemy had, in fact, proved the victor. The attempt to win Sari Bair had definitely failed, and at the cost of 12,000 casualties to the attacking side. At the same time, the invaders had something to show for their resolute offensive, for the Anzac position had been considerably extended in a northerly direction. Demajalik Bair had been secured, and also the high ground between the Sazli Beit and Chailak Deres, which gave elbow-room and which permitted the Anzac position to be joined on to the Suvla position within a few days. The troops concerned in the assaults had been highly tried throughout, as they suffered much from heat and thirst. The Turks also had fought with the utmost grit and courage, their counter-attack on the morning of the 10th being delivered with remarkable spirit and maintained for a considerable time in spite of the murderous gun-fire to which they found themselves exposed.

Observations on General Birdwood's operations from the 6th to the 10th.—That the project of capturing the main ridge of Sari Bair by surprise failed early on the first day of the battle has already been pointed out. All the preparatory arrangements had been devised and carried into effect with masterly skill—it is noteworthy that German accounts of the affair make no mention of the swelling of the Anzac force that took place in anticipation of this offensive, and it may be inferred from this that the first intimation which reached Liman von Sanders that serious events were impending in this particular quarter came to his headquarters when the attacking troops, moving northwards after dark on the 6th, came into collision with the Ottoman outposts amongst the foot-hills near Ocean Beach. The essence of the operation designed by General Birdwood and approved by Sir I. Hamilton, however, was that the crest should be gained at a very early hour on the 7th —before the Turks could call up reinforcements on to the heights. But the stubborn resistance of the enemy—probably not gathered in strong force—on the lower spurs of Sari Bair and in the ravines, during the night of the 6th–7th, coupled with the extreme difficulty of working forward in the dark through such intricate terrain, acted as so fatal a drag upon the assailants that they were unable to make their supreme effort before the defending side had assembled in great numbers.

Under the circumstances, the success achieved on the 8th in

securing a footing on Chunuk Bair, as also the short-lived triumph of the following morning when a couple of battalions for a brief period were in possession of the neck between Chunuk Bair and Hill Q, must be set down as very striking feats of arms. All the advantage of position was on the side of the defenders, and by that time these were prepared and were in formidable strength. The mischance that befell the left assaulting group on the morning of the 9th is instructive, seeing that the failure of this part of the plan was not the result of enemy action but was attributable to topographical causes. The incident illustrates the risks that attend movements in the dark in a broken region. There are grounds for assuming that the non-appearance of this group at the critical juncture exercised a fatal influence over that morning's work as a whole, for had the left been so successful as the centre group, and had it made itself master of even a portion of Hill Q, it is conceivable that the two groups, mutually supporting each other, might have maintained their grip on the all-important crest long enough to admit of reinforcements coming up and making the conquest definitely good. Movements in the dark as a prelude to assault were, however, imposed upon General Birdwood, because his antagonists held dominating positions and were therefore enabled to detect any preparations for attack if these were made by daylight.

German accounts only speak of the 4th and 9th Turkish Divisions having taken part in the fighting of the 7th and 8th, but there must have been other Ottoman troops engaged. Those two divisions are only spoken of as arriving on the heights on the morning of the 7th. That would not account for the enemy forces which the Australian 1st Division encountered at Lone Pine on the 6th, nor those which held their ground about The Neck during the night of the 6th-7th ; nor does it account for the detachments which General Godley's columns had to press back from about the Aghyl Dere, the Sazli Beit Dere and the Chailak Dere that night. The assailants no doubt enjoyed an advantage in respect to numbers during the first twelve hours ; but the difficulties and delays of the night advance from Ocean Beach deprived them of the benefit to be derived from that advantage. On the 8th, 9th, and 10th the Turks were continually gathering strength, whereas General Birdwood received no reinforcements. There seems to be little doubt that the fight for Sari Bair was in reality lost between dark and dawn of the 6th-7th,

THE 13TH DIVISION

owing to the unwonted topographical difficulties which the attacking columns had to overcome in the dark, and owing to the extreme exhaustion in the ranks to which those difficulties gave rise.

The incident of the unfortunate salvo referred to in the footnote to page 206 is instructive, although it is fully realised by tacticians of the day that such contretemps are inevitable. Many similar incidents occurred during the course of the World War, although none possibly had so disastrous a result. The very essence of artillery co-operation with infantry lies in its continuing its shelling up to the very last moment and in its not being afraid to drop its projectiles very close to its own side. In the later stages of the campaign on the Western Front the barrage system and the lifting barrage were executed with wonderful precision and with the very best results. The Ghurkas and South Lancashires had been awaiting the cessation of the bombardment lying quite close up to where the shells were dropping very accurately ; on the bombardment ceasing at the given time they advanced at once and it was after they had won the crest that a perfectly ranged salvo caused all the confusion and loss. There was clearly a misunderstanding somewhere as regards the guns ceasing fire at the given time, and as to their not resuming without some very clear idea what exactly the position was at the front.

In conclusion, it should be stated that the infantry of the 13th Division, commanded by General Shaw, had from the outset of these days of incessant and strenuous combat, vied in its valour and intrepidity as well as in the skill with which battalions and companies were handled, even with the highly practised troops from the Antipodes and from India alongside which it fought. The division had clearly profited by its short experience face to face with the Turks at Helles before being brought round to Anzac. Events on the Western Front had served to indicate the importance of breaking New Army divisions in gradually by contact with the enemy, before committing such troops to hazardous enterprises on a big scale. This was borne out by what occurred in the Gallipoli Peninsula during the August offensive.

The operations at Suvla Bay. Special condition of the landings. —We now come to the story of the third of the three operations which had been designed by Sir I. Hamilton with the intention of using to the best advantage the considerable reinforcements that had been placed at his disposal by his Government. It concerns the landing at Suvla Bay and the events immediately succeeding that successfully conducted undertaking. The manner in which the operations in this locality were executed in their early stages has given rise to warm controversy between highly placed officers engaged in the campaign, and they are on that account somewhat difficult to deal with in edifying fashion at the present stage. Some day a full account of the proceedings will no doubt be officially published ; but in the absence of any such authoritative work of reference it seems expedient to deal in no excessive detail with the facts involved, and to express any views that may suggest themselves in regard to the points in dispute somewhat guardedly. Happily there has been no contention concerning the mode in which the actual disembarkations were conducted, and, seeing that these were effected in face of a certain amount of opposition and were largely carried out in the dark, they undoubtedly represent the most interesting and instructive phase of a memorable series of events.

Special conditions of the landings at this point.—There are one or two matters to which special attention ought, however, to be drawn before the narrative is proceeded with. Thus, it should be remembered that, from the general naval point of view, the conditions attending the descents in August at this new locality in the Gallipoli Peninsula differed materially from the conditions that had prevailed when the Expeditionary Force originally succeeded in winning a way ashore in the previous April. No submarines had been about in April, and there had in consequence been no question whatever then of a possible maritime attack upon the troopships as they approached the scene of action. There was, on the other hand, much less likelihood about mid-summer of bad weather setting in than there had been in the spring, although this particular factor had not in fact influenced the course of events on the earlier occasion. Then again, the land and sea forces had at the time of the first venture been engaging themselves in an enterprise for which there was virtually no tactical precedent with modern armament, whereas at Suvla both the Royal Navy and military headquarters enjoyed the benefit of the valuable experiences that they had acquired at Helles, at Anzac and at Kum Kale. Another circumstance that altered the conditions was that, thanks to an improved air service and to the labours of the Intelligence Department, the attacking side was furnished with much more complete information as to the dispositions of the defending army in August than it had possessed four months before.

Naval preparations in respect to the craft to be employed for getting the troops ashore were also on a more elaborate scale than they had been in April. Then the infantry had relied almost wholly upon ships' cutters hauled by picket-boats. Since that time a number of special vessels of the large lighter class had been sent out, designed for just such a purpose as this. These craft, of which a large number had been constructed in the spring although none were available at the time of the early landings, were fitted with motor engines enabling them to travel five knots under their own power. They were of the nature of large barges of iron plating, which was proof against bullets. A swinging platform projected from the prow, which could be lowered so as to form a broad ramp leading ashore when the lighter was beached stem on. When fully loaded they were calculated only to draw about four and a half feet of water, and would take 500 men with stores, ammunition, and water, or 50 horses, although experience proved that it was better not to ship more than about 360 men. They were christened "beetles" by the troops owing to the appearance of their prow.

In fine weather these lighters could be quite safely towed for considerable distances with troops on board, and they were thus peculiarly well suited for such a trip as that from Imbros to Suvla in August. The idea with regard to them was that transports, cruisers, or battleships would be able to bring them to, or near to, the coast and that they would then be cast off to make the rest of the way under their own power. During the Suvla landing operations they were for the most part towed by destroyers until within a mile or so of their objective. They were largely used during the campaign from this time on.

The orders for the IXth Corps.—In Sir I. Hamilton's orders issued to General Stopford commanding the IXth Corps on the 22nd of July, a special point was made of as few officers as possible being made acquainted with the plan. After indicating the general scheme that the Commander-in-Chief had in mind for his offensive, the strength of the enemy facing the Suvla area was intimated. It was put at five battalions with some gendarmerie, three battalions in the Anafarta villages, and two about Ismail Oglu Tepe and Chocolate Hill, this high ground forming, as appears from Map V, a species of promontory running out into the plain that stretches east and south-east from Suvla Bay and the Salt Lake. There were known to be two heavy guns on this high ground and three field guns, all protected with entanglements and trenches. The German account puts the strength of the Turks at three battalions, two of gendarmerie, with "some guns" and a squadron.

It has already been explained that the force detailed for these operations—the IXth Corps, less the 13th Division and the 29th Brigade of the 10th Division—was starting from the islands of Mitylene, Lemnos, and Imbros, and that the larger part of it, viz. the 11th Division, was coming from the latter point. The plan was that this latter should land first on the 6th of August after dark, with the idea of its all being ashore before daylight. The two brigades of the 10th Division from Mitylene and Mudros would land later. General Stopford was informed that his first objectives would be "the high ground at Lala Baba and Gazi Baba, and the hills near Yilghin Burnu[1] and Ismail Oglu Tepe. It will be necessary to send a small force to secure a footing on the hills due east of Suvla Bay. It is of the utmost importance that Yilghin Burnu and Ismail Oglu Tepe should be carried by a *coup de main* before daylight, in order to prevent the guns which they contain being used on our troops on Hill 305[2] and to safeguard our hold on Suvla Bay. It is hoped that one division will be sufficient for the attainment of these three objectives."

General Birdwood's contemplated operations were then described in some detail, and it was pointed out in the orders how the IXth Corps would be in a position to co-operate effectively with what was to be the main attack upon the enemy. It was hoped that, after the remainder of the corps had landed on the morning of the 7th, this would be able to advance on Biyuk Anafarta and move up the eastern spurs of Koja Chemen Tepe. General Stopford was warned that the landing of sufficient transport to secure mobility for the force would be a matter of great difficulty, and that at first

---

[1] Chocolate Hill.
[2] Koja Chemen Tepe.

everything practically would have to be carried by hand. " Water is plentiful throughout the Anafarta Valley, but, pending the disembarkation of water carts, a number of mules with special eight-gallon water bags will be attached to the units under your command."

The landings.—The plan for the disembarkation of the 11th Division was as follows. The division's three infantry brigades, the 32nd, 33rd, and 34th, were to be put ashore as follows : The 32nd, followed by the 33rd, at Beach C, shown on Map V, and the 34th was to land within the bay at Beach A. The artillery was in due course to be landed at Beach B. The Commander-in-Chief had originally contemplated landing all three infantry brigades south of Nibrunesi Point, where there were extensive stretches of foreshore quite practicable for infantry to land on in fine weather from boats or lighters, but it was subsequently decided (rather unfortunately as it turned out) to put the 34th Brigade ashore within the bay. The landing scheme really hinged upon a very free use of comparatively small craft, as a security against submarines. In this respect, as well as in the employment of the beetles, it differed widely from the plan that had been put into execution at Helles, Kum Kale, and Anzac in April, when the troops, as will be remembered, were brought up to near the landing-places in transports and large warships. The 11th Division being detailed to carry out the landing by night, a complete surprise of the Turks was contemplated.

Nearly all the infantry were conveyed in the beetles from Kephalos Bay in Imbros to the coast near Suvla Bay, each towed by a destroyer. To provide against the contingency of the beetles grounding too far from the shore or meeting with some other misadventure, the flotilla was accompanied by a number of ketches, each in charge of several lifeboats intended to take the troops off the beetles if necessary ; there were picket-boats available to tow the lifeboats to shore if they should be required. The destroyers carried troops in addition to towing the beetles, and the plan was that after a beetle had discharged its living freight on the beach it would return to its destroyer and take off the troops on board of that. The destroyers and beetles were to be followed from Imbros by the two specially belted cruisers *Endymion* and *Talbot*, each with 1000 men on board ; these troops were to be taken off by beetles making a third trip. Two mountain batteries and three field batteries, with their animals, were to follow as a third echelon, the whole conveyed in lighters and horse-boats towed by a sloop and by ketches.

The transfer of the division from Imbros to the beaches assigned was carried out according to programme. The flotilla quitted Kephalos Bay soon after 8 p.m. and the leading beetles appear to have reached the shore about 10 p.m. The 32nd and 33rd Brigades encountered practically no opposition on the stretches of foreshore south of Nibrunesi Point, which proved quite suitable for the lighters although the beaches in themselves hardly deserved the name, being very steep, and awkward also in other respects. It took some hours to put the whole of the two brigades ashore ; but about 2 a.m. two battalions of the 32nd Brigade had already moved north to near Lala Baba which was occupied by some Turkish infantry ensconced in trenches, and had stormed the eminence with the bayonet. This was an important gain, because the 34th Brigade landing at Beach A had been a good deal troubled with musketry from this high ground—musketry fire which took the lighters, and the troops as they landed, to some extent in enfilade. Beach A as a matter of fact had turned out to be a bad landing-place, quite apart from this particular trouble. The water inshore was shallow and several of the beetles grounded some way out, obliging the troops to struggle to land through water as much as four and a half feet deep. Beetles and troops were, moreover, enfiladed from about Gazi Baba as well as from Lala Baba, and the beach itself was sown with land mines which caused casualties and confusion in the dark. The enemy was not in strong force ; but snipers were enterprising and, knowing the ground intimately, made themselves very annoying, with the result that the disembarkation of the 34th Brigade was somewhat retarded.

After the loss of Lala Baba the Turkish outposts withdrew to Hill 10, which had been entrenched. The 34th Brigade began advancing against this hillock (which hardly deserves the name, being merely a very low undulation) some little time before dawn, one battalion diverging northwards to secure the end of the Karakol Dagh. The 34th Brigade was supported by the 32nd, which had turned the interval between landing and the approach of daylight to account by moving along the isthmus between the Salt Lake

ARRIVAL OF GENERAL HILL

and Suvla Bay. (The Salt Lake, it may be observed, was fairly dry at this time of the year, but represented a virtually impassable, sticky marsh over its whole area.) Some delay, however, took place before an attack was launched upon the Turkish detachments on Hill 10 ; soon after dawn, moreover, the hostile artillery opened fire and began to cause casualties. In the end it had come to be broad daylight before the Ottoman infantry had been driven off Hill 10 ; they retired slowly across the plain in an easterly direction, scrub serving to some extent to conceal their movements and their strength. The 33rd Brigade in the meantime remained south of the Salt Lake and about Lala Baba. Two mountain batteries and a field battery were ashore soon after daybreak, and two of the mountain guns promptly came into action on Lala Baba. But the Ottoman artillery was scattered and it proved difficult to locate, so that the arrival of British batteries did little to neutralise the effect of the enemy's shell-fire.

The 10th Division now came upon the scene. A flotilla with the six of its battalions that had assembled at Mitylene—the 31st Brigade and two battalions of the 30th Brigade—arrived at dawn under Brigadier-General Hill, and anchored off Nibrunesi Point. This Irish division had been somewhat unfortunate since quitting the United Kingdom, for its infantry had been split up into three portions, the 29th Brigade proceeding, as we have already seen, from Mudros to Anzac before the start of General Birdwood's offensive, the above-named force concentrating at Mitylene, and the other two battalions of the 30th Brigade with the divisional battalion and the brigade headquarters remaining in camp in Lemnos, together with the divisional commander, Sir B. Mahon and his staff. Since arriving in the Ægean the troops at Mitylene had remained on board their transports in the land-locked inlet which constitutes the better of the island's two famous havens.

General Hill's battalions had during the previous afternoon transhipped from their transports into trawlers and channel steamers, the flotilla had got under way in the evening, and it had covered the 120 miles that had to be traversed exactly according to schedule, so that the troops were ready to begin disembarking as soon as the lighters had become available after discharging the 11th Division. The scheme had originally been that the whole of the 10th Division (except the 29th Brigade)¹ should be put ashore within Suvla Bay and should operate on the left of the 11th Division ; but, in consequence of the landing difficulties that had been experienced by the 34th Brigade owing to the shallows, the naval authorities decided that the infantry from Mitylene must land at Beach C, instead of at Beach A as had been intended.

General Stopford's instructions to General Hill, on learning of this change, were to the effect that he was to support the left of the 11th Division, which was being delayed by the Turkish detachments on Hill 10 and on the outer spurs of the Karakol Dagh. The consequence was that the task of the new arrivals after getting ashore came in the first place to be that of working their way round from Beach C by Lala Baba and the causeway between the Salt Lake and Suvla Bay to somewhere north of Beach A and Hill 10. This fresh disembarkation of infantry at Beach C began a little after dawn, and, as the light improved, it was a good deal interfered with by Turkish shell-fire which proved extremely accurate. The range to the beach had evidently been carefully registered by the enemy, and the troops suffered appreciable losses both on after reaching land and while still in the lighters.

About 8 a.m. the general position of affairs would seem to have been somewhat as follows : The surprise of the Turks had been carried out as contemplated, and, in spite of some delay in getting the troops ashore at Beach A, the landing of the 11th Division had been carried out most successfully in the dark, the trifling opposition of the Turkish detachment on Lala Baba having been brushed out of the way smartly, although not without some loss. There had been some hesitation in dealing with Hill 10, but the position had eventually been carried by the very superior British forces available. The 33rd Brigade was at Lala Baba and south of the Salt Lake. General Hill's troops were disembarking on Beach C, and those first ashore had already assembled under the lee of Lala Baba where there was some shelter from the hostile artillery fire that was causing annoyance all along the line. The Turks were slowly retiring eastwards across the plain towards the high ground on either side of Kuchuk Anafarta. But the advance

---

¹ In speaking of divisions it must be remembered that their artillery had for the most part been sent to Egypt. This was the case with all the 10th Division batteries and with most of those belonging to the 11th Division.

FACTORS DELAYING THE ADVANCE

of the 11th Division was hanging fire, although two of its mountain batteries were in action about Lala Baba and a field battery was getting to work among the sand-hills near Beach C.

Sir I. Hamilton had estimated that the strength of the detachments with which the IXth Corps would have to deal at the outset would be about 4000. That would seem to have been about correct, although, as we have seen, the German account only gives three battalions. Against this exiguous force there were the thirteen battalions of the 11th Division all virtually in action, most of them having already been several hours on shore, while General Hill's force of the 10th Division was in the position of a rapidly growing reserve. Any fighting that had taken place had gone most favourably for the attacking side, and there was every incentive to push on at once and relentlessly. But certain factors militated against the prosecution of a vigorous offensive, and of these due note must be taken.

In the first place, staff arrangements and organisation had been dislocated to some extent by the intermingling of the 11th and 10th Division, although this caused more inconvenience to the 10th Division, which was not in a position to act as early as 8 a.m., than it did to the 11th Division. Then there was the congestion along the shore, coupled with the sandy character of the soil about Beaches C and B where most of the disembarkations were being carried out, to be contended with. The beaches in themselves were suitable enough for discharging the big lighters which played so important a part in the landing operations, so long as it was merely a question of infantry soldiers; but they were steep, narrow, and awkward for landing guns or animals or impedimenta. They were furthermore exposed to a harassing shell-fire, and the fact that nearly everything landed on them had in the nature of things to move flankwards, instead of straight to the front, necessarily aggravated congestion. Yet another cause of delay, and one which was to exert an untoward influence over the operations at Suvla during their critical opening stages, was the difficulty as to water, although the troops did not suffer much from lack of this in the early hours of the day; this water question, however, played so important a part in affecting the issue on the 7th and 8th that it is especially dealt with in Appendix III. About 8 a.m. a fresh flotilla transporting troops appeared in the offing. This was the force from Mudros Bay—the remaining three battalions of the 10th Division, with General Mahon.

Operations on the 7th after 8 a.m.—The infantry from Mudros did not begin to land for some hours, as the naval authorities were opposed to a further disembarkation at Beach A. The capture of Hill 10, and the sturdy advance of the one battalion of the 34th Brigade which had been directed northwards from Beach A about dawn, had, however, induced the enemy practically to abandon the whole of the Suvla Point promontory; this enabled the sailors to reconnoitre, and they discovered a fairly suitable landing-place near Gazi Baba. The Mudros contingent therefore, after a prolonged pause, began disembarking at this new point, which (as it turned out) was not very suitable owing to shallow water that caused the beetles to ground before getting close in. A battalion of the 30th Brigade from Mitylene which had not yet started for shore at Beach C was also transferred to the Gazi Baba landing-place. The disembarkation at this point was interfered with to some extent by the enemy's artillery, the stranded beetles offering a favourable target; land mines caused loss; and the first of the Mudros battalions would not seem to have been in a position to advance from the beach before noon.

Nor had much progress up to that time been made by the 11th Division. The 34th Brigade, supported by the 32nd (which had lost its brigadier, wounded) remained about Hill 10. General Hill's battalions had by midday assembled about Lala Baba, and they then began their awkward flank march northwards along the shell-swept causeway between the lake and the shore where there was no cover, and it was not until after 2 p.m. that this force was ready to advance across the northern Azmak Dere.[1] Two battalions of the 33rd Brigade followed General Hill's column; the remaining two appear to have stopped about Lala Baba as a reserve. Thus at about 3 p.m., when a general advance took place from about Hill 10 and from between that point and the lake,

---

[1] There are two Azmak Deres within a very few miles of each other, as shown on Map V. The Osmanli has singularly little originality in selecting his geographical nomenclature and his rivers are generally called after the supposed colour of their waters—black, white, blue, yellow and red. "Azmak" means blue. The upper valley of the southern Azmak Dere represents an important depression separating Sari Bair and its northern foothills from the Chocolate Hill–Ismail Oglu Tepe promontory of high ground that was to play an important part in the Suvla operations.

CAUSES OF DELAY IN ADVANCE

a force of more than three brigades was getting on the move, two of which had scarcely stirred for six hours although the spirit of the Commander-in-Chief's orders enjoined an extreme activity.

It had become apparent early in the day that the capture of Chocolate Hill and Green Hill was almost imperative, if an effective offensive was to be carried out in the direction of Kuchuk Anafarta and the heights on either side of that village without incurring heavy loss from enfilading fire. The salient formed by those two hills together with the higher hills—Scimitar Hill and Ismail Oglu Tepe— flanked the Suvla plain from the south, just as the Karakol Dagh and Kiritch Tepe Sirt flanked it from the north. But, as will be seen from Map V, the range of heights to the north recedes from the plain as this is crossed from about Hill 10 in an easterly direction ; there do not, moreover, appear to have been any enemy guns emplaced on it, and its occupation was therefore of less vital importance than that of the southern promontory.

The instructions given to General Hill when he arrived off Suvla at dawn had been that he was to operate on the left of the 11th Division ; but this arrangement was altered before his troops came definitely into action. He was directed instead to act on the right of the 34th and 32nd Brigades, and to move against Chocolate and Green Hills, while the two brigades of the 11th Division on his left advanced eastwards and south-eastwards against Kuchuk Anafarta Ova and Sulajik. The inevitable consequence of these dispositions—which had perhaps been rendered necessary by the deliberation of the 34th and 32nd Brigades—was that the inconvenient dispersion of the 10th Division continued and that General Hill's five battalions, after having landed at C Beach, about two miles in a straight line from Chocolate Hill, made a march in the heat of the day of at least five miles right round the Salt Lake before they were in a position to assail that all-important tactical position. The reason for the alteration was no doubt that, by the time that General Hill's force was ready to press forward across the northern Azmak Dere, the 34th and 32nd Brigades were already to some extent committed to their advance across the plain in an easterly direction in extended formation. Could the situation as it had developed by about noon have been foreseen when the contingent from Mitylene appeared off Nibrunesi Point, it would evidently have been better for the contingent to have been directed straight upon Chocolate Hill from about C Beach, taking a line of advance south of the Salt Lake. Nor is it clear why the 33rd Brigade was not employed for action south of the Salt Lake instead of its hanging about Lala Baba, apparently as a reserve. The Commander-in-Chief's orders had spoken of the occupation of Ismail Oglu Tepe by daylight, so as to dispose of the Turkish guns emplaced about there and Chocolate Hill. Even if that was impracticable the situation demanded action as quickly as possible with such troops as were available.

The troops were somewhat exhausted after their night voyage, after the fatigues and excitement of disembarkation, after trudging through the sand and the long waits in the forenoon, and on account of the great heat and the want of water. They had also suffered some loss from shelling and snipers; but as a matter of fact the loss had fallen mainly on two or three of the battalions. The advance was slow and, as General Hill's troops wheeled round the lake before heading straight for their objectives, they were troubled by enfilade fire, so the two battalions of the 33rd Brigade, which had been following in reserve, came up on their left flank to meet this difficulty. Eventually this mixed force, receiving some support from the three batteries that had been landed and the ships' guns, delivered a highly effective attack upon Chocolate Hill and Green Hill towards evening, in spite of thirst and fatigue, and secured them both. The 34th and 32nd Brigades got as far forward as Sulajik and a line extending north from that point.

In the meantime the rest of the 10th Division had moved forward through difficult ground along the Karakol Dagh and Kiritch Tepe Sirt heights, opposed determinedly by a battalion of Turkish gendarmerie. Like the troops further to the south, these battalions suffered much from thirst; but they, nevertheless, made a considerable advance, taking into consideration their late entrance into the fray. By nightfall they had made good nearly three miles of the narrow range of hills, but they do not seem to have been in close touch with the 34th Brigade which formed the left of the 11th Division. The general line ran from their advanced posts southward to the Kuchuk Anafarta Ova and across this by Sulajik to Green Hill—a very different line from that which the Commander-in-Chief had hoped would represent the front of the IXth Corps at the end of the day.

UNSATISFACTORY RESULTS ON THE 7TH   221

The troops were much exhausted at nightfall and had suffered greatly from thirst at practically all points. Very little water had been found, although there existed a number of wells that were discovered afterwards. The arrangements for providing water and bringing it forward, although elaborate and apparently well thought out, had broken down completely owing to unsatisfactory administration and to some little lack of discipline on the part of certain detachments. A fair amount of ground had no doubt been gained eventually; but the advance had taken place so late in the day that by the time darkness had set in there had been no leisure to arrange for pushing forward supplies, ammunition, and so forth, methodically and to good purpose. The situation could not in fact be considered as satisfactory, and, in spite of the success of the landing in the first instance, in no way fulfilled what had been contemplated in the general scheme for the main offensive. The losses do not appear to have exceeded a total of 1000, and they had fallen almost entirely on three or four units.

Comments on the first twenty-four hours of the Suvla operations.
—The two points of special interest in connection with the landing of the 11th and 10th Divisions in and south of Suvla Bay are the fact that most of the infantry were landed by night in presence of the enemy, and that specially constructed lighters provided with their own motive power were used. In so far as the question of landing in the dark is concerned, the experiences of the night of the 6th–7th August offer eloquent testimony to the advantages of a nocturnal disembarkation when opposition is to be expected. The thirteen battalions of the 11th Division got ashore almost without being touched by artillery fire, whereas the 10th Division when landing a few hours later in the daylight was worried by the Turkish shell, and would in all likelihood have been interfered with worse had the hostile gunners not by that time had their attention distracted by a number of other targets. Darkness probably added very appreciably in some respects to the trouble that arose when several lighters conveying portions of the 34th Brigade grounded off Beach A at some distance from the shore, because the obscurity necessarily aggravated difficulties of control and of communication. Still, so long as they remained in the motionless, grounded lighters and while they were making their way ashore from these, the troops at least were not under shell-fire, as they would have been had there

been light; and such musketry as they were exposed to from Lala Baba and Gazi Baba cannot have been so damaging as it must have proved in the daytime. On the other hand, it is reasonable to suppose that the land-mines that were concealed along the shore and which caused some loss, would have been more easily detected and avoided after the sun was up, than by night.

In the absence of detailed statistics as to the exact hour when disembarkation began at the different beaches and as to the hour when the different brigades of the 11th Division had completed their landing, no opinion can well be formed as to whether the actual process of getting the troops ashore was more rapid or less rapid than it presumably would have been had the same operation been taking place by daylight. Those responsible had calculated upon getting the work nearly, if not quite, completed before the moon rose about 2 a.m., and it was apparently only at Beach A that any serious hitch occurred and that all the infantry were not on land some considerable time before dawn.

One of the great hindrances to a night landing on an open beach in an enemy's country will generally be that the sailors find it by no means easy to hit off the appointed spot, in the presumable absence of beacons or of special navigation marks. The Australasian troops, it will be remembered, were not intended to have landed at Anzac Cove on the 25th of April, but at a beach near Gaba Tepe about a mile and a half away; it was largely owing to the current that the flotilla conveying them arrived at the wrong spot, but a background of heights close to the shore must have made it hard to hit off the right point in the dark in any case. Bringing up at the proper locality was facilitated at Suvla by two circumstances. In the first place, the actual voyage from Kephalos Bay was only fourteen miles, whereas the distance from Mudros to Gaba Tepe had been sixty miles. In the second place, Suvla was an easy point to make on a clear night; for the two-miles-wide plain in rear caused Lala Baba to stand out conspicuously, and the lofty promontory of Suvla Point, with the coast receding thence at right angles to the general line of the littoral, indicated the northern limit of the zone of landing operations unmistakably. Besides, there was an ample length of practicable foreshore south-east of Nibrunesi Point, so that where exactly the lighters fetched up was not of vital moment; as for the landing operations inside

Suvla Bay, Lala Baba and the range of hills to the north of the bight made it easy to find Beach A in the dark.

The beetles upon the whole proved a great success, even admitting that their getting aground at some distance from shore both at Beach A and at Gazi Baba created regrettable delay and inconvenience. At Beaches C and B, where these craft could run their bows right on to the foreshore at almost any point, they discharged their passengers very rapidly. They also proved extremely handy when moving under their own power. Vessels of this class—assuming that the actual beaches are favourable to their employment—possess certain obvious merits, where it is a question of disembarking by night in presence of the enemy. One beetle represented practically the equivalent of three tows, of four ships' cutters each, in respect to number of men transported. The beetle also requires far less sea-room than the tows. Supposing, for instance, that three beetles are making for some particular, limited stretch of beach, the risk of collisions and disorder will not be so great as if nine tows—a total of thirty-six cutters—were performing the same service instead.

Confusion is less likely to arise by day than by night. The question of hostile fire has, on the other hand, to be taken into account much more seriously by day than by night. In so far as the enemy's musketry and machine-guns are concerned, lighters of the beetle type would seem to afford troops decidedly better cover than open boats, and the same holds good as regards shrapnel. But this only holds good while the troops approach the beach. Once it becomes a matter of disembarking from the lighter, the troops on board become exposed to concentrated fire (as was the case when the Munsters and Hampshires issued forth from the *River Clyde* during the landing on V Beach), whereas boats offer the enemy a dispersed target. Moreover, even if the lighter provides good cover against shrapnel, a high explosive shell hitting one of them might easily sink it altogether and would assuredly cause many casualties on board. It should be noted that an important point in favour of the beetles used at Suvla was that they could make five knots under their own motor-power; a tow of cutters astern of a picket boat would not travel at anything like that speed.

The great objection to the lighter as compared to the cutter or other ship's boat, however, is its draught. On many beaches—Brighton or Eastbourne at high water for instance—a vessel drawing four and a half feet can run its prow on to the shingle quite comfortably. But if the sea happens to shoal a long way out from the shore—as it does at Brighton and Eastbourne when the tide is out—the lighter is bound to take the ground prematurely, and four and a half feet of water is inconveniently deep for a fully loaded-up infantryman to struggle through. Moreover, the water may turn out to be deeper inshore than it is where the lighter has fetched up, and it will only take a very few additional inches to drown the soldier. This is unquestionably a serious drawback to the employment of such craft. It has to be remembered that a military descent upon the coast of an enemy's country will often perforce take place at some spot where no soundings close inshore have been taken, and of which no thoroughly trustworthy charts exist.

Turning now from the technical conditions that were involved in getting the troops actually to land at Suvla, to the question of their tactical employment on disembarkation, the critic is confronted by a certain divergence in the views that have been expressed by prominent actors in these dramatic events. There has, moreover, been conflict of evidence as to what occurred at given junctures. This makes a review of the operations somewhat difficult. But the outsider who is obliged to form his opinions from the various narratives, official and other, that have appeared, will find it hard to escape from the broad general conclusion that amongst the commanders, the staff and the regimental officers concerned in the landing, and especially amongst those connected with the troops who disembarked by night, the vital importance of a very early advance, and therefore of the initiation of vertebrate offensive action at the first possible moment, was not sufficiently recognised. The enemy would indeed appear to have been taken altogether too seriously during the opening phases of the operation.

Too much was, however, perhaps expected by the High Command, for in his final despatch Sir I. Hamilton writes :—

" The first task of the IXth Corps was to seize and hold Chocolate, and Ismail Oglu Hills, together with the high ground north and east of Suvla Bay. If the landing went off smoothly, and if my informa-

THE DELAY IN ADVANCING

tion regarding the strength of the enemy were correct, I hoped that these hills, with their guns, might be well in our possession before daybreak."

This does strike one as an optimistic forecast. The Ismail Oglu hill, 350 feet high, is situated a good three miles from Beach C, and the later battalions of the 11th Division could hardly hope to be on land before 2 a.m. For troops thrown ashore by night in an unknown country to have occupied this height by 5 a.m. would have been a creditable performance even if there had been no enemy. But there is, on the other hand, a very wide difference between what the Commander-in-Chief had hoped might be achieved by that hour and what was actually accomplished in practice. For at daybreak two whole brigades were only beginning to set about advancing against Hill 10, which was not half a mile from Beach A where one of the brigades had landed. Nor was any forward movement south of the Salt Lake attempted then or at a later hour. During the early hours of the day—from 6 a.m., say, till 10 a.m.—when the heat was not yet trying and when the troops could not have been suffering intensely from thirst, there were thirteen battalions of the 11th Division available to move to the attack. They enjoyed a numerical superiority of at least three to one over the enemy. They were, moreover, sustained by the moral support of part of the 10th Division, already on shore, and the Turks had manifestly already lost the first round in failing to stop the landing and in abandoning Lala Baba. A steady, resolute offensive, set in motion as soon as there was light enough to distinguish the topographical features and to ensure a suitable distribution of the troops, ought to have carried the line forward before noon to points that actually were not made good till late in the afternoon, after an exhausting advance in great heat by a soldiery parched with thirst.

Even supposing that the front had then remained on the line Green Hill–Sulajik–Kuchuk Anafarta Ova, the fact of its advancing so far forward in the forenoon would have left several hours of daylight to get the line properly organised and for bringing forward water, stores, and ammunition. The situation would therefore have been incomparably more satisfactory when night set in, than it actually was on the 7th of August. There is a good deal of analogy between a landing in an enemy's country and crossing a river into territory in hostile occupation, for in either case you require to occupy as large an area of country—to establish as extensive a bridgehead—as possible, and as soon as possible. That fundamental tactical principle does not seem to have been realised by those immediately concerned.

One point, to which reference must be made in this connection, was brought to the notice of the author by certain of the prominent participators in the opening phase of these Suvla operations. It was this. However it came about, the regimental officers and troops in the 11th Division when they set foot on shore had no definite conception of what they were about to do, or of what they were being called upon to face. May not that lethargy that supervened, at the very time when truculent, uncompromising vigour was called for, have been attributable to this circumstance ? The instruments detailed to carry out the project of the High Command were not aware of the vital importance of pushing rapidly forward, nor did they know that the enemy opposing them was the reverse of formidable. Now it was necessary to conceal the nature and the details of the enterprise to the last. News would spread all over the Ægean in no time from Mitylene, Lemnos, and Imbros, peopled as they were with polyglot, largely seafaring, islanders. Every soldier who has become versed in such matters by contact with actual events, realises how imperative confining information to a strictly limited circle is, if you wish to keep your designs secret. The fewer people, be they general-officers or be they drummer-boys, who know what is afoot the better. But this only holds good up to a certain stage in the proceedings. Thanks to the care with which the principle was enforced from general headquarters and from corps headquarters before the Suvla landings, these landings came upon the Osmanlis as a complete surprise. And yet the very reticence and mystification which made the landings a surprise appear to have contributed to some extent to bring about the failure of the operation as a whole.

There can be no question but that, until the flotillas started on their trip from the islands, only a favoured few of the actors in the forthcoming drama could safely be made acquainted with what was contemplated. But, the moment that the armadas weighed, all need for secrecy was at an end. Then, on the contrary, it became in the highest degree expedient that all concerned should learn the

TROOPS UNAWARE OF THEIR TASK

nature of the task to which they were being committed. Ought it not to have been a case of sealed envelopes, of sealed envelopes on a lavish scale? The senior officer on every separate vessel might have had his sealed orders, to be opened as soon as she got into motion. A sketch-plan and a very few general instructions might have sufficed, the significance of rapid progress after landing being emphasised and the weakness of the enemy insisted upon.

It must be remembered that the situation, speaking topographically, was a remarkably straightforward one—Suvla Bay, the Salt Lake, Lala Baba, Chocolate Hill, and the general line of heights which it was so important to secure as soon as possible, were all very well defined. No especial proficiency in map-reading was called for to grasp the essentials. Lights no doubt could not be shown, but an officer charged with sealed orders could easily have conned them over between decks on a destroyer, or down in the hold of a beetle. Having soaked in the information the officer could then have collected the subalterns and non-commissioned officers and have told them what it was so necessary for them to know, and these again would have passed it on to the rank and file. One can imagine how a man who had spent a few months in a mobile column on the veld would have improved the occasion—especially with regard to the weakness of the enemy, and as to the risk of rifle shots by a handful of men in the dark or in the half-light of early morning deceiving and holding up a considerable force, if this allows itself to be bluffed. But there probably were few such practised soldiers aboard the Imbros flotilla, except in the upper grades, in the 11th Division. "We've got to keep pushing for all we're worth, we must get well clear of the beaches before the Turkish gunners have light to see or they'll give us a bad time, and we must get those hills right away before any more of the enemy come up." Every infantry soldier in the division ought to have been infected with this idea before he stepped on shore or waded towards the beach, well aware that brigadiers and staff and those sort of people could be trusted to give the impulse in the right direction.

Still, it has to be remembered that the troops of the IXth Corps who landed at Suvla represented newly constituted formations that had not been even thought of when the European War had broken out, almost exactly a year before. There was no precedent in modern times for a force of anything approaching to the size of three infantry brigades being landed on open beaches in presence of the enemy at dead of night. The 29th Division had performed its great feat of the 25th of April in broad daylight; the French likewise had disembarked at Kum Kale by day; the Anzacs had only begun their landing at dawn. The Suvla venture constituted a new departure altogether, and one that might well have tried the nerve and shattered the cohesion of seasoned troops. Something undoubtedly went wrong after the disembarkation had been most successfully effected. But, even admitting this to be the case, those New Army divisions accomplished much to be proud of between nightfall on the 6th of August and nightfall on the following day.

The events of the 8th.—Before recording what occurred on the British side at Suvla on the 8th, it will be convenient to indicate the action that appears to have been taken by the defenders to meet this new attack upon the Gallipoli Peninsula. We have seen on page 195 that, at the date when Sir I. Hamilton's August offensive started, there were according to German accounts two divisions, the 7th and the 12th, stationed somewhere about the Bulair Isthmus ready to meet danger in that direction of which Marshal Liman von Sanders always appears to have been inordinately afraid. As soon as news of the Suvla landing reached Turkish headquarters, about the same time as intelligence also came to hand of General Birdwood's night advance against Sari Bair, the 7th and 12th Divisions were set in motion, and they apparently proceeded entirely by march route to reinforce the troops that were already on the long line extending from the Kizlar Dagh to near Gaba Tepe, a line which was by far at its thinnest at its northern end, facing Suvla. The German account makes no reference to using ships in the Dardanelles to convey portions of these two divisions to near the scene of action, as had been the case under somewhat similar circumstances when Turkish troops were transferred from the Bulair end of the peninsula to Anzac and Helles on the occasion of the original landing. The 12th Division headed straight for Kuchuk Anafarta, while the 7th on its left made for Biyuk Anafarta and the northern spurs of Sari Bair, and, assuming that they started from near the Bulair lines, the distance would be about thirty miles in either case.

While some of these Ottoman troops were probably further away than the Lines, others may well have been stationed about Gallipoli or even nearer to the new concentration points. Supposing that they started about noon on the 7th, the leading units might have been arriving in the Suvla region fairly early in the day on the 8th. But, as a matter of fact, no reinforcements would seem to have joined the Turkish detachments in this quarter before dark on that day. These had withdrawn their guns and evidently expected attack, and during the whole of the daylight hours of the second twenty-four hours that the IXth Corps spent on the peninsula, it continued to enjoy that great superiority in numerical strength which it had possessed since the landing of the infantry had been completed early in the afternoon of the previous day.

But this infantry had not yet recovered from the effects of the exertions and trials that it had undergone. Nor had the problem with regard to water been overcome. This, as well as food supplies and ammunition, had to be carried from the beaches to the front line by hand, a condition of things that meant a most inconvenient depletion of the fighting ranks, and which was attributable to the landing of transport animals still being seriously in arrear. Some of the units that had joined in the advance on the afternoon of the 7th had, moreover, returned to the beaches. Apart from the weakness of the enemy, the conditions were no doubt somewhat unfavourable for the institution of a vigorous offensive. But, be that as it may, the second day of the IXth Corps' stay at Suvla was, from the fighting point of view, practically a day of rest. Only two movements forward of any note took place. Two battalions of the 32nd Brigade advanced into the hills, one occupying the important Scimitar Hill, and the other, the 9th West Yorks, pushing forward nearly as far as the point Abrikja and a line running north from there; this ought to have represented a very pronounced gain, had further advantage been taken of it. On the extreme left the 10th Division won some little ground on the Kiritch Tepe Sirt early in the morning.

The omission to profit by what was unquestionably a promising tactical situation, in view of the great numerical superiority of the British on this second day, does not appear to have been wholly due to the exhaustion of the troops nor to the disorganisation of the transport service. Weakness in respect to artillery would also seem to have contributed, at a juncture when delay was likely to prove fatal to the prospect of the operations being successful as a whole, towards deciding those in high command to forego attack. It is true that only one field battery and two mountain batteries were yet ashore, and that difficulties of intercommunication were bound to militate against any effective employment of the ships' guns. But the idea that an infantry attack may not be launched against a hostile position without an elaborate bombardment as a prologue, is founded on the assumption that the assailants enjoy no overwhelming superiority of force. The situation was, moreover, emphatically one that demanded unconventional action, and in this connection Sir I. Hamilton pertinently observes in his final despatch :—

" Normally it may be correct to say that in modern warfare infantry cannot be expected to advance without artillery preparation. But in a landing on a hostile shore the order is inverted. The infantry must advance and seize a position suitable to cover the landing and to provide artillery positions for the main thrust. The very existence of the force, its water supply, its facilities for munitions and supplies, its power to reinforce, must depend upon the infantry being able instantly to make good sufficient ground, without the aid of artillery other than can be supplied for the purpose by floating batteries."

Sir I. Hamilton's direct intervention.—The Commander-in-Chief had remained at his headquarters at Imbros on the 7th, satisfied that he could most effectively keep his finger on the pulse of the complex combination of war involving three distinct though interdependent operations to which he was committed, by stationing himself at what was the central point as between Helles, Anzac, and Suvla. Becoming, however, gradually aware from reports coming to hand that the progress of the IXth Corps was very much more deliberate than he had pictured, and that there was consequently a risk of its failing to perform its rôle in the task that was being entrusted to the forces launched on the great offensive north of Gaba Tepe, he decided during the afternoon of the 8th to repair personally to Suvla, and he arrived at corps headquarters, afloat, about 5 p.m. In his final despatch he gives a graphic description of his experiences after landing, and of the sequel. Suffice it to say here that, although General Stopford was most anxious that active operations should be pressed and although Sir Ian urged that even at that late hour orders should be issued for an immediate advance by the 11th Division—under the circumstances this must almost necessarily have meant a night attack—it was not deemed practicable by the divisional general and the brigadiers to get the instructions for such an undertaking out in time, seeing how scattered the force was. They were, moreover, not perhaps altogether unnaturally, indisposed to venture upon nocturnal operations under the conditions then existing and with inexperienced troops. A good deal of doubt, moreover, appears to have existed at corps and divisional headquarters as to where exactly the various infantry units were.

Eventually the Commander-in-Chief ordered that the 32nd Brigade, which was believed to be more concentrated than the others and therefore better situated for promptly resuming the offensive than they were, should act alone. It was to endeavour to gain a footing on the high ground north of Kuchuk Anafarta, before the inevitable arrival of hostile reinforcements had converted the weak Turkish detachments that had been in occupation of the heights all that day into a force capable of offering a stalwart resistance to a determined onset. As a matter of fact, however, the 32nd Brigade was by no means concentrated, for two of its battalions[1] were, as narrated above, on Scimitar Hill and on the high ground about Abrikja and to the north of it, having pushed forward during the day. These units had to be brought back from their advantageous position before the brigade could be launched against its fresh objective. It did not actually start till next morning, and its experiences do not therefore come within the scope of an account of the day's doings on the 8th.

Thus, in spite of the direct intervention of the Commander-in-Chief, the second twenty-four hours of the Sulva venture remained for all practical purposes a day of inaction in so far as fighting was concerned, because the two battalions of the 32nd Brigade which did push on into the hills were virtually unopposed. Much useful work was, on the other hand, got through on the beaches this day in respect to unloading stores, animals, water-cart, and so forth.

[1] One of these, the 6th East Yorks, did not actually belong to the brigade being the divisional pioneer battalion, but was attached to the brigade.

The disembarkation of the 53rd Division was, moreover, begun late in the afternoon and it continued all night, certain of its units taking part in next day's affray.

Comments.—It is not surprising that the situation in this portion of the theatre of operations should have caused Sir I. Hamilton grave concern. He had been confident that the 11th Division would have secured possession of much of the high ground dominating the Suvla Plain, and including the important tactical positions on Chocolate Hill and Ismail Oglu Tepe, at an early hour on the 7th. But at nightfall on the 8th only some of the heights on the extreme left (which were of secondary importance) and Chocolate and Green Hills had been occupied, in so far as the situation was understood on the beach. The encouraging fact that Scimitar Hill and some of the high ground further to the north was likewise in British hands appears only to have been known to the two units which, realising their opportunities, had made good this very valuable position.

Sir Ian had hoped that, after the arrival of the 10th Division on the 7th, the weight of the IXth Corps could have been brought to bear to some extent against Sari Bair from about Ismail Oglu Tepe and Biyuk Anafarta, so as to lend at least some indirect assistance to General Birdwood's forces in their very arduous operations. But no succour of any kind had been afforded to that vital main attack from the Suvla side. We may presume that the Commander-in-Chief had pictured to himself the troops of the IXth Corps, as placed beyond serious anxiety as to their water supply consequent on having mastered the wells that were known to exist about the two large Anafarta villages. But so far from this being the case, he found that those troops at the end of thirty-six hours remained scattered about on the Suvla plain, which, although it was by no means waterless, only provided a few wells far apart and under fire of aggressive snipers. The position of affairs was rendered all the more disquieting from the knowledge that, even if the offensive from the side of Anzac had made gratifying progress in face of rare difficulties and resolute opposition, it had not achieved its object of riveting a grip upon the uppermost ridges of Sari Bair before the enemy could mass his men to hold these coveted heights.

That a great opportunity was lost on the 8th, in spite of the delays that had taken place on the 7th, does not seem to admit of doubt.

OBSTACLES TO ADVANCE

Aeroplane reconnaissance during the day revealed that the Turks were removing their guns, which indeed had remained silent in spite of the attractive targets which the crowded beaches were presenting. Aeroplane reconnaissance also revealed the fact that hostile reinforcements were hurrying from the Bulair end of the peninsula. The troops had had a night's rest of a sort. The importance of capturing Ismail Oglu Tepe—" an abrupt and savage heap of cliff, dented with chasms, harshly scarped at the top, and covered with dense thorn scrub," according to Mr. Masefield—was obvious, seeing that this prominent height dominated the Biyuk Anafarta valley from the north. The occupation of Kuchuk Anafarta would provide the troops that accomplished it with water. The situation was one calling imperatively for vigorous action. Still there is also something to be said on the other side.

The infantry on Chocolate Hill and stretching northwards from thence to Kuchuk Anafarta Ova were gravely handicapped owing to the difficulty in getting up supplies to them across the plain, seeing that everything practically had to be carried by hand. Moreover, the further they advanced on the 8th, or at least early in the day on the 8th, the greater this handicap would necessarily become. Then there was also that water difficulty, which had not yet been overcome. The troops had suffered terribly from thirst on the previous day, and they were still suffering. Some of the few wells found about the plain were filled with corpses put there by the Turks, others were brackish, others were guarded by enemy snipers, and in any case wells were few and far between. The fact of a successful advance to Kuchuk Anafarta on the part of the left of the 11th Division would not provide drink for its right, even supposing that this secured the Ismail Oglu height. The brigadiers, the battalion commanders, and the brigade staffs might be assumed to be better able to judge of the fitness of the troops for a forward movement, than the divisional commander away back on the shore, or the corps commander on board ship, or the Commander-in-Chief, suddenly arrived from an island fourteen miles off, could be. The question is : did brigadiers, regimental officers, and troops realise how much depended upon a prompt advance ? Were they aware that it meant all the difference between success and virtual failure ?

"Thirst and fatigue were forgotten," writes the author of *The Tenth (Irish) Division in Gallipoli,* " as the Fusiliers, exulting in the force of their attack, dashed over trench and communication trench until the crest of the hill was gained." That was the story of how General Hill's infantry had delivered their onset on the previous evening after their trying march round the Salt Lake from Beach C. Thirst and fatigue might likewise have been forgotten on the morning of the 8th had all ranks of the 11th Division been informed of what the strategical and tactical situation so insistently demanded.

The events of the 9th and 10th.—A general attack upon the Ottoman position between the southern Azmak Dere and the heights stretching away north of Kuchuk Anafarta, to be executed by the 11th Division assisted by the 31st Brigade (which had remained in occupation of Chocolate Hill and Green Hill) and some troops of the newly arrived 53rd Division, had been decided upon for the early morning of the 9th, before Sir I. Hamilton intervened with regard to an immediate advance by the 32nd Brigade. The defenders manifestly enjoyed the advantage as regards position, considering that they were holding all the high ground lying east of the Suvla flats except some high ground near Abrikja and the promontory in the hands of the 31st Brigade—as will be seen, Scimitar Hill had been abandoned during the night. The Turks in fact completely overlooked the terrain across which the assailants were called upon to advance.

The operation was timed to commence at 5.30 a.m.; but in consequence of Sir I. Hamilton's intervention on the previous evening the 32nd Brigade, which had been unable to carry out his orders as to an immediate advance, but which had assembled near Sulajik during the night, moved off at 4 a.m. Its objective was the terrain north of the Kuchuk Anafarta gap in the hills, and divisional orders had laid down that the attack was to be led by the 6th East Yorks—the very battalion which had occupied Scimitar Hill the previous day and which had been obliged to withdraw from that point and to retire in the darkness to the brigade rendezvous. The objective indicated to the 31st Brigade on the right of the 32nd was practically the very ground which the two battalions of the 32nd Brigade that had pushed forward on the previous day had occupied and had since abandoned. The 33rd Brigade was to advance on the right of the 31st; but part of this brigade was obliged to start from the beach so early as

2 a.m., as two of its battalions had retired thither after the affray of the 7th; the brigade nevertheless advanced to the attack up to time. The 34th Brigade was on the left of the line, and two battalions of the 53rd Division acted in reserve.

The introductory incidents of the day's affrays were not wholly unpromising, for the 32nd Brigade speedily secured the Baka Baba spurs, and in spite of their sleepless night the 6th East Yorks pressed stoutly up the commanding spur north of Kuchuk Anafarta. On the right, a portion of the 33rd Brigade managed temporarily to master portions of the Oglu Tepe crest, after heavy fighting. But the 9th West Yorks when it advanced towards Abrikja was soon checked, and although some of the 31st Brigade troops struggled on to Scimitar Hill they could not maintain the position. For the enemy was gathering strength from hour to hour and was bringing numbers of batteries into action—a considerable part of the 12th Turkish Division seems to have been on the ground and fully committed to action before the battle reached its height, and these new arrivals threw themselves into the encounter with enthusiasm. In spite of its good beginning the 32nd Brigade was driven back, and, by giving way, it to some extent compromised the troops on its right. Ismail Oglu Tepe and Scimitar Hill were recovered by the enemy as a result of violent counter-attacks, burning scrub caused much confusion, and the assailants eventually fell back at all points. Ammunition replenishment caused serious difficulty during the retirement, and when the engagement gradually died down the 11th Division found itself back practically on the line that it had started from, but with much depleted ranks. The losses on the 7th had been almost insignificant; in this unfortunate action they were very heavy.

It is recorded that Marshal Liman von Sanders had intended that the Ottoman forces should have delivered a counter-attack during the night of the 8th–9th. The Turkish commander who had been placed in charge of operations in this Anafarta area when news came of the Suvla landing appears, however, to have fallen suddenly ill. According to the German account, this contretemps prevented the night attack from materialising. It seems very doubtful, however, whether the Turks were strong enough during the night of the 8th–9th to have assumed the offensive with much prospect of success; if orders for a counter-attack were really issued by the enemy commander-in-chief it would indeed seem to have been an error of judgment. The German work *Der Kampf um die Dardanellen* contains some interesting information as to Turkish movements and as to Liman von Sanders' intentions, but there appear to be mistakes of date in some of its passages. The proposed counter-attack may have been intended for the following night, the 9th–10th, by which time the Turks were in strong force. As will be seen, however, it was the British and not the Turks who attacked on the 10th.

The action of the 9th was upon the whole well contested, but its result was that the IXth Corps suffered a mortifying discomfiture at the hands of their sturdy antagonists, having given these ample time to assemble. Twelve hours' respite from molestation had sufficed to transform the thin line of Moslem defenders of the high ground overlooking the Suvla plain, out of a scattered line of foot soldiers bereft of all artillery support, into a force of all arms that was well qualified to offer an unyielding resistance to the efforts of the British brigades launched against its position on the morning of the 9th. "Time," says Clausewitz, "is on the side of the defence," and on this occasion the defence had been granted time, thanks to a species of torpor which had gripped assailants who, forty-eight hours earlier, had entered upon their venture with all the advantages that the initiative confers when initiative is coupled with surprise.

The confusion that may arise when the ordinary channels of communication are departed from is very well illustrated by what occurred on the afternoon of the 8th and during the night following, with untoward consequences on the 9th. Sir I. Hamilton, after discussing the situation with General Stopford (whose headquarters were on board ship) proceeded to the headquarters of the 11th Division on shore at Lala Baba, and, upon ascertaining there that the 32nd Brigade were fairly well concentrated, gave orders that this should attack as soon as possible. As a matter of fact the brigade was not concentrated by any means, as we have seen, the 6th East Yorks actually being in occupation of Scimitar Hill, and the 9th West Yorks more or less in line to the north, while the remaining battalions were on the low ground about Sulajik and to the north and north-west of that locality. The divisional general, moreover, named the 6th East Yorks as the battalion that was to lead the advance ; it is true that this was the divisional battalion, but it was under the orders of the brigadier of the 32nd Brigade at the time. The result was that the very important Scimitar Hill, which had been occupied without difficulty, was abandoned, and that one of the two battalions which had pushed on a considerable distance during the 8th had to withdraw by night—necessarily a somewhat exhausting process—and by the time that it had reached the rendezvous had to start off to the front and to lead the attack of its brigade about dawn.

The general attack by the 11th Division had been arranged for the morning of the 9th, and the possession of Scimitar Hill from the very start must have been of great advantage—the more so seeing that the Turks reoccupied that eminence, and were able from thence to take in flank the 32nd Brigade when this advanced to the attack on Kuchuk Anafarta. Although the hill was retaken, this was only after tough fighting, and it was only held then for a very short time. The need for action at the earliest possible moment was obvious to the Commander-in-Chief on the afternoon of the 8th, as he was well aware that Turkish reinforcements were on the march and would probably be arriving during the night. But in view of the ignorance that prevailed as to the position of the troops—of which he was unaware—it would perhaps have been better if he had not interfered with the divisional arrangements. The fact that the 6th East Yorks were the divisional battalion might have excused its being especially designated by divisional headquarters, even though it was under the orders of the brigadier of the 32nd Brigade, had divisional headquarters known where it was. But that would not seem to have been the case. The incident is a very instructive one.

The attack on the high ground east of Suvla plain was repeated on the 10th. The operation was on this occasion entrusted to the 53rd Division, supported by the 11th Division. Two whole brigades of artillery were now on shore, and these, seconded by the mountain batteries and by ships' guns, were able to bring a respectable body of fire to bear upon the enemy's commanding positions. But the Turks were now fully prepared and in stronger force than on the previous day ; then many units had only been coming on to the ground as the British advanced and during the ensuing engagement. They had had time to consolidate the position and to strengthen their lines. Therefore, although the 53rd Division gained some ground to start with, it was before long brought to a standstill and was ultimately obliged to fall back to the old lines down in the plain. The losses in this unsuccessful attack were again somewhat heavy. Further frontal attacks offered little hope of success, so General Stopford ordered the troops to dig themselves in on what was practically the line that had been occupied on the evening of the 7th. This had, however, been linked up with the position which the 10th Division had secured on the Kiritch Tepe Sirt ; and during the next two or three days the 31st Brigade was relieved by other infantry and moved off to rejoin its division, from which it had been separated since leaving the United Kingdom.

The splitting up of the 10th Division.—As complaints were made at the time that the 10th Division was unfairly treated in that it came to be so much scattered during, and before, the August offensive, it may perhaps be pointed out that this was the fortune of war and was merely a matter of bad luck. The Commander-in-Chief considered that five brigades of infantry were sufficient for the Suvla operations to start with, and he required an additional infantry brigade for the Sari Bair operations. Therefore, either the 10th or the 11th Division had to be deprived of one brigade for the time being, and the choice fell upon the 10th. There was nothing to complain about in that. As the essence of the Suvla plan was that there should be a surprise by night in force, and as there were good grounds for trying to make the Turks anticipate an attack upon the Asiatic coast from Mitylene, the arrangement under which the whole of the infantry of the 11th Division was assembled at Imbros and shipped across early on the night of the 6th to the Suvla region was the obvious one to adopt. The 11th Division being told off thus, the 10th Division naturally had to proceed in part to Mitylene ; to have sent the whole of the 30th and 31st Brigades thither, together with the divisional battalion, would have created difficulty in respect to shipment thence to Suvla.

In view of the experiences undergone at A Beach during the night of the 6th-7th, there could be no question of landing General Hill's force from Mitylene at such a place in daylight under artillery fire, and, the Gazi Baba landing-place not having been discovered, its relegation to C Beach was practically unavoidable. The anxiety of the corps commander to keep the 10th Division concentrated appears indeed in reality to have been the cause of General Hill's battalions making their troublesome march round the Salt Lake, instead of their being directed on Chocolate Hill straight from their landing-place. Then, by the time that they had assembled near Hill 10, the 32nd and 34th Brigades of the 11th Division were apparently already committed to a somewhat belated movement to their front. Chocolate Hill had to be secured on tactical grounds, so Hill was called upon to march against this as his were practically the only troops available, thus preventing their uniting with the rest of their division to the north. The truth is that, although it may be possible to avoid splitting up units supposing that you have eight or ten of them, it will seldom be possible to avoid splitting at least one of them up during active operations if you only have two at your disposal. It is indeed an elementary military axiom that two infantry units working by themselves are an anachronism, because you have nothing ready to your hand to form a reserve.

Conclusion.—Synchronising as it did with the final defeat of the efforts on the part of General Birdwood's troops to master and to hold Hill Q and the Chunuk Bair ridge, the reverse suffered by the Suvla force on the 10th may be said to have connoted the definite failure of Sir I. Hamilton's boldly conceived design. In so far as the Suvla venture was concerned, the outstanding features of that design had comprised (1) the winning of a landing by surprise, (2) securing a sheltered base on the coast by promptly occupying the high ground, weakly held by the enemy, which dominated the sheltered base within easy artillery range, and (3) intervening thereafter, with a strong military contingent operating from the newly acquired jumping-off place, in the contest that was raging for the possession of the Sari Bair mountain. The first item in the programme—conquest of the landing-place by dint of a surprise—had been triumphantly carried into effect. But the project of the Commander-in-Chief in respect to the early capture of the heights overlooking Suvla Bay had not materialised. Nor had the substantial force that had been thrown on shore in a few hours within and around that bight lent any appreciable succour to the Australasian, British, and Indian troops that were embattled on the mountain ridges not half a dozen miles to the south-east. The activities of the IXth Corps had not indeed even drawn off any of the enemy troops engaged about Sari Bair; and, although the 12th Turkish Division from Bulair hurried to the Anafarta heights, the 7th Division from the same quarter ignored the Suvla threat and made for the more southerly field. The IXth Corps had in fact only performed the first portion of the hard task that had been set it.

A general consideration of the Commander-in-Chief's plan, regarded as a whole, will be deferred till the end of the next chapter, in view of the length of this one. Chapter XII will briefly record the course followed by later aggressive operations in August, operations that were virtually confined to the Suvla area, and that represented a final offensive flicker, before the Dardanelles Expeditionary Force became constrained by its relative inadequacy in fighting potentialities to resign itself reluctantly to a discouraging and unprofitable inaction.

CHAPTER XII

THE CLOSE OF THE AUGUST OFFENSIVE

The situation on the 11th of August.—As pointed out at the end of the last chapter, the events of the 10th marked the definite failure of the scheme of offensive operations for August, as it had been elaborated by the Commander-in-Chief. That scheme had hinged upon effecting a strategical and tactical surprise upon the enemy. Sir Ian's idea had been to secure Sari Bair after unexpectedly and secretly massing forces within striking distance of the objective to accomplish its conquest. Its capture was to serve as a preliminary to advancing from Anzac and Suvla on Maidos and the Narrows of the Dardanelles, while artillery emplaced on the commanding heights that had been secured should exercise domination over the water-way. Bodies of troops, decidedly stronger in numbers than the Turks immediately on the spot, had been gathered together both at Anzac and at Suvla as a result of skilfully conceived and admirably executed concentrations of force. But from neither point had the attack been driven home sufficiently to establish an unqualified tactical superiority on the spot, before Ottoman reinforcements hurrying to the scenes of action from different quarters had succeeded in restoring numerical equilibrium.

General Birdwood's divisions had gone very near to success. They had borne themselves with conspicuous grit and gallantry during a succession of furiously contested affrays, affrays in which the enemy had always opposed them from dominating fortified positions. They had inflicted very heavy losses upon the Turks. But they had also suffered very severely themselves both in officers and in men, and they now stood sorely in need of generous drafts calculated to bring them up to their authorised establishment again. As for the IXth Corps, this had gained its footing at Suvla.

But the line which it had succeeded in occupying and entrenching was not nearly far enough forward to render the newly acquired landing-place thoroughly secure, and it had played no part in the combats for Sari Bair. Moreover, the troops that had made good the new landing-place had suffered heavy losses, whereas they had not inflicted much damage upon the Sultan's soldiery, who were now in great force about the Anafartas and were strongly posted.

General Birdwood for a brief space contemplated a renewal of his attack upon the upper ridges of Sari Bair. But fuller consideration convinced him that offensive operations on any ambitious scale, directed against the Osmanli legions who were crowning the heights overlooking Anzac and Ocean Beach, had become inadvisable. The enemy was too formidable and too well posted to justify further attempts to win the mountain. On the other hand, the desirability of joining up with the Suvla force was manifest. Advance northwards from about Demajalik Bair towards the southern Azmak Dere and the valley of Biyuk Anafarta, moreover, offered a reasonable prospect of success. Consequently such offensive operations as were embarked upon from Anzac during the remainder of August were confined to movements in this direction.

As regards the situation around Suvla Bay, the necessity for the British force that had planted itself down in this area to gain some elbow room, if it were possible, was obvious. Soundings, coupled with a thoroughgoing examination of the foreshore, had established the fact that it would be feasible to construct good landing-places both at Gazi Baba and also on the southern shore of the bay under the shelter of Lala Baba—the bight in fact offered by no means a bad base, if only the Turks could be thrust back off the Anafarta hills so that the newly acquired haven should at least be immune from the effects of hostile field-gun fire. It furthermore was almost imperative that the Ismail Oglu eminences should be wrested out of the hands of the enemy, because guns had been enfilading the Anzac landing-places from thence ever since the Australasian corps had established itself on the outer coast of the Gallipoli Peninsula four months earlier. The Commander-in-Chief consequently made up his mind that the Suvla offensive must continue. He had already ordered the 54th Division, the last of the reinforcements from home, to proceed thither, and its infantry

ACTION OF THE 15TH AUGUST 243

were put ashore on the 11th. Some additional artillery was also landed, and the Anafarta hills became the focus of interest during the third week of August.

Operations from the 12th to the 16th.—On the afternoon of the 12th a brigade of the 54th Division, the 163rd, was deputed to clear some intricate, scrub-clad ground about the Kuchuk Anafarta Ova, this operation being intended as a prologue to a night march that was to be followed by a general attack upon the range north of Kuchuk Anafarta village. But the brigade detailed for the job found the enemy in force and full of fight, the project of the night march and attack was abandoned, and further offensive operations against this part of the enemy's positions on the Suvla front were for the moment deferred. It had, however, become desirable that the troops on the extreme left should gain ground forwards if possible, as that flank of the British line was somewhat thrown back relatively to the positions held in the centre. So steps to overcome this defect in position were decided upon, and in pursuance of that object an attack was undertaken in the Kiritch Tepe Sirt section by the 10th Division on the 15th. Its two brigades were supported by war vessels that bombarded the Turkish right from the Gulf of Saros, as well as by a brigade of the 54th Division which acted on the low ground on the 10th Division's right.

This offensive proved very successful to start with on the left; for, aided by naval gun-fire, the assailants made good a considerable amount of ground on the northern slope of the ridge facing the sea, this in spite of topographical difficulties of no common order and of a stubborn resistance on the part of an enemy abundantly supplied with machine-guns.[1] But on the southern side of the line of hills the heavy fire of the Turks brought movement speedily to a standstill. Activity on the part of the left flank of the IXth Corps had, it appears, been anticipated by the defenders and these were found to be in strong force; Marshal Liman von Sanders is indeed understood to have been on the spot and to have personally superintended the disposal of the reinforcements that were hurried up to confront the 10th Division—in view of the reverses suffered by the IXth Corps on the 9th, 10th, and 12th the enemy naturally anticipated an effort further north on the part of the invading forces. The result of the day's combat was that at nightfall the

[1] See Appendix IV, 6.

left of the division was thrown forward considerably in advance of the right, and that its line of battle resembled the letter Z, with the diagonal line roughly coinciding with the crest of the Kiritch Tepe Sirt ridge—an awkward line, and one that was rendered all the more awkward during the night and the following day by the fact that the Turks were well supplied with hand grenades, whereas the infantry of the 10th Division were not. The upshot on the 16th was that after a somewhat one-sided struggle the battalions which had pressed forward so effectively on the previous day along the coastward side of the ridge, enfiladed as they were and almost threatened in rear, were obliged to fall back to their original line, much diminished in numbers.

This affair offers some points of noteworthy tactical interest. It, for instance, furnishes a good illustration of the value of naval co-operation when the battle conditions are such that the engagement is taking place close to the shore and at right angles to it. As had been the case on the occasion of the struggle of the 12th of May in the Helles area which has been described on page 154, war vessels were able to act against the Turkish flank where it approached the shore; and although the flotilla only comprised two destroyers, their guns pertinaciously worried the enemy holding the slopes of the Kiritch Tepe Sirt range on the seaward side, and they played an important part in promoting the early successes of the 10th Division on that flank. On the other hand, the destroyers could afford no assistance to the battalions of the division that were engaged beyond the crest of the ridge on its southern side, and these were unable to make any progress. The effect of the hand grenades is also instructive. The adversaries had hardly settled down to trench warfare yet in this section of the front; but, owing to the intricate, gully-streaked character of the ground, the combatants speedily got to grips at close range even if it remained a case of open fighting. Such conditions lent themselves readily to bombing work. Better fitted out with these missiles than the British were, the Turks enjoyed a very decided tactical advantage, and of this they made full use.

Sir I. Hamilton's request for large reinforcements.—Sir I. Hamilton had now had time to arrive at a conclusion as to what prospects were left of success, in spite of the discomfiture met with in the second week of August, and he had satisfied himself that heavy

SIR I. HAMILTON REQUESTS REINFORCEMENTS 245

reinforcements were indispensable if he was to carry out the task that his Government had entrusted into his hands; he had already summoned from Egypt the Second Mounted Division of Yeomanry, under General Peyton, who were to act as a dismounted body of troops. On the 16th he telegraphed home to Lord Kitchener at the War Office asking that drafts to the number of 45,000 infantry should be sent out to fill the gaps in the ranks of his depleted battalions, and that 50,000 fresh rifles should be sent as additional formations. The latter figure was equivalent to four fresh divisions at full war establishment, and, with the 45,000 drafts to replace the wastage in the divisions already in the Gallipoli Peninsula, would have given him an army of seventeen divisions—about 190,000 rifles, or double of the 95,000 rifles actually at his disposal when putting forward his demand. Of these 95,000, 25,000 were at Anzac, 40,000 were at Helles, and 30,000 were in the Suvla area. The Turks were believed to have about 110,000 rifles within the peninsula.

But the Home Government was unable to comply with the demands of the Commander-in-Chief, and even the drafts asked for to make good wastage were not sent. Whether 190,000 infantry, backed by the artillery already available, would have gained possession of the heights on the European side of the Dardanelles which dominated the Narrows it is impossible to say. But the decision taken in London to refuse Sir I. Hamilton's request created what was strategically a deplorable state of affairs. It meant that a force that was too small to carry out a successful campaign in the Gallipoli Peninsula, but that was nevertheless large enough to represent a valuable military asset in the Great War, was condemned to remain planted down in an isolated theatre of conflict, depending upon precarious communications, disposed in positions that were tactically most unfavourable, and called upon to operate under conditions that could not be other than discouraging in view of past experiences and of future prospects. The Commander-in-Chief in putting forward his request for substantial reinforcement had forced upon the Home Government a choice between three alternatives—despatch of additional troops to enable the man on the spot to carry out the work that he had been called upon to do; withdrawal of the expeditionary army from the Gallipoli Peninsula; holding on with no hope of success, but with

the certainty of heavy loss from sickness, if not on the battlefield.
There was a good deal to be said for either the first or the second
alternative. There was very little to be said for the alternative
that was actually chosen.

From the 17th to the 20th of August.—Sir I. Hamilton was
naturally much disappointed on receiving the intimation from
London that the reinforcements for which he had asked could not
be sent him. He, however, resolved upon making a fresh effort
to improve the Suvla position and to secure its junction with the
Anzac area, hoping at the same time to gain possession of Ismail
Oglu Tepe, as capture of this hill would constitute an important
step towards securing both Suvla Bay and Anzac Cove from
artillery fire. In view of effecting these objects, he moved the
29th Division round to Suvla from Helles and he also disembarked
the Mounted Division, that was coming from Egypt, in the northern
area. The arrival of the 29th Division, the achievements of which
during the campaign had already been common talk in the United
Kingdom before the troops operating in the Suvla region had started
from home, had, it should be recorded, a most stimulating effect
upon the army that was facing the Anafarta hills, many units in
which had suffered heavily since its landing without their having
much to show for the sacrifices that they had experienced. Problems
of supply and transport had in the meantime to a great extent
been overcome in the newly occupied area, and the number of guns
available, including some howitzers, had been appreciably increased.
The force in the Suvla region now comprised a total of five divisions,
together with a Mounted Division. General De Lisle, previously in
command of the 29th Division, had taken over charge as a temporary
measure, his place at the head of his division being taken by General
Marshall, and on the 21st a fresh attack on an important scale was
undertaken. The engagement took place in presence of Sir I.
Hamilton, although General De Lisle was in executive command.

The battle of the 21st of August.—The special objective of this
offensive operation was the capture of Ismail Oglu Tepe. This
task was assigned to the 29th and 11th Divisions, the 29th Division
advancing on the left from about Chocolate Hill and the ground
immediately on either side of it, while the 11th Division on the
right was to advance in the low ground on the north of the Azmak
Dere, storming the line of trenches which the enemy had con-

structed across this about Hetman Chair. The 10th Division and the Mounted Division were retained as corps reserve. To the 53rd and 54th Division was assigned the duty of holding the front from Sulajik to Kiritch Tepe Sirt. The Anzac force was to co-operate by swinging forward its left from Demajalik Bair towards the Azmak Dere.

But the enterprise to which this considerable army was being committed was manifestly an extremely formidable one. Except in the case of the contingents advancing from just about Chocolate Hill and those starting from Demajalik Bair, it was a question of moving across an open plain overlooked by the positions held by the enemy. The Turks had entrenched themselves at all points, they were fully prepared, they were well equipped, and they were, moreover, in strong force. The artillery support to the assailants,[1] even supplemented as it was by the guns of the warships,[2] was scarcely adequate for an operation of this class. The heat was intense. Scrub fires created serious difficulties to the advancing troops at many points. Finally on the afternoon of the 21st, the time of day appointed for the operation, there was mist which seriously interfered with the development of a really effective bombardment of the hostile position about to be assailed. This was a somewhat serious matter seeing how formidable the position was, also taking into consideration the fact that there were now two heavy and two howitzer batteries available, the fire of which

[1] Thirty-two field guns, eight mountain guns, eight 5-inch howitzers, eight 60-prs.

[2] Owing to Suvla Bay having been netted it was possible to employ unbelted warships within it in support of the troops, and the two battleships *Venerable* and *Swiftsure*, as well as two cruisers, took part in the action from this station. A passage in *A Naval Adventure* throws an interesting light upon their work on this occasion and upon naval bombardments of this kind in general. The ships naturally took the high ground about Scimitar Hill for their target—the low ground about Hetman Chair will no doubt have been invisible, at least from the decks.

"In a short time," we read, "the Turks had to abandon many of their trenches; and if only it had been possible to continue bombardment until the attacking infantry had almost reached their trenches, the 29th Division might have stormed them without much loss. But this was not possible. For one thing the range was too great—over four miles—to make certain of not hitting our own troops. The ships had to cease fire, and this gave time for the Turks to rush back into their trenches and bring their machine guns with them."

A bombardment which stops just when it is going to be of real use is not of much assistance. But guns firing at 7000 yards, or so, range, without forward or overhead observation, will never help an attack much under modern conditions.

might be expected to have a considerable effect. Sir I. Hamilton was disposed at first to postpone the attack on this account, but he decided in the end to let the action proceed as ordered.

Although the operation had been carefully thought out, it went amiss almost from the start. For when the advance began the 11th Division found itself unable to gain any ground along large portions of its front, partly owing to loss of direction by some of its units; it therefore failed to perform its very important share in the preliminary phase of the operation which was to proceed to a general assault of Scimitar Hill and Ismail Oglu Tepe. A battalion of the 29th Division did speedily crown Scimitar Hill, but it was shelled off the height again; and although that division made good some advance beyond Green Hill, the rebuff met with by the 11th Division on its right rendered attempts to push well forward impracticable, and the whole operation was soon brought to a standstill. In the meantime, however, the 2nd Mounted Division was advancing right across the plain from Lala Baba in support, suffering considerably from artillery fire during the movement. On arrival about Chocolate Hill the yeomanry pressed forward eagerly into the fight and they appear to have become a good deal intermingled with the 29th Division. The momentum, however, carried both forward some little distance, in spite of the strenuous resistance of the Turks, and of the heavy losses suffered from fire during a confused movement across broken ground and through patches of burning scrub in the growing darkness. But eventually the whole force had to fall back to its original position, much reduced in numbers.[1]

It was indeed only on the Anzac side that any appreciable gain of ground was made in the course of this general action, which ranks perhaps as the biggest fought during the campaign. There, a mixed force composed of the 29th Indian Brigade, assisted by New Zealand Mounted Riflemen and units from the 10th and 13th Divisions, the whole under General Cox, fought its way forward very nearly to Hill 60, beyond Demajalik Bair, and secured possession of an important well in the low ground to the west of that eminence. The troops were at nightfall holding a position which made it possible a day or two later to join the left of the Anzac

[1] Mr. Nevinson, who was on the ground, gives a clear account of this combat in his *The Dardanelles Campaign*.

front satisfactorily to the right of the Suvla front on the further side of the Azmak Dere.

The casualties suffered by the British in the battle of the 21st of August were particularly heavy, especially in the case of the 29th Division; but the 11th Division and the Mounted Division had also suffered severely. Except near Hill 60 nothing had been gained by these sacrifices. Nor is there any reason to suppose that the Turks, who were on the defensive in dominating and entrenched positions which were not very effectively bombarded, were much diminished in numbers in an engagement in which they could fairly claim to have gained the victory. As it turned out, this was to be the last action on any extended scale that was to take place in the Gallipoli Peninsula, and it has to be admitted that from the point of view of the Allies it was a somewhat unfortunate affair.

The unwonted atmospherical conditions that prevailed during the early part of the afternoon were no doubt a handicap to the attacking side, and it might perhaps have been better to have postponed the attack until the following day. But in that case the presence of the 29th Division would in all likelihood have been discovered by the enemy, and there is always a certain difficulty in changing plans at the last moment when they affect a large force that is in close contact with a hostile army. The tactical situation, moreover, so favoured the Turks that it seems doubtful whether the efforts of the 29th and 11th Divisions and the Yeomanry would have accomplished any satisfactory result, even had there been no mist in the afternoon and even if the advance of the 11th Division had not become distorted owing to faulty direction.

From the 22nd of August to the end of the month.—The forces at Anzac had received a most welcome reinforcement, beginning on the 20th of August, in the shape of the 2nd Australian Division —two infantry brigades, formed of fresh contingents from the Antipodes. The arrival of these troops made it possible to relieve the 1st Australian Division towards the end of the month, and the Australasian army in this portion of the theatre of war consisted thenceforward of three divisions, besides the four mounted brigades. On the 24th of August General Byng arrived at Suvla and took over command, General De Lisle reverting to the 29th

Division, while General Marshall took up charge of the 53rd Division. About the same time Generals Fanshawe and Maude arrived from home, the former taking up command of the 11th Division at Suvla, and the latter that of the 13th Division at Anzac, General Shaw having fallen ill. Thenceforward until the end of the campaign Helles was under charge of General Davies, and Suvla remained under that of General Byng.

One more not unimportant episode in the closing days of August remains to be recorded. As a result of very severe fighting,[1] which lasted from the afternoon of the 27th until the small hours of the morning of the 29th, a composite force under leadership of General Cox gained possession of Hill 60, and by its victory rendered the junction of the Anzac and Suvla armies reasonably secure against hostile efforts from the side of Sari Bair. Even if the extent of ground occupied on this occasion was not great, the affair was of no small local importance. The Turks, moreover, paid a heavy price for their gallant resistance to the onsets of the Australian, New Zealand, and Irish troops who eventually proved their masters in a prolonged trial of stamina. This combat for Hill 60 was destined to be the last serious fight of the campaign.

At the end of the month the position held by the British and Australasians, with the 29th Indian Brigade, represented what was virtually a continuous line of trenches running from near Gaba Tepe in the south up to the shores of the Gulf of Saros at the foot of Kiritch Tepe Sirt. But the link between Suvla Bay and Anzac, although at a considerable distance from the Ottoman lines, was much exposed to shell-fire from Ismail Oglu Tepe and from the upper ridges of Sari Bair. The twelve miles long front was, moreover, at almost all points overlooked by loftier positions in occupation of the Sultan's regiments. Serviceable jetties were being rapidly prepared at Suvla ; but these were open to artillery fire from the enemy's lines. Anzac Cove and jetties to the north of Ari Burnu continued to be exposed to enfilade bombardments from Ismail Oglu Tepe. The anticipation that, with Suvla Bay in British hands, the Allied forces on the western shores of the Gallipoli Peninsula would possess a secure and convenient base during the coming winter, had not been justified owing to

---

[1] Sir I. Hamilton in his despatch describes the preliminary bombardment, somewhat significantly, as "the heaviest we could afford."

the Anafarta hills and Sari Bair remaining in occupation of the enemy. The elaborate scheme of operations devised for August had met with discomfiture, and before proceeding to deal with the closing events of the Dardanelles venture it will be fitting that the merits of that project as a whole should be discussed.

A review of the August offensive as a whole.—There are few matters relative to the Gallipoli drama that have not served as excuse for plentiful discussion in this country, and the majority of the plans elaborated and of the decisions taken in connection with what turned out to be an ill-fated enterprise have been almost savagely animadverted on at times in some quarter or other. But even the least friendly of critics have generally been prepared to concede that, regarded on broad lines, Sir I. Hamilton's conception for his August effort was fundamentally a sound one, deserving of better fortune than in the event attended it. The objections raised to it have for the most part emanated either from the band of believers in descents upon Bulair and Enos, who failed to appreciate the conclusive maritime objections to such a programme, or else from the French, who throughout hankered after operations on the Asiatic side of the Straits.

The Commander-in-Chief was convinced that the key to open the Hellespont was to be found in the Khilid Bahr plateau that dominated the Narrows from the European side. The obstacles that lay in the way of attaining that goal from the Helles area had been demonstrated over and over again from April up till July. The virtual impossibility as a tactical proposition of moving direct towards Maidos from out of the cramped, " fly on a wall " Anzac position, admitted of no dispute. Some new scheme of offensive warfare that hinged upon its inauguration taking place on the outer shores of the Gallipoli Peninsula and at as near a point as possible to the objective—Khilid Bahr—appeared to be dictated by a situation which had practically degenerated into one of stalemate. The project of assailing the Sari Bair heights from the unexpected direction of the littoral immediately north of Anzac, supported by action on the part of a force that was to be landed at Suvla and was to move against the mountain from thence, was perhaps as promising a scheme for securing the purpose in view as could have been devised. Nor in a case like this is the opinion of the adversary to be despised. The Germans have borne a not ungenerous testimony to the merits of Sir I. Hamilton's design. They have taken no little credit to themselves, and have given no little credit to the Turkish commanders and their troops, for bringing to naught so well imagined and so dexterously initiated a thrust.

But while testifying to the approbation that has been expressed in most quarters of the general design, it is perhaps permissible to point out that the plan was based upon decidedly optimistic estimates of the capabilities of the troops who were to carry it out. The High Command, for instance, hoped that General Godley's assaulting columns would crown the topmost ridges of Sari Bair before daybreak on the 7th of August. That hardly took sufficient account of the arduous climb by night that was involved in the operations, nor of the retarding power that even insignificant opposing detachments can exercise on broken ground in the dark. The assumption, again, that the 11th Division would establish itself on the hills overlooking the Suvla flats by the early morning of that same day must be set down as a sanguine forecast, even had the division concerned been composed of a war-trained soldiery. A hint has already been ventured (on page 203) that if their programme had been a somewhat less ambitious one, the forces launched from Anzac against Sari Bair on the night of the 6th–7th might perhaps have fixed their grip firmly upon part of its crest next forenoon and before the Turks had had time to gather strength. Nor can it be denied that, even had the IXth Corps been handled with greater vigour than it actually was, those newly landed troops could not reasonably have been expected to exert any direct influence over the contest for Sari Bair on the first day of the great offensive. General Godley could not at the best hope for more than some little moral support from the presence of battalions that had been thrown ashore by night some half-dozen miles away.

Some urge that Helles ought to have been more freely drawn upon to augment the legions that were charged with the task of breaking through to the Narrows. But there were two obstacles in the way of effecting a redistribution of the available fighting resources in that direction. The water problem, coupled with insuperable difficulties as to concealment, made it virtually impossible to employ more troops at Anzac than actually were assembled there. The amount of ship transport available did not admit of any additional troops being transported by sea on the night of the 6th–7th, nor on the immediately previous nights. Seeing that the 10th and 11th Divisions were inexperienced troops, it has been suggested that they ought to have been exchanged for formations from Helles—say, for the 29th and 42nd Divisions. But here again the shipping difficulty would have arisen. To have effected such a substitution, i.e. to have landed the two New Army divisions at the extremity of the peninsula and to have transferred the 29th and 42nd Divisions from thence temporarily to Imbros, Lemnos, and Mitylene, would have taken considerable time, seeing that the number of trawlers, destroyers, and lighters was limited ; and Sir I. Hamilton was tied down by the dates of arrival of the reinforcements and by the moon. Still, even a single division that was broken to warfare on the Gallipoli Peninsula replacing the unenlightened 11th Division on which so much depended, might have completely transformed the situation at Suvla on the critical 7th and 8th of August, and one does not feel certain that such an interchange would have been wholly out of the question.

The measure of success crowning the efforts of the Anzac force when evening closed in on the 7th undoubtedly fell far short of the Higher Command's somewhat buoyant anticipations, and this was perhaps fatal to the success of the plan. Still the fact remains that the renewed efforts of General Godley's columns on the following morning carried some of the assailants on to Chunuk Bair, and that the ground then won was held for forty-eight hours. On that second day General Birdwood might fairly look for at least indirect support from the side of Suvla, and such aid would have been particularly welcome because it was the left one of the Anzac columns that, after making a highly satisfactory advance, was brought to a standstill and was eventually forced to retire. But on that day the IXth Corps failed to move, and in the meantime General Godley's troops were confronted with strong and growing hostile forces.

On the 9th the Anzac army was the victim of ill-fortune. Those units that won their way that morning on to the crest between Chunuk Bair and Hill Q—a great feat of arms considering the strength of the enemy—were shelled by their own side at the critical moment. The left column lost its way. Such contretemps may always occur where complex tactical operations are in progress in particularly difficult terrain. Still, had they been favoured by better luck, the assailants might possibly even on the third day of combat and without help from Suvla have laid firm hold upon the backbone of Sari Bair. Aid from Suvla, again, had it been forthcoming might have counterbalanced the untoward effects of unfortunately timed gun-fire and of the misadventure to the left column. But ill-fortune and the default of the IXth Corps, together, were too severe a handicap. They turned the scale, and the negative results of that day's combat on the heights decided the issue. By the 10th the Turks were in stronger force than ever, and the Anzac troops had suffered so heavily in the furious affrays of the three previous days that they could hardly hope to maintain their precarious hold upon a patch of Chunuk Bair. Still less could they hope to extend that exiguous conquest of two days before. The Osmanlis no doubt paid somewhat dearly in casualties for their victory on the 10th, but under the circumstances their retention of the Sari Bair mountain was a foregone conclusion. They had gone very near to losing it.

Whether uncontested possession of the upper crests of Sari Bair would have provided a master-key to open all gateways on the road to the Narrows must remain a matter of conjecture. It cannot be said that experience in those theatres of the world-wide conflict that provided a stage for sustained combats—Flanders, for instance, and Verdun and Helles—encourage the theory that a capture of heights such as Chunuk Bair and Koja Chemen Tepe would as a matter of course have rendered further advance practicable. Nor does it necessarily follow that the acquisition of artillery observation posts on this commanding site would have forbidden military use of the Dardanelles to the Turks during subsequent struggles for Maidos and Khilid Bahr. But, that the triumph of the Anzac force in that grim fight of the second week in August would have profoundly modified the situation in the Gallipoli Peninsula, admits of no question. There may have been faults in framing the plan—there undoubtedly were faults in its execution. But it ranks as one of the most remarkable amongst latter-day combinations of war. That it was nipped in the bud constitutes without question a misfortune for the student of the soldier's art in the abstract. Nor will the impartial critic deny that the early August offensive furnished a not unworthy climax to a campaign that had been entered upon without sufficient foresight and that had to be prosecuted with inadequate military resources.

The later events of August hardly call for comment. The battle of the 21st, the biggest general action on land of the Dardanelles adventure, partook of the nature of a forlorn hope, for it was in the main merely an attempt to improve the very unsatisfactory defensive position extending from Gaba Tepe to the Gulf of Saros which the invaders had fortuitously taken up. The plan of attack on that day was unquestionably a somewhat venturesome one, for it amounted in reality to frontal assault upon a commanding position which coincided to some extent with an amphitheatre of high ground. Looked at simply from the tactical point of view, a more promising method of obtaining possession of the heights which overlooked the Suvla plain might have been to have massed forces amongst the gullies and depressions about the Kiritch Tepe Sirt and to have worked forward thence against the left of the Anafarta hills. In such an operation the ships' guns would have been of immense use on the outer flank; but they would have helped little on the southern slopes of the range of heights that rose from the shores of the Gulf of Saros. The drawback to any such scheme of operations would have been that, strategically, it represented an eccentric undertaking launched at the point furthest away from Ismail Oglu Tepe, Sari Bair and the vicinity of the Narrows. Be that as it may, the Expeditionary Force met with defeat on the 21st. Thenceforward the Allies had to rest content with what was virtually a passive rôle, while their adversaries settled down to trench warfare and confined themselves to trying to preserve the strategical and tactical impasse that had resulted from the great August offensive.

CHAPTER XIII

THE THREE AUTUMN MONTHS

The situation at the beginning of September.—The position of affairs in the peninsula was not an encouraging one from the point of view of the Allies at the beginning of September. They had suffered much in the August combats, and the gaps in their ranks remained unfilled. In respect to rifles and to artillery alike, the enemy was in superior force. It was manifest from the course that the campaign had hitherto followed that the expeditionary army was not even on paper strong enough to accomplish its purpose ; nor was there any prospect of its numbers being swelled by reinforcements. The Turks had shown themselves doughty antagonists—skilful marksmen, apt in trench warfare, valiant in fight—and at practically all points they enjoyed the advantage in respect to tactical position. All along the Helles and northern fronts, British, Australasian, and French troops saw themselves confronted by elaborate earthwork systems, without having at their disposal the weight of howitzer fire or of trench-mortar fire needful to render the hostile entrenchments even temporarily untenable. The entire area included in the enclaves that were in the Allies' occupation was exposed to shell-fire, which emanated from concealed pieces that could not be silenced. Finally, autumn was at hand, and autumn would in due course merge into the stormy winter season, when communication from ship to shore at the extremity of the peninsula, at Anzac, and at Suvla would for days on end be rendered impracticable by angry seas.

Another disquieting feature was that the health of the troops was the reverse of satisfactory. They were not perhaps the prey as a body to distempers of a malignant kind ; but the type of malady that attacked them was enervating in its after-effects, and, even when its victims had not actually to be invalided, their fighting potentialities were appreciably diminished for the time being. Disease had indeed been playing havoc in the ranks ever since May, and the fresh units, no less than newly arrived drafts, were proving as prone to its ravages as had been the earlier arrivals. On the other hand, there is reason to believe that the Ottoman soldiery were suffering likewise. Nor indeed is it unlikely that the wastage from medical causes may have been to the full as great in the enemy's ranks as in those of the Expeditionary Force.

There is another point which deserves a word here. The French Government and the French people no longer put trust in the enterprise. As has been mentioned in one or two earlier passages, our neighbours across the Channel had throughout been disposed to favour military effort on the Asiatic shores of the Straits, such effort to be either complementary to, or in substitution of, a peninsular campaign. They could fairly urge at the beginning of September that, even admitting Sir I. Hamilton's decision as to confining operations to the European side to have had much to recommend it, his policy had not after an exhaustive test accomplished what was expected of it. The French contingent under General Bailloud no doubt only represented a fraction (about one-sixth) of the Allied army. It was co-operating loyally as ever with its British comrades over against Achi Baba. None the less, the knowledge that men of affairs in Paris were inclined to look askance at the campaign must have added appreciably to the preoccupations of the Commander-in-Chief in his island headquarters at Imbros.

Still, certain reassuring symptoms were not wanting in the situation. Much admirable work had been, and was being, put in towards consolidating the hold of the Allies on the strips of ground that they had wrested from the Turk. Some additional artillery of medium calibre had been got on shore. Suvla Bay was already transformed into a fairly satisfactory maritime base, protected by wire netting against submarine activities, and on that account a haven where transports of some size could anchor and where their cargoes could be rapidly discharged from the beetles and other craft which now abounded. Two good landing-places had been constructed near Gazi Baba, the outer one known as West Beach; while another landing-place had been devised

s

between D Beach and Nibrunesi Point, where there was good
shelter from southerly winds. The somewhat flimsy trestle structures at Anzac, alongside which small craft could unload in favourable weather, had been solidified; and there were also light jetties
north of Ari Burnu. W Beach and V Beach were transformed into
quite respectable little harbours, especially the latter where the
French had shown great skill in making full use of the *River Clyde*.
Gully Beach had one or two small piers, and a little jetty had been
run out within Morto Bay. Roads had been laid out at all points
within the lines, water arrangements had been developed and
perfected in so far as circumstances admitted, and mountains of
stores were heaped up in the vicinity of every landing-place.
The Royal Navy had, moreover, in its combatant capacity to a
great extent triumphed over the early anxieties caused by the
German U-boats. The monitors and the specially belted cruisers
were proving their merits daily. The large numbers of small vessels
now under Admiral De Robeck's control also compensated to a
great extent for the limitations that had been imposed upon
the traffic of large steamers between the islands and the peninsula
by the submarine menace. Nor, in view of the outrages committed
by their German allies in other quarters, will it perhaps be out of
place to mention here that the Turks scrupulously refrained from
interference with the British hospital ships. One of these stately
ocean greyhounds was often to be seen riding at anchor in Suvla
Bay within easy artillery range of the Ottoman guns dotted about
on Ismail Oglu Tepe and the Anafarta hills.

Early in September the 13th and 54th Divisions changed places,
the 13th Division having properly belonged to the IXth Corps all
along. Some more additional regiments of Yeomanry and of North
Country Horse also arrived from the United Kingdom. But
numbers of small units such as mounted regiments are, piled on
the top of great numbers of other units all of which were far
below strength and without reserves close at hand to make good
wastage as it occurred, were but a poor substitute for the huge
drafts that were in reality needed if the British forces in the
Gallipoli Peninsula were ever to improve their position. To have
made Sir I. Hamilton's army efficient its infantry units required
to be made fully up to establishment, and ample reserves were
required in addition at Lemnos and Imbros so as to maintain a

A QUIET AUTUMN 259

constant dribble of men into the peninsula to replace others removed as wounded and sick. Additional howitzers, together with generous supplies of light trench-mortars and an ample supply of artillery munitions, were, moreover, sorely needed. On paper the Commander-in-Chief disposed of a mighty army. He did not dispose of a mighty army in fact.

An uneventful period in the peninsula from the tactical point of view.—The encounters that were to take place between the belligerent forces during the autumn were confined to insignificant affairs, although the Allies made a point of keeping the enemy busy by dint of raids and demonstrations. Especially amongst the newly arrived English divisions was the spirit of the offensive fostered by minor operations, which served to heighten the moral of the troops. The fruits of this wise policy soon began to be gathered. The efficiency of the new units increased apace and all ranks rapidly gained confidence in themselves. It was indeed very largely due to the methods adopted during the autumn months, when there was little of importance to record in the way of fighting, that, when the delicate and dangerous operation of withdrawing from the peninsula in the winter came to be carried out, commanders and staffs had highly efficient units to deal with, units which acquitted themselves with the very utmost credit, although many of them had not been in existence fifteen months before.

We have seen in the last chapter how eight divisions—the 10th, 11th, 13th, 29th, 53rd, 54th, and the two Australasian—came to be assembled in the northern area during the progress of the August offensive, together with large contingents of dismounted troopers and the Indian brigade, and that a third Australasian division arrived at the end of the month. Only five divisions remained in the Helles region, viz. the 42nd, 52nd, Royal Naval, and the two French. That remained the distribution at the beginning of September, roughly speaking one-third of the army being at the southern end of the peninsula while the remaining two-thirds were divided between Anzac and Suvla. A somewhat analogous disposition of their forces had taken place on the Turkish side; but the ratio as between north and south would rather appear to have been that three-quarters of their formations faced Generals Birdwood and Byng, while one-quarter opposed General Davies. It was much the same in respect to gun-power within the enemy's lines. Although heavy ordnance continued to pound Helles from across the Straits, the bulk of the larger types of guns and howitzers during the autumn months were gathered on the northern front, Anzac especially being at times exposed to severe bombardments which did not, however, cause as much damage as might have been expected. The chiefs of the Ottoman host would seem, quite rightly, to have felt a special anxiety as to the possibility of a successful advance on the part of the Allies somewhere between Kuchuk Anafarta and Gaba Tepe.

The whole of the Expeditionary Force (which, as will be seen later, underwent substantial reductions in October and November) was not present in the peninsula during the autumn period. The sufferings caused by climate before cooler weather set in, the discomforts arising from insufficient water, especially at Anzac, the nerve-shattering effects of a persistent, harassing shell-fire, and the debility resulting from the lighter forms of sickness by which practically the entire personnel was affected, made it expedient that whole brigades, and even whole divisions, should be relieved at a time, and should repair to Lemnos or Imbros to recuperate. This circumstance, coupled with the fact that the numbers of the temporarily indisposed amongst the troops actually on the peninsula diminished the quota of the fit, brought it about that the fighting strength of the Allies always fell far short of the total ration strength of the Expeditionary Force. The ration strength, moreover—as had practically been the case throughout the campaign—fell considerably short of the establishment. This might have constituted a serious danger had the Osmanlis not manifested such marked reluctance to assume the offensive.[1] An unmistakable lack of enterprise on the part of the enemy justified the temporary departures for Lemnos, and it rendered the shortage in respect to establishment less alarming than it must otherwise have been. In so far as the temporary transfers across the Ægean were concerned, the ample tonnage in small craft that was now at the disposal of the naval authorities, permitted these trips to be carried

---

[1] The Turks were no doubt seriously hampered by the activity of the British submarines. These could not prevent traffic across the narrow part of the Dardanelles, but they made direct water communication between the peninsula and Constantinople very hazardous. During the campaign they sunk 2 battleships, 12 gunboats and mine-layers, and 200 transports and supply ships.

out without discomfort to the troops nor hindrance to the supply service.

It may be remarked here that the policy deliberately adopted by Marshal Liman von Sanders at this time—it was virtually a policy of passive defence—was probably based on a desire to conserve personnel. Nor, all things considered, would this policy appear to have been an unwarrantable one under the circumstances. References to the general strategical situation in the World War as a whole have as far as possible been avoided in this volume; but it may be allowable to point out that after the August offensive the condition of affairs had practically degenerated into one of stalemate in the Gallipoli Peninsula. That stalemate, however, favoured the cause of the Central Powers and their Near Eastern allies. Important Entente forces, which were condemned by circumstances to inactivity, were being contained by a Turkish army in a theatre of war that was far removed from the home bases of those forces—France and the United Kingdom. The Dardanelles campaign was proving a greater drain upon the fighting resources of the Allies than if the divisions and the other somewhat heterogeneous military detachments that were fighting under the orders of Sir I. Hamilton had been engaged instead on the Western Front. The German Higher Command no doubt realised this clearly, even if the British Government, which was mainly responsible for the Gallipoli operations, did not. Short of embarking on aggressive action calculated to hustle the invaders of the peninsula back into the Ægean, the non-committal inaction favoured by Liman von Sanders was probably the wisest course that he could have chosen. The German Great General Staff would indeed in all likelihood have been well content if a military impasse at the outer portals of Constantinople, such as prevailed in the autumn of 1915, had continued to immobilise large Allied and large Turkish forces right on to the end of the war.

Such spasmodic activity as was displayed by the opposing sides during the autumn period was almost invariably the direct outcome of the offensive spirit animating the British and the French troops. Their enterprises were on a small scale—the most important attack delivered during these months was one carried out by the 156th Brigade of the 42nd Division near Krithia on the 15th of November. But they had something to show for their policy of alarms and excursions by the end of November, seeing that on that date the line both at Suvla and at Helles had been advanced on the average quite a quarter of a mile from its position immediately after the August offensive, and that the 11th Division on the extreme left had pushed forward double that distance. At Anzac the Australians developed a marked aptitude for mining operations, at which they proved more than a match for the Osmanli; but from the nature of the ground they were not able to advance their front very appreciably at any point. The gains of ground at Suvla, on the other hand, proved particularly useful in that they tended to advance the line in some sections from the levels on to sloping ground, which was a matter of importance when heavy rains began to fall with the approach of winter; for these deluges converted portions of the plain into a morass and at times flooded the defences down on the flats.

The rains also caused much inconvenience at other points, the shelters and dug-outs not infrequently having been sited in the troughs of gullies down which the water rushed in cataracts in wet weather, although such contretemps had been foreseen and provided against by many units. Indeed the most memorable incident to break the monotony of the autumn months that befell the belligerents took the shape of a furious gale on the 27th of November, which is said to have been almost without precedent for violence at that time of the year.

The blizzard of the 27th of November.—The storm was accompanied by torrential rain which lasted for twenty-four hours, and the continuous downpour was followed by hard frost and a blizzard. It was especially the troops at Suvla who suffered from this fierce atmospheric disturbance, in consequence of the lack of protection against the icy blast in that area and of the inundation of its low-lying ditch-systems. The watercourses were converted into raging torrents, the excavations became conduits, all means of communication were for the time being interrupted, the defence works were in places almost obliterated, and several soldiers were drowned in the rush of waters. The 29th Division, and particularly its 86th Brigade, were the worst sufferers, as their lines were sited in the basin of the northern Azmak Dere where there was a veritable inundation. Drenched as they were by the deluge and the floods, the troops suffered terribly afterwards from the cold, many

THE GREAT BLIZZARD

collapsing from exposure and exhaustion. The casualty list, which included nearly 50 per cent of the 29th Division, amounted to 200 deaths and to 10,000 sick who had to be evacuated from the peninsula; there is reason to believe, however, that the Turks suffered even in greater degree, some of their dead being washed down into the British trenches at Suvla.

Much damage was furthermore done by the tempest to the fragile piers and unsubstantial breakwaters on which the Allies so much depended, and a number of barges and of kindred craft foundered or were seriously injured. The facilities for landing and embarkation at Helles were greatly reduced for the time being. The harbour that had laboriously been created at Kephalos was wrecked, the ship which had been sunk to form the breakwater going to pieces and everything afloat under its lee being washed up high and dry on shore. That memorable hurricane of the 27th of November served as a significant warning of what was to be expected should the Expeditionary Force tarry much longer on the littoral on which it had planted itself down eight months before.

The Balkan situation between April and October.—While the situation in the Dardanelles arena of conflict was signalised by no event of importance from the tactical point of view during the autumn months, the strategical situation underwent a profound alteration during the same period consequent upon political and military occurrences in other fields. Up till November, 1915, Turkey remained to all intents and purposes completely cut off from its German and Austro-Hungarian confederates. Warlike stores, it is true, had been percolating through in limited quantities from Central Europe via Roumania and Bulgaria ever since the Sultan started hostilities; but the Ottoman Empire was in reality almost as much obliged to depend on its own resources as if it had been an island State engaged in war with a foe possessing undisputed command of the sea. Those conditions were, however, completely transformed by what took place in the Balkans during the autumn, and an entirely new state of affairs had arisen by the date when autumn gave place to winter.

In the early days of the Dardanelles venture the military situation in the east of Europe had differed fundamentally from the state of things that obtained towards the close of 1915. At that time Russian armies were in the position of having overrun large part of Galicia, of having captured the renowned stronghold of Przemysl, and even for some weeks of threatening Cracow. The legions of the Central Powers, it is true, had portions of Russian Poland under their heel, but neither side could upon the whole claim to have definitely obtained the upper hand in the main eastern theatre of war. That the Russian prospects were in the highest degree precarious owing to their insufficient munitions' supplies, was known only to those behind the scenes. The Greek and Bulgarian Governments may have been in possession of secret information on the subject, but the people of the Balkans in general accepted the situation as it was shown on the map, and did not in the least anticipate a dramatic collapse of the Tsar's military forces during the coming summer. Serbia, moreover, had during the previous winter inflicted a humiliating defeat upon the hosts of the Dual Monarchy, at a juncture when these had already penetrated far into King Peter's dominions. So that, in appearance at least, the outlook of the Entente in the East and the Near East had seemed to be by no means unpromising outwardly when, first, Admirals Carden and De Robeck, and then General Sir I. Hamilton, committed formidable fighting forces of the Allies by sea and land to the campaign for the Straits.

Following upon the miscarriage of the purely naval undertaking, and after it had become manifest that, in spite of its having solved the initial problem of effecting a landing, the Expeditionary Force was effectually held in check, strenuous efforts to bring Bulgaria into the war against the Central Powers and the Ottoman Empire were instituted by the diplomatists of the Entente. Inducements were likewise held out to Greece for that kingdom to throw its lot in with the Allies against its time-honoured foe, the Turk. These negotiations might have achieved their object—if they had, their success must have exerted a tremendous influence over the course of the fight for the Dardanelles—had not the armies of Germany and of Austria-Hungary early in the summer fallen upon the hosts of the Tsar, with an overwhelming superiority in artillery and ammunition at their command. The Russian bubble was pricked. Within a very few weeks Galicia had been practically cleared of the Muscovite invaders. Warsaw fell. The great places of arms, Novo-Giorgevsk and Brest-Litovsk, yielded without a struggle. A couple of months had scarcely passed before the "honours easy" situation in the main eastern theatre of war had been converted into one that permitted the conquering legions of the Central Powers, after a triumphant progress which had carried them to the Dvina and the Pripet marshes, to gird their loins for a blow to be delivered in an entirely new direction.

The effect upon the wavering Balkan peoples of these stirring events in the north was immense. One more example was set up in support of the dictum of history that it is not the wiles of the ambassador that count in time of war, but the achievements of the belligerent armies. All prospect of Bulgaria or Greece joining the Entente came to an end, and the British and French Governments had perforce to acknowledge to themselves that if they were going to force the Dardanelles they would have to do it unassisted. Nor was this all. The position of Serbia, ally of the British Empire and the French Republic, suddenly became one of imminent peril. The Russian debacle had liberated vast numbers of enemy troops and made them available for employment in other fields. The correct strategical policy for the Central Powers to adopt in the early autumn clearly was to overthrow once and for all the weak and isolated little Slav State whose frontiers coincided with those of the Dual Monarchy on the south—and to have done with it. That policy the Central Powers adopted.

The Bulgarians, moreover, were embittered rivals of the Serbs, so that, when great German and Austro-Hungarian forces swarmed into Serbia from the north early in October, Bulgaria suddenly mobilised and joined in the fray from the east. King Peter's armies found themselves in hopeless plight from the outset. They were overborne in several encounters. They lost most of their artillery and of their impedimenta. They were herded southwestwards in disorder into the mountain fastnesses on the confines of Montenegro and Albania. A possibility of Salonika actually falling into the hands of the Central Powers had to be faced by the Allies, for Greece, although bound to Serbia by a solemn compact, declined to fulfil her engagements. There appeared, however, to be some hope of disentangling the remnants of the beaten Serbs by a Franco-British advance from that great port, and the planting down of troops of the Entente in southern Macedonia promised at the worst to fend the enemy off from the western Ægean. The only Allied contingents immediately available were engaged in the Gallipoli Peninsula or were resting in the islands of Imbros and Lemnos. So it was decided to call upon Sir I. Hamilton to furnish an advanced force for Salonika. The 1st French and 10th British Divisions were detailed for this new duty, and they left for the new theatre of war early in October.

The effect of the overthrow of Serbia on the Dardanelles campaign. —But it was not only in respect to diversions of force from the peninsula and the islands that the Serbian disaster affected the Dardanelles operations. The triumph of the Central Powers south of the Danube, coupled with the accession of the Bulgarian kingdom to their side, put an end to the isolation from which the Ottoman Empire had been suffering since the outbreak of hostilities. Although some little time must elapse ere railway communication could be restored, it was obvious that as soon as this had been accomplished material of war of all kinds from Essen and Skoda and other arsenals of Central Europe would pour through Bulgaria towards Thrace and the Golden Horn, and that the arrival of these munitions must sooner or later vastly enhance the difficulties under which the Allies were labouring in the Gallipoli Peninsula. Even as it was, Suvla, Anzac, and Helles were constantly suffering from bombardments from which there was practically no escape. The transformation that was taking place in the strategical situation in the Near East suggested that the position of Sir I. Hamilton's force clinging to narrow strips of Turkish littoral would in time become impossible, and the French Government, bent on a Macedonian campaign, began to press insistently for an abandonment of the Dardanelles undertaking.

The British Government had been in two minds ever since the August rebuff with regard to the prosecution of a campaign from which they had at one time hoped much. Had the decision rested with soldiers and sailors there would probably have been no halting between two opinions—the policy that was actually adhered to for a time would in all likelihood have been rejected without hesitation. For, from the military point of view, there was in reality no middle course between despatching sufficient reinforcements of all kinds to render victory secure, and withdrawing the Expeditionary Force. But the Cabinet in London was obliged also to take into consideration the effect that an incontinent abandonment of the enterprise might have in regions where British

SIR C. MONRO TAKES COMMAND

prestige was an asset not lightly to be relinquished, although the event proved that the solicitude of Oriental experts on this head was not justified. Be that as it may, the War Council in England would not during October go further than to cable out to Sir I. Hamilton on the 11th asking him for an estimate of the losses which would be involved in the evacuation of the peninsula. " On the 12th," writes Sir Ian in his final despatch, " I replied in terms that such a step was to me unthinkable." Thereupon the Government decided to recall him, as a step towards obtaining a fresh and unbiassed opinion on the question of an early withdrawal, and they appointed a new Commander-in-chief of the Mediterranean Field Force.

Sir I. Hamilton relieved by Sir C. Monro.—The choice of the British Government fell upon General Sir C. Monro, who was at the time at the head of the First Army in France. Sir I. Hamilton received orders on the 16th to return home, and he sailed on the following day, making over command temporarily to General Birdwood. After a few days in London, engaged in study of the situation in the Ægean as interpreted at the War Office, General Monro left to take up his new appointment, and he arrived at Imbros on the 28th and took over charge. In addition to the troops in the peninsula and the islands, this charge included the 10th Division together with certain other British detachments that had proceeded to Salonika.

His predecessor had been called upon to undertake a task of extraordinary difficulty and had been obliged to carry on his campaign under disheartening conditions. Although the very essence of an enterprise such as the military conquest of the Dardanelles by a force arriving by sea lay in effecting a surprise, the conditions at the start had been such that the enemy was both fore-warned and fore-armed. The consequence had been that, although a landing had been effected on the Gallipoli Peninsula by a very fine feat of arms, the enemy had been able to bring Sir I. Hamilton's forces to a standstill before these could establish themselves in a dominating situation, had been able to entrench himself in tactically favourable positions, and had bid defiance to the invader. During the months of trench warfare that ensued, the Expeditionary Force had throughout lacked the artillery resources that are almost indispensable if a line of fortified ground is to be pierced under present-day conditions, its units had not from start to finish been kept up to establishment, and the reinforcements which its chief demanded arrived—when they did arrive—too late.

Sir I. Hamilton when he pronounced evacuation to be unthinkable was no doubt very largely actuated by concern as to the effect that such a confession of defeat would create in the East in general —a concern shared by many others, although as it turned out the solicitude entertained in some quarters on this account was exaggerated. He could not but be influenced to some extent by distress at the idea of all that his troops had suffered and that they had accomplished, going for naught. But he would also seem to have felt an excessive apprehension as to the tactical difficulties of effecting a withdrawal from the peninsula—as did many experienced soldiers on the spot and elsewhere at the time. It should not, at the same time, be forgotten that there are sailors and soldiers, whose opinion is worth having, who hold to this day that the policy recommended by his successor and eventually most skilfully executed ought not to have been adopted, and that the effort to gain possession of the Straits ought to have been proceeded with.

General Monro's instructions and his conclusions.—In his despatch of the 6th of March, 1916, which records the course of events while he was holding command of the Mediterranean Expeditionary Force, Sir C. Monro explains that his duty on arrival was in broad outline : (a) To report on the military situation in the Gallipoli Peninsula. (b) To express an opinion whether on purely military grounds the peninsula should be evacuated, or whether another attempt should be made to carry it. (c) To suggest the number of troops that would be required to carry the peninsula, to keep the Straits open, and to take Constantinople. The new Commander-in-chief did not take long to make up his mind. On the 3rd of November he telegraphed to Lord Kitchener at the War Office to say that he could see no military advantage in our continued occupation of the peninsula, and that in his opinion steps ought to be taken to evacuate it.

His impressions after visiting the peninsula he summarises shortly in his despatch, as follows :—

" The position occupied by our troops presented a military situation unique in history. The mere fringe of the coast-line had been secured.

The beaches and piers upon which they were dependent for all requirements in personnel and material were exposed to registered and observed artillery fire. Our entrenchments were dominated almost throughout by the Turks. The possible artillery positions were insufficient and defective. The force, in short, held a line possessing every possible military defect. The position was without depth, the communications were insecure and dependent on the weather. No means existed for the concealment and deployment of fresh troops destined for the offensive—whilst the Turks enjoyed full powers of observation, abundant artillery positions, and they had been given the time to supplement the natural advantages which the position presented, by all the devices at the disposal of the Field Engineer."

General Monro goes on to say that he was also guided in arriving at his conclusions by the state of health of the troops, by the shortage of officers competent to take command of men, by the impossibility of giving the force proper rest owing to shell-fire, and by the fact that yeomanry and mounted troops had perforce been called in to act as substitutes for infantry. But his outspoken view as to the virtual impracticability of the undertaking to which his army stood committed, is of special interest.

"(a) It was obvious that the Turks could hold us in front with a small force and prosecute their designs on Baghdad or Egypt or both.

(b) An advance from the positions we held could not be regarded as a reasonable military operation to expect.

(c) Even had we been able to make an advance in the peninsula, our position would not have been ameliorated to any marked degree, and an advance on Constantinople was quite out of the question.

(d) Since we could not hope to achieve any purpose by remaining on the peninsula, the appalling cost to the nation involved in consequence of embarking on an overseas expedition with no base available for the rapid transit of stores, supplies and personnel, made it urgent that we should divert the troops locked up on the peninsula to a more useful theatre."

One comment on this clear and uncompromising pronouncement suggests itself. It does seem open to question whether the assumption that the Turks could hold the Expeditionary Force with much inferior bodies of troops was entirely warranted by the circumstances, and in any case there was little likelihood of the enemy adopting such a course. That the Allied army which had intruded itself into the Gallipoli Peninsula had ever since its arrival caused serious apprehension to the Sublime Porte and to the Teutonic officials who had established so effective a control over the Sultan's affairs, does not admit of doubt. The danger to the capital might not be imminent, and yet the authorities charged with maintaining the safety of the State could not afford to run the slightest risks when a place of such paramount strategical and political importance as Constantinople was at stake. The menace, such as it was, pointed too directly at the very heart and focus of the Empire to permit of the least laxity in respect to defensive countermeasures. So long as a further advance on the part of the invaders could not be regarded as wholly impracticable, the situation, as it was bound to be viewed by the Ottoman Government and its military chiefs, demanded that considerable bodies of Turkish troops should be on the spot to make certain of defeating any such attempt were it to be made.

It may be pointed out that the position of affairs in the British Isles at this same period provided a counterpart to that which held good at the Dardanelles. An army was maintained in the United Kingdom during the whole of the World War for no other purpose than for meeting the very remote contingency of hostile invasion. It was fully realised that the eventuality which was being provided against was so unlikely to occur, that it might almost be regarded as out of the question. But those responsible had to bear in mind that the results would be fatal if it did occur, unless there were military forces available in the country to bring the invaders to a halt. You do not, after all, take the same precautions when you only have a few coppers about you as you do when you have a sheaf of bank-notes in your pocket, although the chances of being robbed may be no greater in the one case than in the other.

Government indecision ; Lord Kitchener proceeds to the Ægean.—Having despatched a soldier of high rank and of great experience of war in its most recent phases to take over command of the Expeditionary Force, for the express purpose of his furnishing them with a perfectly unbiassed report on a situation that obviously gave cause for anxiety and that furthermore cried aloud for a prompt decision as to the policy to be followed, the British Government would not be guided by that soldier's advice when they got it. They remained immersed in hesitation, and Lord Kitchener proceeded to the theatre of war to consider the position of affairs afresh and then to acquaint his Cabinet colleagues with his views. He left England early in November for Mudros where he met the British High Commissioner in Egypt and General Maxwell who commanded the troops in that country, as well as General Monro and other superior officers. He made an inspection of the Gallipoli fronts, arrived at very much the same conclusion as General Monro had arrived at a fortnight earlier, and in due course reported his opinion to the Home Government.

But irresolution still prevailed in Downing Street, although time was passing. Winter was approaching apace. If there was as yet no direct evidence that the Central Powers were getting munitions through by way of Bulgaria to the Turkish armies, it was safe to assume that the produce of such military traffic must soon make its presence felt in the Gallipoli Peninsula. The French were insisting upon the withdrawal of their other division from Helles at an early date. But even the intelligence of the great gale of the 27th of November, with its dire effects on portions of the troops and its destructive results to landing stages and small craft, failed to convince the Executive in London that the sands were running out and that they were jeopardising the safety, and even the existence, of a considerable army by their vacillation. It is, however, only fair to place on record that one reason for procrastination in arriving at a decision, was the unwillingness of the naval authorities to assent to the abandonment of Helles, whereas General Monro had advocated unconditional evacuation. There may have been something to be said from the sailor's point of view for retaining a military hold on the southern extremity of the peninsula, but, be that as it may, General Monro was cabled to so late as the 3rd of December to enquire whether he would be able to undertake an offensive, if reinforced. His reply was in the negative.

Partial withdrawal ordered.—Then, at last, on the 8th of December the Commander-in-Chief received instructions from London, directing him to withdraw his forces from Anzac and Suvla. But he was ordered to leave troops at Helles. It will be noted that by that date nearly six weeks had elapsed since the general had communicated to the Home Government his considered opinion that evacuation was the only sensible course to adopt.

Leaving the question of the retention of Helles out of the question, the reluctance of the British Cabinet to consent to the abandonment of the Dardanelles enterprise would appear to have been due to three principal causes. They naturally sharnk from relinquishing an undertaking which had been entered upon with no little confidence, which had been prosecuted with devoted gallantry by soldiers drawn from most parts of the Empire, and which had been made memorable by the deplorable loss of life that it involved. They dreaded the effect which such a confession of defeat might exert throughout Oriental regions where the upholding of British reputation was of vital import. They conjured up in their imaginations a tactical disaster at the moment when the armies should be vacating their precarious positions on the enemy's shores. As regards this last point it must, however, be remarked that, in the absence of any modern precedent to go by, military opinion had long inclined to the view that an embarkation under the nose of a vigilant and resolute foe must in ordinary circumstances prove a most perilous operation of war.

The sailors' insistence on the retention of Helles.—As the importance which the naval authorities attached to the continued occupation of Helles protracted the Government's deliberations concerning Dardanelles policy, some observations on this point will not be inappropriate. It is a little difficult to understand why the sea service should have been so anxious for persistence in holding the toe of the peninsula. Under the maritime conditions existing in the Ægean at the time, and under those to be anticipated in the early future, the value of naval bases in close proximity to the mouth of the Straits was obvious. But the floating forces of the Allies had Tenedos, Imbros, and Lemnos at their disposal as it was, all three of them islands situated within touch of the water-area to be watched and controlled. Nor had Helles hitherto been used to any appreciable extent as a place of refreshment and repair by fighting ships great or small. The coves known as W Beach and V Beach were under shell-fire from the high ground beyond Krithia and about Achi Baba, Morto Bay was even more exposed to the enemy's artillery, and ships at rest offer particularly attractive targets to the shore gunner. The idea that Helles would provide some sort of advanced naval base would hardly seem to have been responsible for the attitude taken up by the Admiralty on the question.

But it has to be remembered that, so long as Allied troops clung to the extremity of the peninsula, their presence there precluded the possibility of the Turks emplacing mobile guns or howitzers at, let us say, Sedd-el-Bahr or De Tott's Battery. Weapons of that sort at work in that neighbourhood would be in a position to molest light craft engaged in watching the outlet of the Dardanelles or in examining the lower reaches of the waterway. The very fact of the force under General Davies quitting the spot, would automatically liberate a number of pieces of this type, and these the enemy might employ for firing seawards. Naval craft had not, it is true, been suffering much from this kind of annoyance since early mine-sweeping days; but this comparative immunity could be attributed to the Ottoman artillery being too much taken up with bombarding the Allies' land positions to pay attention to vessels that were on the move and were therefore hard to hit. This possibility at all events did provide a reason for holding on to Helles—even if the reason was not a very convincing one.

This, however, must not be forgotten. The Royal Navy had, as Sir I. Hamilton had happily expressed it in one of his early despatches, been father and mother to the army during the Dardanelles campaign, and if troops were to remain in the peninsula the cares of parenthood could not be shuffled off by the Senior Service. Its personnel and its material would have to remain servants to a considerable body of troops isolated on an inhospitable shore. Neither the landing of soldiery and stores, nor yet the evacuation of sick and wounded had at all times proved quite a simple matter up to date. Nor were such responsibilities likely to become less exacting and arduous in the winter months, when the provisional harbour-works that had been set on foot were likely to be swept away at any time, and when all communication with the shore might be interrupted for periods lasting over several days. Clinging on to Helles inevitably meant maintaining a strain on the resources of the Allied fleets. Would its results repay this ?

General Monro's digest of the communications situation at the peninsula.—Some quotations from Sir C. Monro's despatch of the 6th of March have been given in the course of this chapter, and before closing it and proceeding to deal with the evacuation of the peninsula, it seems worth while to include in it his summary of the work that had to be carried on on the communications of the army that had been landed on the shores of the Ægean. Although only intended to describe the situation during the time that he was in command, his account may almost be said to cover in many respects the whole period of the land campaign. It runs as follows:—

"Before concluding this inadequate account of the events which happened during my tenure of command of the forces in the Eastern Mediterranean, I desire to give a brief explanation of the work which was carried out on the line of communications, and to place on record my appreciation of the admirable work rendered by the officers responsible for this important service.

On the Dardanelles Peninsula it may be said that the whole of the machinery by which the text-books contemplate the maintenance and supply of an army was non-existent. The zone commanded by the enemy's guns extended not only to the landing-places on the peninsula, but even over the sea in the vicinity. The beaches were the advanced depots and refilling points at which the services of supply had to be carried out under artillery fire. The landing of stores as well as of troops was only possible under cover of darkness. The sea, the ships, lighters and tugs took, in fact, the place of railways and roads with their railway trains, mechanical transport, etc.—but with this difference, that the use of the latter is subject only to the intervention of the enemy, while that of the former was dependent on the weather.

Between the beaches and the base of Alexandria, 800 miles to the south, the line of communications had but two harbours, Kephalos Bay on the island of Imbros, 15 miles roughly from the beaches, and Mudros Bay, at a distance of 60 miles. In neither were there any piers, breakwaters, wharves or storehouses before the advent of the troops. On the shores of these two bays there were no roads of any military value, or buildings fit for military usage. The water supply at the islands was, until developed, totally inadequate for our needs.

The peninsula landing-places were open beaches. Kephalos Bay is without protection from the north, and swept by a high sea in northerly gales. In Mudros harbour transhipments and disembarkations were often seriously impeded with a wind from north or south. These difficulties were accentuated by the advent of submarines in the Ægean Sea, on account of which the Vice-Admiral deemed it necessary to prohibit any transport or store-ship exceeding 1500 tons proceeding north of Mudros, and although this rule was relaxed in the case of supply ships proceeding within the netted area of Suvla, it necessitated the transhipment of practically all reinforcements, stores and supplies —other than those for Suvla—into small ships in Mudros harbour. At Suvla and Anzac, disembarkation could only be effected by lighters

and tugs, thus for all personnel and material there was at least one
transhipment, and, for the greater portion of both, two transhipments.

Yet, notwithstanding the difficulties which have been set forth
above, the army was well maintained in equipment and ammunition.
It was well fed ; it received its full supply of winter clothing at the
beginning of December. The evacuation of the sick and wounded was
carried out with the minimum of inconvenience, and the provision of
hospital accommodation for them on the Dardanelles line of communications and elsewhere in the Mediterranean met all requirements.
The above is a very brief exposition of the extreme difficulties with
which the officers responsible were confronted in dealing with problems
of peculiar complexity. They were fortunate in being associated in
their onerous and anxious task with a most competent and highly
trained naval staff. The members of the two staffs worked throughout
in perfect harmony and cordiality, and it was owing to their joint
efforts that the requirements of the troops were so well responded to."

General Monro's observations with regard to the army being
maintained in equipment and ammunition perhaps hardly apply
fully to the early days of the land campaign. The water difficulty had always been a source of anxiety at Anzac, and there was
but a short supply all through the summer. Nor could it be
asserted that the evacuation of the sick and wounded was carried
out with a minimum of inconvenience during the weeks immediately
following the first landing, at a stage when appliances were still
of a very makeshift order and when the administrative services
were grappling with a situation for which, through no fault of
theirs, no sufficient provision had been made. But during the last
six months of the stay of the Expeditionary Force on the Gallipoli
Peninsula the operations in rear of the fighting fronts proceeded
smoothly, except on occasions of exceptional stress such as during
the August offensive.

CHAPTER XIV

THE EVACUATION OF ANZAC AND SUVLA

General Monro's instructions to General Birdwood.—The Commander-in-Chief had realised that the British Government must sooner or later make up their minds and order a withdrawal from the peninsula or at least from part of it. He had therefore towards the end of November ordered General Birdwood to draw up a scheme for carrying such an operation out should retirement be decided on. The general principles upon which evacuation was to be effected he sketches in his despatch of the 6th of March, 1916, and the passage deserves to be quoted.

" I had in broad outline contemplated soon after my arrival on the peninsula that an evacuation could best be conducted by subdivision into three stages.

The first, during which all troops, animals and supplies not required for a long campaign should be withdrawn.

The second, to comprise the evacuation of all men, guns, animals and stores not required for defence during a period when the conditions of weather might retard the evacuation, or in fact seriously alter the programme contemplated.

The third or final stage, in which the troops on shore should be embarked with all possible speed, leaving behind such guns, animals and stores as were needed for military reasons at this period.

This problem with which we were confronted was the withdrawal of an army of a considerable size from positions in no case more than 300 yards from the enemy's trenches, and its embarkation on open beaches, every part of which was within range of Turkish guns, and from which, in winds from the south and south-west, the withdrawal of troops was not possible.

The attitude which we should adopt from a naval and military point of view in case of a withdrawal from the peninsula being ordered, had given me much anxious thought. According to text-book principles and lessons from history it seemed essential that this operation of evacuation should be immediately preceded by a combined naval and military feint in the neighbourhood of the peninsula, with a view to distracting the attention of the Turks from our intention. When endeavouring to work out the concrete fact how such principles could be applied to the situation of our forces, I came to the conclusion that our chances of success were infinitely more probable if we made no departure of any kind from the normal life which we were following both on sea and on land. A feint which did not fully fulfil its purpose would have been worse than useless, and there was obvious danger that the suspicion of the Turks would be aroused by our adoption of a course, the real purport of which could not have been long disguised."

We have seen in the last chapter that General Monro was enabled on the 8th of December to issue definite orders to General Birdwood that the evacuation of Anzac and Suvla was to be proceeded with at once. It was thereupon decided that, if weather permitted, the final abandonment of these portions of the peninsula should take place on the night of the 19th–20th. It may be remarked, however, that already during the opening days of the month and before the issue of these orders, some steps were being taken towards reducing numbers ashore by a process of weeding out sickly men, or rather by encouraging these to report themselves sick and thus to enable the medical authorities to draft them off to the islands; such methods were not, however, always successful, for the troops in general, and especially the Australians and New Zealanders, manifested little inclination to quit the front if they could help it. Moreover, to accustom the enemy to the period of quiet nights which would necessarily form part of the proceedings leading up to final evacuation should withdrawal be decided on, scarcely a shot was fired by the invaders after dark during the first ten days in December. If some of the troops realised that they might shortly quit the peninsula for good and all, the forces as a whole had no idea of the position of affairs and did not know what was the reason of this nocturnal inactivity. It was facilitated by the fact that during the closing days of November and the early days of December the Turks showed no enterprise, although their artillery was often busy and caused the British and the Anzacs a good deal of annoyance at times.

General Monro's reference to lessons gathered from history in the passage quoted above from his despatch, evidently relates to the question of making a feint elsewhere when preparing for any sudden operation that is to partake of the nature of a surprise—a very common practice in land warfare or when undertaking a landing in hostile territory. Military and naval annals, up to the time of the evacuation of the Gallipoli Peninsula, threw little light upon the problem that the Commander-in-Chief and General Birdwood were setting themselves to solve; as a matter of fact there was really no precedent for such an operation under modern conditions. The retirement from Corunna in 1809 did, it is true, afford an example of carrying out an evacuation virtually in presence of the enemy; but that enemy had been very roughly handled in battle before the troops took to their ships and was hardly in a position to molest the embarkation; the embarkation, moreover, took place within a harbour. M'Clellan's withdrawal from Harrison Landing on the James River in 1862 was scarcely interfered with, although his army had been hustled back on that place by Lee and Jackson; the Confederate forces had, however, for the most part been suddenly transferred northwards for the invasion of Maryland. But going back to a somewhat earlier date, our own military history provided an example—the affair of St. Cas in 1758, when half the force that had been left by General Bligh as rearguard to cover the embarkation of the remainder was either killed or taken during a final sanguinary struggle on the beach. Withdrawals by sea from hostile soil in face of the enemy have been unusual events in war, and the plan of making feints elsewhere with the object of facilitating the evacuation seem to have played no part in such few instances of this type of operation as have occurred in modern times.

General Birdwood's general plan.—However ill-advised the decision of the Home Government may have been in respect to retaining Helles, that decision at least offered the advantage that for the moment it somewhat lightened the responsibilities of the naval and military authorities in charge of the Dardanelles operations. A withdrawal such as these had been charged to carry out necessarily absorbs shipping in various forms. Under the circumstances actually obtaining in the Ægean, it meant the employment of a huge fleet of small craft, as well as of a great

GENERAL BIRDWOOD'S PLANS

number of boats. Having only Anzac and Suvla to deal with reduced the strain that was being placed on the naval resources by quite one-third. That in itself was a not unwelcome relief, and it appreciably facilitated the framing of his arrangements by General Birdwood, in consultation with Admiral Wemyss.

It was decided to carry out the evacuation of both areas in driblets, night after night, from the 10th to the 17th, and to embark roughly half of what remained on the following night ; so that when the final very critical operation of withdrawing the troops in front line and getting them away by boat during the few hours intervening between the closing in of complete darkness on the 19th and the first streak of dawn on the 20th came to be accomplished, practically no troops or material should remain to be dealt with other than the minimum of infantry, of artillery, and of engineers necessary to hold the positions during the 19th, together with such munitions and stores as were to be abandoned. Atmospheric uncertainties had, moreover, always to be taken into account while elaborating the plans. Winds from south or from south-west might be expected at this season of the year, and if these attained even moderate force they would stop all communication between ships and shore at Anzac and about Suvla Point, while if they developed in violence even embarkation within Suvla Bay near Lala Baba would become impracticable.

Then again, it was imperative that what was going on should remain unknown to the Turks who, it will be remembered, overlooked the Allies' positions at almost all points and whose airmen, even if they were not particularly enterprising, did none the less conduct reconnaissances from time to time over the areas occupied by the forces that were to disappear. That the fighting line and the trenches held by the invaders should remain occupied to the very last moment, however thinly, was furthermore an essential feature in the scheme contemplated by the Commander-in-Chief and worked out by General Birdwood and his staff.

But although that was fully intended, it behoved those responsible to consider whether some form of interior lines, or of reduit, covering the beaches from which the troops who should remain to the last were to embark, ought not to be constructed. In the southern area the fighting front was so near Anzac Cove, where the final embarkation must take place, that scarcely any measures of this kind were adjudged to be called for, although a keep was created on the hills immediately overlooking the cove. But at Suvla, where the lines were traced considerably further out, General Byng made special arrangements. He divided his front into two sectors, one to the north and the other to the south of the outlet joining the Salt Lake with Suvla Bay. He had a regular system of rear defences laid out. The northern extended from the "D" in "Karakol Dagh" (*vide* Map V) through Hill 10 to the lake. The other stretched from the southern portion of the lake to the "n" in "Sand," while Lala Baba was especially fortified. "These lines were only to be held in case of emergency," writes General Monro, "the principle governing the withdrawal being that the troops should proceed direct from the trenches to the distributing centres near the beach, and that no intermediate positions should be occupied except in case of necessity."

From the 10th to the 18th of December.—The Allies had not at all times been favoured with the best of luck during previous months of campaigning for the control of the Dardanelles. Still in one respect fortune had smiled on them as a rule. They had almost always enjoyed fair weather at junctures that were critical and when a calm sea was of vital importance, and this proved to be the case again during the days immediately preceding the evacuation of the peninsula by the Australasians and the IXth Corps. Such wind as there was blew off shore and the waters remained placid in spite of the inclement season, so that the highly delicate operation of removing troops and impedimenta from exposed beaches and jetties in the dark proceeded for more than a week, virtually without interruption. Night after night, working to a carefully drawn-up scheme, General Godley commanding at Anzac and General Byng commanding at Suvla lightened themselves of part of the personnel and of the material under their respective charge. What was embarked was transported to the islands, and the Osmanlis had no idea of what was going on almost under their very noses. Care was taken to foster the notion in the minds of the enemy staff that the situation within the British and the Australasian lines was normal. Such indications of permanency as were likely to attract Turkish attention by day were turned to account to mislead the foe. Hostile observers whether they were perched on the hill-tops, or lurked in camouflaged recesses in front line, or were carrying out reconnaissance by aeroplane, noted troops moving up from the beaches in ordinary relief and detected supplies being pushed forward to the front line in the usual methodical fashion. Some animals were even landed, and an enemy aeroplane one day soared overhead just as a few mules were being disembarked at Anzac. Occasional bursts of musketry or machine-gun fire suggested to the enemy that their opponents still meant business. And although guns and howitzers were being quietly withdrawn by night from their hidden emplacements, generally on the principle of reducing batteries first to sections and then to single guns, the Turkish troops scattered along the front from the bluffs overlooking the Gulf of Saros to Gaba Tepe were deceived as to the waning strength of the invaders' artillery by the swelling of the volume of fire from the pieces left. Firing remained at a minimum at night so as to keep the enemy accustomed to quiet during the dark hours in view of the final evacuation.

The operation, taken as a whole, was carried out on the principle of removing first whatever might be looked upon as of least importance from the fighting point of view, while also removing brigades and particular units which could be spared. Men who were not thoroughly fit, non-combatant units, animals that would not be needed during the last day or two, stores of ammunition, engineer material and ordnance requisites—there were vast accumulations of such both at Anzac and at Suvla—departed during the first four or five days. After that, whole infantry units selected for embarkation in advance were got away, and guns and howitzers were quietly withdrawn, run down to the beaches and shipped off to the islands. All this involved heavy work and close supervision on the beaches, which in the case of the left Suvla sector were placed especially under Brigadier-General Percival, and in that of the right sector under General Marshall. Quantities of stores were destroyed at Anzac on the 17th and 18th by an accidental conflagration.

Admiral Wemyss, who was temporarily in naval charge owing to Admiral de Robeck being ill, in his despatch of the 22nd of December which describes how the evacuation of Anzac and Suvla was carried out, explains that on each of the last two nights over 10,000 men had to be removed from either area, and he indicates the perils attending the undertaking had bad weather set in ; the period of calms during mid-December had enabled light piers to be constructed for the special purpose of accelerating the withdrawal at the last.

"A southerly wind of even moderate force," he writes, "at any time during this period must have wrecked piers, and have caused considerable loss among the small craft assembled for the operations, and would have necessitated the embarkations being carried out from open beaches. Such loss of small craft would have made anything in the nature of rapid evacuation an impossibility, and would have enormously increased the difficulties. To cope with such an eventuality a reserve of small craft up to 50 per cent would not have been too great; actually the reserve maintained had to be much smaller.

Interference by the enemy would have been most serious, as the beaches were fully exposed to shell-fire, and the damage inflicted to personnel, small craft, piers, etc., might have been most serious, as he would have had no inducement to husband his ammunition. Under such conditions it is most improbable that anything except personnel could have been evacuated. Casualties would have been heavy and the removal of the wounded out of the question. To meet the latter possibility, arrangements were made to leave the hospital clearing-stations intact, with a proportion of medical staff in attendance, and thus ensure that our wounded would not suffer from want of attention, which the enemy, with all the goodwill in the world, might have been unable to supply. It was also arranged that in such circumstances an attempt would have been made to negotiate an armistice on the morning after the evacuation to collect and, if possible, to bring off our wounded. Fortunately neither of these two dangers matured, but the probability of either or both doing so made this stage of the operations most anxious for all concerned. The final concentration of ships and craft required at Kephalos was completed on the 17th of December, and in order to prevent enemy's aircraft observing the unusual quantity of shipping, a constant air patrol was maintained to keep these at a distance. Reports of enemy submarines were also received during these two days; patrols were strengthened, but no attacks by these craft were made."

In the case of Anzac, most of the preliminary work (as also that on the nights of the 18th-19th and 19th-20th) was done at the cove itself, although removals were also carried out from the piers on Ocean Beach just to the north of Ari Burnu. The Suvla area had, as stated on page 280, been divided into two sectors; that on the right (facing the enemy) had been placed in charge of

General Maude, and its main embarking place was in Suvla Bay at the "o" in "Shallow" in Map V; that on the left, under General Fanshawe, had two embarking places near Gazi Baba and also a newly constructed little harbour on the northern side of the extremity of Suvla Point. Everything up to the morning of the 18th worked smoothly alike at Anzac and Suvla, and, although the enemy shelled the beaches from time to time both by day and by night, the damage done was small and little interruption to the evacuation operations was caused. An enormous amount of personnel and material had been got away. The troops holding the long twelve miles' front had shrunk numerically to insignificant proportions, and the number of guns still left merely represented the skeletons of a proportion of the batteries that had formerly been emplaced in these areas. The weather remained extraordinarily favourable, and commanders, staffs, and troops could fairly congratulate themselves upon what had been accomplished, and were in a position to look forward with some confidence to the development of the final scenes in the unrehearsed drama. It may be added that—in so far as can be judged from published narratives emanating from the enemy's side—neither Turks nor their German advisers had the slightest idea that, of the forces which had been opposing them on what they called the Northern and Anafarta Fronts, most of the artillery and the animals, enormous quantities of stores, and more than half of the infantry personnel, had disappeared since the beginning of the month.

The final evacuation of Anzac.—It will be convenient to deal with the final withdrawals from Anzac and from the Suvla area separately. Both evacuations were carried out on analogous lines in most respects, and it had been arranged that on the last night the front trenches at Suvla and on the left of the Anzac position would be vacated simultaneously at 1.15 a.m. But there were some features that distinguished the operations of General Godley's force very markedly from the work being carried out simultaneously under the orders of Generals Fanshawe and Maude a few miles off to the north-west.

Nearly 11,000 officers and men had been taken off during the night of the 18th–19th, the work finishing at 5.30 a.m., and by daylight the beaches had resumed their usual appearance. About 11,000 of all ranks remained. The front line of the Anzac command stretched from the southern Azmak Dere valley to the southern end of Brighton Beach. It was being held intact, but very thinly. The withdrawal of the troops in this area presented an especially embarrassing problem owing to the general trace of the fighting front in respect to the shore, and to the position of the embarking points in relation to the fighting front. That this was so becomes apparent at a glance if Map V be examined. From the Azmak Dere north of Hill 60 to about Chatham Post measures a distance of some five miles or so, and the front followed a line running less than a mile from the sea at all points except north of the Aghyl Dere. The troops were to embark mainly at Anzac Cove, a few being taken off at a pier a little north of Ari Burnu, that is to say they had to assemble at localities that were not opposite to the middle of the front, but that were opposite to the right centre of the front. Moreover, the embarking points were less than a mile in direct line from the Turkish positions abreast of them and in a sense overlooking them. The consequence was that the troops on the extreme left were called upon to make a flank march of about three and a half miles to get to their boats and beetles. In the event of the Turks discovering what was afoot and of their delivering a vigorous thrust towards Anzac Cove from about The Neck or from their positions further to the south, the distance that the enemy would have to traverse to approach the beach, or to bring an effective musketry to bear on it from the heights overlooking it directly, was merely a matter of a very few hundred yards.

The ground furthermore was extremely broken, and it was especially awkward on the left and in the left centre, seeing that the troops falling back on that flank would be traversing to some extent a succession of transverse spurs and gullies. At one point in the left centre, known as "The Apex" resting on an offshoot of Rhododendron Spur, the advanced trenches were high up in the hills, involving a steep descent. These difficulties were, however, overcome to some extent by the elaborate system of road and track communications that had been laid out, and by the fact that the moon on the night of the 19th–20th afforded fair light. Owing to the distance to be covered from about Hill 60,[1]

[1] 400 Indian infantry on the low ground about the Azmak Dere were by special arrangement moved off to the embarking places near Nibrunesi Point, coming under General Maude's orders.

the detachments that were to remain there longest must quit their positions at a considerably earlier hour than the detachments holding such points as Quinn's Post. Were the abandonment of Hill 60 or of trenches near it to be detected by the enemy, the discovery might encourage the Turks to press forward at points further south, and might lead to the overthrow of the thin line that was still holding the front directly covering the beaches, before the troops from the far-off left had completed their flank march.

It had very reluctantly been decided that a few pieces of artillery which were high up and in forward positions would have to be abandoned ; these kept up a lively fire during the day, to which the Ottoman guns responded with some vigour, the beaches being somewhat heavily shelled at times. The men were instructed to show themselves freely so that the enemy should fail to notice how few of them there in reality were. Vigilant watch was kept by the aeroplanes to prevent any hostile aviators approaching and taking note of the situation. To prevent the noise of tramping over rocky patches and over places where timber had been laid down being heard when the retirements were in progress during the night, a carpeting of sacks was made use of at such points.

All three Australasian divisions were represented in the final scene, as were also the mounted brigades from the Antipodes. What may perhaps be called the post of honour—the sections of front nearest to Anzac Cove about Pope's, Quinn's, and Courtney's Posts and stretching thence southwards towards Lone Pine—were held by battalions of the 2nd Australian Division, which had only arrived after the severe fighting of August was over. Australian Light Horse were on the extreme right towards Chatham and Tasman Posts. Hill 60 and adjoining trenches were held by Norfolk and Suffolk Yeomanry and Welsh Horse, with the Ghurkas who were to embark in the Suvla area on the extreme left. New Zealand Mounted Riflemen, the 4th Australian Brigade and Australian Light Horse were on their right. The Apex was in the hands of New Zealanders. The schedule of movements had been drawn up with meticulous care. The exact hour at which each detachment was to quit its post, the route that it was to follow, and the point at which it was to dovetail into other bodies of troops streaming in the same direction had been worked out with infinite pains. Every precaution had been taken that subordinate commanders should be in possession of clear and detailed instructions, and it is indeed scarcely an exaggeration to say that every rank-and-file soldier engaged in this very delicate operation of war knew exactly what he was to do at any given hour of the night. The plan, describing it in broad outline, was to call in the troops on the flanks first and to continue to hold the line in the right centre—the sector where the fighting front ran nearest to the embarking places—for some time longer. The whole was governed by the understanding with Suvla that the front line trenches on the left must be held till 1.15 a.m. Yet even from the flanks the retirement was to be very gradual. Detachments were, moreover, in pursuance of progressive withdrawal all along the front, already to be on their way towards the beaches even from the right centre, within an hour of complete darkness setting in, i.e. before eight o'clock.

The weather proved propitious, for the night was still and the sea calm, while fleecy clouds drifting across the full moon served to shroud the unwelcome brilliancy of its illumination to some extent. Embarkation started about 8 p.m. and from the outset it proceeded virtually without the slightest hitch. Slender detachments, composed of specially chosen men, remained scattered along the front until 1.30 a.m. The Turks were in the meantime giving no indication that they realised what was in progress; the occasional crack of fixed rifles, that were discharged by a mechanical device from abandoned trenches, deceived the enemy and fostered the illusion that the defences were occupied as usual. As each detachment finally quitted any particular enclave of trench the men also fired their rifles off. To this sputtering musketry the enemy merely replied in his usual desultory fashion.

By 1.30 a.m. the troops who still held those parts of the front line that remained occupied had been reduced to a very few hundred resolute men, and at 2.30 a.m. Chatham Post on the extreme right near Brighton Beach was abandoned. Lone Pine was evacuated about 3 a.m., and by 3.30 a.m. Pope's, Quinn's, and Courtney's Posts, which had been held for some time longer, were no longer tenanted, the entire front line was clear, and the detachments that had been clinging to those very important positions directly covering Anzac Cove in the centre were hurrying down the familiar tracks that led to the place of embarkation. Rifles left in position still chattered fitfully, and although hostile infantry were ensconced at some spots

within a very few paces of the empty trenches in this sector, the
Turkish watchers evidently remained in complete ignorance that
their antagonists had so deftly slipped away.

Then of a sudden, about 3.45 a.m., the air was rent with a
tremendous report. A series of mines about the head of Monash
Gully had been exploded by the engineers, and the Turks evidently
at last detected that there was something out of the ordinary
afoot. For artillery, machine-gun, and rifle fire was opened by
them on the trenches all along the line—a mere waste of ammunition, as the trenches had been evacuated some time before. The
rearmost Australasian detachments were already pouring on to
the beach and were speedily afloat, and the naval officer in charge
was able to report all clear to Admiral Wemyss at 4.15 a.m. The
retirement had in fact been wholly unmolested by the enemy, and
the total casualties suffered during the night amounted to three men
wounded, a few stragglers being taken off by picket boats at dawn.
The Turks did not open fire on the beaches till about 5.30 a.m.

Four 18-pounder guns, two 5-inch howitzers, one 4·7-inch gun,
one anti-aircraft gun, and two 3-pounder Hotchkiss weapons were
abandoned, all of them representing ordnance already worn out ;
the pieces were, however, rendered wholly unserviceable before
departure. Fifty-six sorry mules had to be left behind, as well
as a few damaged vehicles that were set on fire before they were
abandoned. Large quantities of stores, however, could not be
carried off. It was not considered advisable to set these alight
before retirement, but a heavy bombardment was opened upon
the dumps near the shore after day had broken, and by this
means a conflagration was caused. The bombardment both
here and at Suvla was, however, cut short by Admiral Wemyss,
who feared a hostile submarine attack, as the presence of enemy
underwater craft was known ; but one of the specially protected
cruisers remained off Anzac and claimed to have caused considerable loss to the Turks when these began swarming down from the
hills to take possession of such booty as had not been destroyed by
fire. According to German accounts considerable accumulations
of undamaged stores were captured, and it is possible that the fires
started by the naval bombardment may have caused less destruction than appeared to be the case according to boardship observation. Owing to the nature of the area, and to the extent to which

the whole position was overlooked, it had been impossible to very largely reduce some of the magazines of stores up in the hills, and the Turks no doubt acquired a certain amount of loot from these.

The evacuation of Anzac had proved a greater success than even the most sanguine on the side of the Allies had anticipated. All the movements had been carried out according to schedule. There had been no confusion at any point, neither in clearing the trenches, nor between different parties converging in the dark by hill tracks towards the beach, nor yet at the points of embarkation where enshipment had proceeded like clockwork. The withdrawal had proved a triumph of foresight and of organisation. The troops had, however, been favoured by a spell of exceptionally favourable weather. On the very next day, the 21st, it came on to blow hard from the south-west, so that the Anzac force, as also that at Suvla, had little more than twenty-four hours to spare in effecting their remarkable evacuation.

Comments on the final evacuation of Anzac.—It will be agreed that the behaviour of the weather was a matter of paramount importance on the occasion of the final departure from Anzac. The beaches were completely exposed, and even a moderate on-shore breeze would have made embarkation almost impracticable and would have upset all arrangements on the night of the 19th–20th. The enemy manifestly had not on the 19th discovered how large a portion of the force had been withdrawn during previous days, but the hostile staff might well have obtained an inkling of the position of affairs had evacuation been compulsorily postponed on the critical night. Bad weather might, moreover, have lasted several days—it often does in the winter in the Ægean. Nor was this the only danger. There was always the possibility of the wind getting up during the night, after a considerable part of the garrison that had held the position on the 19th had embarked, and after, say, Hill 60 and other outlying positions had been abandoned. Had that taken place the Turks must next day have discovered how the land lay and might well have overpowered the troops that had been left in the lurch on shore.

A point that should be borne in mind in the case of the Anzac evacuation, as also in that of the simultaneous retirement from Suvla and of the subsequent departure from Helles, is that darkness under such circumstances does not help the withdrawing

EVACUATION OF ANZAC 289

force merely in that it conceals movements. The Anzacs could also count upon darkness lending them valuable aid supposing the enemy to discover that evacuation was in progress, because it was bound to hamper their antagonists in pursuit. The elaborate trench systems and their barbed-wire protection offered the adversary a serious obstacle at night, even supposing the trenches to have been abandoned. The fear of mines and the impossibility of finding and cutting electric connections in the dark could be depended upon to delay the enemy. This had been foreseen by the Commander-in-Chief and General Birdwood. Assuming the Osmanlis to have traversed the Anzac trench systems, following up the retiring troops, they would be moving in unknown country, whereas the withdrawing detachments would be following well-known tracks, and darkness would be altogether in their favour. But The Neck and adjacent Turkish positions were so near to the embarking points that these difficulties would be likely to impede the Ottoman forces less at Anzac than would be the case under similar conditions at Suvla, where the enemy would be starting at a distance of three miles or so from the beaches.

In so far as the question of slipping away unnoticed out of trenches in the close vicinity of hostile positions is concerned, it may be remarked that an example of such an operation had been provided in Flanders at the end of April, 1915. General Plumer had managed to withdraw two divisions by night out of the trenches near Ypres and to introduce them into a position some distance back, unnoticed by the enemy. But very good arrangements are required if such a retirement is to be entirely uninterrupted, and it takes efficient troops to carry out this class of operation successfully.

Although the matter was not put to the test, the immediate surroundings of Anzac Cove offered certain especial advantages to the retiring side, supposing that its movements had been discovered betimes by the enemy and that the Turks had followed the departing troops up closely. On the steep hillsides overhanging the cove, the Osmanlis would have offered a fine target to the warships, lighted up as their movements would have been by the powerful searchlights of the naval forces. Searchlights indeed may prove in themselves a by no means ineffective weapon in a case like this, owing to the dazzling effect of their rays upon troops

U

who come within their beams and are obliged to face them ; given more level ground about the embarking place than existed at Anzac Cove, the searchlights would, if used, be not unlikely to dazzle the retiring troops equally with their pursuers—it would not be a case of the embarkation proceeding below the level of the beams. On comparatively level ground the task of firing over the heads of embarking troops at an enemy endeavouring to prevent their departure would also necessarily be a more delicate operation for ships' gunners, than where the ground rises steeply from the foreshore, as at Anzac ; and this would be particularly the case during a night retirement. The risk of firing into the fugitive force will always act as a deterrent to the warships under such circumstances. At St. Cas (the affair alluded to on page 278) Commodore Howe—the hero of the "Glorious First of June" many years later—who was in naval command and who had come ashore when the situation on the beach was becoming critical, was obliged, as the French pressed their attacks relentlessly home, to signal to the fleet to stop firing for fear of hitting their own men. That affray took place in daylight. It is easy to imagine the difficulty that boardship gunners would experience under at all analogous circumstances supposing the struggle to be proceeding in the dark, or the arena to be merely illumined by searchlights.

The final evacuation of Suvla.—As at Anzac, the fighting line along the Suvla front on the evening of the 19th of December was the same as what had been held for some weeks, and, except at its northern end on the Kiritch Tepe Sirt, it was practically the line which had been taken up when the severe fighting of August came to an end, having only been pushed forward slightly in the meantime at most points, as a result of the nibbling offensives practised by the various divisions that had at different times occupied the trenches. From the seaward slopes of the Kiritch Tepe Sirt on the extreme left, the front followed a wavy course running west of Aghyl down into the upper basin of the northern Azmak Dere and from thence across the Kuchuk Anafarta Ova to a little east of Sulajik. South of Sulajik it took the line to the neck between Chocolate and Green Hill and beyond that ran south-eastwards to the southern Azmak Dere, east of Kavaklar, where it came in contact with the Anzac front. This represented a length of about five miles.

EVACUATION OF SUVLA

The northern end of the front on the Kiritch Tepe heights was (as is shown on Map VI) about three miles and a half from Suvla Point and rather less from the West Beaches, the localities where the left half of General Byng's command was to embark. About Sulajik the front was only two miles from the embarking places about Nibrunesi Point whence the right half of the Suvla force was to depart, while the front further to the south was somewhat further off from that point of departure. Thus the last troops to quit the trenches had in all cases to march fully two miles to reach their boats, while on the extreme left the distance was quite three and a half miles.

When General Birdwood received his definite instructions from the Commander-in-Chief to evacuate Anzac and Suvla, General Byng had under his command five divisions, with some additional troops. The 11th Division had been on the extreme left of the line since the end of August; on its right was the 29th Division under General De Lisle; to the right of this again was the 53rd Division under General Marshall; occupying Chocolate Hill and some low ground to the south towards the southern Azmak Dere was the 13th Division under General Maude; on the extreme right was the 2nd Mounted Division under General Peyton. That represented twelve infantry brigades and some regiments of horse. The whole of the 53rd Division, together with the 86th and 87th Brigades of the 29th Division had, however, been withdrawn before the 18th, as well as the 34th Brigade of the 11th Division. On that day the line was held as follows, proceeding from left to right along the front : 32nd Brigade, 33rd Brigade, 88th Brigade, 39th Brigade, 38th Brigade, 40th Brigade, Mounted Troops. Of these, the first four brigades on the left were to embark about Suvla Point under arrangements made by General Fanshawe, while the two remaining brigades and the mounted troops were to embark near Nibrunesi Point under the orders of General Maude. General Maude furthermore had most of the artillery that still remained ashore in his sector, as the main gun position ever since the first landing in this area had been about Lala Baba.

It is proposed to describe the final operations at the Suvla Point end in some detail as they so well illustrate how a considerable body of troops can be withdrawn by sea at night although in close touch with the enemy, at a minimum sacrifice in men, animals, and material. But before doing so it will not be out of place to point out that in many respects the problem of withdrawing General Byng's force from the two extremities of Suvla Bay differed very materially from that with which General Godley and his subordinate commanders were confronted in the Anzac area. In the first place, owing to there being two distinct embarking places and to their position in respect to the general line of the fighting front, the troops under Generals Fanshawe and Maude were not called upon to make anything resembling a flank march to reach the boats, such as the Australasian detachments about Hill 60 and Demajalik Bair were obliged to carry out.[1] In the second place, the two promontories at either extremity of Suvla Bay were naturally favourable positions for rearguards to protect in the event of the retirement being followed up. In the third place, it was possible for the last troops holding the trenches all along the Suvla front to quit these practically simultaneously, whereas at Anzac the trenches on the left were abandoned two hours before Pope's Hill and Quinn's Post were finally relinquished which made the operation as a whole more complicated. Furthermore, the front line at Suvla was not dominated by the hostile positions at close range to at all the same extent that the front line was at Anzac. It is well to bear these factors in mind, as helping to explain why the evacuation of General Byng's corps was carried out with much less sacrifice of material than was that of General Godley's very awkwardly situated troops.

The withdrawal of the left sector of the Suvla force.—There were three points of embarkation about Suvla Point, viz. Suvla Cove at the extreme end, and West Beach and Little West Beach inside the bay by Gazi Baba. Of these, West Beach was the most convenient in view of the works that had been established during the occupation, but Little West Beach was favourable enough, and Suvla Cove, as being the most sheltered, was selected for the embarkation of the last detachments of the 32nd Brigade which were to cover the final withdrawal of all. The practice of giving names to all roads, paths, crossing places, etc., names which came to be very

---

[1] The march of the 400 Indian troops, and some of the mounted troops on the extreme right of the right sector, was to some extent a flank movement, but not at all to the same extent.

GENERAL FANSHAWE'S SECTOR

well known to all concerned, greatly facilitated the issue of intricate orders such as were necessary for an operation such as that which the troops under General Fanshawe's charge were called upon to carry out on the nights of the 18th–19th and of the 19th–20th. It is only proposed to give details as regards the final night's work.

As will be seen from Map VI, the 32nd Brigade on the extreme left occupied in front line the seaward slope of the Kiritch Tepe heights, and, thanks to enterprises undertaken during the previous two months, its trench system formed a somewhat pronounced salient pushed forward in advance of the general front. The trenches of the 33rd Brigade followed almost a straight line down the southerly face of the ridge, joining on to those held by the 88th Brigade near the bottom. These joined on to the trenches occupied by the 39th Brigade in the plain, the latter extending southwards across the Kuchuk Anafarta Ova to near Sulajik. The line of demarcation between General Fanshawe's area and General Maude's area ran roughly east from the embouchure of the Salt Lake to a short distance north of Sulajik. The special defence line that had been prepared, which is shown as " 2nd Line " on Map VI, extended from the shore beyond the Karakol Dagh to the Salt Lake. The " 3rd Line " only extended across the area held by the 32nd and 33rd Brigades within the promontory north of Suvla Bay ; there was no 3rd Line for the 88th and 39th Brigades. But, as it turned out, neither the 2nd nor the 3rd Line came to be seriously occupied during the night of the 19th–20th. It has to be remembered that the Kiritch Tepe–Karakol Dagh ridge was extremely rugged, cut into by dongas and ravines which cannot conveniently be shown on a sketch map, and that the communications marked on Map VI represented in some cases well-marked roads constructed during the past three months, but in others were mere paths ; down in the plain there was less need for regularly constructed routes, and less difficulty when moving off them in the dark. The 32nd and 33rd Brigades were to embark at Suvla Cove and West Beach, while the 88th and 39th Brigades on their right were to embark at Little West Beach.

Two field batteries and one mountain battery had been emplaced on the high ground occupied by the 11th Division, but by the night of the 18th–19th only three sections were left (at the positions shown on Map VI), and in the course of the withdrawal on that

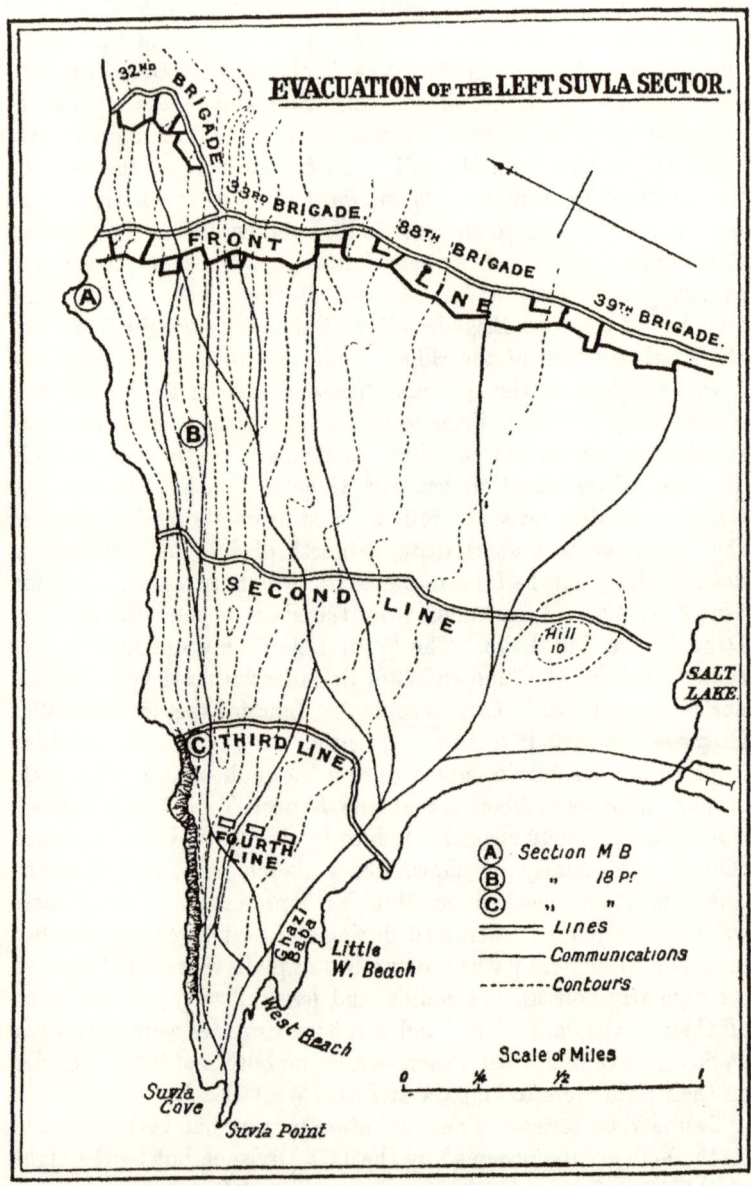

MAP VI.—EVACUATION OF THE LEFT SUVLA SECTOR

GENERAL FANSHAWE'S SECTOR

night the sections were reduced to one gun each ; a similar plan had been adopted with one field battery emplaced on Hill 10. Practically everything requiring animals to carry it was removed during that night, and the mules were nearly all embarked. The four infantry brigades were reduced by 6090 of all ranks, including attached gunners, engineers, medical personnel, etc.—rather more than half of the total numbers that had remained on the morning of the 18th. The embarkations began immediately after dark on the evening of the 18th and they were completed before 3 a.m., all having proceeded most satisfactorily.

During the 19th the dumps of rations collected at various points were destroyed by puncturing the tins, soaking contents with paraffin and fixing automatic arrangements for firing ; it had been necessary to leave stores of supplies near the front in the event of bad weather setting in at the end, but there was now every appearance of the calm continuing. Wells were destroyed during the day and tanks broached. Every care was taken during the day that the commanders of all detachments, and any individual officers or men told off for special duties in connection with the coming night's operations, had their schedules and orders and were fully acquainted with the programme that they had to carry out, that they understood the movements of neighbouring detachments, and so forth. A complete system of cable communications had been laid down extending from the front-line trenches back to Suvla Cove, and these would admit of General Fanshawe's headquarters keeping touch with the four brigade headquarters, and for these keeping touch with their battalions and details as withdrawal progressed. Control stations had been set up at points where the main routes to be followed by the retiring troops crossed the rearward defensive positions, so that the precise whereabouts of detachments on their march to the embarking places could be ascertained ; it was arranged that each officer in charge of a control station would, on the last detachment passing through, report the fact and would then disconnect the telephone and proceed to his embarking place. This communication system had been tested during the night withdrawal of the 18th–19th and had worked most satisfactorily.

The numbers left in the area under General Fanshawe's orders at dusk on the evening of the 19th were calculated to be 5114 of all ranks, besides divisional staff, of whom 4614 were in front line, holding about two and a half miles of trenches. The strengths of the four brigades, with the details attached to them, varied between 1035 and 1630—the latter the figure of the 32nd Brigade under General Dallas. This brigade was occupying the advanced salient on the extreme left of the line and was thus furthest from its embarking place at Suvla Cove.

For some days prior to the 19th a uniform method had been followed in regard to artillery and trench-mortar fire after dark, and exactly the same procedure was followed after dark on the 19th. Trenches were relieved as usual, late in the afternoon, and working parties were sent up with tools; tins used for carrying water were conveyed up to the front trenches after dark with the usual noises, and patrols were sent out at one or two points to make a show of activity. There had, moreover, usually been a destroyer lying off the shore opposite the extreme left flank of the line, ready to assist with shell-fire should the enemy show any signs of liveliness on the outer slopes, and this vessel fired a few rounds after dark at the Turkish trenches. Occasional bursts of machine-gun and rifle fire were indulged in during the early part of the night. Especial frameworks of barbed wire had been got ready, to be drawn into communication trenches to block these should the Turks discover that their adversaries were retiring and should they follow the retirement up. To deaden the sound as parties quitted the front trenches, the men's boots were as far as possible to be wrapped in sacking. The mines in advance of the front line were made active at 6 p.m.

The first detachments began to move quietly off from the front line about 5.30 p.m., an hour when it was just dark enough to conceal their departure, and by 7.15 p.m. the troops in the front trenches had already been reduced in number from 4614 to 3241. The three guns that remained on the high ground had completed their customary evening shoot by 7.35 p.m. and they thereupon moved off, the mountain piece having to follow a very awkward track until it reached the nearest main communication leading to the rear; the field gun which remained on Hill 10 was withdrawn about the same time. At this hour the 2nd Line was being held by 200 men of the 32nd Brigade across the high ground, and by 200 men of the 88th Brigade on Hill 10. The first embarkation

GENERAL FANSHAWE'S SECTOR

commenced both at West Beach and at Little West Beach at 7.15 p.m. ; the troops detailed for this arrived well up to time, enshipment by means of beetles commenced at once, and the work was carried through without difficulty and most expeditiously—as was also the case in the later embarkations.

Between 7.15 p.m. and 9.45 p.m. a great reduction in the numbers in front line took place, the total falling during these two and a half hours from 3241 to 877. Allowing for non-combatants, staff and so forth, it may be assumed that, subsequently to 9.45 p.m., there were not more than 800 infantrymen, machine-gun men, and trench-mortar men to hold a front of fully two and a half miles. From this time on till towards 1.15 a.m., when the trenches were to be finally quitted, was the critical period in so far as risk of a hostile infantry attack was concerned ; but the danger to the force as a whole necessarily decreased from hour to hour, if we take into consideration the difficulty that the enemy would find in advancing in the dark across very broken ground, cut up as it was by trenches and intersected in places by barbed wire. The Turks would not know where the roads were and must move much more slowly than the retiring British. Beyond occasional sniping the enemy was, however, showing few signs of life, and was affording no indication of having observed what was going on within their opponents' lines. Bivouac fires were carefully made up as the troops moved off ; and the men still left in occupation of the trenches were instructed to make the customary trench noises, and they occasionally let off a few rounds. Trench mortars and a few machine-guns still remained in position, firing from time to time. The advanced dressing stations had been withdrawn at 9 p.m. and proceeded partly direct to the embarking places, and partly took up positions in rear of the 2nd Line as a temporary measure. The second embarkation began according to programme at 9.45 p.m.

The final stage approached. The trench mortars were all withdrawn from the front about 11.15 p.m., and half an hour later the detachments of the 32nd Brigade in occupation of the advanced salient fell back from this to the old line abreast of the 33rd Brigade under special arrangements, so that the whole of the groups still left in front line, numbering now 677 of all ranks, were able to move off simultaneously at 1.15 a.m. in accordance with General Fanshawe's programme. The enemy still displayed no signs of activity, although some of the supply dumps had by this time been fired under special orders received from corps headquarters. It had been intended that the 2nd Line should be held if necessary; but as the enemy was quiescent all along the front, the troops marched straight to the beaches. The third embarkations began at 1.15 a.m. and the fourth about 3 a.m., the last of the 39th Brigade (330 men), of the 88th Brigade (187 men), and of the 33rd Brigade (255 men) being timed to pass the 2nd Line, or to withdraw from it, at 2 a.m. Of the 32nd Brigade 200 men had taken up position at the 4th Line at 1.15 a.m. to act as final rearguard to the embarking troops; the last of the troops of this brigade from the front line (230 men) were timed to pass the 2nd Line at 2 a.m. like those of the other brigades. The fourth embarkation was carried on between 3 a.m. and 4.30 a.m., and at 4 a.m. the supply dumps down on the shore were fired; by that time the whole of the 33rd, 39th, and 88th Brigades were afloat.

The 200 men of the rearguard left by the 32nd Brigade at the 4th Line were ordered down to Suvla Cove at 4.30 a.m., and they embarked at once in a beetle, pushing off about 5.15 a.m.; Generals Fanshawe and Dallas with the signalling detachment were taken off at the same time in a picket boat. Everything at the beaches had worked smoothly during the night, the naval arrangements having been admirable throughout till the very end; but by a singular coincidence the transport which was to have conveyed the last detachments and the staff across to Imbros sailed without them, and these had to make the fifteen miles' voyage from Suvla Point to Kephalos Bay in the picket boat and lighter; the weather being calm this presented no difficulty. Every man, gun, vehicle, and animal had been withdrawn, and only one or two men had been wounded by accidental bullets during the night. It had not been possible to remove the cables; but all the ammunition had been got away, and the few stores left behind were in full blaze as the last of the troops quitted the shore, leaving merely an insignificant, undamaged booty for the Turks to seize when they eventually advanced.

The warships opened a bombardment on the abandoned trenches as soon as it was light, and the enemy promptly followed suit, showing thereby that the trenches had not been seized. The Turkish artillery also fired on the burning dumps apparently under the impression that the conflagrations were accidental. Only then would the Osmanlis seem to have realised that their antagonists had disappeared, although, as will be seen in the quotation given from an anonymous German staff officer on page 303, it is claimed that they had become aware of the retirement early in the night. The navy also directed fire on the dumps on the beaches, and by the same means they destroyed four beetles which had been driven ashore during the gale at the end of November mentioned on page 262, and which it had not been found possible to get off again. The enemy does not appear to have occupied the Suvla Point promontory until after 9 a.m., being kept at a distance by the belted cruiser which remained off the coast after the rest of the naval flotilla had (as already mentioned on page 287) retired to Kephalos for fear of enemy submarines. The withdrawal of the left sector of the Suvla force had been effected with remarkable precision, in perfect order and in brilliant style.

The withdrawal of the right sector of the Suvla force.—General Maude's arrangements for retiring the troops from the right sector were drawn up on analogous lines to those framed by General Fanshawe, and the story of the operation need not therefore be told in detail. About half of the 38th and 40th Brigades and the mounted troops still left, together with a large amount of impedimenta and some guns, embarked on the night of the 18th–19th; nearly the whole of the troops still left in the sector on the 19th occupied the trenches throughout that day. The beach inside of Nibrunesi Point, which was protected by a sunken vessel and was furnished with a good pier, was a favourable point for embarking troops and material, and C Beach was also used to some extent. All that it was proposed to remove on the night before the final evacuation was got afloat without difficulty by 3 a.m. It included two field howitzers, and four field guns. The Turks made some good practice at C Beach and the pier on the 19th, smashing one span of the pier.

The scheme for the final night was that the troops should all retire by the southern side of the Salt Lake to the embarking places. It was considered necessary to keep two howitzers in action on Lala Baba, as well as eight field guns, so as to deceive the enemy and also so as to support the infantry in case the enemy should deliver an attack during the day anywhere between the northern line of heights and the right of the Suvla front. The withdrawal of the howitzers and six of the guns began as soon as it was dark enough to hide movements of men on the hill from the Turkish lines two miles away, a few rounds having been fired during the day, as usual; they were embarked especially at Little West Beach. The two remaining guns were withdrawn at 8 p.m.

The hour for the final retirement from the front trenches was fixed for 1.15 a.m., so as to coincide with the withdrawal of the troops in front line in the left sector. The programme contemplated holding the second line if necessary, which, as already stated, included Lala Baba and entrenchments running diagonally from the Salt Lake across to B Beach. But, as in the left sector, the precautions taken to hoodwink the Turks, the care with which the schedules of movements had been drawn up, the dexterity displayed by subordinate leaders in carrying out their delicate tasks, and the admirable discipline of the rank and file, caused the abandonment of the front line to remain unnoticed by the opposing side. Consequently the last detachments to quit the trenches were able to move straight through to the place of embarkation. Special arrangements had been made for passing them through the defensive system stretching across the isthmus south of the Salt Lake. 100 men with 3 machine guns held this line, and 250 men with 6 machine guns held Lala Baba. But these troops had no work to do, and were able to move down to the beach about 3 a.m. and to embark at 4 a.m.—an hour and a quarter earlier than the rearguard in the northern sector got afloat at Suvla Cove. The supply dumps about the beach were ignited at the same time. As in the evacuation of the northern sector, every man, gun, vehicle, and animal was brought off, and there were no casualties.

The arrangements for rendering the few abandoned stores useless to the enemy were very complete and the material was in a blaze as the last of the troops quitted Suvla Bay. A short but brisk bombardment by the warships as soon as day broke completed the destruction. As far as could be ascertained the enemy remained as entirely unaware in the right sector that the invaders had slipped away, as was the case in the left sector. The action of the navy apparently first made the Turks acquainted with the dramatic change that had taken place during the night watches almost within a stone's throw of their sentries. They had been particularly busy digging and improving wire entanglements during the night, and appear to have expected attack in the morning.

Comments on the evacuation of the Suvla area.—The most significant feature in the withdrawal of General Byng's forces from the Suvla area was the situation created on the 19th, when practically the whole of the infantry still left was occupying a line of trenches nearly five miles in length, without reserves, the number of rifles not much exceeding 8000. The only support was provided by a very small number of guns and some trench mortars. It is strange that neither here nor at Anzac does the enemy appear to have had the slightest idea that there was so little in front of him on that date, and that such huge withdrawals of men, guns, vehicles, and material of all kinds had taken place during the previous few days. Served by more numerous and more enterprising aviators, the Turks must have discovered the true position of affairs, and if so they would surely have delivered a furious attack upon the thin line of invaders. That is a point worth noting, because what occurred during this first evacuation of the Gallipoli Peninsula must not be taken as an assured precedent.

The plan actually adopted proved emphatically the right one. It is difficult indeed to see what other method could have achieved so remarkable a success. A retirement by stages, with the idea of opposing the enemy advancing in pursuit, would inevitably have meant delay; and, although the winter nights were long, the last of General Fanshawe's troops, as it was, only got away on the morning of the 20th a short time before dawn. But the essence of the plan was that the enemy should remain wholly unaware that retirement was in progress. Supposing the Turks had attacked about 10 p.m.—and in the earlier days of the Gallipoli campaign they had shown a marked bent for night attacks and had delivered these with great determination—they might easily enough have broken through at certain points, seeing how weak were the detachments that were spread out at that hour along the extended line. The assailants would thereupon have realised that their foes were in full retreat and would surely have made desperate efforts to follow up, in spite of the mines, of the barbed wire, and the trenches, and of the difficult terrain at least in the northern sector. Much would then have depended upon whether the 2nd Line had been effectively taken up, upon the rate at which the Turks moved in the dark and upon whether the 2nd Line would hold. Supposing the 2nd Line to go, the triumphant Osmanlis would have been able to get very near to the embarking places. Still, the Suvla Point promontory, as also the peculiar topographical conditions about Lala Baba and the fortified isthmus to the south, would have greatly favoured rearguard work, and it is likely enough that even under such untoward conditions the greater part of the personnel left in the Suvla area on the 19th could have been got away by daybreak, before a heavy rifle fire could be brought to bear by the enemy on the embarking places.

But the most serious danger to be anticipated, supposing that the enemy should discover that the troops in the front trenches were retiring or had retired, did not lie in what their infantry might do in the way of harassing retreat and of bringing musketry or machine-gun fire to bear on the beaches. It lay in the possibility of the Ottoman artillery opening a furious bombardment of the beaches, which were accurately registered from the enemy's gun emplacements. Realising that their antagonists were evacuating the Suvla area, the Turks would have been justified in using up pretty nearly the whole of their artillery ammunition in a final effort to do as much damage to the retiring forces as possible. This might have caused serious loss and confusion, beetles might have been sunk alongside the jetties, the jetties might have been seriously damaged, and the embarking process might have been so much retarded as to give the Osmanli infantry time to come up with the later echelons of the British ere these could be got afloat. This held good both in the northern and the southern sectors at Suvla, and it held good likewise during the subsequent evacuation of Helles. At Anzac, as we have seen, the position was somewhat different; but there also a heavy bombardment of the beaches while the withdrawal was in progress on the night of the 19th-20th would have been in the highest degree inconvenient.

Looking at the problem of embarkation in presence of the enemy in the abstract, it is well to remember that the conditions at Suvla, as also at Anzac (and also later on at Helles, although not to the same extent in the latter case), during the withdrawals of the Allied forces from the Gallipoli Peninsula scarcely supply typical examples of a military operation of this particular kind. Such an operation will, as a rule, be the epilogue to some strategical or tactical failure. The enemy will be alert and on the watch and will be endeavouring to improve upon his previous successes. He will be fully aware that the troops opposed to him are trying to escape, and he will press them for all he is worth. The Suvla force had been in occupation of the trenches that it held to the last for several weeks, and the Turks were satisfied to maintain a passive defensive. They appear indeed to have been keeping somewhat careless guard. Sir J. Moore's army was enabled to effect its embarkation undisturbed after its strategical retreat from Sahagun, as a result of the victory of Corunna. General Bligh's little force at St. Cas, on the other hand, had to fight it out while embarkation was actually in progress, it met with a minor disaster in spite of vigorous naval assistance, and, although conditions of armament and of tactics have undergone a transformation since that day, the affair on the Brittany coast perhaps provides a more pertinent example of an evacuation by sea in face of the enemy than do the operations on the shores of the Ægean on the night of the 19th-20th of December, 1915.

The German account.—It was given out at the time from German sources that the invaders had been hustled off the peninsula from Anzac and Suvla, suffering heavy losses in personnel and material. This story is repeated by an anonymous staff officer of Marshal Liman von Sanders in *Gallipoli. Der Kampf um den Orient*, and, as the account of the withdrawal given in this chapter has been based entirely on British sources of information, it seems in accordance with the fitness of things to quote what the staff officer in question has to say. The passage may be translated as follows :—

" On the night of the 19th-20th of December information reached the higher command from the Northern and Anafarta Sectors " (Anzac and Suvla areas) " that the enemy was abandoning his advanced positions. Orders were instantly given for a general attack on this front. The enemy was unable to offer effective resistance at any point. Where he tried to hold his ground he was overwhelmed. Line after line of defence fell into our hands. The shore was alive with a multitude of troops, artillery was brought up and poured shot and shell into the crowded hostile ranks; the confusion was terrible. Those who escaped the holocaust rushed to the boats, which put off in disorder and hurried helter-skelter to the ships."

The reader is entitled to take his choice between the story as it is related by the German staff officer and as it has been related in foregoing paragraphs. But to show that the staff officer's interpretation of the operations was not universally accepted within the Turkish lines, it may be permissible to give the view of a German correspondent who was with the enemy on the night of the evacuation, which is quoted by Mr. Nevinson in his book on the campaign. " So long as wars exist," wrote this correspondent in the *Vossische Zeitung* on the 21st of January, 1916, " the British evacuation of the Ari Burnu and Anafarta fronts will stand before the eyes of all strategists of retreat as a hitherto quite unattained masterpiece." Marshal Liman von Sanders in the interview recorded in Appendix IV also tells a different story from that of his staff officer.

CHAPTER XV

THE EVACUATION OF HELLES

The decision to withdraw from Helles.—His Majesty's Government had been, as we have seen, in a condition of painful indecision as to what course to pursue in respect to the Dardanelles venture ever since September, and they had not been prepared, when they did make up their minds, to do the thing thoroughly.

The naval situation did not change appreciably during December. Any arguments that could be put forward at the beginning of that month for maintaining a military grip upon the extremity of the Gallipoli Peninsula, remained equally cogent in its closing days. But the signally successful evacuation of the two northern areas would seem to have modified the views of the home authorities concerning the position at the Straits, and certain noteworthy changes that took place at the War Office about Christmas time helped to decide the issue. For orders were despatched to General Monro on the 28th to carry out a withdrawal from Helles, and the matter was at once taken in hand by him in consultation with General Birdwood, who still commanded the Dardanelles forces, and with Admiral de Robeck. General Davies was in immediate command of the troops that were to be removed.

While granting that there was something to be said from the naval point of view for keeping a footing at the toe of the peninsula and on the European side of the mouth of the Straits, it can fairly be insisted that the military objections to such a course were conclusive. Relieved of all anxiety as to the Anzac and Suvla fronts whence the Narrows had so long been menaced, the enemy was now in a position to concentrate the whole of the land forces at his disposal in this theatre of war against General Davies' divisions. It was, moreover, inevitable that the Turkish artillery facing Helles would sooner or later receive substantial accessions of strength, quite apart from the pieces that could be moved across from the northern area ; the Central Powers were in a position to despatch heavy ordnance with abundant ammunition from the German and Austro-Hungarian factories to Thrace for service at the Dardanelles. The entire Helles area was swept by shell-fire from the north and also from the east across the Dardanelles, and the possibility existed that the enemy would in due course assemble such a weight of guns and howitzers as to render the Allies' position at the extremity of the peninsula wholly untenable owing to artillery fire alone. In any case, losses were bound to be extremely heavy from this cause even if there were no active operations, and the landing of stores might be rendered virtually impracticable except at night. An especially severe bombardment on the 24th of December afforded the troops holding this unprofitable position a foretaste of what might be expected later. Moreover, the longer the position was held, the more difficult would it become to evacuate the troops should withdrawal be eventually decided upon.

The problem.—Generals Birdwood and Davies were now called upon to deal with a situation which, if in some respects a less anxious one than that which had been disposed of so effectively at Anzac and Suvla in mid-December, in reality presented a decidedly more difficult problem.

It is true that Helles enjoyed, from the point of view of evacuation, certain distinct advantages as compared with Anzac and even with Suvla. There was, for instance, a considerable choice of embarking points at Helles, Gully Beach, X Beach, W Beach, V Beach, and Morto Bay all being available. The three latter were decidedly better sheltered than Anzac in case of bad weather, W Beach with its fairly solid little breakwater could be made use of even with moderately strong south-westerly winds, thanks to sunken ships V Beach was well protected in ordinary weather, and Morto Bay, apart from danger of hostile shell-fire, was serviceable under almost any atmospheric conditions. Owing to the direction of the front line (extending from about Fusilier Bluff to the Kerevez Dere) in relation to the embarking places, retirement would naturally be carried out direct to the rear, there would be no occasion for a flank march such as the troops about Hill 60 and Demajalik Bair had been called upon to carry out on the night of the 19th–20th of December, the withdrawal from the front trenches at the last could therefore be carried out simultaneously all along the front if thought desirable. Then again, General Davies enjoyed the benefit of the experiences gained during the evacuation of the two northern areas; Admiral de Robeck and his subordinates had likewise learnt useful lessons while the clearing of Anzac and Suvla was being effected. Furthermore—and this was a point of considerable importance—the trench systems at Helles were decidedly more elaborate than those which had been created in the northern areas, because (largely owing to the advances which had taken place on several occasions) there actually were several lines in existence. These several lines would constitute very awkward obstacles for an enemy to traverse in the dark, assuming—as it was safe to do—that the final retirement would take place by night. All these were points to the good.

But there was also another side to the picture. Marshal Liman von Sanders was almost as well able to appreciate the situation as this presented itself to General Monro and Admiral de Robeck as were the authorities now called upon to effect the withdrawal, and he must have realised that there was at least a strong likelihood of an evacuation of Helles. General Davies was, moreover, face to face with relatively far stronger forces in respect to numbers and to artillery than those which had been opposing the Anzac and Suvla armies when these were quitting the peninsula. The Turks had naturally received great encouragement from what had occurred in the northern areas; they were in a much more aggressive mood than they had been during the first three weeks of December, their patrols were showing enterprise and activity, and hostile aircraft were operating with increased energy and daring. Most important of all, however, was the fact that the difficulty of carrying out a withdrawal by surprise had been vastly increased owing to the warning that the enemy had received at Anzac and Suvla, because the opposing troops would be likely to maintain much more careful guard than had been the case when the attenuated forces under Generals Godley and Byng had slipped away so cleverly on the night of the 19th–20th of December. It must also be remembered that General Davies could scarcely hope to enjoy such good luck in respect to weather as had favoured the Anzac and Suvla forces, from the date on which their evacuation had been definitely ordered up to the climax of their dramatic operations.

The situation on the 28th of December.—The Commander-in-Chief had foreseen the likelihood of orders arriving from home for the evacuation of Helles, and on the 24th of December he instructed General Birdwood to make all preliminary preparations for such an operation. By that date the damage done to the landing-places at W and V Beaches on the occasion of the gale at the end of November had been made good. Orders had come early in December for the transfer of the 2nd French Division under General Brulard from the Gallipoli Peninsula to Salonika; and by the 21st the greater part of the infantry of that division had already been taken out of the line, the Royal Naval Division replacing the troops so withdrawn in the right sector of the front. In addition to the French still left, and to the Royal Naval Division under General Paris, the troops at Helles on the 24th consisted of the 29th Division that had been transferred in the latter part of the month from Suvla under General de Lisle, the 42nd Division under General Douglas, and the 52nd Division under General Lawrence. The 11th Division and the 13th Division, troops just withdrawn from Suvla, were available as a reserve in the islands. Arrangements had already been made for the removal of the 53rd and 54th Divisions and of the three Australasian divisions, as well as of the mounted troops, from the islands to Egypt.

General Birdwood at once arranged with General Brulard to relieve the French infantry still in front line, so as to escape the inconveniences of divided command. But it was agreed at the same time that the French artillery still in the peninsula should be lent to the VIIIth Corps under General Davies and should in case of evacuation only be withdrawn at the same time as the British artillery was removed. Besides a number of 75-mm. field guns, this French artillery included six old heavy guns that had done very valuable service in combating the hostile artillery on the Asiatic side of the Straits during the previous months, but which were practically worn out.

General Monro's instructions with regard to the carrying out of the evacuation.—In his despatch of the 26th of January, 1916, describing the withdrawal of the troops, Admiral de Robeck gives the following summary of the instructions given by General Monro

GENERAL MONRO'S INSTRUCTIONS

on the occasion of his conference with the admiral and General Birdwood on the 28th of December :—

" In considering the evacuation of the Helles position it was laid down by Sir Charles Monro, for the guidance of the army, that :

(a) The withdrawal should be conducted with the utmost rapidity, the final stage being limited to one night.

(b) Every effort should be made to improve embarkation facilities at as many points on the coast as could be used, other than " W " and " V " Beaches.

(c) Every endeavour should be made to evacuate as many as possible of the following : British—18-pounder guns,[1] 4·5-inch howitzers, 60-pounder guns, 6-inch guns. French—75-mm. guns, heavy guns. Also artillery ammunition and such small arm ammunition as could safely be withdrawn before the final stage.

(d) The period of time which must elapse before the final stage could be undertaken would be determined by the time required to collect necessary shipping and to make essential preparations ashore (work on beaches, pathways, etc.) taken in conjunction with the necessity for evacuating the superfluous personnel and as much as possible of the material mentioned in (c).

(e) During the " intermediate stage," the duration of which would be determined by the foregoing considerations, such other animals, material, stores, and supplies as could be embarked without prolonging this period would also be evacuated.

Forty-eight hours before the evacuation was completed the number of men remaining on the peninsula was to be cut down to 22,000. Of these 7000 were to embark on the last night but one, leaving 15,000 for the final night ; at the request of the military the latter number was increased to 17,000.[2] As few guns as possible were to be left to the final night, and arrangements were made to destroy any of these which it might be found impossible to remove or which, by reason of their condition, were considered not worth removing."

The Commander-in-Chief also expressed a wish that animals and vehicles as well as the artillery above named should be got away, in so far as was compatible with reasonable safety to personnel, and that the troops from the front trenches should on the last night withdraw straight to the beaches, and should not take up an intermediate position unless they were to be seriously molested, thus

---

[1] Territorial divisions (42nd and 52nd) had the semi-obsolete 15 pr.
[2] These figures do not appear to be correct, *vide* p. 316.

following the precedents set at Anzac and Suvla. He at the same time explained the course which he thought ought to be adopted as regards deceiving the Turks :—

"The situation on the peninsula had not materially changed owing to our withdrawal from Suvla and Anzac, except that there was a markedly increased activity in aerial activity over our positions and the islands of Mudros and Imbros, and that hostile patrolling of our trenches was more frequent and more daring. The most important factor was that the number of heavy guns on the European and Asiatic shores had been considerably augmented, and that these guns were liberally supplied with German ammunition, the result of which was that our beaches were being continuously shelled, especially from the Asiatic shore. I gave it as my opinion that in my judgment I did not regard a feint as an operation offering any prospect of success. Time, the uncertainty of the weather conditions in the Ægean, the absence of a suitable locality, and the withdrawal of small craft from the main issue for such an operation, were some of the reasons which influenced me in the decision at which I arrived. With the concurrence of the Vice-Admiral, therefore, it was decided that the navy should do their utmost to pursue a course of retaliation against the Turkish batteries, but to refrain from any unusually aggressive attitude should the Turkish guns remain quiescent."[1]

General Monro had selected Mudros as his headquarters from the outset, General Birdwood making his at Imbros from the date of his taking over command of the Dardanelles Army. On the 30th, the Commander-in-Chief, having received orders from home that he was to hand over charge of the Mediterranean Force and was to resume command of an army in France, broke up his headquarters at Mudros and proceeded to Alexandria. He made over command at Cairo on the 9th of January to his successor, the evacuation of Helles having (as will be seen) been completed during the previous night. He had realised from the time of his arrival in the Ægean at the end of October that a withdrawal from the peninsula was imperative, and he had the gratification of remaining in general control of the very complex operation of evacuation to the end, and of knowing before laying down his responsibilities that the task had been triumphantly accomplished.

The preliminary stage of the operation.—Two brigades of the

[1] Sir C. Monro's despatch of the 16th March, 1916.

PREPARATIONS FOR EVACUATION

13th Division, already experienced in the art of evacuation by sea in presence of an enemy, were shipped across from Imbros on the 29th of December in relief of the 42nd Division. As a means of deceiving the Turks as to what was in contemplation, it was given out in published orders that this transfer of troops was part of a general relief of the VIIIth Corps by the IXth Corps gradually to be carried out. General Maude's division took over the left of the line—the stretch of trenches between the Great Gully and Fusilier Bluff, with some ground also to the right of the gully. The front next to the right of the 13th Division was in occupation of the 29th Division; to the right of that again was the 52nd Division; while on the extreme right, in occupation of the sector previously held by General Brulard's French division, was the Royal Naval Division. It had been in contemplation to bring the 11th Division over from Imbros in relief of the 29th; but this arrangement was not carried out in the end, although a brigade of the 11th Division was held in readiness to be shipped across should its services be required. The French infantry still left within the area took ship between the 2nd and 4th of January and proceeded to Mudros, and the 86th Brigade of the 29th Division left on the night of the 3rd–4th.

General Lawrence was chosen to supervise actual embarkation operations on the military side, naval arrangements being placed in the hands of Captain Staveley, R.N. Both officers were furnished with especially selected staffs to assist them. General Birdwood had furthermore placed the services of some of the staff officers who had gained experience in the withdrawals from Suvla and Anzac at the disposal of General Davies.

Work was at once taken in hand at the beaches in respect to increasing the facilities for effecting rapid embarkation. It was proposed at the outset to make use of Gully Beach, X Beach, W Beach, and V Beach. The pier at Gully Beach was therefore thoroughly repaired, having been little used latterly. Six piers were put in hand at X Beach. Many important improvements were effected at the last at W Beach; a couple of ships had been sunk, end on to each other, beyond the outer extremity of the breakwater pier running out from Cape Tekke, which protected the beach from the west; a floating bridge was taken in hand to connect the end of the pier with these hulks, and arrangements were made on these to admit of troops being taken off them both on their outer and their inner side. There were also three other shorter piers at W Beach; these were considerably improved by the engineers. The pier arrangements at V Beach had been greatly developed by the French during recent months, providing better shelter than existed at W Beach, with superior jetty facilities; besides the *River Clyde*, dating from the original landing, there were now sunk as block ships the French battleship *Massena* and another vessel; useful work was nevertheless carried out during the first few days of January at this beach also in improving means of embarking in lighters. In such constructions as were taken in hand subsequent to the 29th of December, the object ever particularly kept in mind was the devising of means to accelerate the rate at which personnel would be able to embark in the beetles on the last night of evacuation.

The total number of officers and men on shore to be embarked in due course was in round numbers 40,000 of all ranks, with 150 guns, on the 29th of December; there were furthermore 4500 animals to be got off if possible, besides great quantities of valuable stores, of ammunition, and so forth. The evacuation of men who were not thoroughly fit, of guns, of animals, of certain non-combatant services, and of war material of all kinds began at once. A Greek Labour Corps, which had been performing very useful service on the beaches, was embarked on the pretext that the shelling was for the present too severe to justify their remaining, the men being told that they would be brought back as soon as the Turkish guns had been silenced. The withdrawal of the artillery was carried out on the same lines as at Suvla; four-gun batteries were reduced to two guns each, and later on to a single gun, the artillery personnel being shipped off as the number of guns diminished. Actual departures from the beaches and piers for practical purposes only took place by night.

The work was continuous, the weather, as will be seen below, serving fairly well for loading-up operations at the shore end, but proving less propitious on certain nights for transferring the personnel, animals, and stores from the lighters to the "carrier ships" lying further out. The beach parties were engaged all day long in loading up the beetles so that these should be ready to move off to the store-ships after dark. The operations had to

PREPARATIONS FOR EVACUATION

be interrupted on several occasions by day on the appearance of enemy aeroplanes, which were showing ever-increasing activity although the invaders in general held command of the air. On such occasions animals and transport that happened to be moving down to the beaches turned hastily round and proceeded in the opposite direction, and loading up at the piers and lighters was converted into discharging work for the time being; animals were even taken out of the lighters on some occasions so as to deceive the hostile reconnoitrers. As it turned out, only W and V Beaches were actually used, although it had originally been intended to carry out evacuation work at X and Gully Beaches as well.

All this time the bouts of shelling of the beaches and the trenches on the part of the enemy were recurring with a growing frequency and were conducted with ever-developing intensity, in spite of effective reply from monitors and cruisers, so that the average number of daily casualties from this source kept on the upward grade.[1] Alike about Achi Baba and on the further side of the Straits the Turkish gunners had accurately registered their pieces on W and V Beaches, and heavy bombardments were carried out by day and by night at uncertain intervals, showing that the enemy realised, or assumed, that preparations for withdrawal were in progress. The guns on the Asiatic side firing high-explosive shell were particularly troublesome; heavy howitzers were emplaced near Kum Kale at the very end. "That the actual loss of life from this fire was very small," Admiral de Robeck remarks in his despatch, "borders on the miraculous; the beach parties were completely exposed, and piers and foreshore were constantly hit by shell while officers and men were working on them; even when resting in the dug-outs security from enemy fire could not be assured, and several casualties occurred under these conditions."

In the meantime, special defensive positions were chosen and were prepared in view of possible eventualities at the last; they were designed for accommodation of small detachments, whose task would be to maintain themselves in them for a short time. General Maude selected a suitable line for covering Gully Beach, that locality having at the time been told off as the place of embarka-

[1] The monitors generally lay under cover of Rabbit Island, and when they issued out devoted their attention especially to the enemy artillery on the Asiatic side of the Straits.

tion of what would be left ashore of his division on the last night. Certain detached positions covering X Beach, W Beach, and V Beach were prepared. The old lines which extended right across the peninsula, and which represented fronts that had been held successively by the invaders at different times during their gradual advance to the trenches now in their occupation, were repaired to some extent, and gaps occurring in the lines of barbed wire were filled up at important points. A fresh line of posts extending across from De Tott's Battery to near Gully Beach was established. Finally a small "keep" was designed at Cape Tekke to which it was proposed that men who should be left behind by any chance on the last night should repair; food and water were arranged for here, the idea being that it might possibly be feasible to get such a party off subsequently. All communications that were not to be used on the last night were gradually barred at points where they passed through the defensive lines, and arrangements were made for closing at the last moment the communications to be left open, after the final parties had passed through. "Controls" were to be established at these points in telephonic communication with divisional headquarters, as at Suvla (*vide* page 295).

As the withdrawal of the whole of the heavy guns that were in the habit of replying to the Turkish guns would have made the enemy suspicious, it was decided to retain, and to destroy at the last moment, one British 6-inch gun and the six French heavy guns mentioned above—the latter with the full approval of General Brulard; it was foreseen that it would be impossible to remove these pieces on the last night. From the date of the order of evacuation being issued, the rate of artillery fire was reduced to that which the number of guns to remain on the last day would be able to keep up. At the same time it was arranged that all rifle fire and hand-grenade throwing should cease nightly at 11.30 p.m., as it was intended that the final detachments should quit the trenches at 11.45 p.m. on the last night; there was to be no activity after that hour unless the enemy became very aggressive. The object of these orders was to accustom the Turks to a period of quiescence on the British side each night after 11.30 p.m. This plan produced the desired result. The opposing side followed suit, and during the last few nights before the Helles force quitted the peninsula hostile activity after 11.30 p.m. was practically confined to the long-range bombardments of the beaches.

The unfavourable weather.—Reference has been made above to the losses and the annoyance caused on the beaches by the Turkish artillery fire, and to the delays caused at times by the appearance of enemy aviators. But a much graver cause of anxiety and of inconvenience arose from the weather conditions, which had become much less settled than had been the case while the Anzac and Suvla forces were effecting their withdrawal. The apprehension which the possibility of strong winds and rough seas had caused to Admiral Wemyss during those operations has been referred to on page 282, but still days and nights were, as it turned out, then to be the rule. That he had had good grounds for solicitude had, however, been shown on the 21st of December and again on the 24th, days which were signalised by some very boisterous weather. That break marked the close of the spell of calms which had prevailed during the middle weeks of the month, and heralded a period of atmospheric disturbances occurring at short intervals for some time to come.

Strong north-easterly winds lasted all day on the 2nd and 3rd of January and during the following nights. The 4th was calm; but a change came on that evening, and it blew a gale from the north-east during the night which only gradually died down in the course of the following day; on the 6th the weather was favourable. Owing to the direction of the wind being off-shore at W and V Beaches on the occasions of its blowing with force during these days and nights, actual embarkation work at the shore-end was not much interfered with; but the rough water and strong wind outside rendered the transhipment of animals and stores from the lighters on to the larger vessels that were to transport these to the islands a labour of considerable difficulty, involving frequent minor delays which in the aggregate served to throw the whole programme of movements back. After the rough night of the 2nd-3rd, some of the personnel that ought to have been got aboard the bigger ships during the dark hours was embarked by daylight on the following morning, and in the morning the French also managed to get a quantity of animals afloat from V Beach after creating a smoke screen by igniting a haystack on shore. During the night of the 4th-5th a lighter, fully loaded up with transport vehicles and mules and their native Indian drivers, was swept out to sea; but it fortunately fetched up on Rabbit Island and was got off again by a war vessel.

Gully Beach and X Beach could not have been used on the nights of the 1st–2nd, 2nd–3rd, and 4th–5th; nor might embarkations at those localities perhaps have been feasible even on the night of the 5th–6th; but it had not been intended to use those points on the outer coast of the peninsula except at the end. Although the unsettled weather caused serious delays, these represented nothing approaching to what they might have meant had the wind during the first few days in January blown from the south or the south-west, instead of being northerly. The fact remained, however, that great quantities of material and a good many animals which the naval and military staffs had hoped to have sent afloat by that date still remained on shore on the 6th. Moreover, by an unfortunate contretemps, a horse-ship had been sunk by a French battleship in collision, and this threw out all calculations as to the rate of evacuation of animals. It therefore became necessary on the morning of the 6th to review the position of affairs, in view of the course of events during the previous few days and of the threatening atmospheric conditions.

Change of plan as to the final evacuation.—The plan agreed upon by the naval and military authorities at the start had been that only 13,450 troops with about 25 guns should be left ashore on the last day, 6000 troops and the same number of guns being taken off on the night before. The scheme was that the bulk of the troops and all the guns left for the last two nights were to embark at W and V Beaches, but that, although Gully Beach and X Beach were not to be used on the penultimate night, all that was left of the 13th Division and a portion of the 29th Division were to be embarked at those two points on the last night of all—about 3000 of all ranks at Gully Beach and about 950 at X Beach. But the experiences of the previous two or three days and nights decided General Davies (who had issued orders in the above sense on the 3rd) on the 6th to propose some very important alterations in the plan.

In the first place, the unsettled state of the weather justified the fear that two successive favourable nights would not present themselves, and that, should the programme be carried out as

CHANGE OF PLAN

contemplated for the last night but one, a force of only 13,450 of all ranks, with very few guns, might be left to hold a front of 8000 yards for some days. There would be a strong likelihood of the enemy detecting its weakness. Then there was also the question as to the wisdom of using Gully Beach and X Beach at all. Those two embarking places could not be depended upon with strong winds from the north such as had been experienced since the 1st of January, although under such conditions withdrawal by way of W and V Beaches might be perfectly practicable ; while they were just as exposed as the two others during periods of bad weather from the south or south-west. It was, moreover, pointed out that any assembling of boats or shipping, or a conspicuous development in respect to piers, at those points might if observed by the Turks serve to disclose the fact that evacuation was in progress, because those beaches on the outer side of the peninsula had been very little used during recent months. General Davies therefore proposed that the number of troops and guns to be withdrawn on the last night but one should be reduced, and that the force to be left for evacuation on the final night should be fixed at 17,000 of all ranks, with a total of 54 guns (including those which it had been decided to destroy). He further proposed that the project of using Gully and X Beaches should be abandoned.

The additional strain thrown upon W and V Beaches, were these suggestions to be adopted, demanded careful consideration on the part of the naval authorities. They, however, came to the conclusion that the difficulty created by having to embark about 6500 additional troops and a larger number of guns at those localities could be met by employing destroyers alongside the sunken ships, leaving the previously made arrangements with regard to the disposal of the beetles to stand, subject to some slight modifications. It was agreed that the use of X Beach should be given up and that the bulk of the 13th Division should embark at W Beach instead of at Gully Beach on the last night, but that the final detachments of that division to quit the trenches should be taken off at the latter point. General Birdwood gave his sanction to this change of plan, and General Davies issued fresh orders at once to meet the revised programme. Work at X Beach was suspended, and the engineers engaged at that point were transferred to W and V Beaches to make certain alterations necessitated by the new programme. The naval authorities had to revise many details, in conjunction with the military staff; but they nevertheless had their fresh schedules drawn up and communicated to all concerned during the morning of the 7th. It was decided that, subject to change in the weather conditions, the nights of the 7th–8th and 8th–9th were to be the two last nights of withdrawal; but under the revised scheme the importance of the penultimate night had been considerably reduced.

Events of the 7th.—Apart from vigorous shelling of the beaches and from activity on the part of hostile aviators, the enemy had not shown much sign of life during the past few days, except in the form of liveliness on the part of patrols and of some increase in artillery work against the trenches. But about noon on the 7th the Turks suddenly opened a very heavy bombardment of the stretch of front held by the 13th Division, especially to the left of the Great Gully, and at the same time they directed a heavy shell-fire from across the Straits against the trenches that were being held by the Royal Naval Division. The artillery attack upon the lines occupied by the 13th Division proved to be the heaviest that had hitherto been encountered on the peninsula, while the Turkish pieces also played freely upon the sectors held by the 29th and 52nd Divisions. This lasted until about 5 p.m., and the bombardment was intensive between 3 p.m. and 3.30 p.m.; considerable damage was done to parapets and communication trenches, and telephone communication was interrupted. At 3.30 p.m. two mines were fired near Fusilier Bluff and it was then seen that the Turkish trenches were full of men. An assault upon the lines held by the 13th Division appears to have been intended; but when the Osmanlis did make a half-hearted attempt to advance they were soon driven back again by the accurate fire to which they were subjected at the hands of the 13th Division. General Davies' weakness in artillery owing to a number of guns having already been withdrawn was compensated for this day by the fire from a supporting squadron consisting of monitors and destroyers, which was able to act effectively against the enemy's flank. The casualties suffered by the British in the affair only amounted to 164, these falling almost entirely upon the 7th North Staffords, whose section of trenches was much knocked about by the enemy's concentrated shell-fire directed on that particular point. The enemy is believed to have lost heavily from the naval guns, owing to being massed in the trenches opposite the 13th Division which were very effectively taken in enfilade.

The Turks would not seem to have been well-advised in selecting the left flank of the British line for delivering an attack, seeing that fire from the warships was likely to be particularly troublesome to the assailants in that portion of the front. That Marshal Liman von Sanders adopted such a plan certainly suggests that he was entirely unaware that a large part of the British artillery had been withdrawn and that the British commander on shore was very dependent upon naval assistance in consequence. All arrangements were made to reinforce Helles by a brigade from Imbros when the hostile bombardment of the trenches began; but the move was not carried out when it became apparent that the expected Ottoman offensive was petering out.

There seems to be little doubt that from the invader's point of view this affair was a most fortunate one. The Turks clearly intended either to deliver a serious attack, or else to make a reconnaissance in force so as to ascertain whether their opponents were holding their trenches in strength. Whatever was intended —and in this connection the quotation from a German account given on page 326 is not without interest—the result would seem to have convinced the enemy that the defenders of the British front were gathered in amply sufficient numbers to give a good account of themselves, and it is reasonable to suppose that General Davies' antagonist came to the conclusion that afternoon that, even supposing the invaders to contemplate an early retirement from Helles, such an operation was not actually imminent.

The day's combat did not in any way interfere with the programme for the coming hours of darkness. The night turned out fine and calm, and before dawn on the 8th the dwindling British army had been cut down by a further 2300 of all ranks, by nine guns, and by 880 animals. This reduced the numbers of personnel and guns remaining to the figure that had been fixed between General Davies and the naval authorities as the force that should remain to be removed on the last night.

The situation on the 8th.—During the eight nights between the 31st of December and the 8th of January, 15,975 officers and men, 85 guns, 2667 horses and mules, and great quantities of ammunition, ordnance stores and other forms of war material had been embarked. But, owing to the delays that had been caused on some nights by unfavourable weather, a considerable number of animals that it had been hoped to get off still remained on shore, and there were such vast accumulations of material that much of it must have been abandoned in any case.

"It would have been possible, of course," Sir C. Monro wrote in his despatch, "by extending the period during which the process of evacuation proceeded to have reduced the quantity of stores and material that was left behind on the peninsula, but not to the degree that may seem apparent at first sight. Our chances of enjoying a continuity of fine weather in the Ægean were very slender in the month of January; it was indeed a contingency that had to be reckoned with that we might very probably be visited by a spell of bad weather which would cut us off completely from the peninsula for a fortnight or even longer.

Supplies, ammunition, and material to a certain degree had therefore to be left to the last moment for fear of the isolation of the garrison at any moment when the evacuation might be in progress. I decided therefore that our aim should be primarily the withdrawal of the bulk of the personnel, artillery, and ammunition in the intermediate period, and that no risk should be taken in prolonging the withdrawal of personnel at the final stage with a view to reducing the quantity of stores left."

The 8th was fine and calm, but the glass had fallen and the wind was inclined to back. It was, however, decided that the final embarkation should be undertaken that night, and all necessary arrangements in anticipation of that operation which required to be put in effect during the day, were therefore carried out.

The arrangements for the coming night were briefly as follows:—

The 13th and 29th Divisions (except the last parties of the 13th Division to quit the trenches) were to embark at W Beach, the route to be followed by the detachments of the 13th Division being by the road which had been constructed along the shore below the bluffs, while the 29th Division took a route more inland. The forming-up place for the 13th Division was just north of Cape Tekke, while that of the 29th Division was at the head of the little gully leading down to W Beach (*vide* Map II, p. 70). The last parties of the 13th Division were to embark at Gully Beach. The 52nd and Royal Naval Divisions were to embark at V Beach, the forming-up place being beside the old castle on its north-western side ; two distinct routes leading from the front to the forming-up place had been arranged for.

There were to be three trips each from W and V Beaches, 4000 being taken off at W Beach and 3200 at V Beach by the first trip, 3246 from W and 2795 from V by the second trip, and 1596 from W and 1611 from V by the third trip ; the numbers to be taken off at each trip decreasing, as shown, allowed for accidents to destroyers, beetles, and so forth. Only one trip, equivalent in respect to the hour to the third at the other two beaches, was to take place from Gully Beach, 670 being allowed for. The strengths of the divisions and other troops were, 13th Division 3645, 29th Division 4145, 52nd Division 2845, Royal Naval Division 4445, Artillery 700, and various base details, beach parties, etc., 1138, making a grand total of 17,118. Of these 8842 were to be taken off at W Beach, 7606 at V Beach, and the 670 at Gully Beach. The troops for the first trip were to reach their forming-up places between 7 p.m. and 7.30 p.m., and those for the second trip between 10.30 p.m. and 11 p.m. The hour for the remainder to reach their forming-up places was not definitely fixed. This must depend upon the time taken to reach the forming-up places by routes that were not quite the same length in each case, the detachments all quitting the front trenches simultaneously at 11.45 p.m. The third trip included beach parties, engineers working at the piers, special staffs, and so on, as well as the forces mentioned below as detailed for the beach defences.

During the afternoon special forces, consisting of 600 men from the 29th Division and of 400 men from the Royal Naval Division, took up position along the lines of special defences that had been established to cover W and V Beaches. Arrangements had been made that the piles of stores at various points which it had not been possible to remove to the beaches should be ignited by time-fuses set to act about the hour that the last troops would be embarking. An especial staff was told off to destroy the great dumps of ammunition, ordnance stores, engineer material, supplies, etc., near the two beaches. Orders were also issued for the destruction, as far as practicable, of animals that it would be impossible to embark, as also for the complete demolition of the guns that were to be left behind, before they were finally abandoned.

The final evacuation.—By the time that darkness closed in the wind was from the south, but was as yet of little strength. At 7 p.m. General Davies shifted his headquarters from the shore to H.M.S. *Triad*, which was connected with the land by cables, so that he remained in close touch with the various divisional headquarters and with General Lawrence. The troops for the first trip arrived in good time and their embarkation commenced at 8 p.m. By 9 p.m. " the wind had freshened considerably, still blowing from the south ; a slight sea got up, and caused much inconvenience on the beaches."[1] The work nevertheless proceeded everywhere without a hitch, except at the hulks in extension of the W Beach breakwater. The floating bridge connecting these with the breakwater became very unsteady in the choppy water, which delayed the passage of the troops on to the hulks from which they were to be taken off by destroyers. Various devices were tried to get over the difficulty during the next two or three hours ; but beetles kept fouling the bridge and damaging its structure, and in the end, after 3000 troops had been safely got off at this point and the sea by this time being decidedly rough, it was decided to abandon this method of embarkation. The naval officer in charge at W Beach was satisfied by that time that he could get off all the troops still to come without it. Embarkation was in the meantime proceeding quite satisfactorily at the other W Beach piers ; and progress was particularly satisfactory at V Beach, where the arrangements that had been hastily made after the change of plan of the 6th for using the two sunken French vessels as embarking places, proved most effective. By 10.30 p.m. fourteen British guns and all the French 75's had been embarked at V Beach. The second trip began, well up to schedule time, at 11.30 p.m.

At 11.45 p.m. the last detachments quietly moved out of the advanced trenches all along the front and proceeded direct to their forming-up places. As had been the case at Suvla, the men's boots were muffled with sacking and every precaution had been taken to keep the enemy in ignorance that anything unusual was in progress ; as on previous nights a certain amount of rifle fire and grenade throwing had been kept up until 11.30 p.m. Various

---

[1] Sir J. De Robeck's despatch.

THE FINAL EVACUATION

devices for firing fixed rifles from time to time were set in action before the detachments filed out of the trenches, and lights and fires were left burning. On the last detachments passing through the different controls the communications were in each case blocked and the mines that had been laid down were made active. At no point was there, however, the slightest indication that the enemy had detected that the trenches were no longer tenanted. The Turks were indeed particularly quiescent on this night and there was less bombardment of W and V Beaches than had been the case on any night for some time previously ; the few shell that did plunge down did no harm whatever. The last detachments from the front began to arrive at the forming-up places at W and V Beaches about 1.30 a.m., and the beetles told off for the third trip at once started taking them off, but under ever-increasing difficulties caused by wind and swell. As there was no sign of hostile activity orders were sent at 1.45 a.m. to the covering forces in occupation of the beach defences to move down to the embarking places. In the meantime the last detachments of the 13th Division, having had less distance to go, had arrived at Gully Beach before 1 a.m. and they were all embarked in their beetles by 1.45 a.m., ready to push off to the cruiser *Talbot*.

The weather was growing rapidly worse, and the first and only alarming contretemps occurred at Gully Beach, where the swell caused serious trouble and where one lighter with its living freight on board got aground and could not be refloated, although the troops were able to disembark in safety. This was communicated to the chief embarking officer who immediately despatched a fresh beetle to replace the one ashore. But after some little delay General Maude, noting that the sea was getting up, decided to march the disembarked detachment to W Beach, where they arrived at 3.15 a.m. He and his divisional headquarters, following in rear, had considerable difficulty in getting through the entanglements, as all gaps had been closed.

"After a temporary lull," Admiral de Robeck wrote in his final despatch, "the wind again increased, and by 3 a.m. a very nasty sea was running into W Beach. It was only by the great skill and determination displayed by the beach personnel that the embarkation was brought to a successful conclusion, and that all the craft except one steamboat (damaged in collision) got away in safety." The delay caused by the lighter load of the 13th Division gave rise indeed to great anxiety. The last gun had been shipped from V Beach soon after 2 a.m. and work at that point was completed by 3 a.m., that better protected embarking place feeling the effect of the rising sea less than was the case at W Beach. But at W Beach the question at the end almost became one of minutes, and getting the last troops and the beach staff taken off came to be a decidedly critical operation. All the troops were clear at 3.45 a.m., however, without serious mishap, although the utmost difficulty was experienced in getting the last few beetles and boats away owing to the heavy seas running into the harbour. The naval beach personnel then left. Unfortunately one magazine that had been prepared for destruction appears in the hurry at the end to have been fired somewhat prematurely, for it blew up before all the boats were clear and one sailor was killed by the debris. This was the one serious casualty that occurred in this most remarkable operation; amongst the troops one man was hit by a spent bullet and three met with accidents while embarking.

The anxieties of the vice-admiral, it should be mentioned, had been considerably increased during the night by the knowledge that a hostile submarine was at large. The battleship *Prince George*, which had taken off about 2000 troops together with the headquarters of the 29th Division, and which was sailing for Mudros, was actually struck by a torpedo that failed to explode. Under the circumstances it was decided to modify the project for bombarding the evacuated positions from the sea, that had been contemplated.

The arrangements that had been made by the military for igniting the dumps of stores and for blowing up the magazines proved (except for the premature explosion mentioned above) most satisfactory as far as could be judged from afloat. The conflagrations and concussions that ensued were apparently the first intimation received by the Turks that General Davies' force had withdrawn. Red Verey lights were then discharged from the enemy trenches, this firework display apparently representing a preconcerted signal to place the Ottoman forces on the alert should it be discovered that evacuation was in progress; and a brisk artillery fire was opened upon the empty British trenches and on the beaches, which was maintained until 6.30 a.m. The enemy

THE FINAL EVACUATION

had been particularly quiet between midnight and 4 a.m., and there is every reason to believe that General Davies' plan of shutting down trench activity nightly at 11.30 p.m. during the period immediately preceding the final embarkation, had effected its purpose.

Leaving out of account four serviceable 15-pounders which had been destroyed earlier in the month, the ordnance that was abandoned comprised the one British 6-inch gun and the six old French heavy guns already mentioned, together with ten other worn-out 15-pounders; all these pieces were blown up. Besides the artillery, 508 animals (most of which were shot) were left on the peninsula, with a number of vehicles and considerable quantities of appliances, ordnance stores and food supplies. Steps had been taken to destroy all the material by burning, and there is reason to believe that very little fell into the hands of the Turks in serviceable condition; but the goods left behind and destroyed none the less represented a large sum of money. Still, the financial sacrifice involved was a matter of trifling importance to set against the memorable achievement involved in successfully extricating an army of some 40,000 men out of such a trap as the Helles area represented, in presence of superior forces in a position to foresee the operation which their antagonists were carrying out.

The withdrawal of the troops from the advanced trenches and the embarkation of 17,000 men and 35 guns on the last night were a veritable triumph of finished staff work on the part of the navy and the army. They were only made possible, however, by the high standard of discipline that prevailed amongst all ranks of the land forces. The most praiseworthy feat of all, however, lay in the getting off of so large a body of soldiers, under weather conditions such as prevailed on the night of the 8th–9th of January, 1916, from embarkation points so exposed to the winds and the waves as were W and V Beaches, almost without a single mishap. The handling of the destroyers alongside the blockships in a strong onshore wind raising choppy seas, was the admiration of the military, while the crews of the beetles managed their awkward craft in broken waters with a rare combination of nerve, skill, and judgment. That under such circumstances not a single soldier was drowned, and that the operation was actually completed in less time than had been anticipated when framing the programme, constitute a performance which the Royal Navy have every reason to be proud of, and for which the army that was served so well have every reason to be grateful.

The German version.—A German staff officer's account of the withdrawal from Anzac and Suvla was given at the end of the last chapter, and it may not be out of place to quote here the same author's story of the evacuation of Helles.

" On the afternoon of the 7th of January, Marshal Liman von Sanders came to the conclusion that the decisive moment had arrived for bringing the Gallipoli campaign to a satisfactory termination. A terrific drum fire from the whole of the artillery served for a finale to the months' long infernal concert. The enemy must have guessed that the fateful hour was at hand. When the fire of the Turkish batteries ceased for a moment, the hostile commander-in-chief, General Monro, adopted a desperate expedient to disengage his troops. He offered up his best regiment, the Staffordshire, to certain death, sending it forward to meet the Turks and to provide the opening scene in the melancholy drama which, under the title of the ' glorious retirement from Gallipoli ' was to make its Don Quixote progress though the journalistic forest of the Entente press. And indeed, had it not been for the ever active hostile fleet, not an enemy would have left the soil of the peninsula alive. On the night of the 8th–9th the enemy succeeded in extricating himself from the clutches of the strenuously pursuing defenders under protection of the warships, but at the cost of abandoning enormous masses of munitions and provisions, the counting of which took weeks. A fully loaded transport was struck by heavy shell and sank. Only a handful of those on board were saved."

The author goes on to give a glowing description of the vast captures in material that compensated the Osmanlis and their German advisers for the escape of the stricken remnants of the invading army.

Widely as this version of the business differs from the account given in preceding paragraphs of this chapter, it is worth noting that there are certain points of resemblance between the two stories in respect to matters of detail. As to the violence of the bombardment of the 7th of January there appears to be agreement between the contending sides. General Monro was in Egypt on that day ; still, a mistake of that kind is natural enough and would not in itself seriously discredit the anonymous staff officer's tale.

The special reference to the Staffordshire Regiment, with its gratifying tribute to the efficiency of the corps, is deserving of attention, seeing that it was the 7th North Staffords who suffered by far the most heavily of any battalion engaged, although their losses arose from the concentrated bombardment to which their section of trenches was subjected and not under conditions such as the German writer portrays. Even the tragedy of the fully loaded transport sunk by shell with disastrous loss of life, finds some sort of counterpart in Admiral de Robeck's mention of a steamer that foundered after collision on the last night. We can leave it at that. Marshal Liman von Sanders' version (Appendix IV) does not agree with that of his staff officer.

Comments on the operation.—The evacuation of Helles provides a particularly instructive illustration of the extent to which an operation of this kind is dependent upon weather conditions. Although General Davies was not favoured with such good fortune in this respect as had been Generals Godley and Byng in their withdrawals from Anzac and Suvla, he can hardly be called unlucky considering the season of the year at which he was called upon to retire from the peninsula. The strong winds that prevailed in the north-eastern Ægean on certain days and nights of the first week of January, 1916, blew from the north-east and north, from which point W and V Beaches were sheltered ; it was only on the last night of all that a breeze set in from the south which increased in force as the minutes passed until, in the small hours of the morning, it threatened to prohibit the embarkation of the last few detachments left ashore—at a stage of the proceedings, moreover, when the regular lines of defence had been abandoned, when the artillery remaining serviceable was already afloat, and when the situation ensured that the enemy would concentrate a violent and accurately directed shell-fire in the morning on the marooned residue of what a week before had been a formidable army.

As it was, and although the general direction of the wind even when strong favoured the embarkation of animals, munition, and supplies in boats and lighters at the two beaches in use for the purpose, a large amount of war material had to be left behind. The enemy also enjoyed the satisfaction of laying hands upon several guns ; although these, it is true, had been rendered wholly unserviceable. Had the wind, on the contrary, come from the south or south-west on the occasions when it was blowing fresh during the preliminary stage, not only would the embarkation of horses and armament and stores have been wholly impracticable, but the piers that had been especially contrived to facilitate the work would inevitably have broken up, greatly retarding proceedings on the calm days and making the embarkation of 17,000 men on the last night a virtual impossibility.

There finally supervened the disquieting atmospheric conditions of the hours of darkness of the 8th-9th. Had the "very nasty sea" spoken of by Admiral de Robeck in his despatch been running, let us say, at 10 p.m., instead of the weather only creating those untoward conditions by about 3 a.m., the bulk of the troops could not have been got off, although a considerable proportion would by that hour already have embarked. It would have become impossible to use the lighters at a stage when the work was only about one-third completed, even if the piers had stood, and the blockships at W Beach would have ceased to serve at an earlier hour than was actually the case, because the connecting bridge between them and the shore would have become useless so much the sooner. It is continuous battering by the seas that gradually smashes structures up—they may hold together for half an hour or an hour, but will be totally wrecked by three or four hours of heavy weather. It may be admitted that wind and waves rise more suddenly and quickly in the Mediterranean than in most waters, but the evacuation of troops in presence of the enemy must always be largely dependent upon atmospheric conditions.[1]

The remarkable success that attended the British naval and military operations at Helles at the beginning of 1916, as also the similar operations at Anzac and Suvla a few days earlier,

[1] This was shown by the minor disaster which befel a body of British troops at Ostend in 1798 already referred to on p. 55. They landed on the shore north of the town and performed the task assigned to them—the destruction of the lock-gates of the Bruges canal. But when they returned to the beach about noon on the following day, with the enemy approaching in force, they found an awkward surf beating. The second-in-command (General Eyre Coote, nephew of the famous Indian general, was in command but was wounded) wrote in his despatch that they had "attempted to get off some companies, but the boats soon filled with water and it was with extreme difficulty that the men were saved." The upshot was that, attacked in superior numbers, the little force consisting of 60 officers and 1076 rank and file had to surrender.

reflected the utmost credit upon all who were concerned in the evacuations on the spot. But it would be absurd to pretend that the invaders of the Gallipoli Peninsula were not lucky in the matter of the weather when they came to depart, or to suggest that the happy sequel to operations of a critical nature relieved the home authorities of a very heavy responsibility for having refused to act upon the recommendation of General Monro when he reported in favour of complete withdrawal at the end of October.

The motor lighters proved a great success under somewhat difficult conditions on the last night at Helles. Leaving the question of broken water entirely out of the question, it seems doubtful if some 16,600 officers and men could have been got off from W and V Beaches during the course of a single winter's night but for these craft. A force of that strength would have represented rather more than five hundred 30-foot cutter loads—say, 130 tows —besides special horse-boats for the guns. Even if it had been possible to bring off five trips within the hours of darkness, that would mean about twenty-six tows to each trip, with only about 700 yards of beach space available, or less than 30 yards to the tow. It would also mean that about 130 cutters would be loading up and lying off 700 yards of beach, manned by men of whom probably very few would be watermen, and in the dark. Add to this such weather conditions as prevailed on the night of the 8th–9th of January after the first three or four hours of darkness, and it is easy to picture the confusion that would almost certainly have occurred. Some of the cutters would assuredly have been swamped; others would have been dashed ashore on the beaches; there must have been loss of life amongst the military, even if the numbers of the drowned were not large. The beetles, it should be added, proved of the utmost use during the earlier stages, when material was being embarked.

As far as the embarking forces and the naval forces were able to judge, the enemy made no attempt to follow up the last detachments to quit the front trenches (although that is not the impression that the German account quoted on page 326 conveys). Assuming this to be correct, the reason for it—apart from the various special precautions taken in the trenches, the devices to deceive the Turks, the skill displayed by detachment leaders, and the military virtues displayed by the troops—possibly was that the opposing side had persuaded itself, as a consequence of the engagement of the previous day and of the uncompromising front displayed by the 13th Division on that occasion, that no immediate withdrawal of the invading army from the Helles area was in contemplation. If appreciation of the situation took that form within the Ottoman lines, the enemy outposts may have been exercising less vigilance than usual and than would otherwise have been the case. The change in the direction of the wind may also have suggested to Marshal Liman von Sanders and the Turkish staff that evacuation on this particular night was, on the face of it, improbable ; those very atmospheric conditions which caused such trouble on the beaches may indeed from this point of view have been a blessing in disguise.

The enemy may, no doubt, have become aware about midnight, or a little later, that the British trenches were empty and may have been creeping forward during the small hours under great difficulties arising from the lines of excavations, the barbed-wire and the blocked communications. But in that case some of the " booby trap " mines would surely have gone off, and the reports would have been heard ; a heavy artillery fire would also surely have been opened on the beaches. The fact that the Turks discharged lights and opened bombardment, as soon as the dumps of stores were ignited and the magazine of explosives and ammunition blew up towards 4 a.m., does suggest that only then did they have any inkling that their antagonists had slipped them for a second time. As a matter of fact, it is extremely doubtful whether the enemy, even if the evacuation of the front trenches had been observed at the last, could have interfered appreciably with the embarkation except by long-range gun-fire directed on the beaches. Advance in the dark across the lines of obstacles which the British trenches created must have been extremely slow, and the mines would have proved very disconcerting. It was artillery fire on the beaches and not infantry pursuit that General Davies feared, and it was the rising wind, far more than the Turks, that gave just grounds for anxiety during the last four hours of the famous evacuation of the extremity of the Gallipoli Peninsula.

The change of plan arrived at upon General Davies' representations on the 6th of January was unquestionably a judicious step. It is true that there is no reason to suppose, in view of the torpid attitude displayed by the Turks on the 8th, that the increase in the British force left in the Helles area on that day by some 4000 men and several guns made any difference from the point of view of security, while it added appreciably to the amount of work that had to be got through on the beaches under somewhat difficult conditions on the following night. But although activity on the part of the enemy was not unexpected on the 6th, the abortive Ottoman offensive of the 7th, with its depressing experiences for the Ottoman leaders and troops, could not be foreseen when the alteration of programme was agreed to by the naval and military authorities. One of the arguments used in favour of introducing the modification in arrangements was that two successive nights of favourable weather could not be depended upon; although embarkation was in the event possible both on the 7th–8th and the 8th–9th, there was not much to spare on the latter night. In view of what occurred at Gully Beach at the end, it seems very doubtful whether anything like the total number of troops which it had been in contemplation to take off at that point under the original scheme, could have been embarked there. The work at X Beach was intended to be completed fairly early under the first programme, and at an hour when there cannot have been much sea running on the night of the 8th–9th. But under the weather conditions of early January it would certainly have been risky to place much dependence on embarking places which were exposed whether the wind blew from the north or the west or the south, and when the piers would have been hasty improvisations.

In concluding this account of the withdrawal from Helles, General Monro's summary covering that operation and also the withdrawals from the northern areas may fittingly be quoted. "The entire evacuation of the peninsula had now been completed. It demanded for its successful realisation two important military essentials, viz. good luck and skilled disciplined organisation, and they were both forthcoming to a marked degree at the hour needed. Our luck was in the ascendant by the marvellous spell of calm weather which prevailed. But we were able to turn to fullest advantage these accidents of fortune."

CHAPTER XVI

SOME OUTSTANDING LESSONS OF THE CAMPAIGN

The vital necessity of exhaustive examination of the conditions before embarking on a warlike adventure, and of evolving a comprehensive plan of campaign for its conduct.—The most significant lesson taught us by the story of the operations with which this volume deals is not one illustrative of the art of war, as that expression is ordinarily interpreted by the sailor or the soldier. It is not a lesson concerned with tactics, nor with strategy, nor yet with the technicalities that are of absorbing interest to the naval or the military expert. It is not a lesson that needs to be instilled into the youngster at Dartmouth, nor at Woolwich, nor at Sandhurst. But it nevertheless goes to the very root of the principles on which war policy must be conducted if a cause is to triumph. The lesson is one to be learnt by the statesman rather than by the fighting man ashore or afloat, and it amounts to this : If they wish the realm that they govern to overcome its enemies in times of national emergency, rulers of a country must take exhaustive counsel with professional advisers, and they must see to it that those professional advisers are given full opportunity to state their case unhampered by political interference.

It is no use mincing matters about the Dardanelles. The discomfiture of the Allies in their campaign for the Straits was primarily due to their fighting forces having been committed to a ticklish adventure without adequate forethought. A martial operation of an altogether abnormal kind was undertaken without searching investigation of the whole of the factors that bore on the contemplated enterprise. The plan of campaign decided upon at the start—what there was of it—only dealt with a portion of the project that those responsible for commanding action to proceed had in mind, and it was drawn up on the assumption that an entirely novel scheme of making war was necessarily going to succeed. Hostilities between embattled nations are too serious a business to be conducted in this haphazard fashion. The published Report of the Dardanelles Commission discloses that no joint naval and military scheme for carrying out the undertaking was laid before the British Government before the fleets were launched on their attack, nor apparently was this considered necessary. The document leaves it to be inferred that the General Staff, as representing military opinion, was never called upon to formulate its considered views as to the merits of the plan proposed by Admiral Carden and accepted by the Admiralty, although the project manifestly bespoke military as well as naval considerations.[1] The Government in fact committed a cardinal blunder at the very outset. The deliberate, creeping method of attack upon the defile was perhaps from the sailor's point of view a sagacious one, even if the method failed when put in practice. But its advocates—naval and civilian—would seem to have overlooked one point of vital importance. The essence of the plan was that it would take some weeks to complete, and that fact in itself rendered it in the highest degree objectionable from the soldier's point of view. Such conditions necessarily afforded the enemy time for preparation, and they made it certain that if the warships were to fail and if it were then to be decided to try military effort instead of, or in supplement of, naval effort, the difficulties in the way of the army would be vastly increased.

Nor was that the only error committed by the Government in leaving the military aspect of the contemplated operations out of account. It does not seem to have been realised that the attack of coast defences, that operations which bring floating force into collision with enemy troops, create not a naval but an amphibious situation. If it was to be the warships of the Allies that were to force the Straits, it was the Turkish army with its forts and its artillery that represented the principal obstacle in the way. The

[1] The writer can vouch for it that the matter was never considered jointly by the Naval War Staff and the General Staff at the War Office. Had it been, he is confident that the idea of a purely naval attack, either in the nature of trying to rush the passage or in the form that the attack actually took, would have been abandoned in deference to the representations that the soldiers must have made. For the military objections were manifest and were overwhelming.

dangers that the British and French vessels would encounter from concealed ordnance, to which the ships' guns would be unable effectively to reply, was a point likely to be far more apparent to soldiers than to sailors, seeing the extent to which the system of employing guns and howitzers from hidden positions has entered into land tactics of late years.

Be that as it may, the result of the British Government's irrational procedure was that the fleet operations began at a juncture when there were no troops available to assist in major, or even in minor, degree. The affair indeed started at a season when the landing of troops, had there been troops, was bound to be rendered particularly difficult owing to unsettled weather conditions. All this, moreover, only takes into account the attempt to conquer the actual Dardanelles. The project for accomplishing this particular object was, however, only part of what was in reality an almost entirely undigested scheme. The forcing of the Straits was only supposed to be a preliminary to operations that were to supervene further ahead—the passage of the Bosphorus, occupation of Constantinople, and so on—and goodness only knows what would have happened had Admiral de Robeck beaten down the Turkish defences on the 18th of March and had he passed up the Narrows. But the sequel never materialised and the struggle of 1915 was consequently confined within somewhat narrow limits.

The conduct of war in these latter days has become exceedingly complex, as a result of advance in science, and it is studied by its professional exponents to an extent hardly dreamt of a few decades ago. Efficiency on the water or in the field, armament, resources of all kinds, skilled leadership—all these factors count towards achieving victory. But, other things being the same, it is the belligerent who has the more carefully of the two prepared his plans in advance, and who has provided for all eventualities more completely than his opponent as a result of foresight and of calculation, who will prove the conqueror. Talented and voluble civilians sitting round a table do not provide an auspicious machinery for devising plans of campaign. That is work for experts, and it is work that requires to be grappled with very methodically and at infinite pains. Cabinets, War Councils, Dardanelles Committees, and kindred executive gangs are generally composed entirely, or almost entirely, of persons, who if they have any knowledge of war at all, are merely furnished with that modicum of it that is so dangerous a thing. The most important lesson taught by the Dardanelles affair is that governments should leave the contriving of military and naval operations to those who understand them, that they should make certain that plans of campaign have been exhaustively elaborated before these are put in execution in face of the enemy, and that they must never allow the importance of an end in the conduct of war to blind them to an absence of the means requisite for securing that end.

The great size of modern armies tends to impair the effectiveness of amphibious forms of war.—Although the Dardanelles campaign does not perhaps drive the lesson home so forcibly as do certain other sets of operations that have taken place during the World War, the struggle for the Hellespont does suggest that in these days, when whole nations take the field and when armies consequently muster as vast multitudes, command of the sea cannot be turned to account to such good purpose in connection with land operations as was formerly the case. The liberty of action which maritime control will sometimes confer upon a military commander has of late years formed a popular theme for the expositions of writers and lecturers on the art of war in this country. Such incidents as Sir J. Stuart's descent upon Calabria in menace of Reynier's communications which heralded the Battle of Maida, as the transfer of the Allies' forces from Varna to the Crimea by sea while the Russians had to conform by an arduous land march, as the shipping of McClellan's legions from the James River to near Washington when Lee invaded Maryland in 1862, as the sudden appearance of Suliman Pasha in the Shipka Pass in 1877 after a voyage from the Adriatic to Thrace, and as the landing of Japanese troops near Port Arthur in 1894 and their facile capture of that coast fortress, have in the past served to illustrate the efficacy of command of the sea in amphibious operations.

But the more dramatic amongst historical incidents which come properly under this designation have generally been affairs on, what we should now regard as, an insignificant scale. Louisbourg and Quebec were conquered by military contingents which according to present-day ideas were numerically almost contemptible. The army which landed near Copenhagen in 1807 and compelled the Danes to deliver up their fleet, did not approach the strength of an army corps as we reckon one to-day. Sir A. Wellesley had barely 17,000 men, all told, under his orders in his extraordinarily successful campaign of Vimiera, which hinged so greatly upon difficult disembarkations on the storm-swept western littoral of Portugal. Indeed, even the expeditionary force under Marshal St. Arnaud and Lord Raglan which put ashore north of the Alma and initiated the Crimean War, only numbered some 60,000 men, with, moreover, an exceedingly small proportion of artillery and of cavalry. It stands to reason that sudden maritime descents upon an enemy's coasts can be more readily effected with small than with large armies, and that, the more numerous be the forces detailed for such ventures, the less likely is it that full value will be obtained from the element of surprise which is the essence of that class of enterprise.

The Gallipoli operations were carried out on a greater scale than any previous undertaking of at all analogous kind. Our forces that assembled in South Africa from 1900 to 1902 were, it is true, larger than the invading army was in the Gallipoli Peninsula, and the Japanese likewise landed much bigger hosts in Manchuria and Korea during their duel with the Russian Empire. But in both those contests the belligerent who was carrying out hostilities beyond the seas had harbours at his disposal in the theatre of war, and the disembarkations were in either case carried out throughout without interference by the enemy. It may be urged that the transport of troops across the seas is in the present day much facilitated by the size of the vessels that are used for the purpose, and by the conveniences of all kinds that have been introduced for facilitating the taking in and the discharge of personnel and goods, as compared to the days of the Peninsula and the Crimean War. But against this has to be set the fact that armies of the twentieth century require far more paraphernalia and appurtenances than was formerly the case, and that military forces committed to an adventure on foreign soil without their recognised quota of such impedimenta, are more than likely to come to grief. Sir I. Hamilton was always badly off for guns as compared with his antagonists ; and although this circumstance was mainly attributable to the right type of ordnance and of ammunition not being available in requisite quantities, it was also partly due to difficulties in landing such artillery as was to hand.

NEED OF ADVANCED BASES

Means of communication are so backward within the dominions of the Caliph that the Turks and their German advisers were never able to assemble more than a fraction of the total of the Osmanli land forces on a war footing in the environs of the Dardanelles—and this in spite of the vital strategical importance of the defile from the Ottoman point of view. Thanks, however, to the great resources in personnel at the disposal of the Seraskierate, owing to the existence of universal service, Marshal Liman von Sanders had many divisions under his orders, and so the condition of the struggle compelled the Allies to place a large army in the field and thereby to throw a great strain upon their shipping resources of all kinds. The scale upon which the invasion had perforce to be carried out rendered all movements deliberate, and caused concentrations to be slow. Consequently, certain of those advantages which are apparently conferred upon military forces when they contrive the invasion of hostile territory from the sea, were automatically lost. Dardanelles experiences in this matter are, it is true, suggestive rather than compelling. But the story of the operations gives at least some indication as to what a maritime descent upon the coasts of a great military state that is furnished with ample railway communications, would be likely to mean.

An advanced base needed in case of a maritime descent upon an enemy's shores.—One point has been brought into great prominence by the events with which this volume deals. Maritime invasion of a distant country—assuming the enemy to be in the military sense formidable and that there is no harbour available for the invaders within the prospective theatre of operations—is virtually impossible unless some secure advanced base is held or can be acquired. In the hazardous undertaking to which the Allies committed themselves in the Ægean early in 1915, they enjoyed one great advantage. The island of Lemnos with its spacious haven, and that of Imbros situated close to the Gallipoli Peninsula and offering a fairly well sheltered anchorage, were at Sir I. Hamilton's disposal. One has but to imagine what the conditions would have been had those islands not existed, to realise what a leading, if unobtrusive, rôle they played in the campaign.

The expansion in the dimensions of modern armies, and the developments that have taken place in respect to military impedimenta, have made advanced bases virtually indispensable. Abercrombie's expedition, which has been referred to in Chapter IV in connection with the famous landing in Aboukir Bay, stood across the Mediterranean from Marmarice Bay in Anatolia, and the troops were straightway landed in face of the enemy. But it is doubtful whether it would have been feasible for Sir I. Hamilton to have transferred his army direct from Alexandria to the Helles and Anzac beaches, although in point of time the distance from Egypt to the Dardanelles in 1915 was less than that from Marmarice to Aboukir in 1800. Nor should it be forgotten that the landing on the 25th of April took place before the arrival of the enemy's submarines in Ægean waters.

It is no exaggeration to say that the attack upon the Dardanelles hinged upon those two islands, Lemnos and Imbros. Secure from hostile attack and conveniently placed in regard to the actual scene of fighting, they provided priceless advanced bases for the expeditionary army. Stores were gathered together there. Transhipments took place under their shelter. Station hospitals, rest camps, and kindred establishments were created on their shores. Mudros Bay, moreover, served as rendezvous and rest house to the naval forces as well as the expeditionary army. Those two island bases also acquired an added importance as military depots, owing to the landing-places on the peninsula being at the mercy of enemy bombardments all the time that the campaign lasted.

The influence of the submarine upon undertakings of the Dardanelles type.—The story of the campaign subsequent to the month of May, 1915, illustrates the effect that hostile submarines may exert upon the course of invasions of an enemy's country from the sea. It has been remarked above that, but for the islands, it might have been impracticable to have carried out the military attack upon the Gallipoli Peninsula at all. The appearance of the U-boats in the Ægean rendered the possession of Lemnos and Imbros more valuable than ever. We have seen that the use of ocean-going transports to convey the troops and stores to the peninsula was promptly abandoned after *Triumph* and *Majestic* succumbed to the torpedo, and that thenceforward this service was performed almost entirely by small craft. Under such circumstances advanced bases that are capable of being rendered unassailable by submarine attack become absolutely essential.

INFLUENCE OF SUBMARINES

The course of the World War has shown that the submarine is not unconquerable. Experience has proved that by means of special devices in the shape of nets and of mines, stretches of water can be rendered virtually immune from its depredations. The history of the struggle at sea has shown that, by utilising immense flotillas of small vessels aided by an enterprising and efficient air service, damage inflicted by hostile underwater craft can be kept well within bounds in almost any maritime area. But it is manifest that their introduction as instruments of war must tend as a broad general rule to render maritime descents upon an enemy's shores more difficult to carry into effect than they were before.

It has always been recognised that the transport of troops across the seas during hostilities is in principle only permissible if the state carrying out the operation enjoys maritime command ; but so long as opposing submarines are about, maritime command is necessarily merely relative and cannot be complete. The invasion of hostile territory may be almost said to presume convoys of troopships offering particularly favourable objectives to the underwater vessel. It suggests transports lying at anchor which must provide tempting targets for the torpedo. One of the great advantages of Suvla Bay was that it could after a time be protected by nets. An argument that was occasionally put forward for transferring operations to the Bulair Isthmus was that, by similar arrangements on a much larger scale, it would be possible to render the upper end of the Gulf of Saros safe. But it is necessarily more difficult to adapt such methods to the conditions of a perfectly open stretch of coast like Anzac than to those of a bight ; and in any case it must take time to carry the construction out.

Comparative ineffectiveness of boardship gun-fire against shore targets.—The somewhat disappointing character of what the Allies' naval artillery accomplished when acting against forts, against trenches, and against hostile troops engaged in battle, has been touched upon here and there in preceding chapters. Indeed, the unsatisfactory results obtained by sea power on the very first day of the campaign—the virtual failure of a relatively speaking formidable squadron to settle the coast batteries that defended the entrance to the Straits for good and all—were to be reproduced in various forms throughout the months of stirring naval and amphibious warfare that was to follow in this theatre of operations. The tremendous effect produced by our sailors' gunnery at the affair of the Bight, on the occasion of the trapping of Von Spee's armament off the Falkland Islands, and on the day of Jutland, prove that any shortcomings of our warships in their efforts against the coast of the Gallipoli Peninsula and against targets ashore within the Dardanelles, cannot be attributed to bad shooting nor yet to defective technique. Such discomfitures as were met with must be set down to the abnormal conditions that supervene when floating force is pitted against the land.

Only a limited number of artillery officers in this country had realised before the World War to what an extent the efficacy of their arm in combat depended upon " close-up " observation of fire. There had been ample discussion as to the virtues of co-operation between guns and infantry, it is true. The importance of such concert was fully recognised. How it ought to be secured in principle as a tactical proposition was a matter of general agreement. But the practical methods of arriving at the desired end had not been grappled with. We know better now. We have learnt that in the absence of really intimate observation of fire, that without telephonic communication between the eyes of the battery —projected far to the front of the position where the guns are in action—and the battery itself, the only means of obtaining edifying results are to be found in aerial observation, if that be practicable.

Now, when it is a case of warships that are engaging targets ashore, close-up observation of fire can only be established conveniently if the targets happen to be near the water's edge, or else if circumstances admit of the vessels steaming in to short range. You can hardly send in some little craft—say a motor launch—to cruise about, observing, half a mile or so from a coast battery which your battleship is engaging at 10,000 yards range, because the enemy will sink the launch with a big shrapnel or by dint of a few rounds from some anti-torpedo-boat gun. Supposing, on the other hand, the objective to be situated three or four miles inland (like Chocolate Hill and Ismail Oglu Tepe on the 21st of August) it may be feasible to overcome the observation difficulty by sending an observing party ashore to go forward on foot ; but it will be difficult for them to communicate what they see to their ship. The telephone arrangements made use of by the land gunner might be introduced; but it would not be easy to improvise such a system suddenly for the purpose of bridging the gulf between a ship off the coast and a party a mile or two inland. The consequences of a lack of forward observation may cause projectiles from supporting vessels to do serious damage to the troops in the middle of a general action; and although such contretemps are not wholly unknown where land batteries are working in conjunction with other arms, they generally nowadays only occur when the friendly infantry is very close to the target. Or lack of forward observation may oblige the ships' guns to cease fire just when this is most wanted—as happened on the 21st of August.

Bearing in mind the imposing calibre and the unquestionable might of the ships' guns that the Allies had at their disposal, it can hardly be said that this monster ordnance achieved commensurate successes, except when its targets happened to be exceptionally easy to hit—as for instance Sedd-el-Bahr Castle when *Albion* battered its ancient walls on the morning of the 26th of February, and the trenches overlooking X Beach when *Implacable* on the previous morning had crept in to within short range and let them have it with a will. Moreover, the fleet, as was to be expected, did scarcely anything against concealed howitzers and guns, and they were able to effect less than might have been expected towards easing the wearing strain that was suffered by the troops at Helles and Anzac, and, later, in the Suvla area, at the hands of artillery equipments that were incomparably less powerful than the armament carried by the monitors and belted cruisers.

There was nothing new in this. On the contrary, the history of war abounds in instances of naval ineffectiveness when coping with military force. Most soldiers who had devoted attention to the subject had indeed foreseen that the advance in the science of armament need not necessarily alter the tactical relations as between land and sea very appreciably, and that former experiences of warfare of this class, although carried out with ruder appliances and with less accurate and less potent weapons, would be found still to hold good. The events of the campaign showed that they were right, and this is one of its most significant lessons. Still, in this connection it is necessary to make one radical reservation.

Aeronautics introduce new factors into operations of war, and there is reason to suppose that they will in the future exert considerable influence over amphibious contests. Although aircraft played a part in the fight for the Straits it was not a very important part. That does not prove that a flying service may not in future campaigns render fleets more formidable in amphibious combats than they proved to be in the struggle for the Hellespont. Aerial observation was of use on certain occasions during the naval attacks upon the Narrows in March, and it enabled *Queen Elizabeth* to sink a Turkish transport off Maidos. But air power was not seriously turned to account with a view to its prosecuting accurate, scientific, communicated observation in the interests of the attacking guns, until after the appearance of the U-boats was already restricting naval activity. In the later stages of the campaign this form of observation was employed rather by the batteries on shore than by the ships' gunners.

Vital importance in the case of a maritime descent upon hostile territory of securing a large area immediately on landing.—One lesson that is impressed upon us with signal force by the story of the Dardanelles campaign has already been expatiated upon in earlier chapters, and the point need perhaps hardly be laboured further here. That lesson is that when you are conducting an invasion by sea of an enemy's country with prospect of meeting opposition, it is imperative for you to secure as extensive an area of ground as possible near the landing-place with the utmost despatch. Had a considerably larger tract been conquered at any one of the three localities where the Gallipoli landings took place, within a few hours of the commencement of disembarkation—at Helles, or at Anzac, or at Suvla—the effort against the peninsula might conceivably have accomplished the primary object of the campaign, and the Narrows might have been wrested out of the keeping of the Turk. Resistance proved too strong to be brushed aside at Helles. Grim opposition coupled with topographical difficulties of no common order served to confine the space won at Anzac to exceedingly restricted limits from the very start. In the case of Suvla, a number of circumstances which have been commented on in Chapters XI and XII combined to prevent the occupation of essential positions which were weakly held by Ottoman troops when the invaders first set foot on shore. The result was, however, practically identical in all three cases. A footing was gained—and that was all.

NEED OF ELBOW-ROOM ON LANDING 343

A landing in an enemy's country bears, it may be observed, a marked resemblance to the passage by troops of some great military obstacle which is only traversable by armed forces at certain indicated localities—a mighty river, say, or a range of mountains, or a stretch of desert wilderness. The principal difference indeed is that in the case of the river, or of the range, or of the desert, the enemy may be able to assume the offensive on your side of the obstacle ; a maritime descent, on the other hand, postulates a situation that imposes the defensive upon the adversary. In this latter case the sea creates the obstacle; and, owing to the conformation of normal littorals, the practicable landing-places are usually limited in number, and they thus present the counterpart of points where the river may be bridged, or where tracks fit for troops traverse the hills, or where chains of wells permit of a multitude of men crossing the desert. It is an accepted tactical and strategical axiom that, when forcing the passage of a military obstacle, reaping the fruits of preliminary success hinges upon securing ample space on its further side as soon as may be, so as to admit of the army deploying as accessions swell its numbers, and so as to ensure that the issues from the defile shall not be under hostile fire. It is just the same in the case of the landing. You stand in need of elbow-room, and your points of disembarkation, as well as the exits leading immediately outwards from them, require to be out of range of hostile projectiles.

But that is not all. As with the river, or the range, or the desert, success will often be contingent on surprise. It will be a question of debouching unexpectedly on the enemy's side of the obstacle and while the foe is still weak in numbers at the point which you select. Once your antagonist ascertains your intentions, he is likely to hold some precious trump cards in his hand. He may be in a position to gather his forces from all sides; whereas you are for some time hampered by having to get your troops and impedimenta across bridges, or through mountain defiles, or along desert tracks, or on to terra firma out of ships. The enemy is not unlikely to be able to mass the bulk of his forces adjacent to the scene of action a good deal more rapidly than you can. So your task during the early hours is to secure as big a " bridgehead " as circumstances permit. You require also to make yourself master straightway of favourable positions where your leading troops, weak as they must be, will be able to sustain themselves against superior numbers until those reinforcements have joined up which, it is to be assumed, you have at command—for otherwise you presumably would not be venturing on an offensive on the further side of the obstacle. It is all fairly obvious—at all events in theory.

The position warfare (or trench warfare, as it has come to be called in view of experiences on all fronts during the World War) which appears to be an almost automatic consequence of the great progress that has taken place in the science of armaments of late years, provides a fresh incentive for securing a maximum of space immediately, when effecting a landing in an enemy's country. Anzac illustrates this principle. It will be remembered that, although General Birdwood's forces did contrive to extend the area in their occupation flankwards, they virtually stood still in so far as advance directly inland from the starting-point was concerned. The line Russel's Top—Quinn's Post—Pimple was secured within a few hours. What was virtually that same line remained the battle-front from the night of stress which succeeded the 25th of April, down to the early hours of that memorable December morning when the shrunken parties of Australians, who were holding this mile or so of sterile crag and naked ridge to the last, stole silently away in the darkness and made for their boats.

A reasonably defensible line taken up by efficient troops who are fitted out with the weapons of to-day, can, experience of the World War has proved, be maintained almost for certain so long as the enemy does not mass a prodigious weight of artillery to batter the line with. This feature in contemporary tactics is due to the magazine rifle and to the machine-gun. Accepting the above as an axiom, the advantage of thrusting your bridgehead as far as possible outwards seems to stand to reason. The position hastily occupied at the start ought to be tenable for the few days that will in most cases elapse before the reinforcements shall have disembarked, which are required first to make the line secure and then to permit of an offensive onwards with an army presumably superior to that which the enemy will have been able to gather together.

Reserves to replace wastage must be provided on the spot in the case of distant campaigns.—Amongst the various factors that con-

DEPOTS MUST BE CLOSE AT HAND

tributed to bring about a miscarriage of the Entente Powers' efforts to obtain mastery over the Dardanelles, not the least potent was their inability to maintain the expeditionary army at its proper establishment. The point has been dealt with in former chapters, and it teaches us an important lesson with reference to the conduct of war under analogous conditions. A nation embarking upon a military adventure to take place in some region far removed from the home country, and in the course of which losses are likely to be heavy, should collect ample reserves in, or near, the theatre of war, upon which the commander can draw to replenish his ranks.

The requirements in respect to location of draft-producing depots for prosecuting the Dardanelles operations, differed widely there from what was appropriate in France and Belgium during the World War. The belligerent armies in action on what we came to call the Western Front—French, British, German, and Belgian—were all fighting within a day or two by rail and sea from their homes. So long as the personnel, trained and equipped, was in existence, the despatch of drafts from Germany or from the United Kingdom to Flanders or Artois was merely a question of hours. But warfare on the shores of the Ægean was quite a different story for the French, and even more so for the British. To carry on the campaign in the Gallipoli Peninsula effectively, huge depots of officers and men ought to have been available in the islands of Imbros or Lemnos, ready to despatch reinforcements to depleted units at the scene of action at a few hours' notice. Because the reserves were not where they ought to have been, because they were located away back in France and the British Isles, they were invariably weeks behind time when they were wanted. We are here assuming that the troops actually did exist somewhere. But as a matter of fact there was always a shortage of trained men during 1915, at least as far as this country was concerned, and the way in which Sir I. Hamilton was starved for drafts was perhaps unavoidable.

The truth is that, to despatch a division to a distant theatre of war fitted out with all its paraphernalia of personnel and material, but deprived of those reinforcing resources in officers and men that are bound to be needed as soon as the division gets to work, is to court disaster. Such dispositions mean that—possibly within a very few hours of its first taking the field—the division may have become, and will remain, a mere framework, without vitality, without efficacy, and without worth. An army that has degenerated into a mere aggregate of non-combatant clusters, because its combatant services have melted away in the furnace of battle and because their wastage has not been made good, is an imposture and an anachronism. Even in the case of a fighting unit, it must be remembered, a portion of the personnel is inevitably employed in rear and out of the firing line ; this portion is apt to remain numerically constant, although the numbers in the firing line diminish ; and the consequence is that the comparative combatant potentialities of the unit as a whole depreciate out of proportion to its actual losses in action. There are few things, moreover, more discouraging to a battalion, or to a squadron of horse, or to a battery of artillery, than to see its ranks evaporating without observing any signs of their being replenished. From every point of view, in fact, the maintenance of those establishments which experience has proved to be fitting is a matter of cardinal military importance. But such maintenance will only be assured if ample reserves of personnel are planted down within, or reasonably near to, the arena of operations.

Conclusion.—Events that preceded and that occurred during the struggle for the Straits teach us other lessons besides those that have been particularly touched upon in this chapter. Some of them have been discussed in earlier passages scattered through the volume. Others may suggest themselves to its readers. The Dardanelles operations were indeed charged throughout with instruction for the thinker on the methods of war. Were it not that they represent merely one episode in the greatest of all international conflicts, the various incidents that signalised the contest would be conned over by the professional fighting men of all lands to the full as keenly as of late years have been the annals of the American Civil War, the history of the Franco-German duel of 1870–71, and the records of the hostilities between Russia and Japan in the Far East.

An official account of the fight for the Hellespont will, we may assume, appear in due course, elucidating many matters that to-day remain obscure and bringing to light factors bearing on the issue that are at present only realised by those who were fully behind the scenes. Still, even as it is, we know enough about what occurred to be in a position to appraise the principal occurrences of the campaign fairly correctly, and to justify our deducing theories from them as to the principles which govern certain aspects of the naval and the military art. The attempt to reach Constantinople made by the Entente Powers in 1915 ranks as one of the most remarkable martial undertakings recorded in history. Not one set of operations that can be named since the conquest of Canada, so nearly embodies the ideal of amphibious warfare. On the side of the Allies, admirals and generals were continually being called upon to grapple with novel tactical and administrative problems of rare complexity. Their opponents, labouring as they were under a crushing responsibility and hampered by indifferent land communications and an inefficient military system, remained undismayed and managed to keep their flag flying in spite of all. The withdrawal of the British and Australasian forces from the Gallipoli Peninsula furnishes an illuminating example of what method, combined with foresight, will accomplish when war-experienced and well-disciplined troops under mettlesome leadership serve as the material to be handled by a competent staff. Nor, if the annals of campaigns ancient and modern be ransacked for deeds of heroism and of grit, will there be found a more inspiring story than the immortal tale of the first landing by Sir I. Hamilton's troops on Turkish soil hard by the Dardanelles.

APPENDIX I

LIST OF AUTHORITIES CONSULTED

Official Despatches of General Sir I. Hamilton, General Sir C. Monro, Vice-Admiral Sir J. de Robeck, and Vice-Admiral Sir R. Wemyss.
Nelson's History of the War.—J. Buchan.
The Dardanelles Commission Report, Part I.
" The Times' " History of the War.
The Straits Impregnable.—S. de Loghe.
Last Cruise of the Majestic.—G. Goodchild.
What of the Dardanelles ?—Granville Fortescue.
Two Years' War in Constantinople.—H. Stuermer.
Australia in Arms.—P. F. E. Schuler.
From Gallipoli to Baghdad.—W. Ewing.
Gallipoli.—J. Masefield.
Experiences in the Dardanelles.—E. Pebody.
The Diary of a Padre at Suvla Bay.—Rev. D. Jones.
The Immortal Gamble.—Comdr. A. T. Stewart and Rev. C. J. E. Peshall.
Trenching at Gallipoli.—J. Gallishaw.
The Tenth (Irish) Division in Gallipoli.—Major B. Cooper.
At Suvla Bay.—J. Hargrave.
The Truth about the Dardanelles.—J. Moseley.
With the Fleet in the Dardanelles.—Rev. H. C. Price.
With the 29th Division in Gallipoli.—Rev. O. Creighton.
Ashmead Bartlett's Despatches from the Dardanelles.
With the Zionists in Gallipoli.—Lieut.-Colonel J. H. Paterson, D.S.O.
The Big Fight.—Captain D. Fallon, M.C.
A Naval Adventure.—Fleet-Surgeon J. T. James, R.N.
At Antwerp and the Dardanelles.—Rev. H. C. Foster.

APPENDIX I

Gallipoli Diary.—Major G. S. Gillam, D.S.O.
The Dardanelles Campaign.—H. W. Nevinson.
On Four Fronts with the Naval Division.—Surgeon G. Sparrow, M.C., R.N., and Surgeon J. N. Macbean, M.C., R.N.
Three Years of Naval Warfare.—R. H. Gibson.
British Campaigns in the Near East.—E. Dane.
Antwerp to Gallipoli.—A. Ruhl.
Inside Constantinople.—L. Enstein.
Secrets of the Bosphorus.—H. Morgenthau.
From Berlin to Baghdad.—G. K. Schreiner.
L'Expedition des Dardanelles.—C. Stienon.
Combat d'Orient. Dardanelles-Salonique (1915-16).—Capitaine Canudo.
Dardanelles, Serbie, Salonique.—J. Vassal.
Les Compagnons de l'Aventure.—A. Tudesq.
Deux années de guerre navale.—René La Bruyère.
Gallipoli. Der Kampf um den Orient.—Von einem Offizier aus dem Stabe Marschalls Liman von Sanders.
Der Kampf um die Dardanellen.—Major E. R. Prigge.
Im Turkischen Hauptquartier.—P. Schweder.

APPENDIX II

ORDER OF BATTLE OF THE EXPEDITIONARY FORCE
(exclusive of artillery)

The British and Australasian Divisions are enumerated in order of arrival in the Gallipoli Peninsula.

29th Division

86th Brigade.—2nd Royal Fusiliers; 1st Lancashire Fusiliers; 1st Royal Munster Fusiliers; 1st Royal Dublin Fusiliers.

87th Brigade.—2nd South Wales Borderers; 1st K.O.S.B.'s; 1st Royal Inniskilling Fusiliers; 1st Border Regiment.

88th Brigade.—2nd Hampshire; 4th Worcesters; 1st Essex; 5th Royal Scots.

Royal Naval Division[1]

1st Naval Brigade.—*Anson* Battalion; *Howe* Battalion; *Hood* Battalion; *Collingwood* Battalion.[2]

2nd Naval Brigade.—*Hawke* Battalion; *Nelson* Battalion; *Drake* Battalion; *Benbow* Battalion.

Marine Brigade.—Chatham Battalion; Plymouth Battalion; Portsmouth Battalion; Deal Battalion.

---

[1] Owing to the very heavy casualties that the division suffered and to the difficulty in filling the gaps, it was reduced from three brigades to two comparatively early in the operations, certain amalgamations taking place. In the autumn and at the time of the evacuation the 1st Brigade was composed of the *Drake, Nelson, Hawke* and *Hood* Battalions, and the 2nd Brigade comprised the *Howe* and *Anson* Battalions and 1st and 2nd Battalions of Royal Marines.

[2] Did not arrive till the end of May.

APPENDIX II 351

1st *Australian Division*

1st (New South Wales) Brigade.—1st, 2nd, 3rd, and 4th N.S. Wales Battalions.

2nd (Victoria) Brigade.—5th, 6th, 7th, and 8th Victoria Battalions.

3rd Brigade.—9th Queensland, 10th South Australian, 11th West Australian, and 12th Tasmania Battalions.

Australian and New Zealand Division

4th Brigade.—13th N.S. Wales, 14th Victoria, 15th Composite, and 16th Composite Battalions.

New Zealand Brigade.—Auckland, Canterbury, Wellington, and Otago Battalions.

1st Australian Light Horse Brigade.—1st, 3rd, and 4th Light Horse.

42nd *East Lancashire Division*

125th (Lancashire Fusilier) Brigade.—5th, 6th, 7th, and 8th Lancashire Fusiliers.

126th (East Lancashire) Brigade.—4th and 5th East Lancashire ; 9th and 10th Manchesters.

127th (Manchester) Brigade.—5th, 6th, 7th, and 8th Manchesters.

29th Indian Brigade.—1/5th and 1/6th Ghurka Rifles ; 2/10th Ghurka Rifles ; 14th Sikhs.

52nd *Lowland Division*

155th (South Scottish) Brigade.—4th and 5th Royal Scots Fusiliers ; 4th and 5th K.O.S.B.'s.

156th (Scottish Rifle) Brigade.—4th and 7th Royal Scots ; 7th and 8th Scottish Rifles.

157th (Highland Light Infantry) Brigade.—5th, 6th, and 7th Highland Light Infantry ; 5th Argyle and Sutherland Highlanders.

13th Division

38th Brigade.—6th Royal Lancashire ; 6th Lancashire Fusiliers ; 6th South Lancashire ; 6th Loyal North Lancashire.

39th Brigade.—9th Warwick ; 7th Gloucester ; 9th Worcesters ; 7th North Stafford.

40th Brigade.—8th Royal Welsh Fusiliers ; 4th South Wales Borderers ; 8th Cheshire ; 5th Wiltshire.

Divisional Battalion.—8th Welsh.

11th Division

32nd Brigade.—9th West Yorkshire ; 6th Yorkshire ; 6th York and Lancaster ; 8th West Riding.

33rd Brigade.—6th Lincoln; 6th Border Regiment; 6th South Stafford ; 9th Notts and Derby.

34th Brigade.—8th Northumberland Fusiliers ; 9th Lancashire Fusiliers ; 11th Manchester ; 5th Dorset.

Divisional Battalion.—6th East Yorkshire.

10th Division

29th Brigade.—10th Hampshire ; 6th Royal Irish Rifles ; 5th Connaught Rangers ; 6th Leinster.

30th Brigade.—6th and 7th Royal Dublin Fusiliers ; 6th and 7th Royal Munster Fusiliers.

31st Brigade.—5th and 6th Royal Inniskilling Fusiliers ; 5th and 6th Royal Irish Fusiliers.

Divisional Battalion.—5th Royal Irish.

53rd Welsh Division

158th Cheshire Brigade.—4th, 5th, 6th, and 7th Cheshire.

159th (North Wales) Brigade.—4th, 5th, 6th, and 7th Royal Welsh Fusiliers.

160th Brigade.—4th Queens ; 4th Royal Sussex ; 1st Hereford ; 10th Middlesex.

APPENDIX II

54th East Anglian Division

161st Norfolk and Suffolk Brigade.—4th and 5th Norfolk; 4th and 5th Suffolk.

162nd East Anglian Brigade.—5th Bedford; 4th Northampton; 1st Cambridge; Herts Battalion.

163rd Essex Brigade.—4th, 5th, 6th, and 7th Essex.

The 2nd Mounted Division

1st South Midland Brigade.—Warwickshire Yeomanry; Worcestershire Yeomanry; Gloucestershire Hussars.

2nd South Midland Brigade.—Buckinghamshire Hussars; Berks Yeomanry; Dorset Yeomanry.

North Midland Brigade.—Derbyshire Yeomanry; Notts Yeomanry; South Notts Yeomanry.

London Brigade.—City of London Roughriders; 1st County of London Yeomanry; Surrey Yeomanry.

Divisional Troops.—Westminster Dragoons; Herts Yeomanry.

3rd Australian Light Horse Brigade.[1]—2nd, 5th, and 7th Light Horse.

2nd Australian Light Horse Brigade.[1]—8th, 9th, and 10th Light Horse.

New Zealand Mounted Brigade.[1]—Auckland Mounted Rifles; Canterbury Mounted Rifles; Wellington Mounted Rifles; Otago Mounted Rifles.

2nd Australian Division

5th Brigade.—17th, 18th, 19th, and 20th Battalions.

6th Brigade.—21st, 22nd, 23rd, and 24th Battalions.

Troops that arrived after August. Newfoundland Battalion; Scottish Horse; 1st and 2nd Lovat's Scouts; East Kent, West Kent, Sussex, North Devon, Devon and West Somerset Yeomanry.

[1] These arrived at various dates between May and July.

FRENCH FORCES

1st Division[1]

1st Metropolitan Brigade.—175th Regiment; Composite Regiment of Zouaves and Foreign Legion.

Colonial Brigade.[2]—4th Colonial Regiment; 6th Colonial Regiment.

2nd Division[1]

3rd Metropolitan Brigade.—176th Regiment; 2nd African Regiment (Zouaves).

Colonial Brigade.[2]—7th Colonial Regiment; 8th Colonial Regiment.

Two Regiments of Chasseurs d'Afrique.

[1] Each division had six batteries of "75's" and two of mountain guns.
[2] The Colonial regiments were made up partly of battalions of French Colonial troops and partly of Senegalese battalions.

APPENDIX III

THE ARRANGEMENTS MADE WITH REGARD TO WATER FOR THE SUVLA LANDING

The serious difficulties that arose as to water after the landing had taken place at the beaches at Suvla were mainly due to the problem of distribution to the troops, and not to any failure to provide water. The arrangements for its provision were as follows :—

A tank steamer, towing water lighters, accompanied the 11th Division from Imbros, its arrival being timed for daybreak. Another vessel carried hose, tanks, and troughs, as well as water-pumps and the requisite ordnance stores for developing any wells and springs that might be found. The design was that the lighters were to bring up at the beaches and were to be emptied by pumps and hose. But several of the lighters grounded some way from the shore, and in some cases the hose was pierced by thirsty soldiers, so that the supply even on the beaches did not reach the volume anticipated. The plan was that after the lighters and tank-ship were emptied they would return to Imbros, to fill up afresh from the parent water-ship stationed there.

For purposes of distribution a large number of mules had been specially provided, and most elaborate arrangements had been made in respect to assembling receptacles in the shape of petrol tins, milk cans, camel tanks, and water bags, sufficient having been procured to contain 100,000 gallons. Neither mules nor water-carts were, however, landed during the first hours after disembarkation had commenced, and the consequence was that the troops that had advanced from the beaches were entirely dependent upon what could be carried by hand in water bottles and so forth during the greater part of the day on the 7th of August. When the serious position at the front in respect to water was ascertained, the landing of the artillery horses was stopped so as to accelerate getting ashore the mules intended to carry the receptacles to the troops. But all this took time, with the result that the men suffered very greatly from thirst in most sections of the line. Considerable delay took place in landing the material on board the vessel carrying troughs and hose, as well as special gear for sinking wells.

The organisation in respect to bringing the lighters full of water to the shore was in the hands of the Royal Navy. Drawing the water from the lighters and distributing it on shore was in the hands of the army. As regards the latter operation Sir I. Hamilton writes in his final despatch : " Undoubtedly the distribution of this water to the advancing troops was a matter of great difficulty, and one which required not only well worked-out schemes from Corps and Divisional Staffs, but also energy and experience on the part of those who had to put them in practice. As it turned out, and judging only by results, I regret to say that the measures actually taken in regard to the distribution proved inadequate, and that suffering and disorganisation ensued."

APPENDIX IV

MARSHAL LIMAN VON SANDERS' VIEWS AND STATEMENTS

Since this volume was sent to press, an interesting report of an interview with Marshal Liman von Sanders which took place towards the end of November, 1918, at Constantinople has appeared in a number of journals in this country. The various points, which were then raised by the enemy commander-in-chief during the land campaign for the Dardanelles, are briefly dealt with below.

1. The marshal remarked : " The attack on the Straits by the Navy alone, I don't think could ever have succeeded owing to the mines. I proposed to flood the Straits broadcast with mines, and it was my view that these were the main defence of the Dardanelles, and that the function of the guns in the forts was simply to protect the minefields from interference." Many sailors and soldiers in this country will agree with the view that a sufficiency of mines would make the passage of the Straits virtually impracticable, so long as the defenders had searchlights, field-guns, and howitzers to oppose to the mine-sweepers. The point, however, suggests itself that the Turks may not have possessed sufficient mines to " flood " the channel " broad-cast " with such engines of destruction. The drifting mines certainly proved very effective in the general action of the 18th of March ; but the Ottoman Government was none too well supplied with munitions at that time.

2. " If I had been the attacker instead of the defender of the Dardanelles," the marshal continued, " I would not have landed at Cape Helles and Anzac. I should have made the principal landing on the coast of Asia Minor from Tenedos. There you have, first of all, a convenient base close at hand, while by only two

days' march you would be in rear of the Dardanelles forts which can only fire seaward. At the same time I should have landed on the neck of the Gallipoli Peninsula close to the Bulair lines. So strongly did I expect that the British would choose those places that when I took command a month before the landing I posted two of my six divisions opposite Tenedos, two on the peninsula, and two at Bulair."

It may be remarked that if Sir I. Hamilton had chosen to try landings at Besika Bay and Bulair, he would have been doing exactly what his opponent thought he was going to do, and that is what a commander generally avoids if he can. But there were other strong objections to selecting those points for attack, which have been pointed out in Chapter IV. The only two practicable beaches " close to the Bulair lines " are of very limited extent and the wider of the two is outside the lines. A landing undertaken there in presence of two hostile divisions would have been a much more difficult operation than the landings at Helles and north of Gaba Tepe—which proved quite difficult enough. The most obvious tactical lesson that is taught by this campaign as regards landings in presence of an enemy is the necessity of getting the troops ashore very rapidly and of gaining ground at once—in other words of landing on a broad front. That was impossible at Bulair, although it might have been feasible at and near Besika Bay and Yukyeri Bay. Marshal Liman von Sanders indicates one serious objection to operating on the Asiatic side of the Straits when he says that it would take two days' march to get in rear of the forts ; one day's march would do it from Helles, and half a day's march from Gaba Tepe, judged merely by distance and not taking opposition into account in any of the three cases.

3. With regard to the Suvla landing the marshal said he would have preferred to make it between Anzac and Helles, because there the peninsula is narrower and the Turks at Helles could have been attacked from the rear. Possibly Sir I. Hamilton would have preferred it too, had there been any place to land ; but this would not seem to have been the case—the information at his disposal at all events did not suggest that there was any suitable spot for disembarking a large force rapidly between Gaba Tepe and Gully Beach.

4. Marshal Liman von Sanders put his force at Suvla on the

APPENDIX IV 359

7th of August at only two battalions, two squadrons and two batteries of old guns (a somewhat lower total than which is given in Chapter XI), and he considered that if the British troops had pressed hard they would have won the heights. That is an interesting admission.

5. He stated that when the push was made for Chunuk Bair he rushed a division across from the Asiatic side, which would have been blown to pieces by the British guns if it had arrived only half an hour later. It is not clear what date this refers to, but it sounds as if that date was the 8th of August; a division could scarcely have been got across from the Asiatic side and hurried on to the Sari Bair mountain by the morning of the 7th. But it was no doubt the case that much depended upon time during the encounters of the Anzac force with the enemy on the 7th and 8th, and possibly also on the 9th ; not until full particulars are known from the enemy's side will it be possible, however, to piece together properly the story of the great four days' fight for the Sari Bair mountain.

6. The marshal quoted the case of an attack by the Allies at Kiretch Keui, three days after the Suvla landing, as having been "touch and go." This probably refers to the attack of the 10th and 54th Divisions on the 15th of August (dealt with on pages 243 and 244), there being a mistake of date. No village known as Kiretch Keui is shown on our maps, but there may have been such a place somewhere ahead of our lines across the Kiritch Tepe Sirt.

7. He entirely agreed with the wisdom of the British decision to evacuate the peninsula, and he stated that he was constantly being reinforced so that at the end he had twenty-one divisions. This hardly calls for comment, but the figure as to the number of divisions is worthy of note.

8. The marshal spoke highly of the arrangements made by his adversaries for the final evacuation at Suvla, and he stated that when his patrols sighted red flares on the beach it was thought for a time that fresh troops were being landed. The flares referred to no doubt were the burning dumps. He mentioned that when the Turks advanced they suffered serious loss from our mines ; this perhaps accounts for the deliberate movements of his troops on the morning of the 20th of December, and it is a tribute to the

efficacy of this particular form of defence in the case of a withdrawal from trenches by night.

9. He claimed to have seen the preparations for evacuation going on at Helles, but he stated that he was never able to guess on which day it would actually take place. If that was so, how comes it that his troops displayed such torpor at night and fell in so readily with their opponents' plan of knocking off rifle-fire and bombing about midnight ? With twenty-one divisions available and only about 8000 yards of front to watch, it ought surely to have been possible to relieve the Ottoman forces in the trenches at frequent intervals so as to ensure their being on the alert. There must have been laxity somewhere. The marshal's foot-soldiers could not, it is true, have interfered very effectively with the British embarkation after midnight on the 8th-9th; but, had they observed an appropriate vigilance, they ought to have become aware that the trenches in front of them were untenanted very soon after the last of the retiring detachments slipped away. The Turkish artillery could then have been warned and their shell might have caused very serious havoc on the beaches, where personnel was being got aboard the beetles and into boats under considerable difficulty owing to the heavy seas.

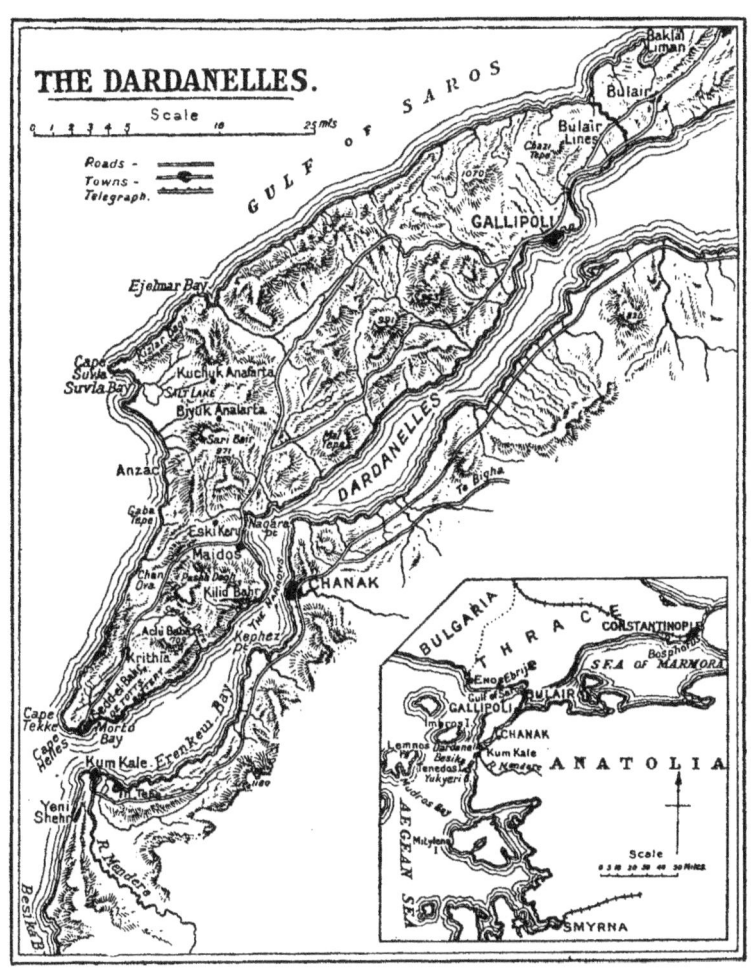

MAP VII.—THE DARDANELLES
MAP VIII (inset).—GENERAL

www.ingramcontent.com/pod-product-compliance
Lightning Source LLC
Chambersburg PA
CBHW031131160426
43193CB00008B/108